Twin Star Exorcists

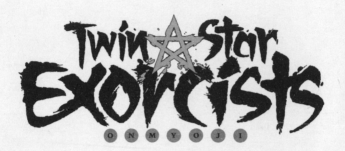

ONMYOJI

Twin ☆ Star Exorcists
ONMYOJI

17

STORY & ART
YOSHIAKI SUKENO

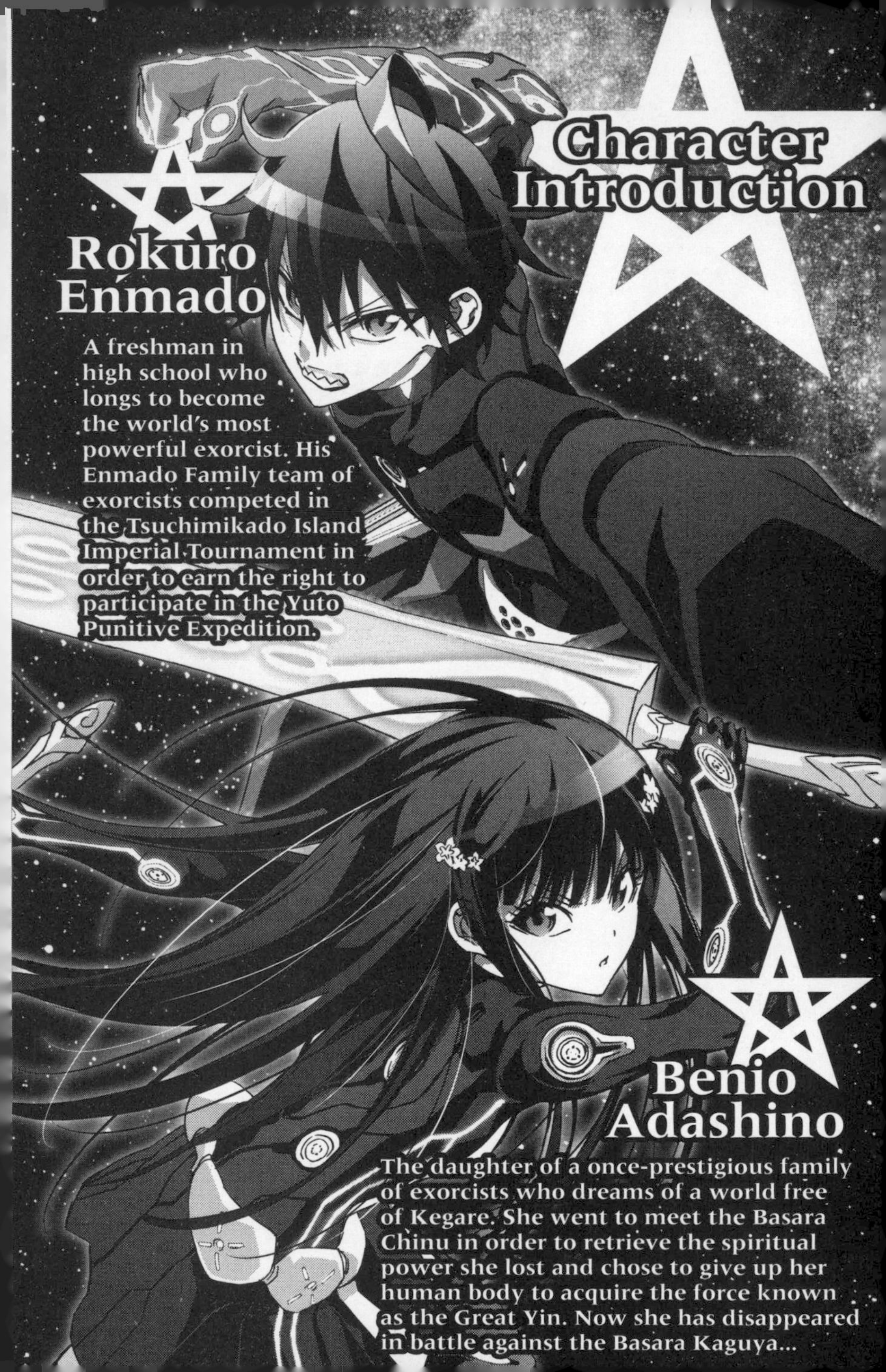

Character Introduction

Rokuro Enmado

A freshman in high school who longs to become the world's most powerful exorcist. His Enmado Family team of exorcists competed in the Tsuchimikado Island Imperial Tournament in order to earn the right to participate in the Yuto Punitive Expedition.

Benio Adashino

The daughter of a once-prestigious family of exorcists who dreams of a world free of Kegare. She went to meet the Basara Chinu in order to retrieve the spiritual power she lost and chose to give up her human body to acquire the force known as the Great Yin. Now she has disappeared in battle against the Basara Kaguya...

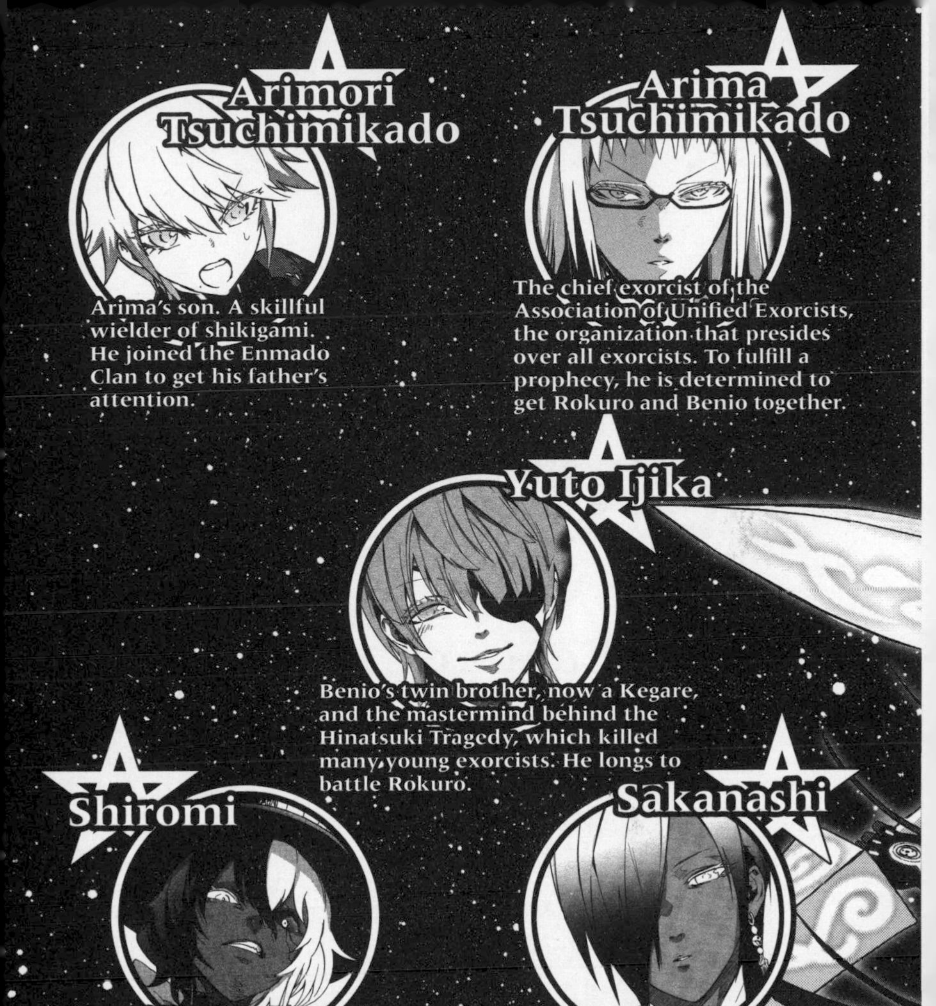
Arimori Tsuchimikado
Arima's son. A skillful wielder of shikigami. He joined the Enmado Clan to get his father's attention.
Arima Tsuchimikado
The chief exorcist of the Association of Unified Exorcists, the organization that presides over all exorcists. To fulfill a prophecy, he is determined to get Rokuro and Benio together.
Yuto Ijika
Benio's twin brother, now a Kegare, and the mastermind behind the Hinatsuki Tragedy, which killed many young exorcists. He longs to battle Rokuro.
Shiromi
The fifth-ranking Basara. He participated in the latest raid and launched an attack on Rokuro and his friends.
Sakanashi
The second-ranking Basara after Chinu. During the last raid, he simultaneously attacked five locations at once.

Story Thus Far...

Kegare are creatures from Magano, the underworld, and it is the duty of an exorcist to hunt, exorcise and purify them. Rokuro and Benio are the Twin Star Exorcists, fated to bear the Prophesied Child who will defeat the Kegare. Their goal was to go to Tsuchimikado Island to get revenge on Yuto, the mastermind behind the Hinatsuki Tragedy and Benio's brother.

After two years, Rokuro has qualified to go to the island, but Benio has lost her spiritual power and must remain behind. Rokuro establishes his own clan, the Enmado Family. Having proved their mettle at the Imperial Tournament, they are permitted to join the Yuto Punitive Expedition. But suddenly a group of risk-level SS Basara appear in an upper layer of Magano! Yuto Ijika and four other Basara attack five locations. Rokuro and his friends head toward them to fight back, but even the powerful, experienced Ioroi Family and Miku Zeze have already been annihilated...

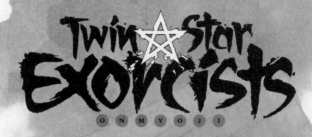

Twin Star Exorcists

O N M Y O J I

EXORCISMS

17

ONMYOJI have worked for the Imperial Court since the Heian era. In addition to exorcising evil spirits, as civil servants they performed a variety of roles, including advising nobles by foretelling the future, creating the calendar, observing the movements of the stars, measuring time...

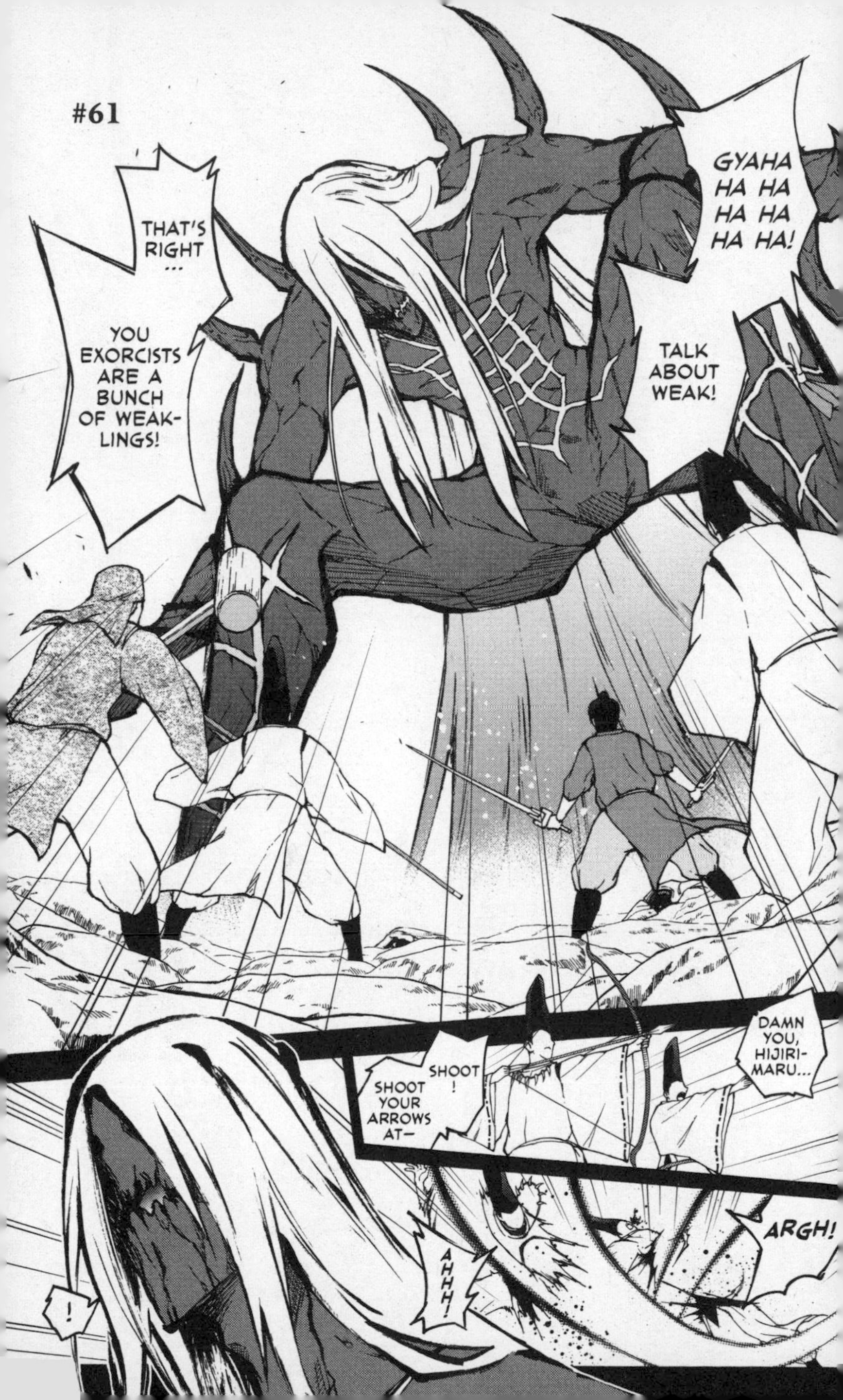
#61
GYAHA HA HA HA HA HA HA!
TALK ABOUT WEAK!
THAT'S RIGHT...
YOU EXORCISTS ARE A BUNCH OF WEAK-LINGS!
DAMN YOU, HIJIRI-MARU...
SHOOT!
SHOOT YOUR ARROWS AT—
ARGH!
AHHH!
!

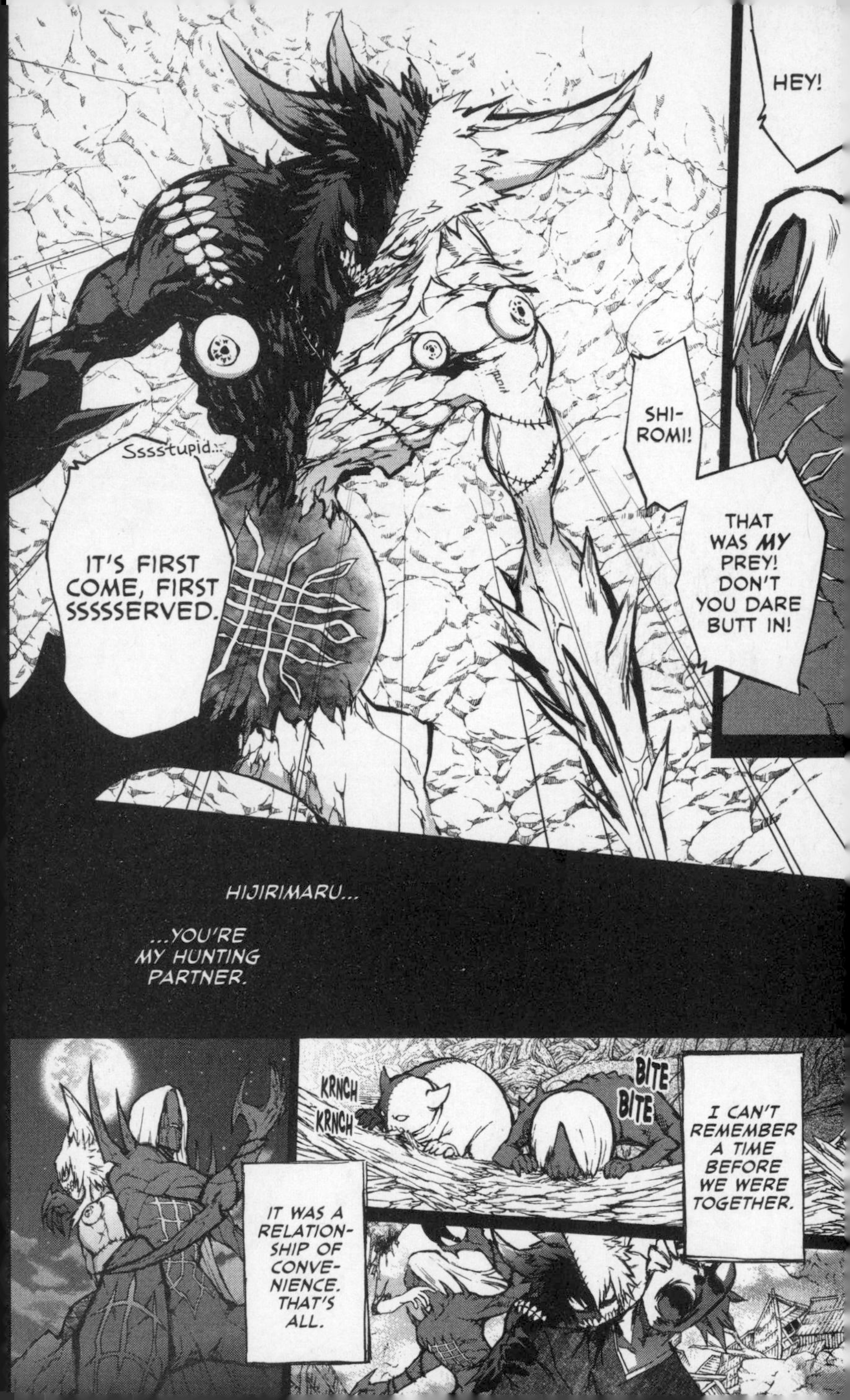
HEY!
THAT WAS *MY* PREY! DON'T YOU DARE BUTT IN!
SHI-ROMI!
Sssstupid...
IT'S FIRST COME, FIRST SSSSSERVED.
HIJIRIMARU...
...YOU'RE MY HUNTING PARTNER.
BITE BITE
I CAN'T REMEMBER A TIME BEFORE WE WERE TOGETHER.
KRNCH KRNCH
IT WAS A RELATIONSHIP OF CONVENIENCE. THAT'S ALL.

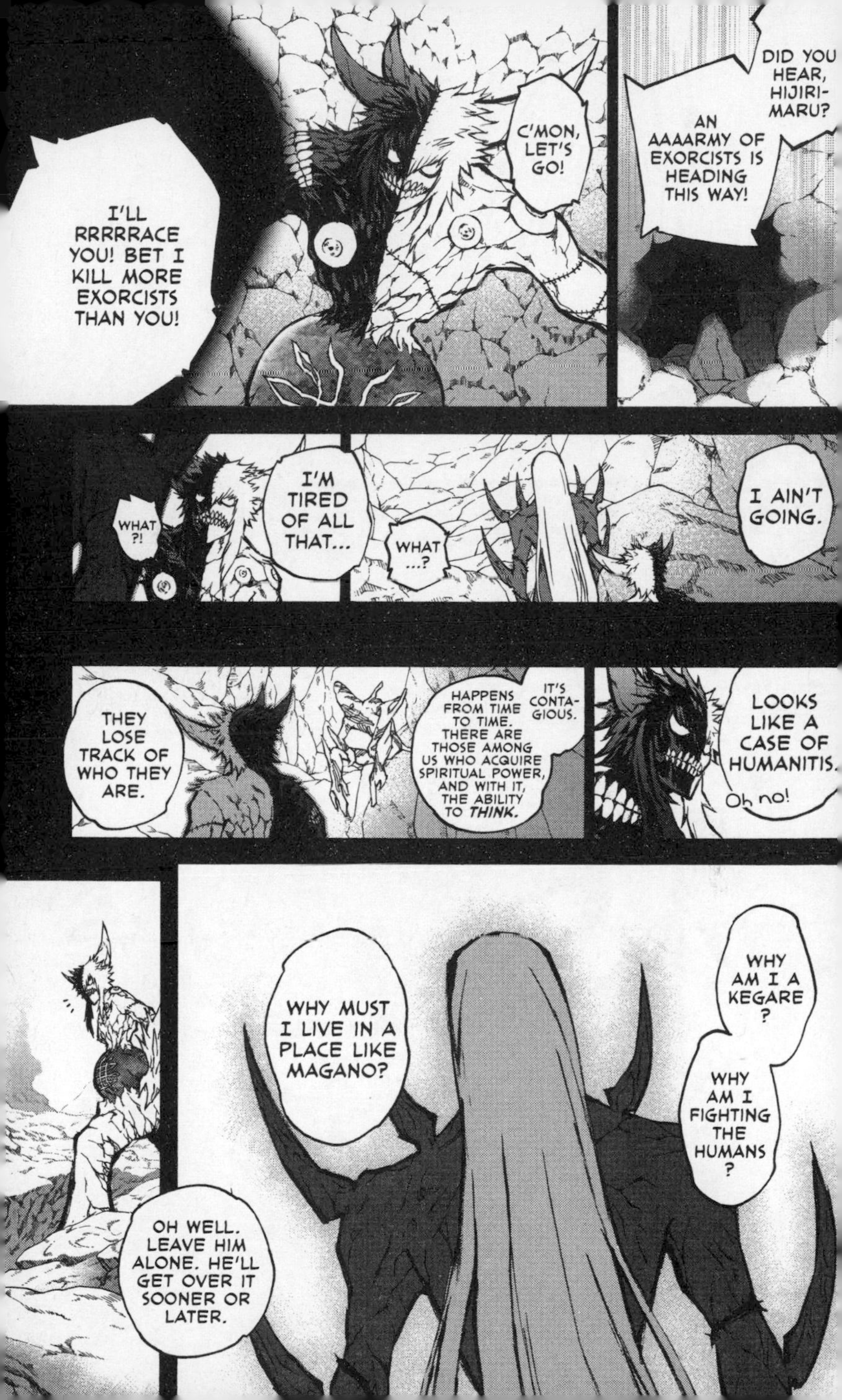

DID YOU HEAR, HIJIRI-MARU?
AN AAAARMY OF EXORCISTS IS HEADING THIS WAY!
C'MON, LET'S GO!
I'LL RRRRRACE YOU! BET I KILL MORE EXORCISTS THAN YOU!
I AIN'T GOING.
WHAT ...?
I'M TIRED OF ALL THAT...
WHAT ?!
LOOKS LIKE A CASE OF HUMANITIS.
Oh no!
IT'S CONTAGIOUS.
HAPPENS FROM TIME TO TIME. THERE ARE THOSE AMONG US WHO ACQUIRE SPIRITUAL POWER, AND WITH IT, THE ABILITY TO *THINK.*
THEY LOSE TRACK OF WHO THEY ARE.
WHY AM I A KEGARE?
WHY AM I FIGHTING THE HUMANS?
WHY MUST I LIVE IN A PLACE LIKE MAGANO?
OH WELL. LEAVE HIM ALONE. HE'LL GET OVER IT SOONER OR LATER.

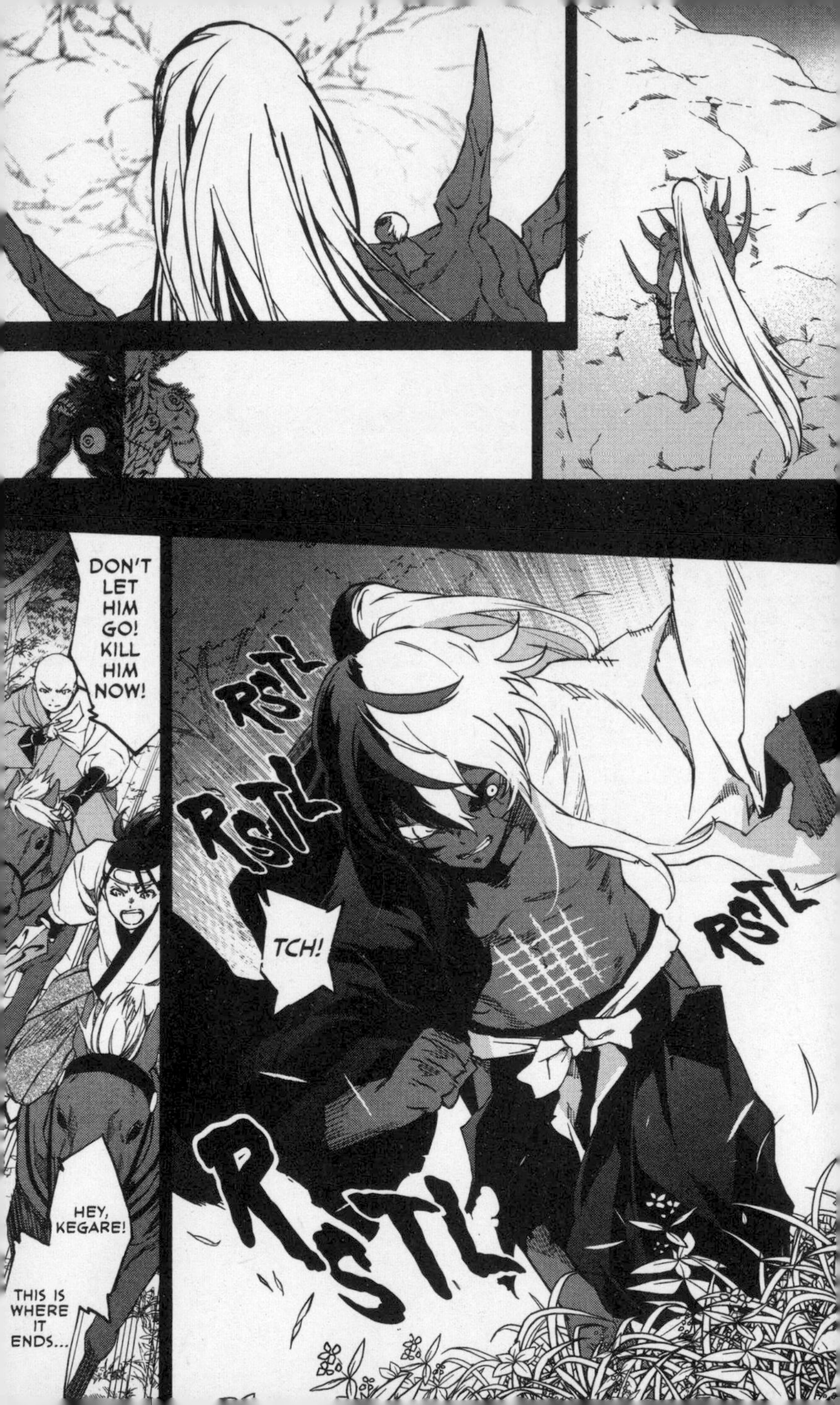
RSTL
RSTL
RSTL
TCH!
RSTL
DON'T LET HIM GO! KILL HIM NOW!
HEY, KEGARE!
THIS IS WHERE IT ENDS...

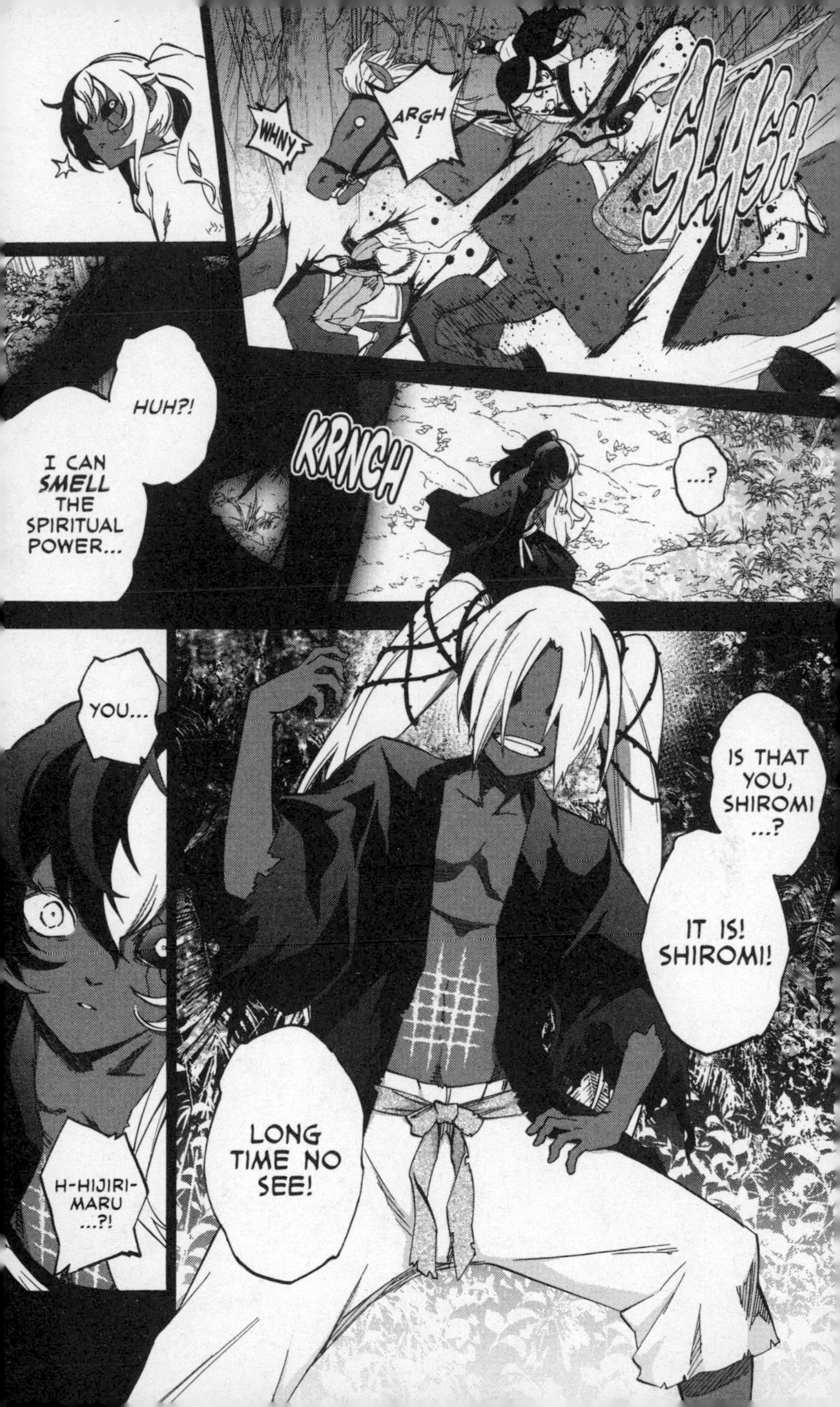
SLASH
ARGH!
WHNY
...?
KRNCH
HUH?!
I CAN SMELL THE SPIRITUAL POWER...
IS THAT YOU, SHIROMI ...?
IT IS! SHIROMI!
LONG TIME NO SEE!
YOU...
H-HIJIRI-MARU ...?!

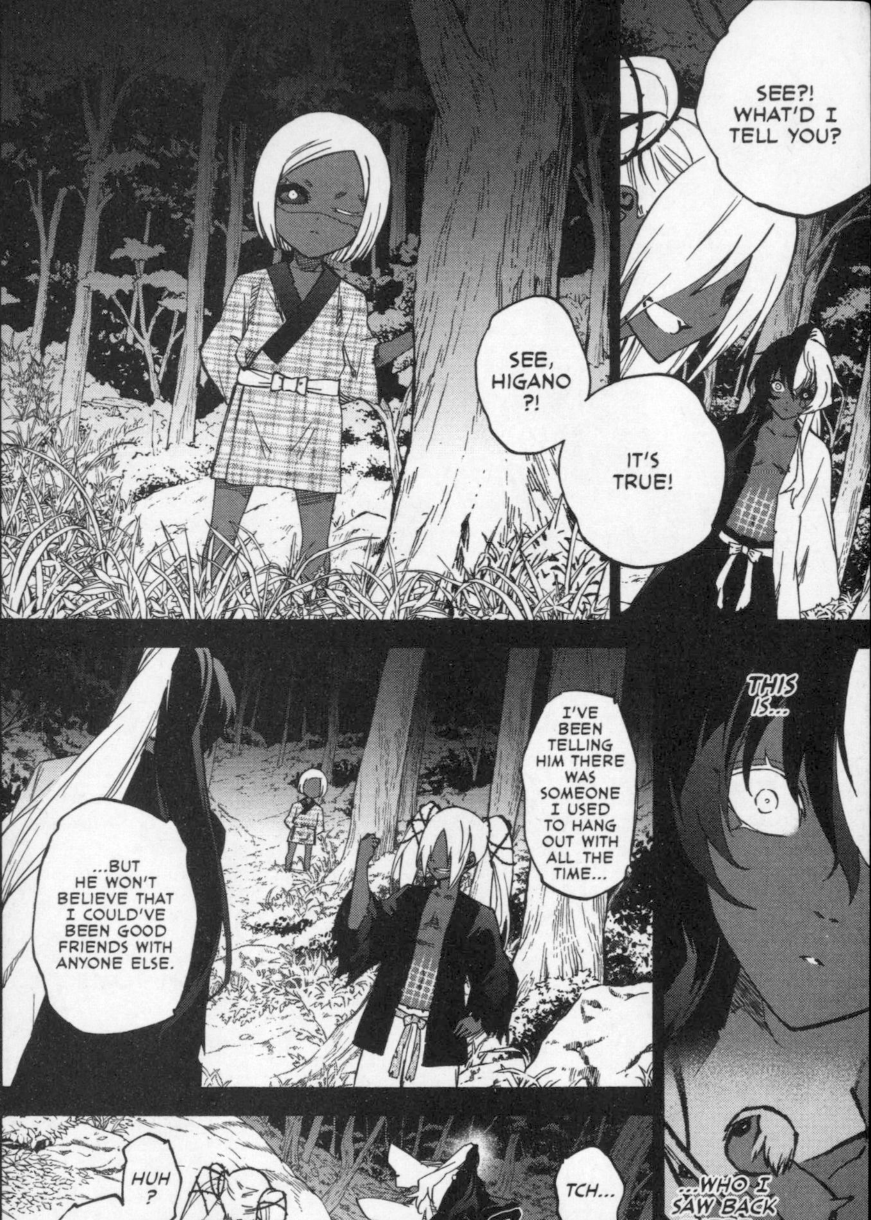
SEE?! WHAT'D I TELL YOU?
SEE, HIGANO ?!
IT'S TRUE!
THIS IS...
...WHO I SAW BACK THERE...
I'VE BEEN TELLING HIM THERE WAS SOMEONE I USED TO HANG OUT WITH ALL THE TIME...
...BUT HE WON'T BELIEVE THAT I COULD'VE BEEN GOOD FRIENDS WITH ANYONE ELSE.
TCH...
RSTL
HUH ?
HEY, SHIROMI!

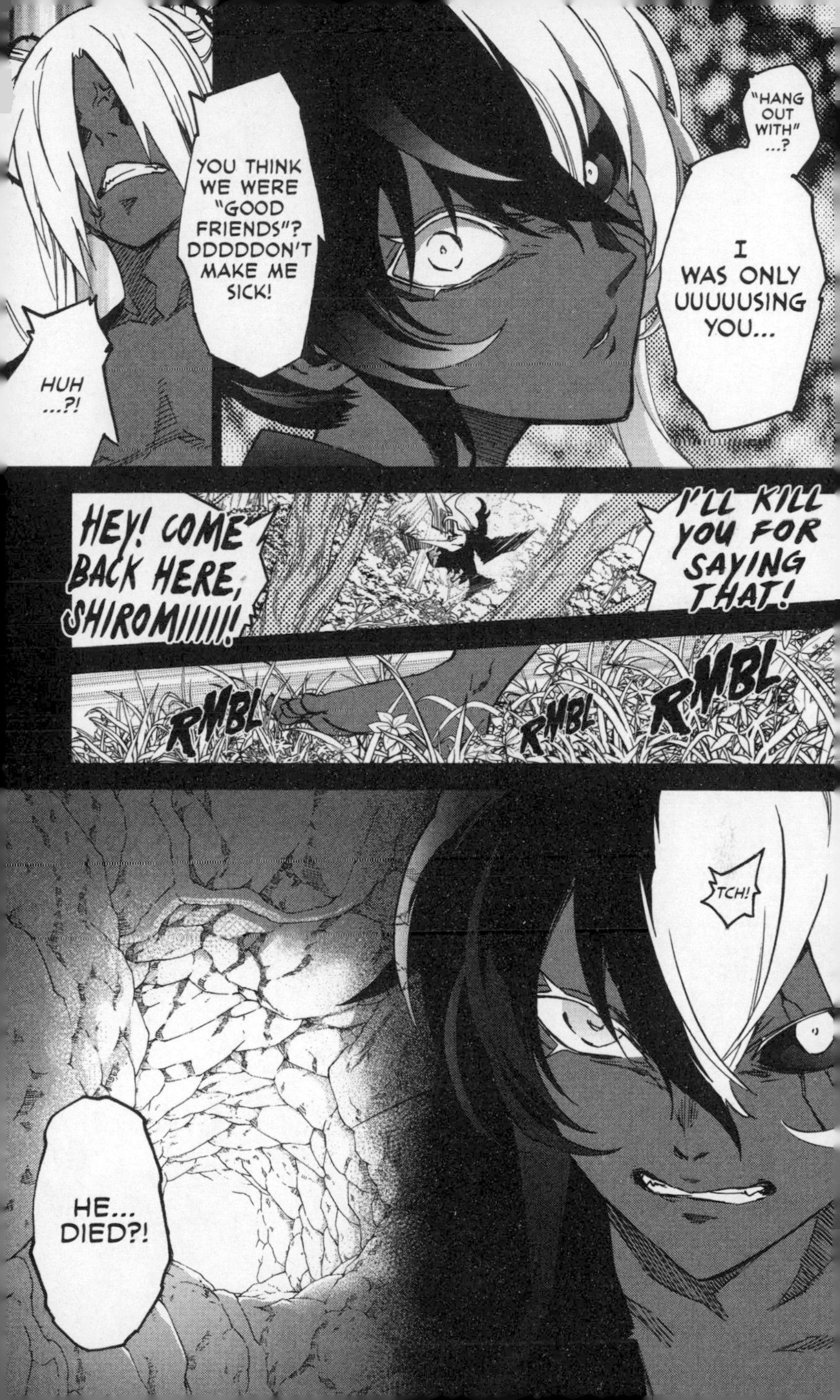
"HANG OUT WITH"...?
I WAS ONLY UUUUUSING YOU...
YOU THINK WE WERE "GOOD FRIENDS"? DDDDDON'T MAKE ME SICK!
HUH...?!
I'LL KILL YOU FOR SAYING THAT!
HEY! COME BACK HERE, SHIROMI!!!!!!!
RMBL RMBL
RMBL
RMBL
TCH!
HE... DIED?!

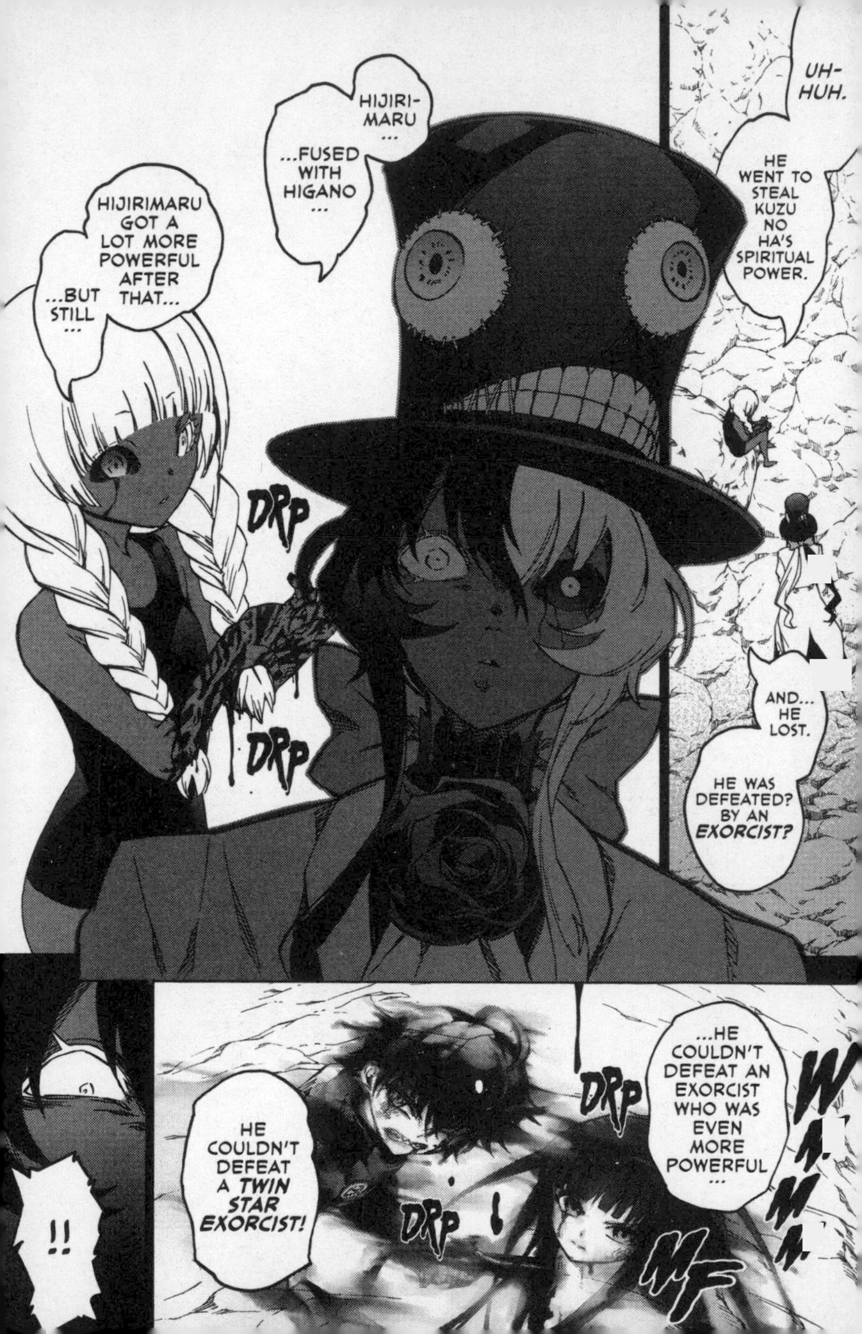
UH-HUH.
HE WENT TO STEAL KUZU NO HA'S SPIRITUAL POWER.
AND... HE LOST.
HE WAS DEFEATED? BY AN *EXORCIST?*
HIJIRI-MARU...
...FUSED WITH HIGANO...
HIJIRIMARU GOT A LOT MORE POWERFUL AFTER THAT...
...BUT STILL...
DRP
DRP
...HE COULDN'T DEFEAT AN EXORCIST WHO WAS EVEN MORE POWERFUL...
DRP
HE COULDN'T DEFEAT A *TWIN STAR EXORCIST!*
DRP
!!

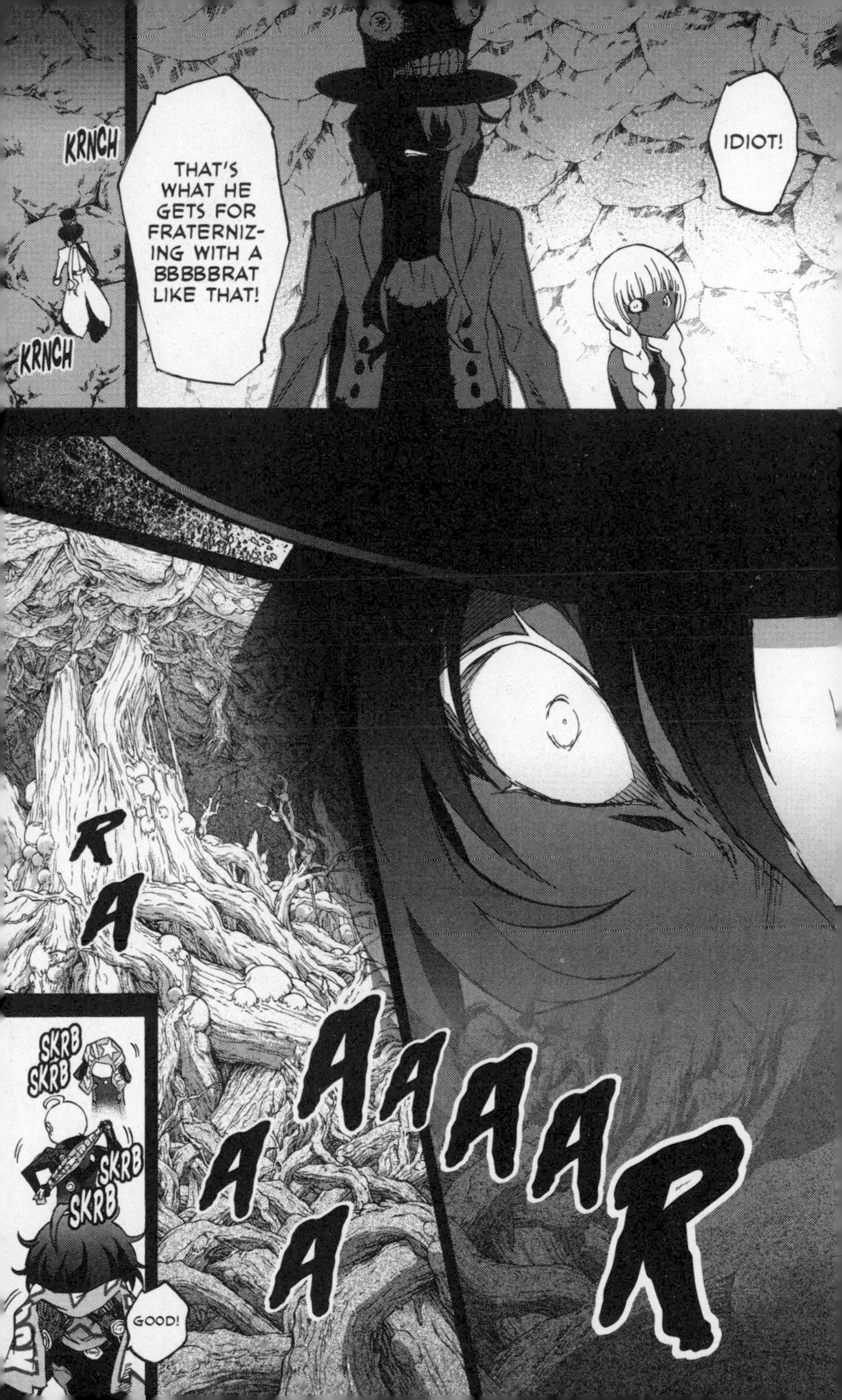
IDIOT!
THAT'S WHAT HE GETS FOR FRATERNIZ-ING WITH A BBBBBRAT LIKE THAT!
KRNCH
KRNCH
RAAAAAAAAR
SKRB SKRB
SKRB SKRB
GOOD!

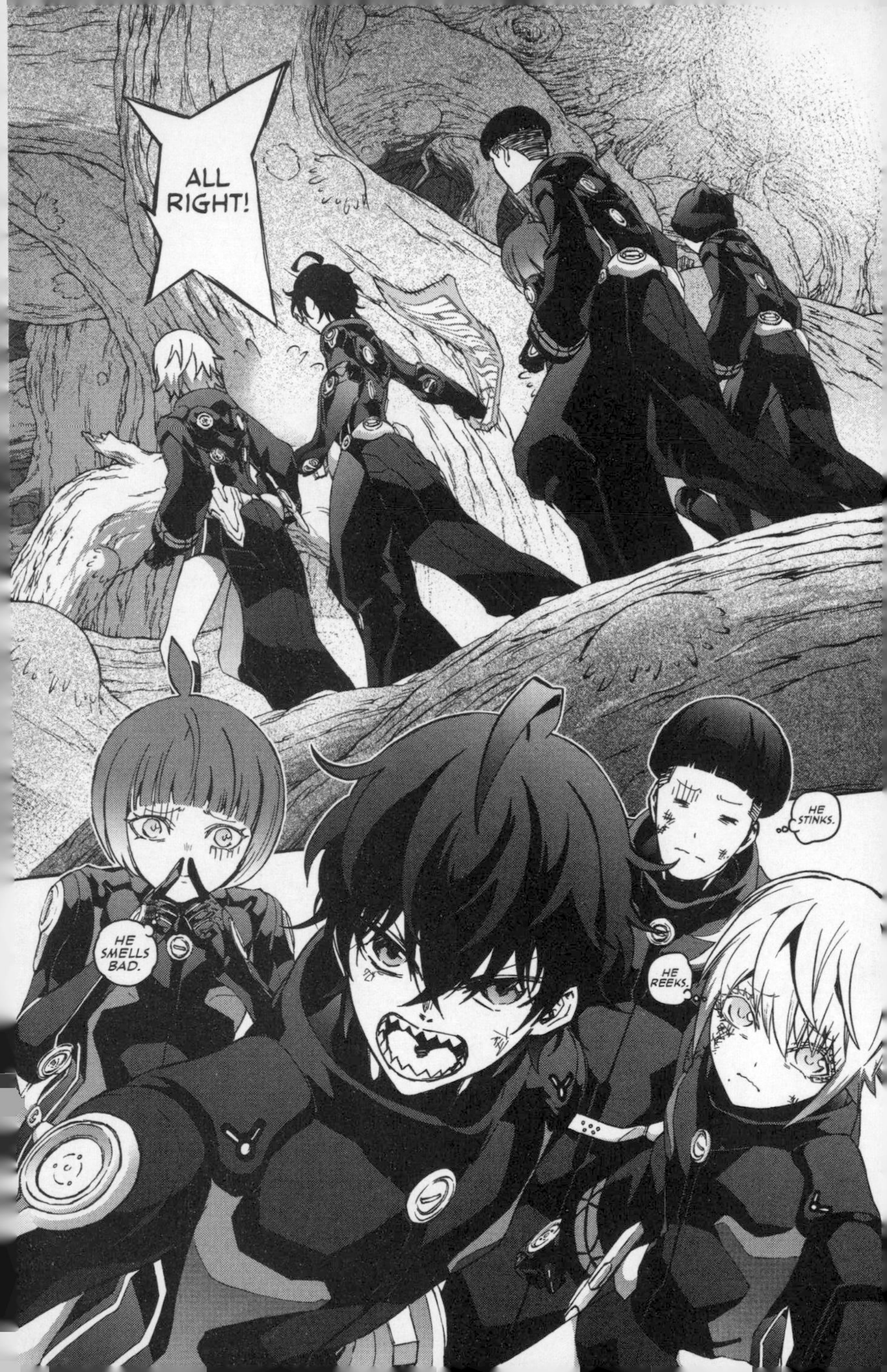
ALL RIGHT!
HE STINKS.
HE REEKS.
HE SMELLS BAD.

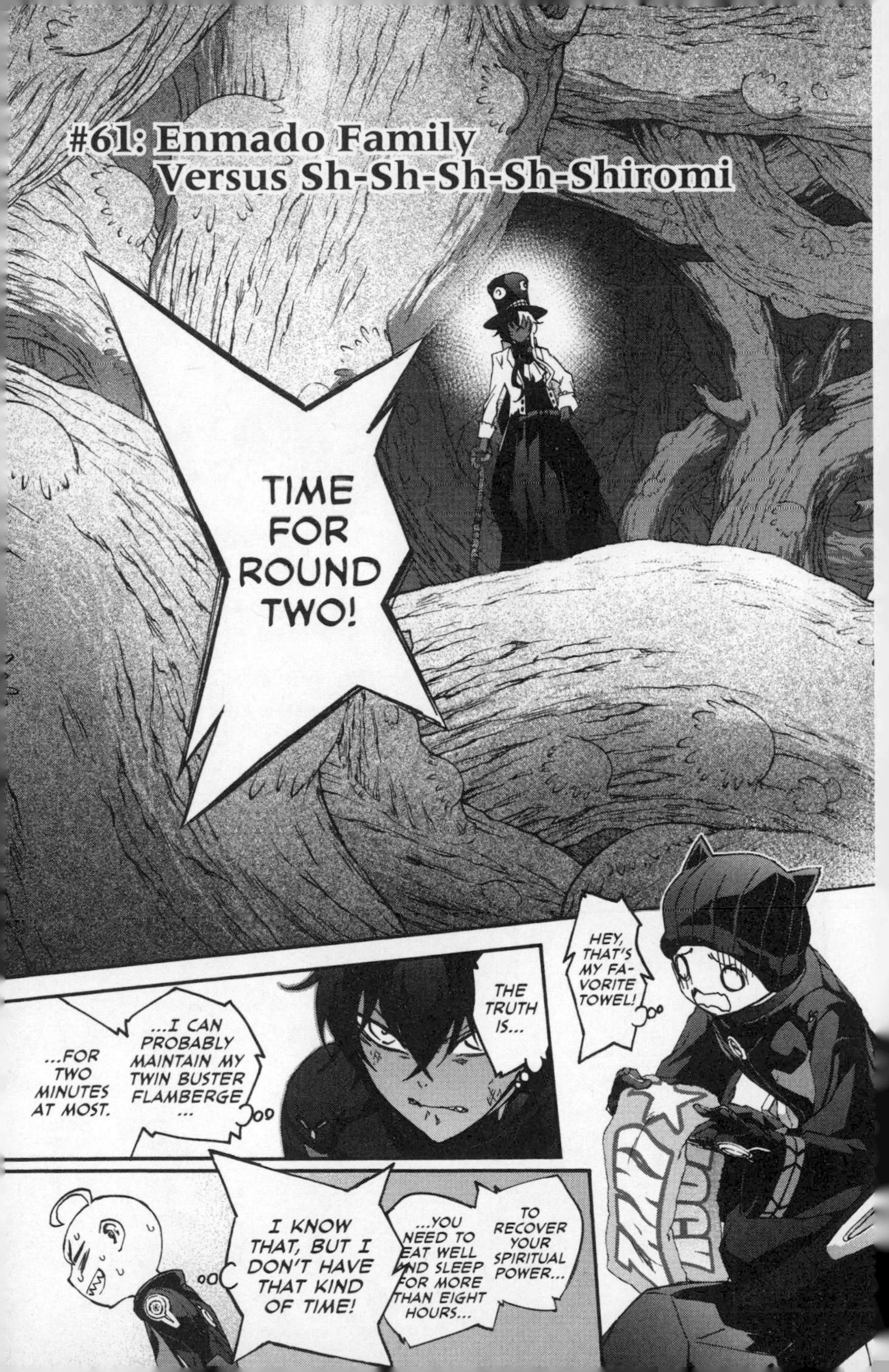
#61: Enmado Family Versus Sh-Sh-Sh-Sh-Shiromi
TIME FOR ROUND TWO!
HEY, THAT'S MY FAVORITE TOWEL!
THE TRUTH IS...
...I CAN PROBABLY MAINTAIN MY TWIN BUSTER FLAMBERGE...
...FOR TWO MINUTES AT MOST.
TO RECOVER YOUR SPIRITUAL POWER...
...YOU NEED TO EAT WELL AND SLEEP FOR MORE THAN EIGHT HOURS...
I KNOW THAT, BUT I DON'T HAVE THAT KIND OF TIME!

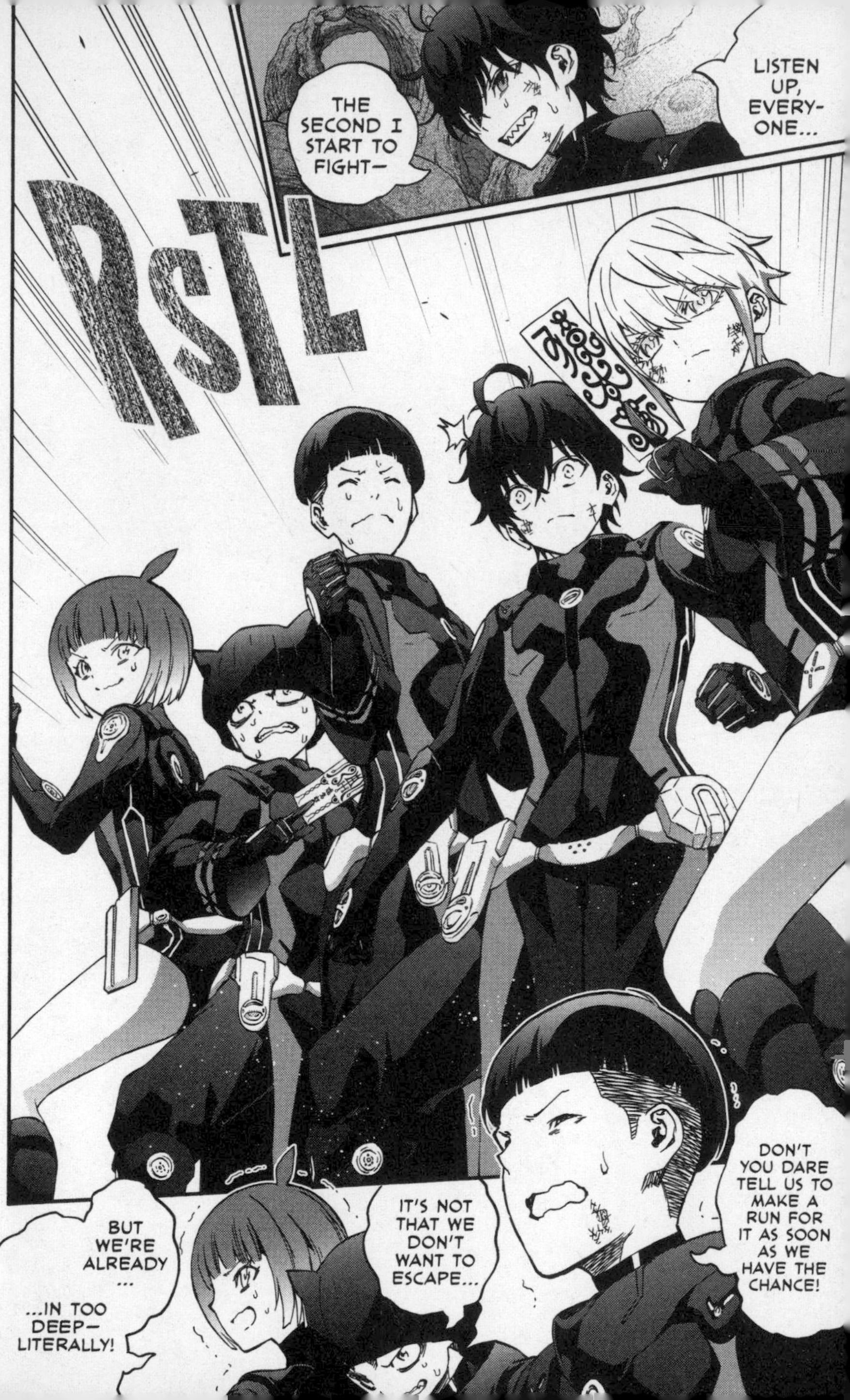
LISTEN UP, EVERYONE...
THE SECOND I START TO FIGHT—
RSTL
DON'T YOU DARE TELL US TO MAKE A RUN FOR IT AS SOON AS WE HAVE THE CHANCE!
IT'S NOT THAT WE DON'T WANT TO ESCAPE...
BUT WE'RE ALREADY ...
...IN TOO DEEP— LITERALLY!

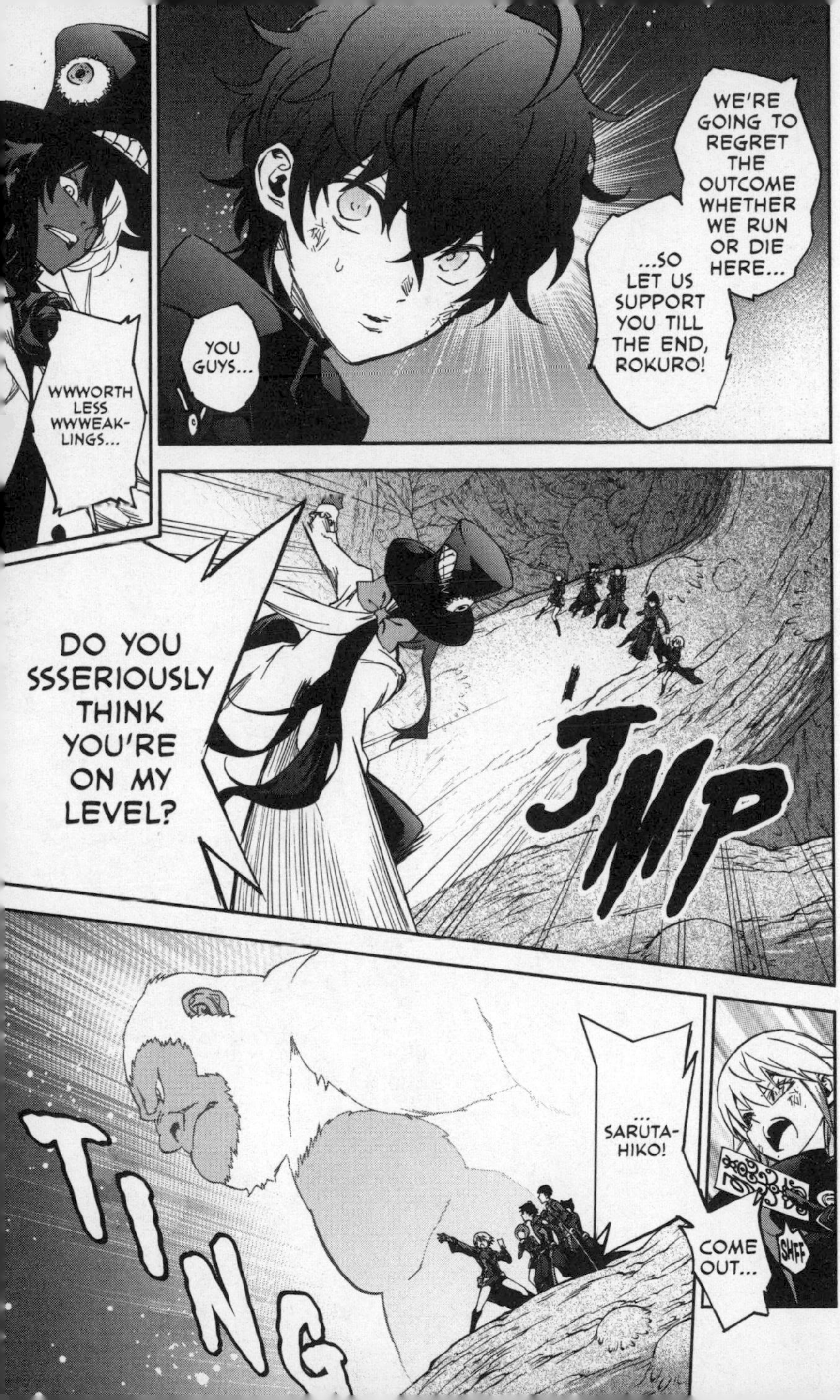
WE'RE GOING TO REGRET THE OUTCOME WHETHER WE RUN OR DIE HERE...
...SO LET US SUPPORT YOU TILL THE END, ROKURO!
YOU GUYS...
WWWORTH LESS WWWEAK-LINGS...
DO YOU SSSERIOUSLY THINK YOU'RE ON MY LEVEL?
JMP
COME OUT...
SHFF
...SARUTA-HIKO!
TING

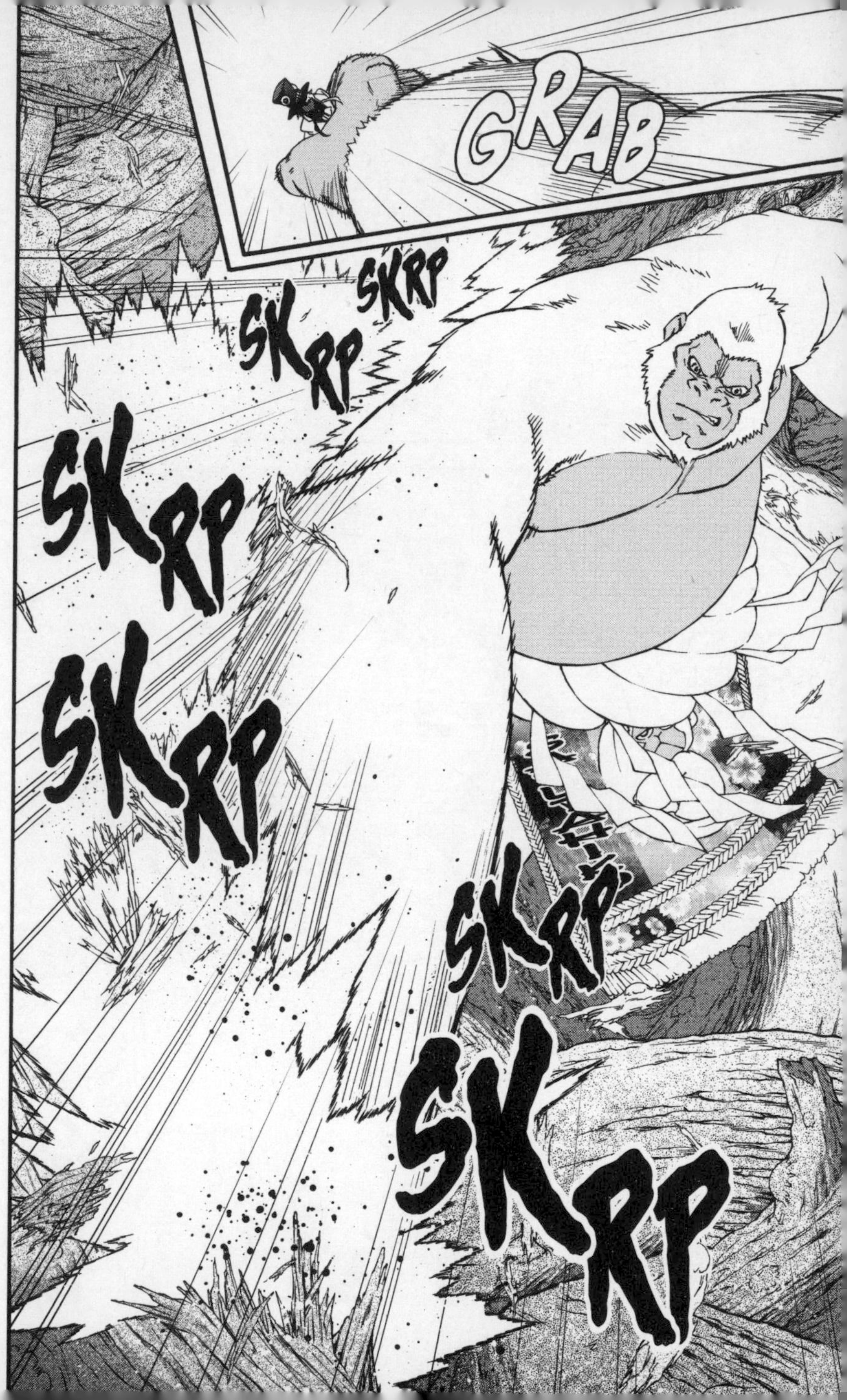
GRAB
SKRP
SKRP
SKRP
SKRP
SKRP
SKRP

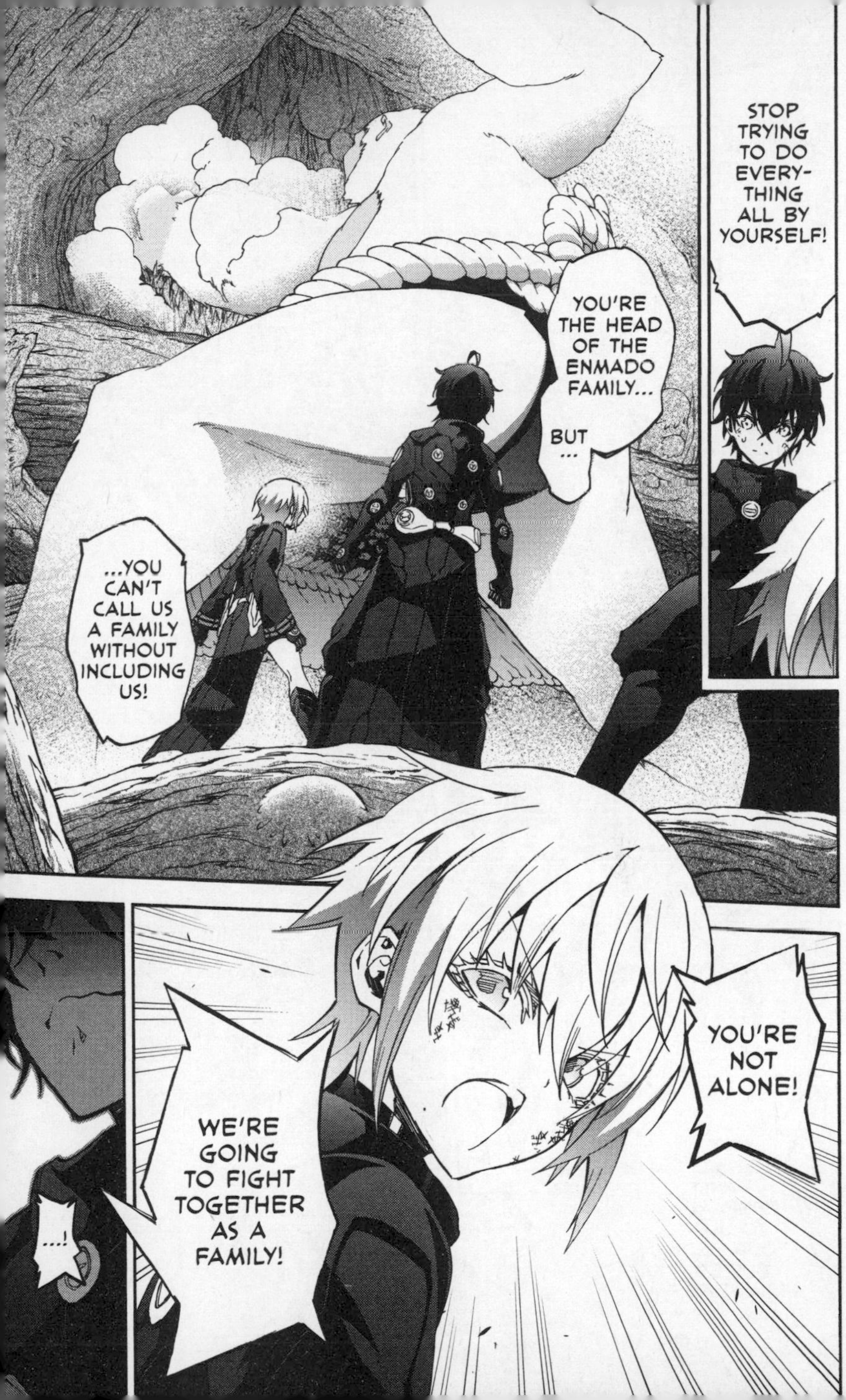
STOP TRYING TO DO EVERY-THING ALL BY YOURSELF!
YOU'RE THE HEAD OF THE ENMADO FAMILY...
BUT ...
...YOU CAN'T CALL US A FAMILY WITHOUT INCLUDING US!
YOU'RE NOT ALONE!
WE'RE GOING TO FIGHT TOGETHER AS A FAMILY!
...!

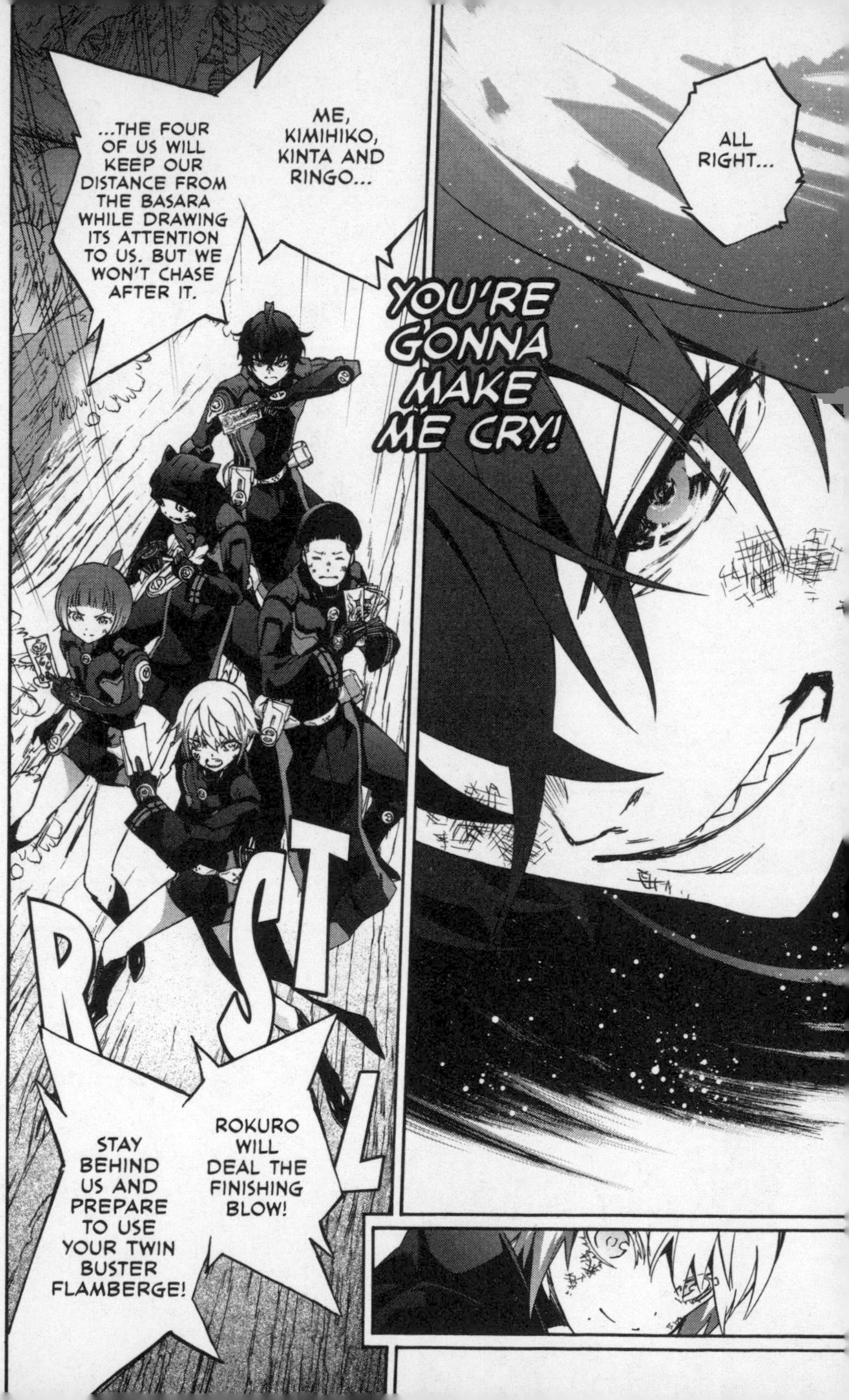
ALL RIGHT...
YOU'RE GONNA MAKE ME CRY!
ME, KIMIHIKO, KINTA AND RINGO...
...THE FOUR OF US WILL KEEP OUR DISTANCE FROM THE BASARA WHILE DRAWING ITS ATTENTION TO US. BUT WE WON'T CHASE AFTER IT.
RSTL
ROKURO WILL DEAL THE FINISHING BLOW!
STAY BEHIND US AND PREPARE TO USE YOUR TWIN BUSTER FLAMBERGE!

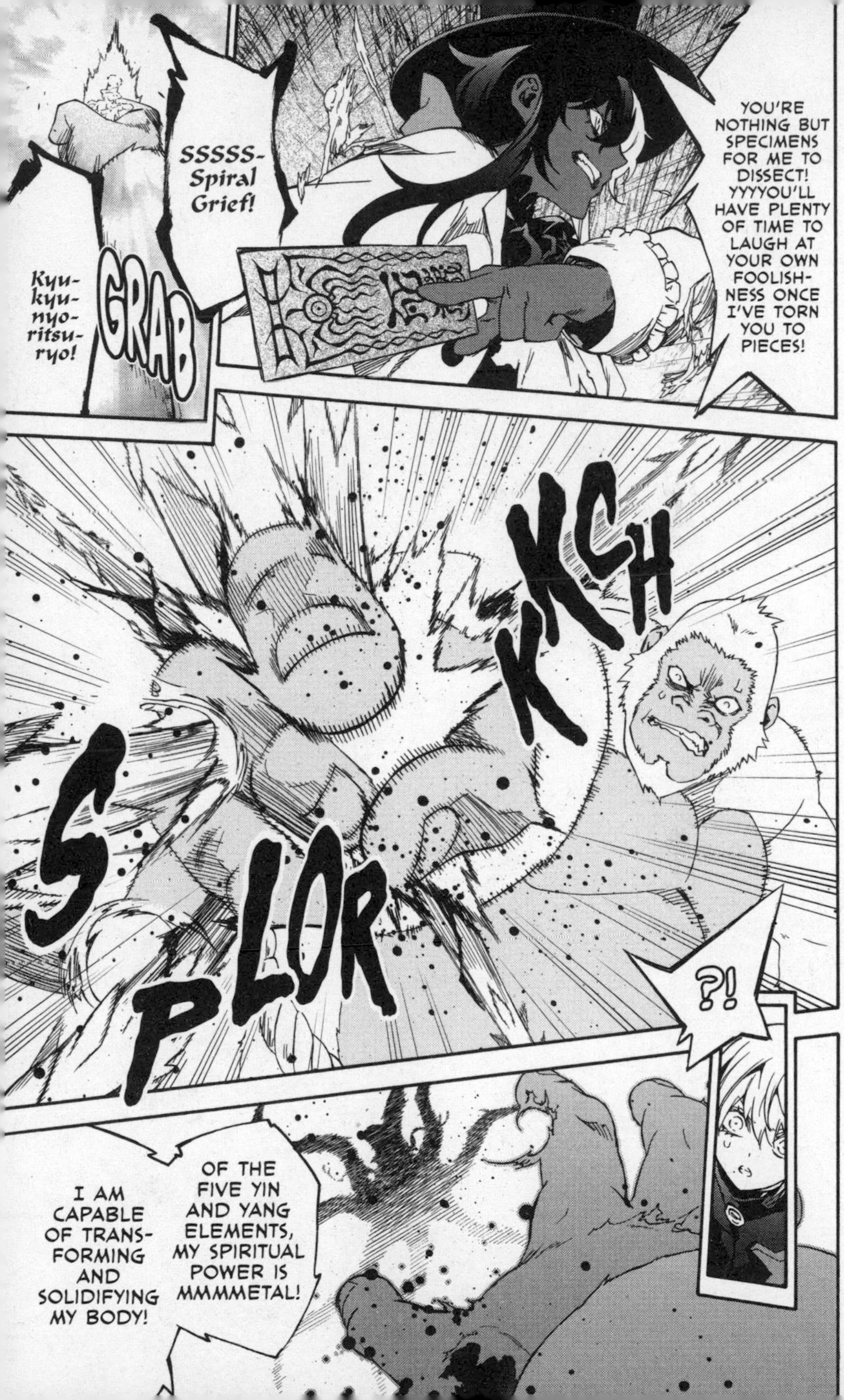

YOU'RE NOTHING BUT SPECIMENS FOR ME TO DISSECT! YYYYOU'LL HAVE PLENTY OF TIME TO LAUGH AT YOUR OWN FOOLISHNESS ONCE I'VE TORN YOU TO PIECES!
SSSSS- Spiral Grief!
GRAB
Kyu-kyu-nyo-ritsu-ryo!
KKCH
SPLOR
?!
OF THE FIVE YIN AND YANG ELEMENTS, MY SPIRITUAL POWER IS MMMMETAL!
I AM CAPABLE OF TRANSFORMING AND SOLIDIFYING MY BODY!

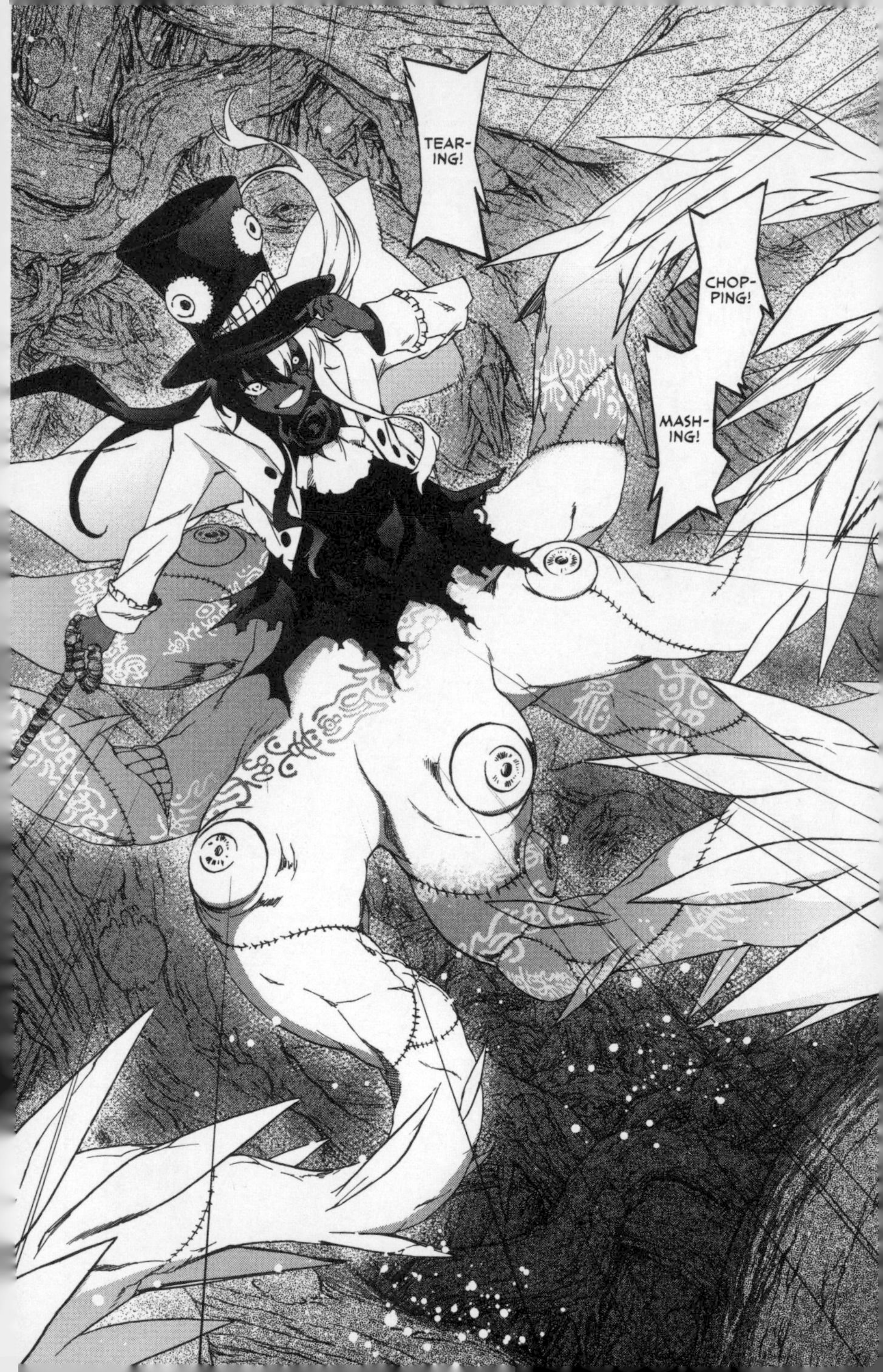
CHOP-
PING!
MASH-
ING!
TEAR-
ING!

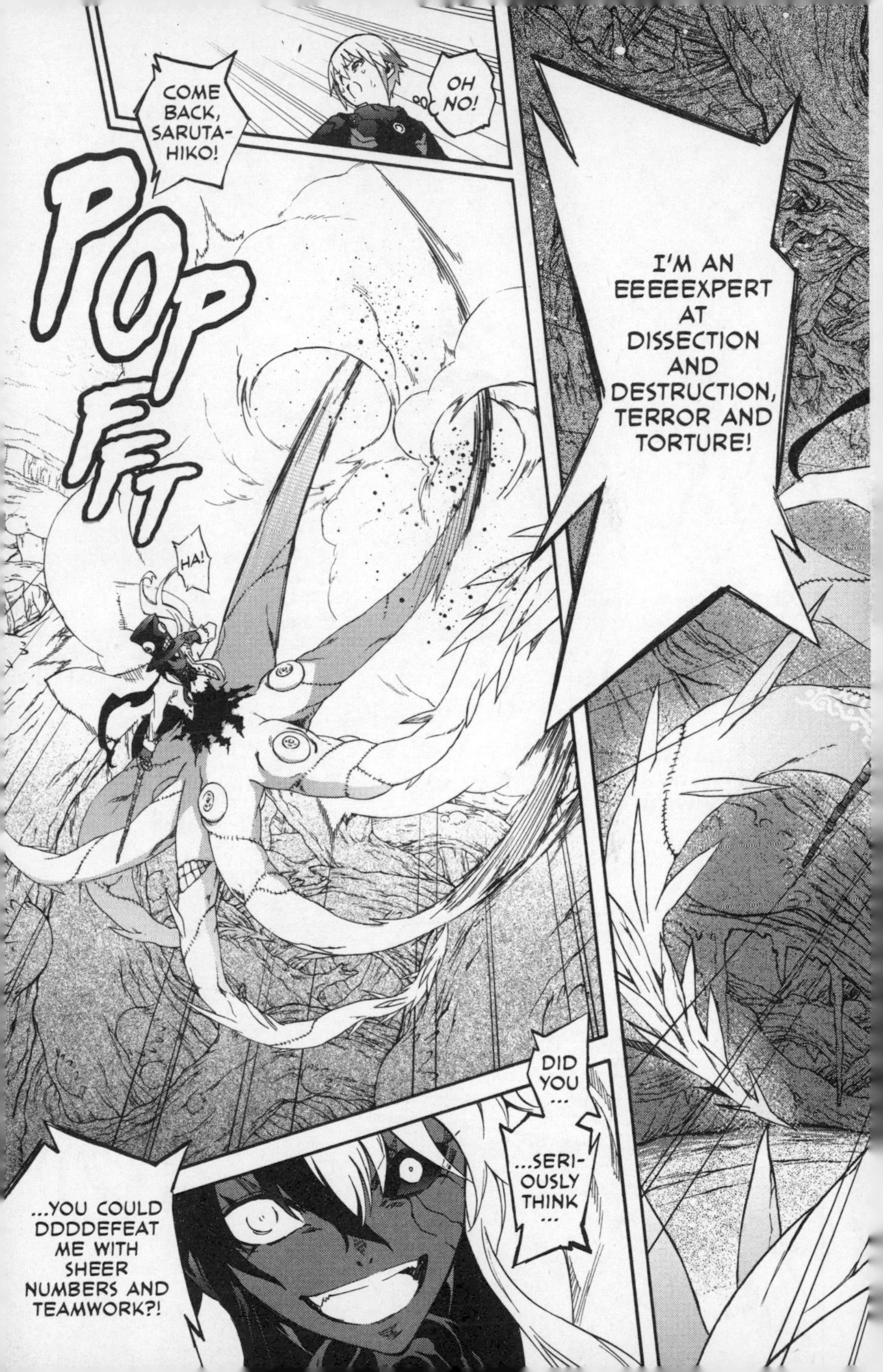
I'M AN EEEEEXPERT AT DISSECTION AND DESTRUCTION, TERROR AND TORTURE!
OH NO!
COME BACK, SARUTA-HIKO!
POP
FFT
HA!
DID YOU...
...SERI-OUSLY THINK...
...YOU COULD DDDDEFEAT ME WITH SHEER NUMBERS AND TEAMWORK?!

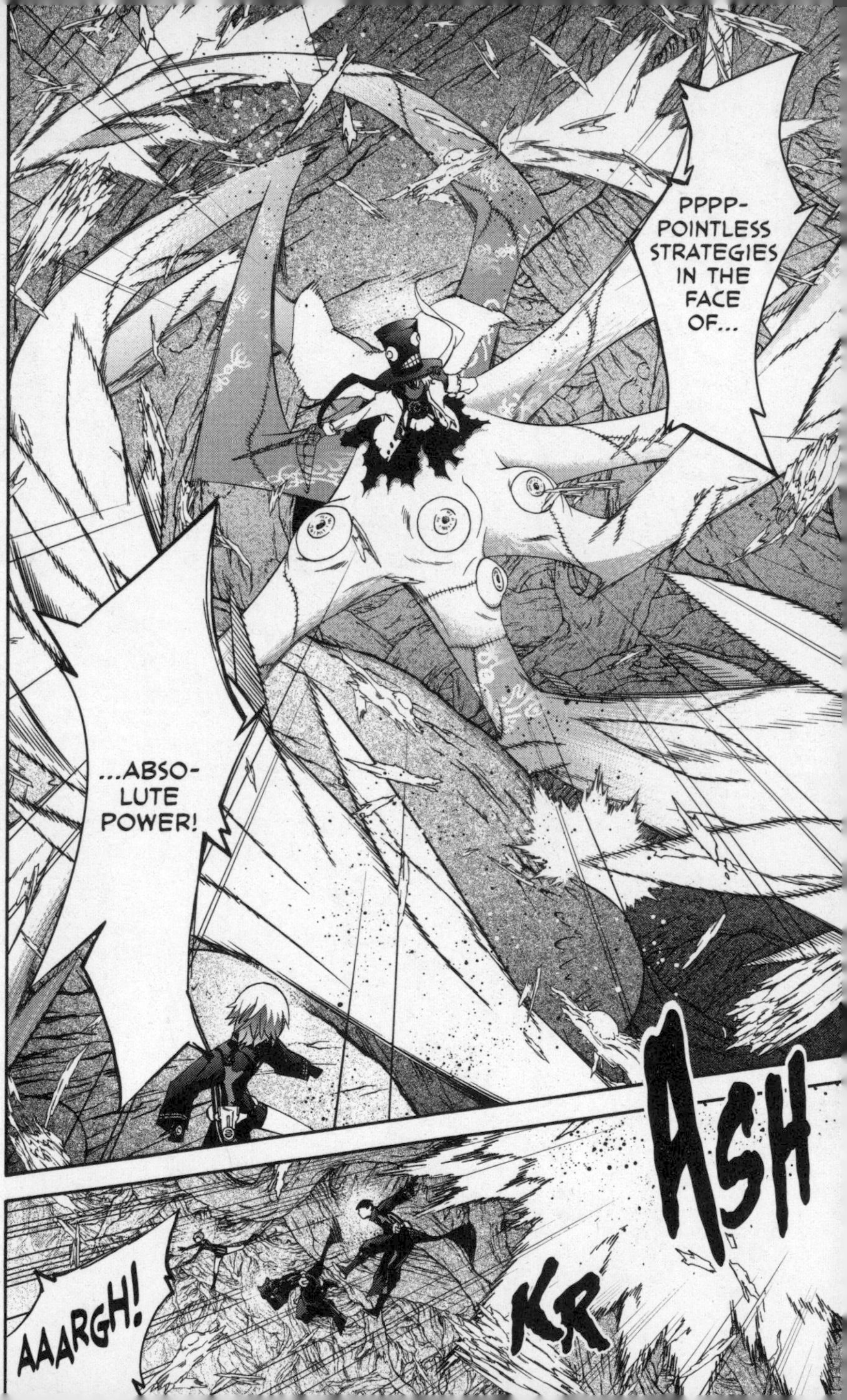
PPPP-POINTLESS STRATEGIES IN THE FACE OF...
...ABSOLUTE POWER!
KRASH
AAARGH!

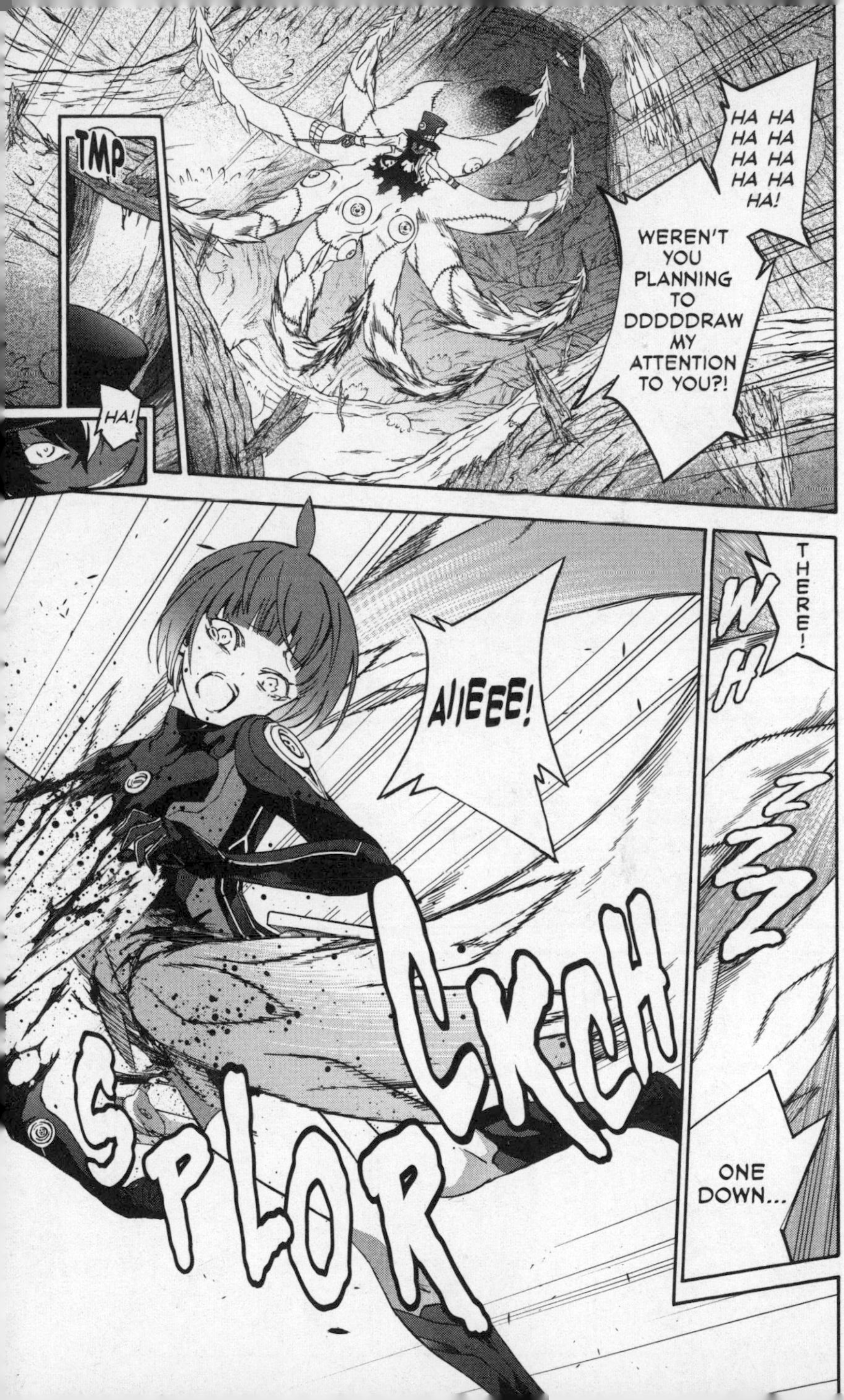
HA HA HA HA HA HA HA HA HA!
WEREN'T YOU PLANNING TO DDDDDRAW MY ATTENTION TO YOU?!
TMP
HA!
THERE!
WHZZZ
ONE DOWN...
AIIEEE!
SPLORLKCH

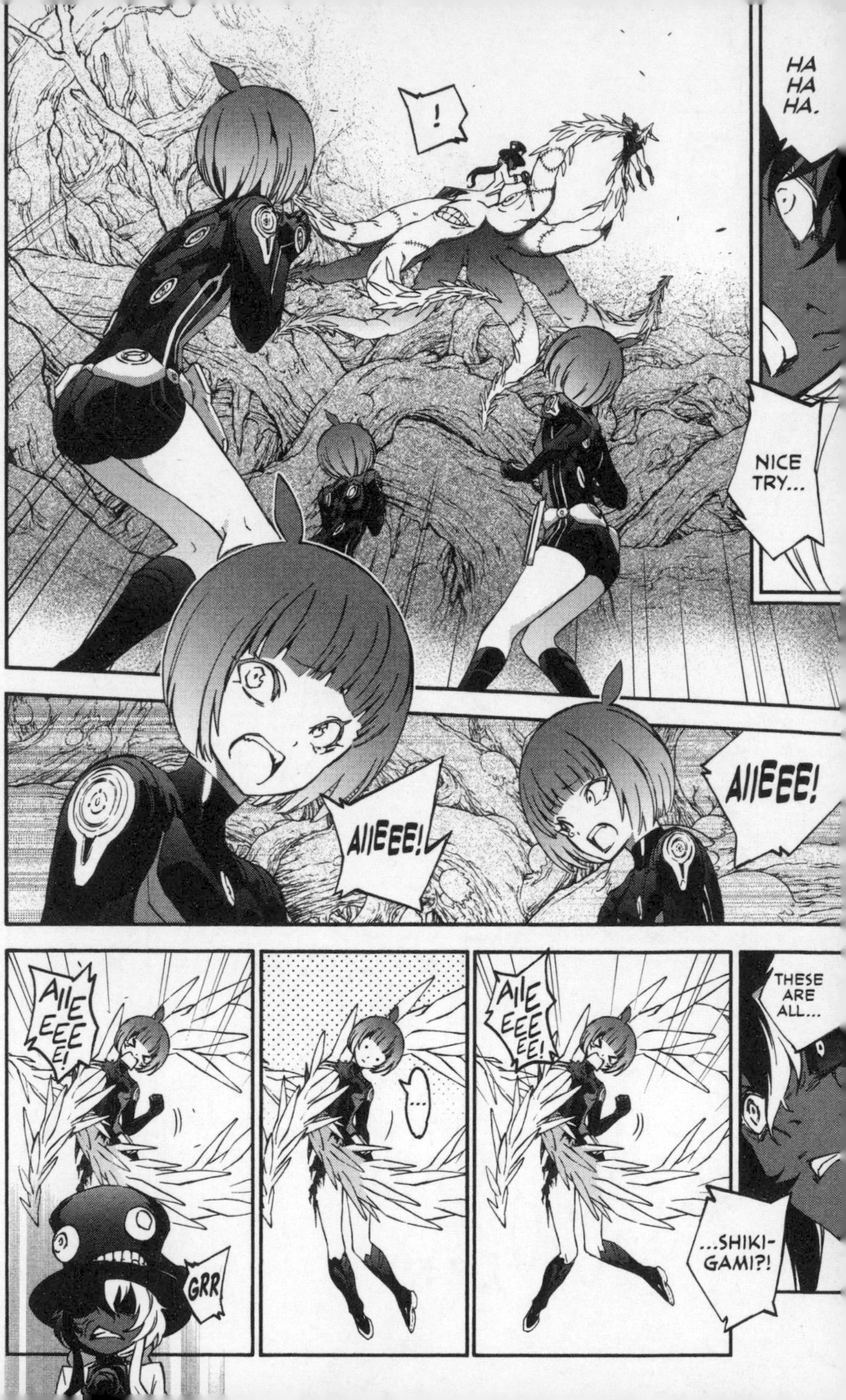
HA HA HA.
NICE TRY...
!
AIIEEE!
AIIEEE!
THESE ARE ALL...
...SHIKI-GAMI?!
AIIEEEEEE!
...
AIIEEEEEE!
GRR

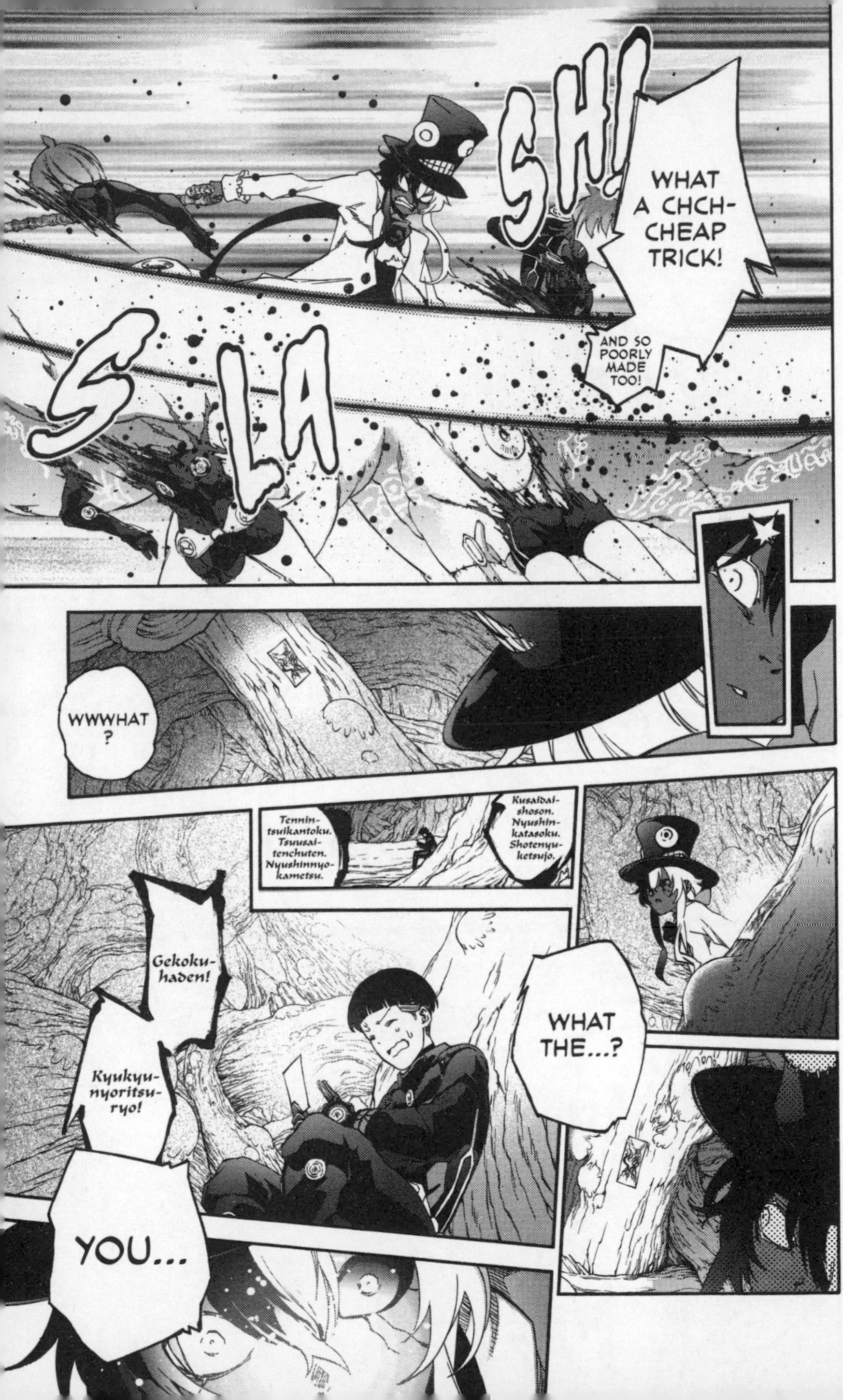
WHAT A CHCH-CHEAP TRICK!
AND SO POORLY MADE TOO!
SLA
SH!
WWWHAT?
Kusaidai-shoson. Nyushin-katasoku. Shotenyu-ketsujo.
Tennin-tsuikantoku. Tsuusai-tenchuten. Nyushinnyo-kametsu.
WHAT THE...?
Gekoku-haden!
Kyukyu-nyoritsu-ryo!
YOU...

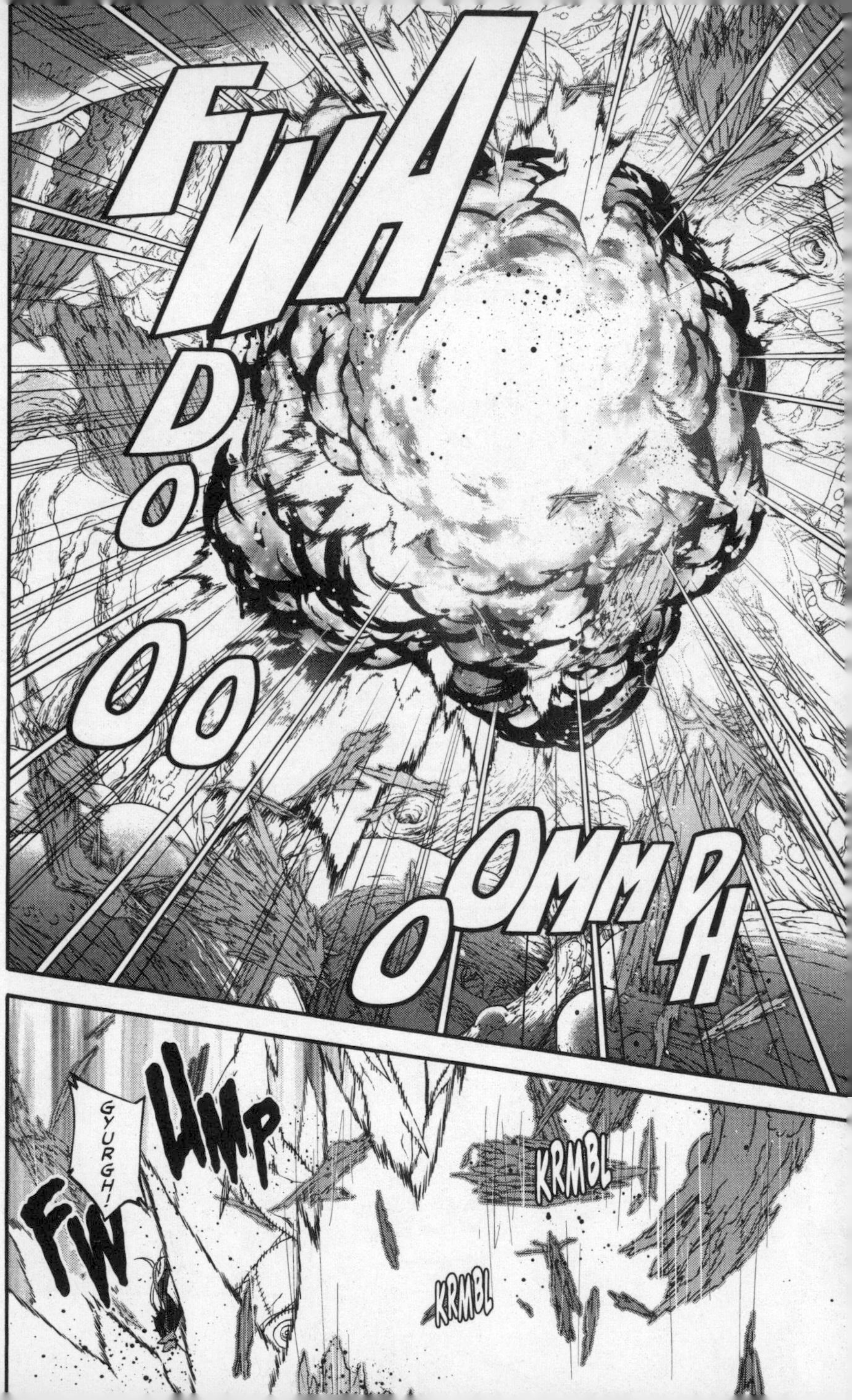
FWA
DOOOOOMM PA
KRMBL
FWUMP
GYURGH!
KRMBL

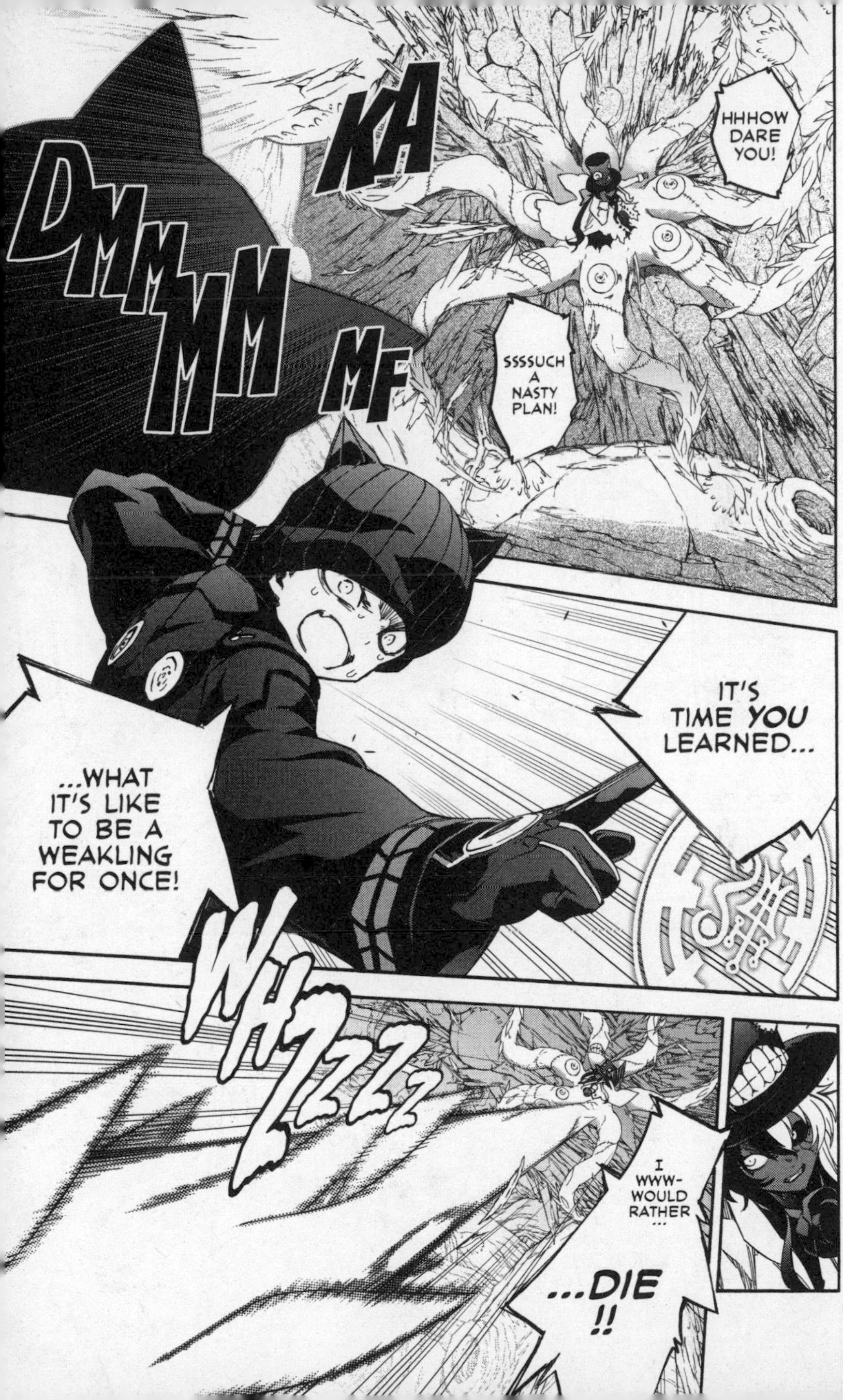
KA
HHHOW DARE YOU!
SSSSUCH A NASTY PLAN!
DMMMMMMF
IT'S TIME YOU LEARNED...
...WHAT IT'S LIKE TO BE A WEAKLING FOR ONCE!
WHZZZZ
I WWW-WOULD RATHER ...
...DIE !!

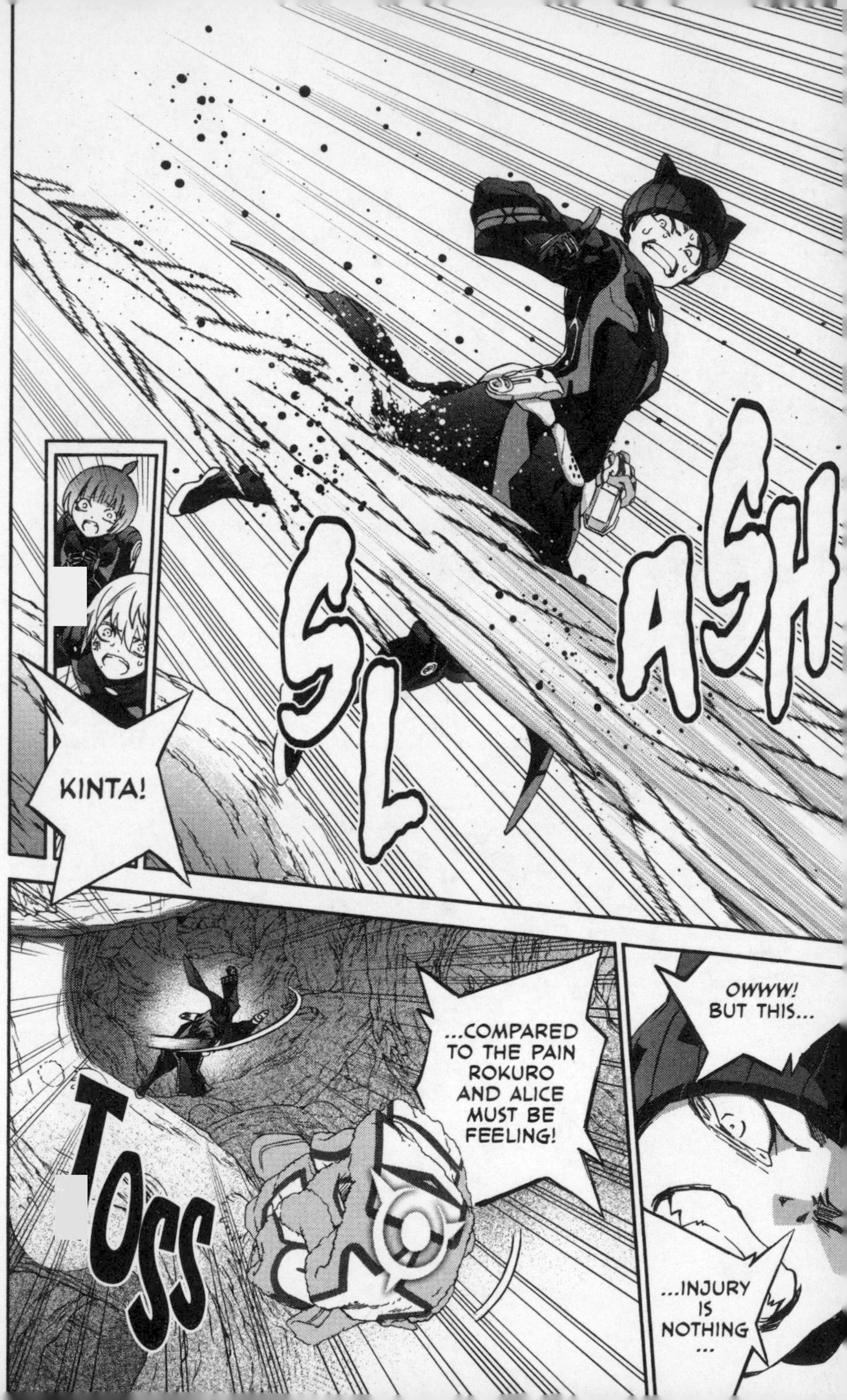
SLASH
KINTA!
OWWW! BUT THIS...
...INJURY IS NOTHING...
...COMPARED TO THE PAIN ROKURO AND ALICE MUST BE FEELING!
TOSS

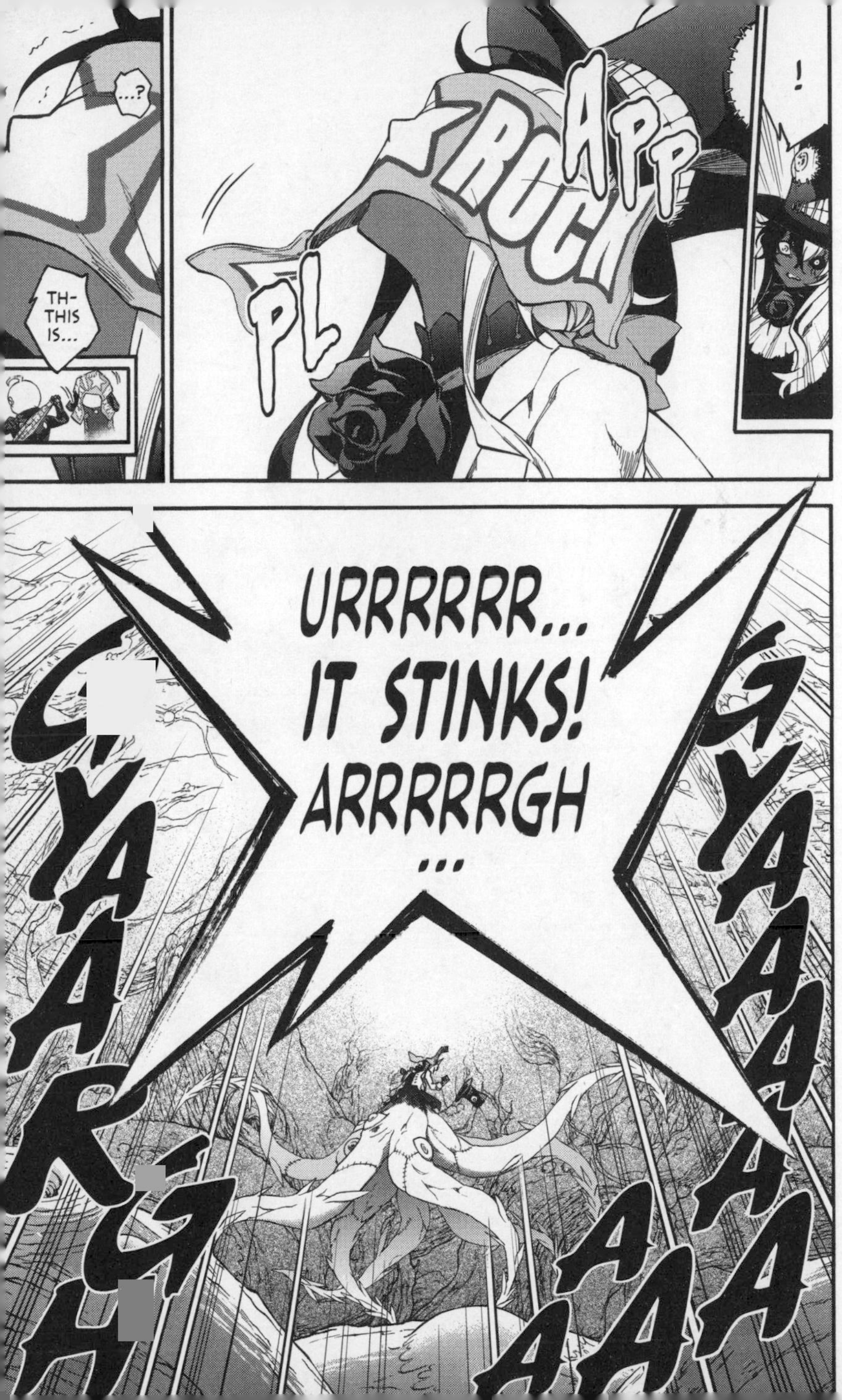
!
...?
TH- THIS IS...
URRRRRR... IT STINKS! ARRRRRGH ...

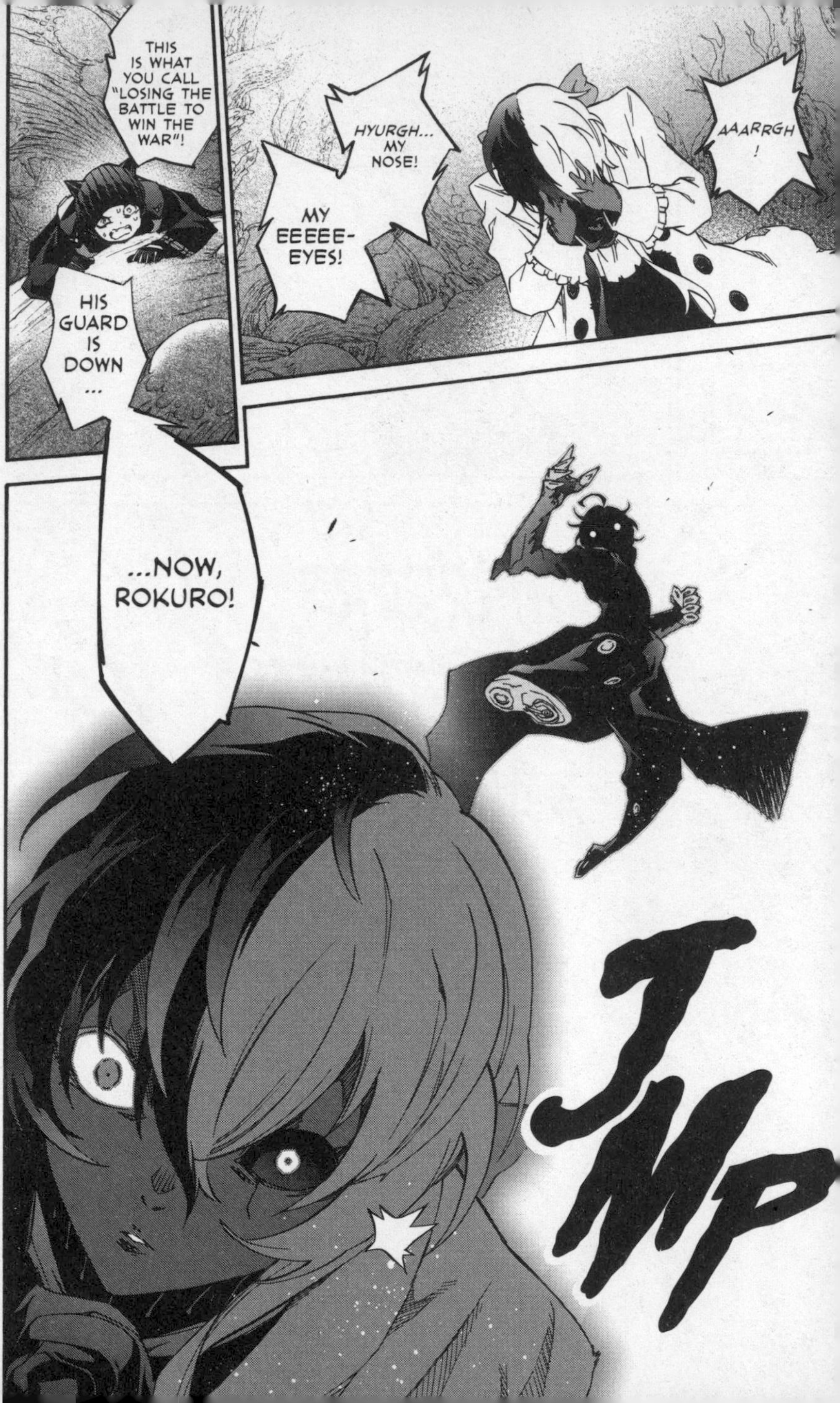
AAARRGH!
HYURGH... MY NOSE!
MY EEEEE-EYES!
THIS IS WHAT YOU CALL "LOSING THE BATTLE TO WIN THE WAR"!
HIS GUARD IS DOWN ...
...NOW, ROKURO!

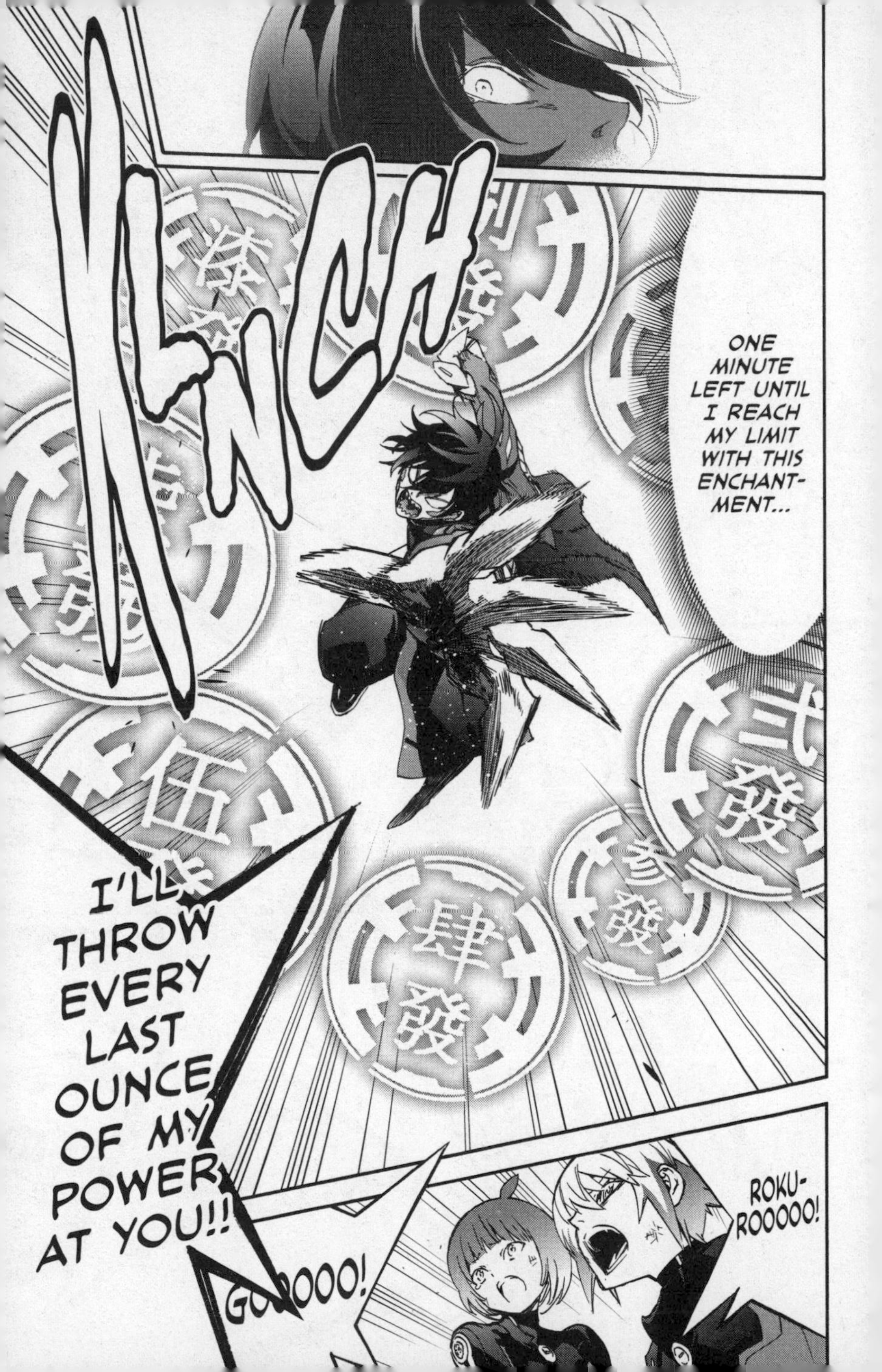
ONE MINUTE LEFT UNTIL I REACH MY LIMIT WITH THIS ENCHANT-MENT...
I'LL THROW EVERY LAST OUNCE OF MY POWER AT YOU!!
ROKU-ROOOOO!

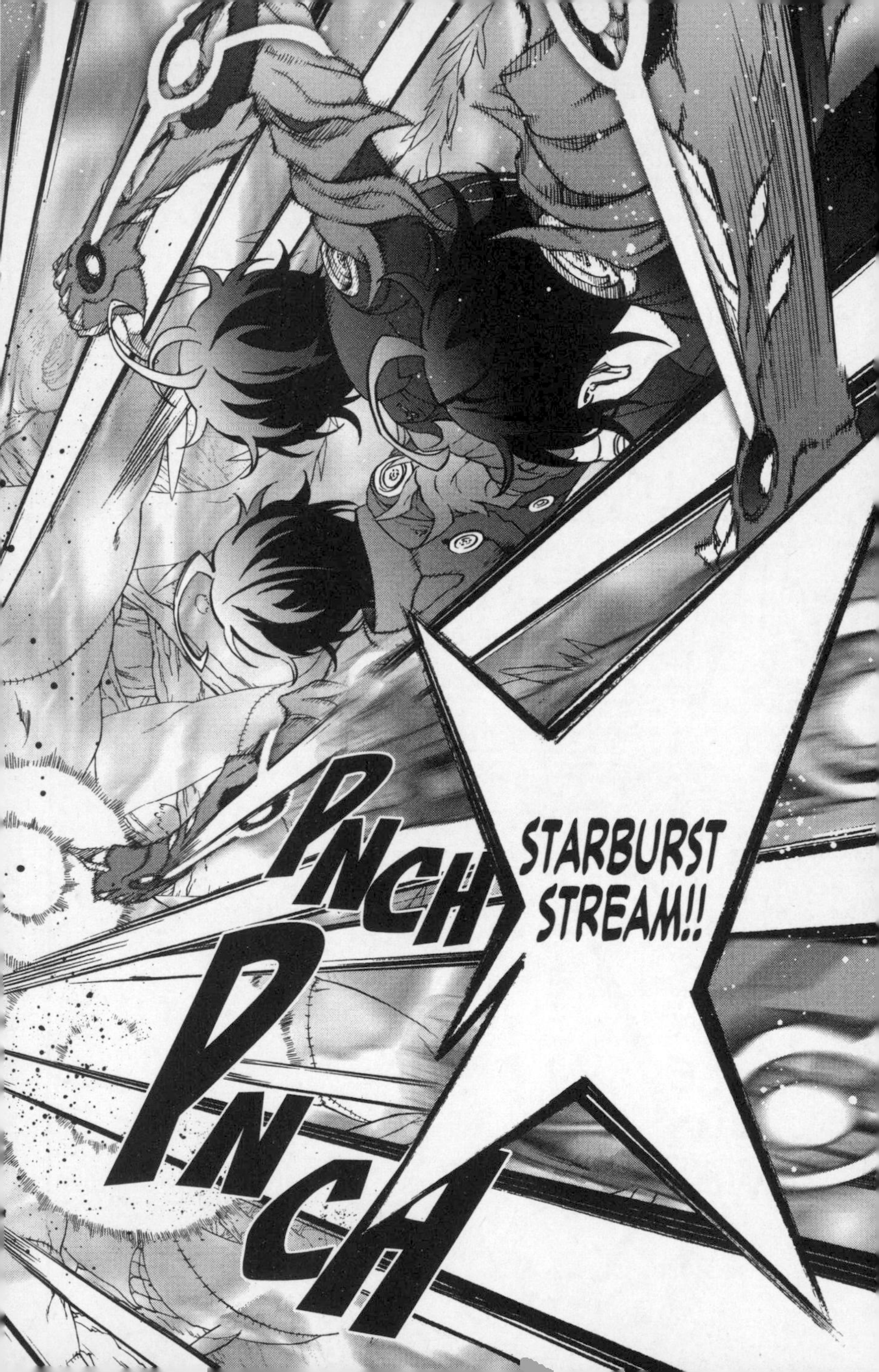
STARBURST STREAM!!

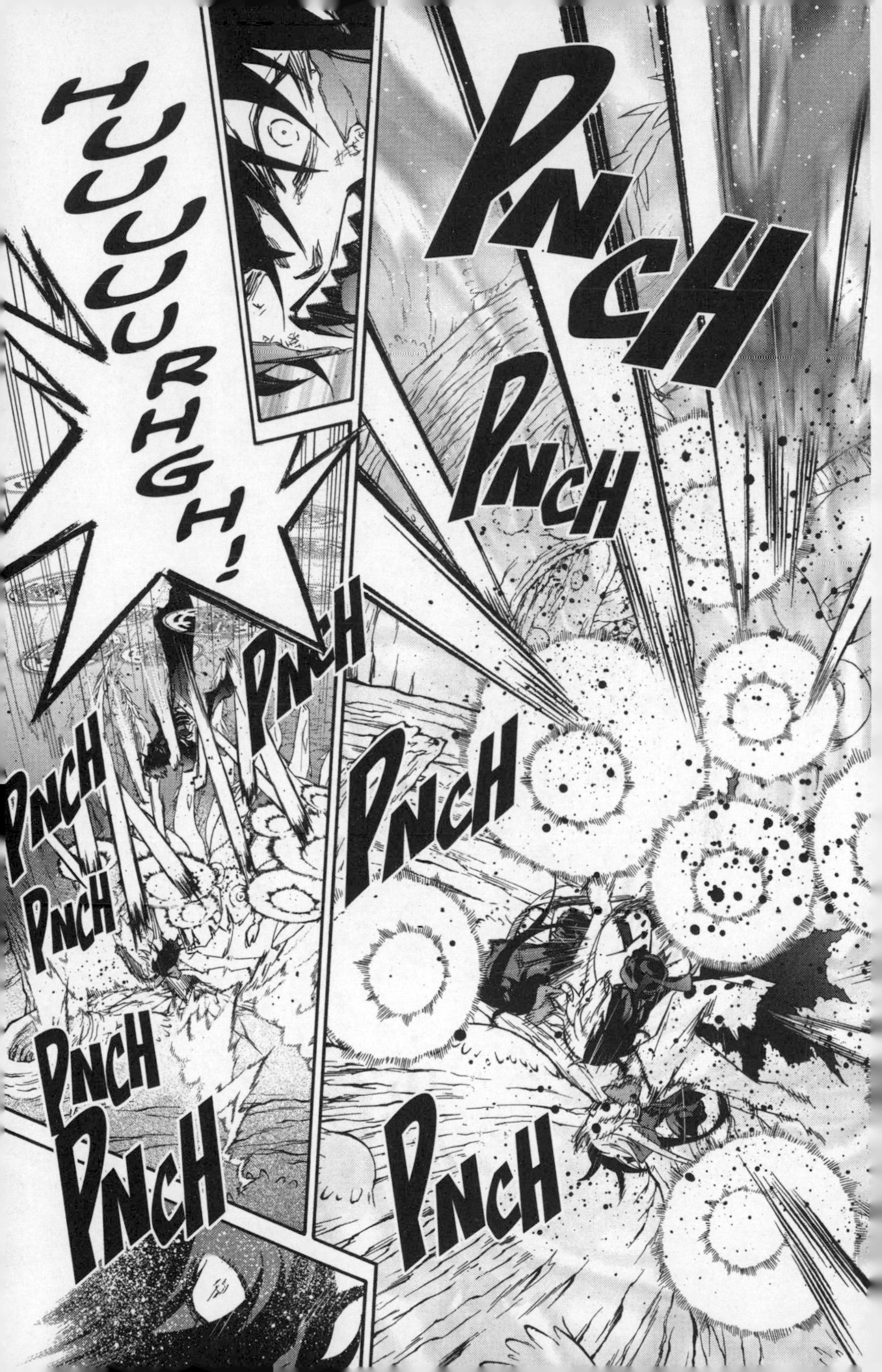
PNCH
PNCH
HUUURRHGH!
PNCH
PNCH
PNCH
PNCH
PNCH
PNCH
PNCH

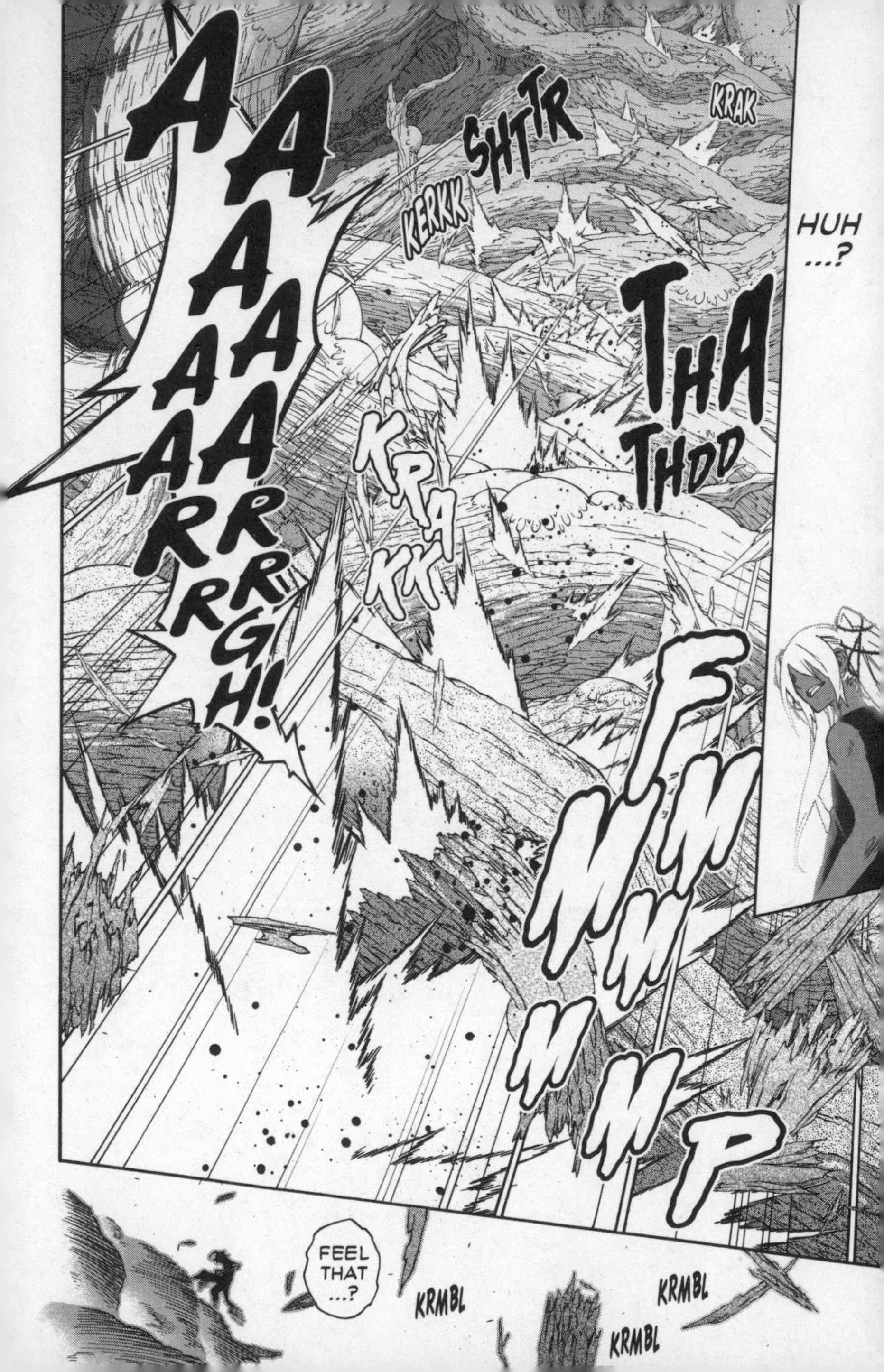
HUH ...?
AAAAAAAAARRRRGH!
KRAK
SHTR
KERKK
THA
THDD
KRAKK
FMMMMMMP
FEEL THAT ...?
KRMBL
KRMBL
KRMBL

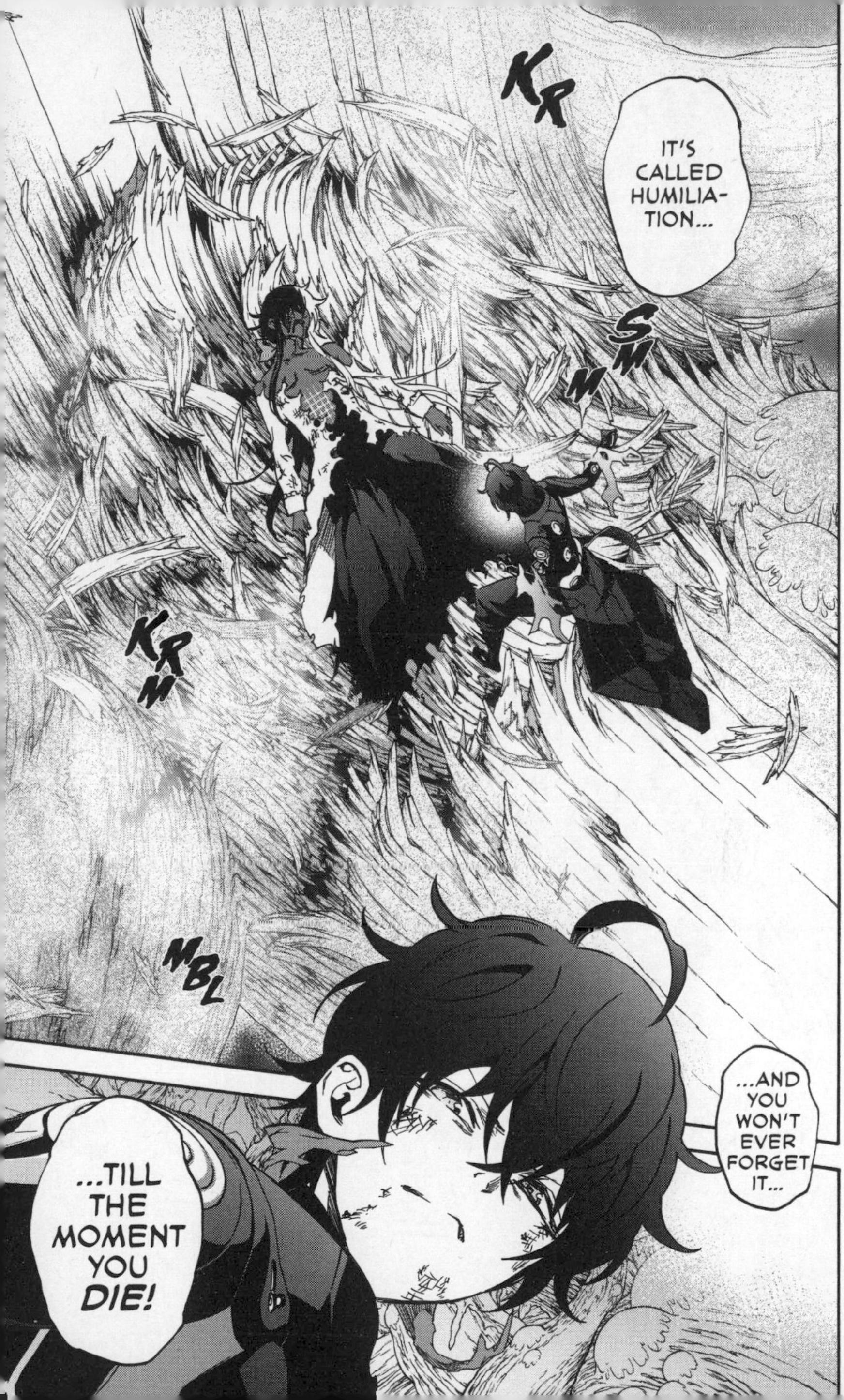
KR
IT'S CALLED HUMILIATION...
SMM
KRM
MBL
...AND YOU WON'T EVER FORGET IT...
...TILL THE MOMENT YOU *DIE!*

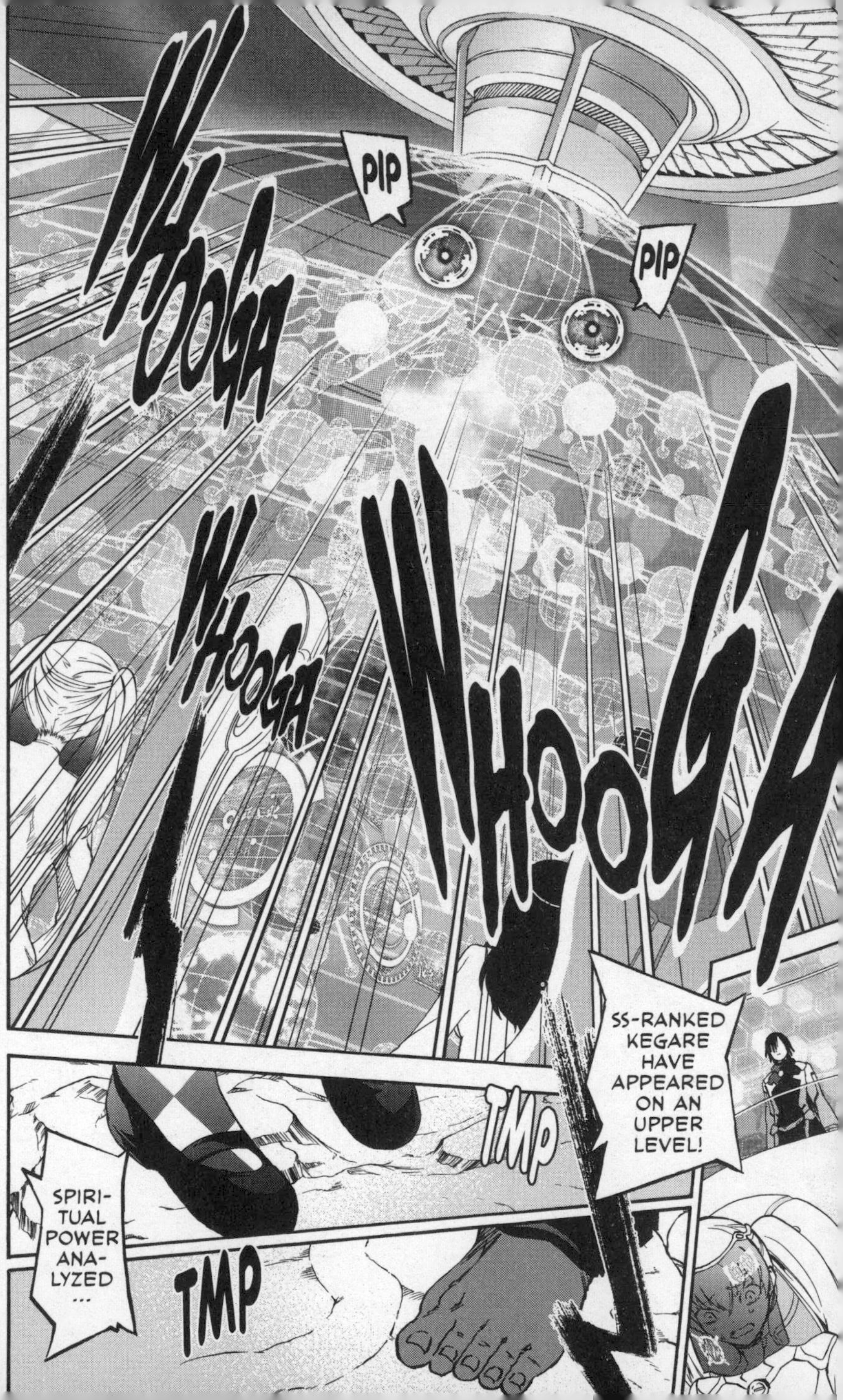
PIP
PIP
WHOOGA
WHOOGA
WHOOGA
SS-RANKED KEGARE HAVE APPEARED ON AN UPPER LEVEL!
TMP
SPIRI-TUAL POWER ANA-LYZED...
TMP

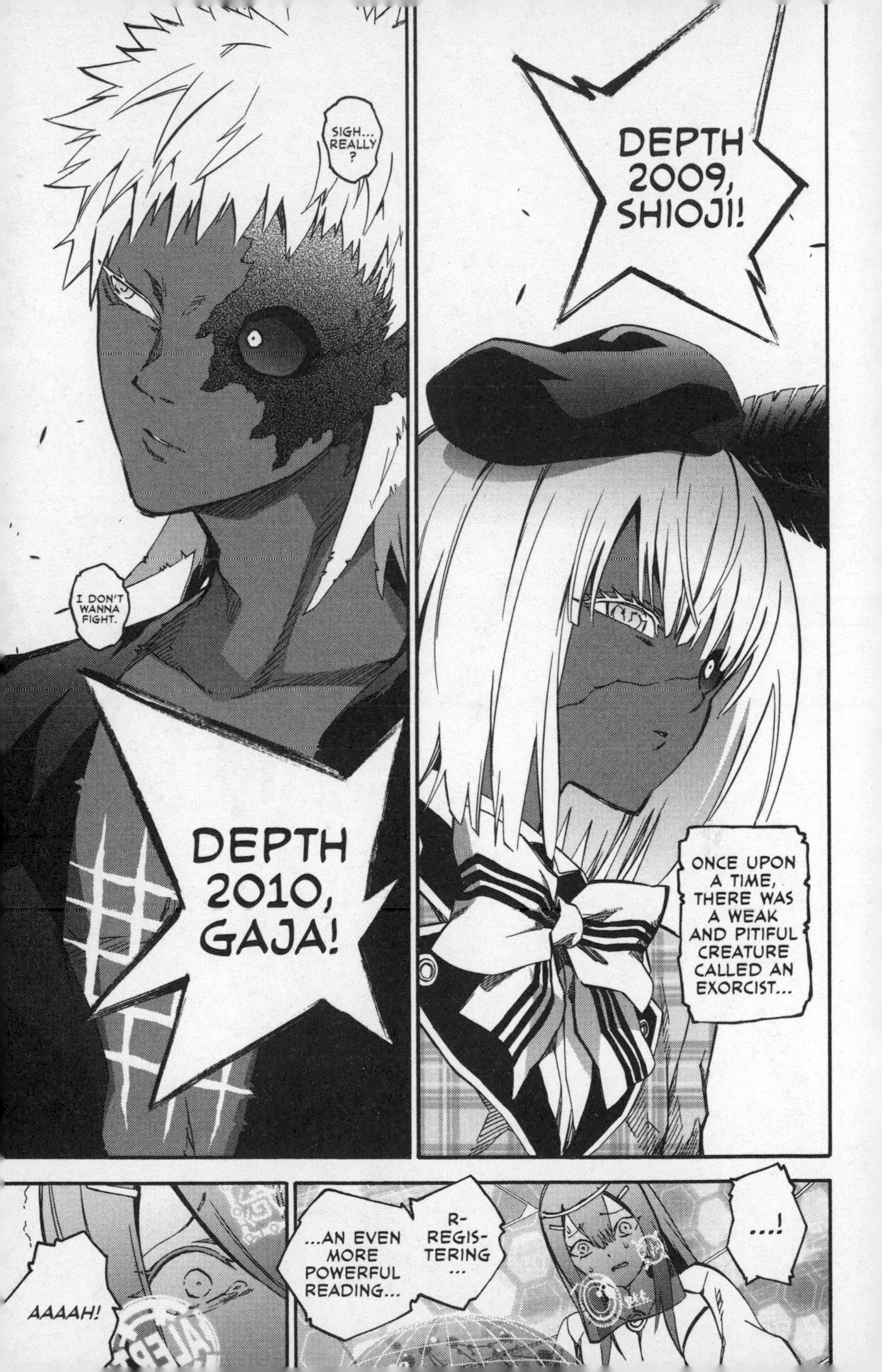
DEPTH 2009, SHIOJI!
ONCE UPON A TIME, THERE WAS A WEAK AND PITIFUL CREATURE CALLED AN EXORCIST...
SIGH... REALLY?
I DON'T WANNA FIGHT.
DEPTH 2010, GAJA!
...!
R-REGISTERING...
...AN EVEN MORE POWERFUL READING...
AAAAH!

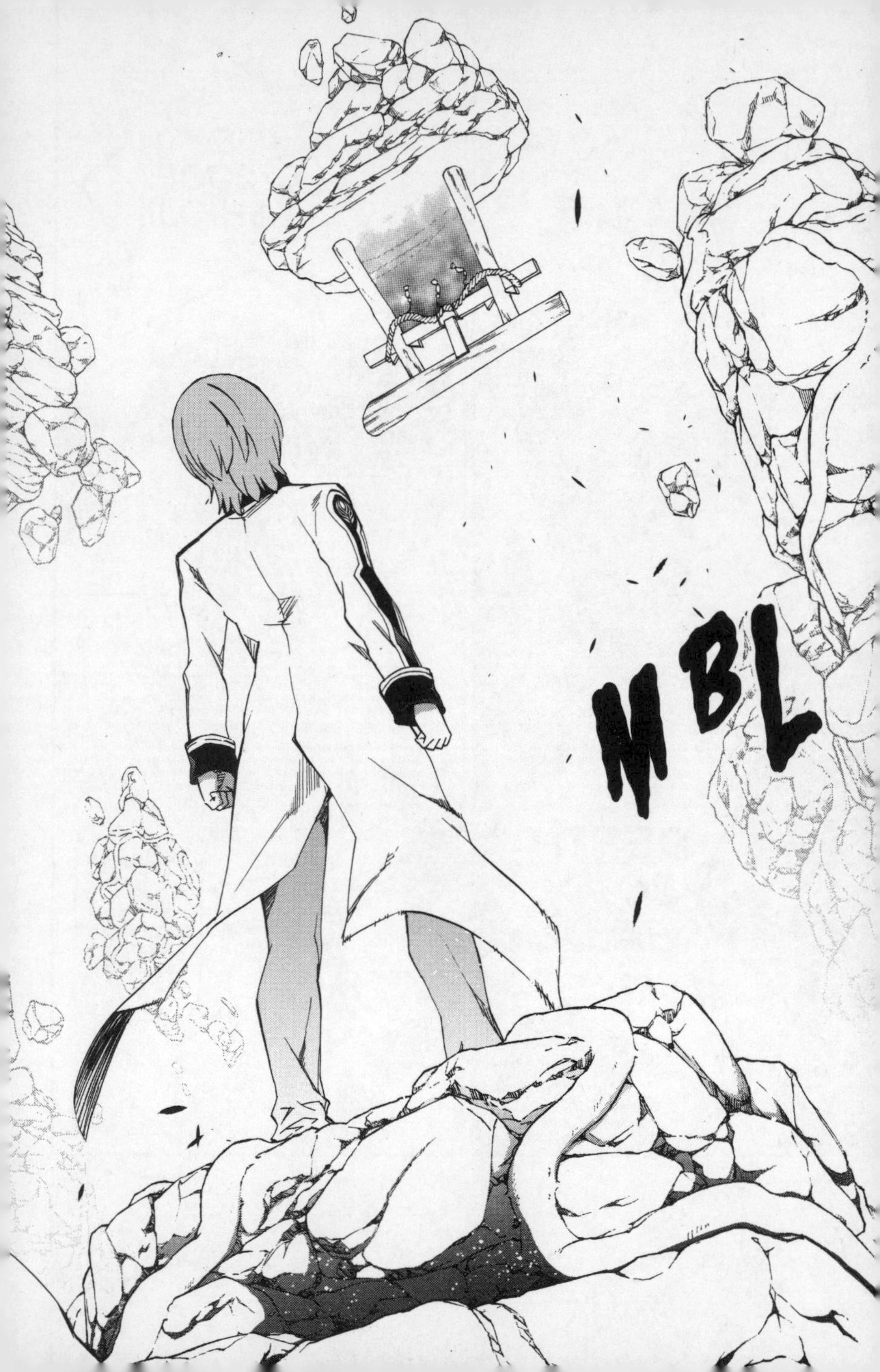
MBL

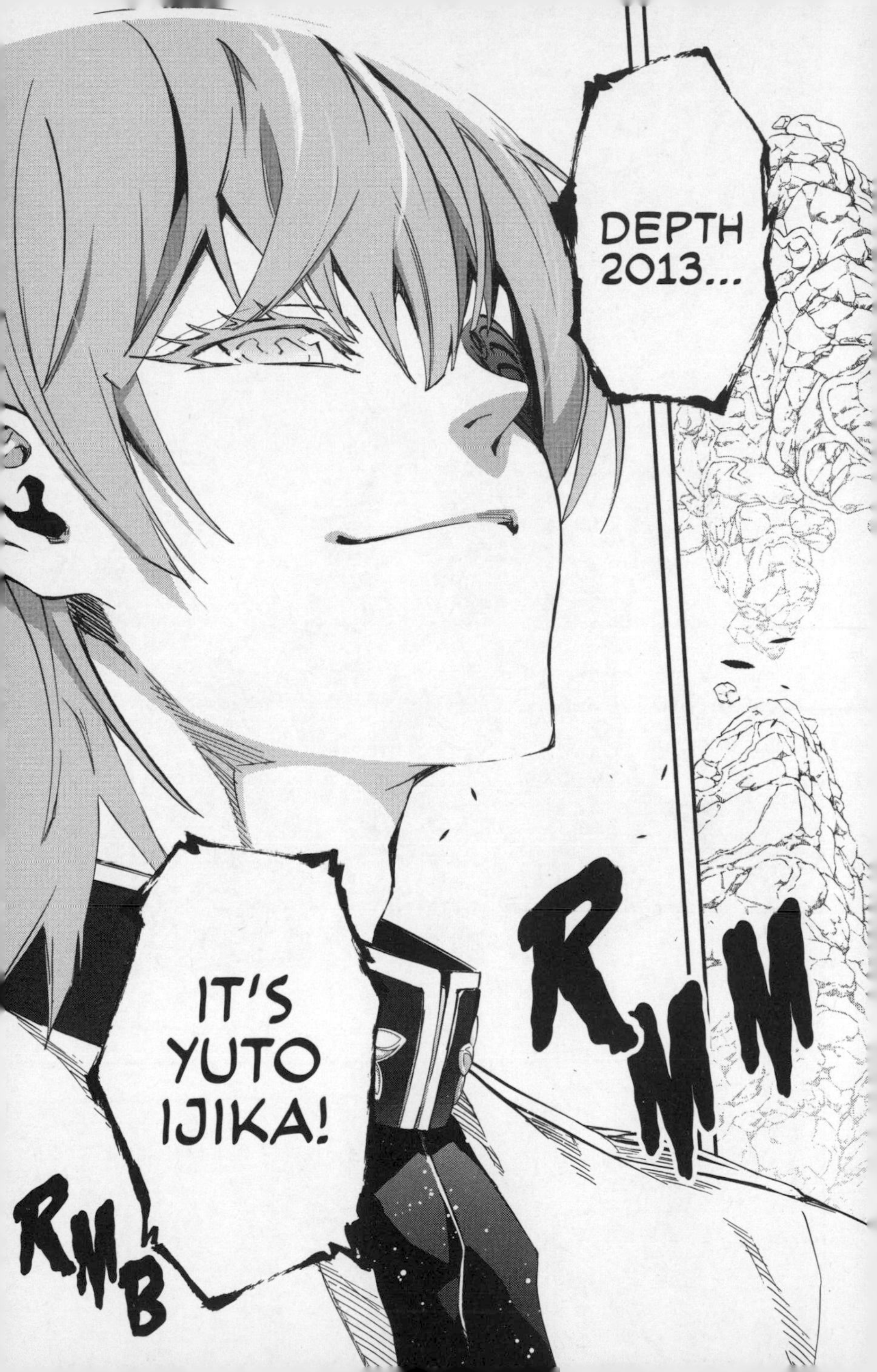
DEPTH 2013...
RMMM
IT'S YUTO IJIKA!
RMB

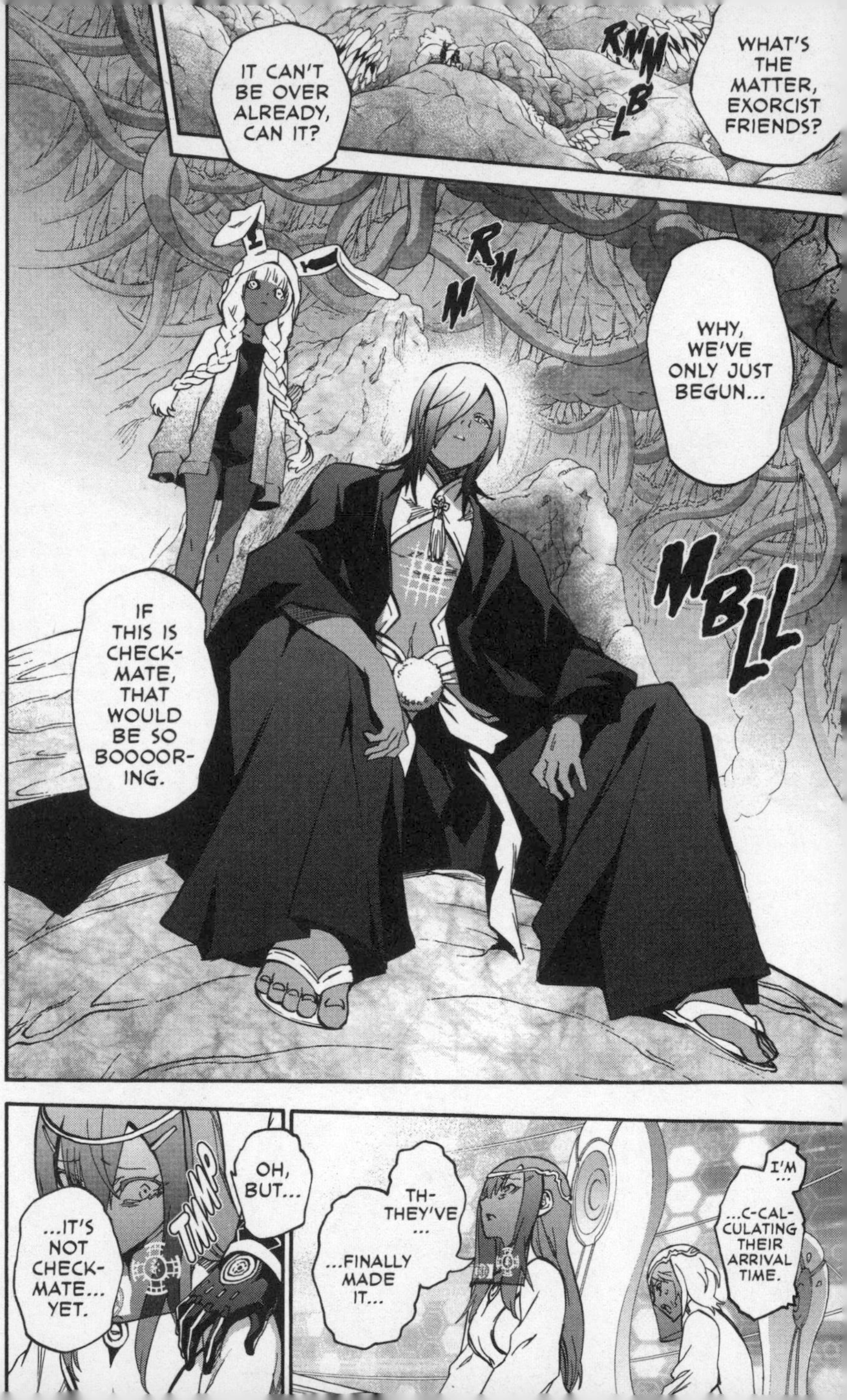
WHAT'S THE MATTER, EXORCIST FRIENDS?
RMMBL
IT CAN'T BE OVER ALREADY, CAN IT?
WHY, WE'VE ONLY JUST BEGUN...
RMM
MBLL
IF THIS IS CHECK-MATE, THAT WOULD BE SO BOOOOR-ING.
I'M ...
...C-CALCULATING THEIR ARRIVAL TIME.
TH-THEY'VE ...
...FINALLY MADE IT...
OH, BUT...
TMP
...IT'S NOT CHECK-MATE... YET.

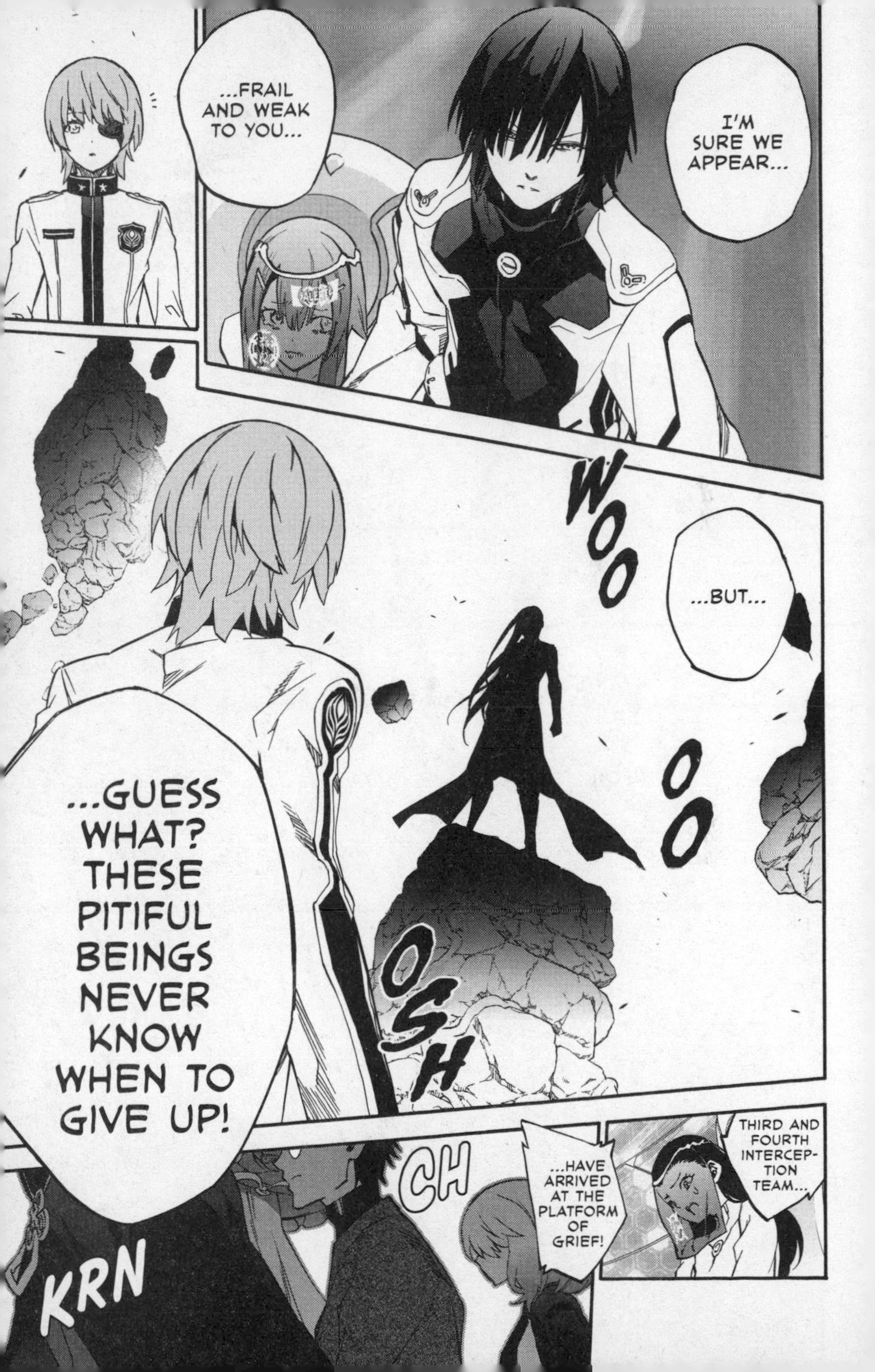
I'M SURE WE APPEAR...
...FRAIL AND WEAK TO YOU...
WOOOOOSH
...BUT...
...GUESS WHAT? THESE PITIFUL BEINGS NEVER KNOW WHEN TO GIVE UP!
THIRD AND FOURTH INTERCEPTION TEAM...
...HAVE ARRIVED AT THE PLATFORM OF GRIEF!
CH
KRN

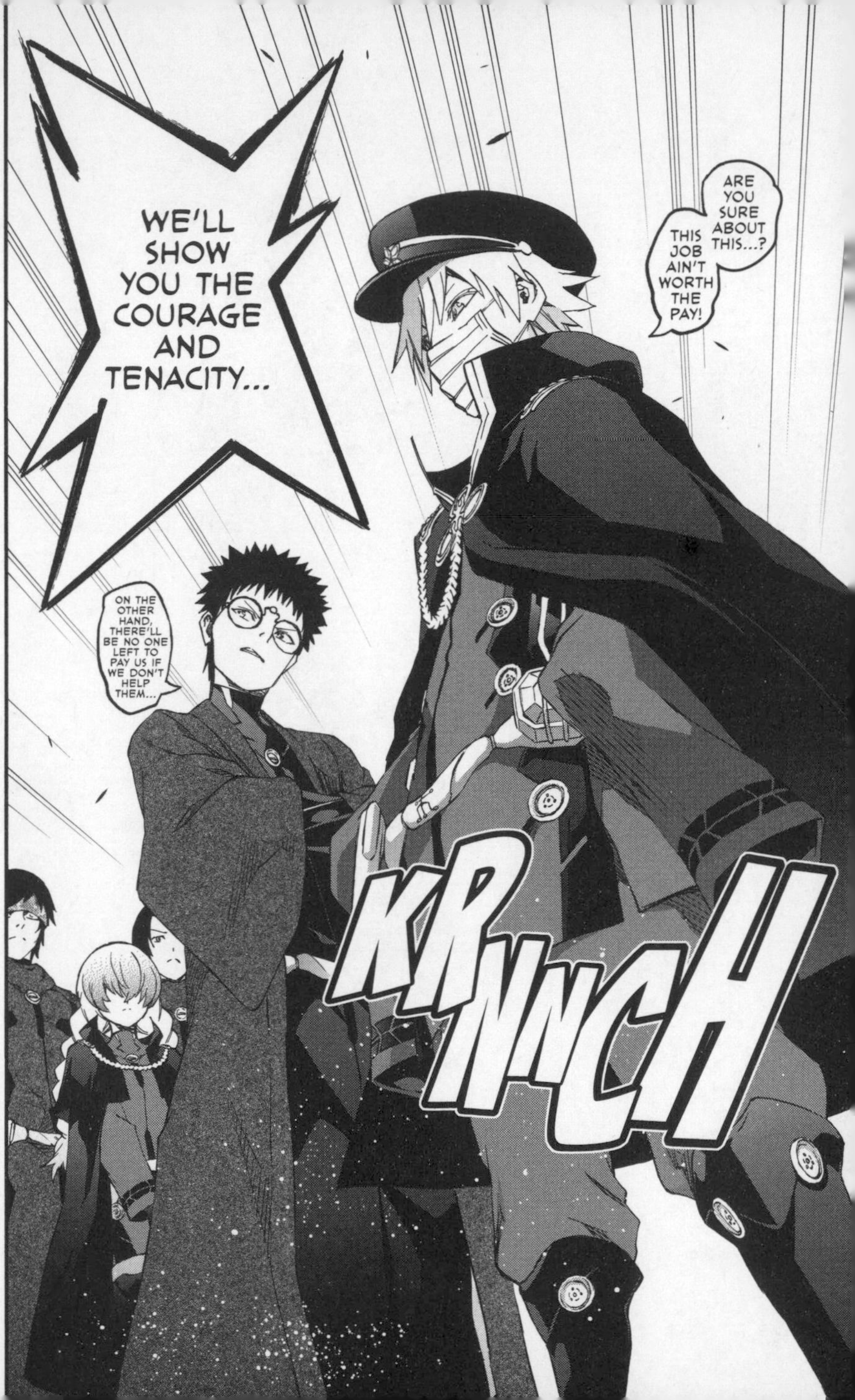
ARE YOU SURE ABOUT THIS...?
THIS JOB AIN'T WORTH THE PAY!
WE'LL SHOW YOU THE COURAGE AND TENACITY...
ON THE OTHER HAND, THERE'LL BE NO ONE LEFT TO PAY US IF WE DON'T HELP THEM...
KRNNCH

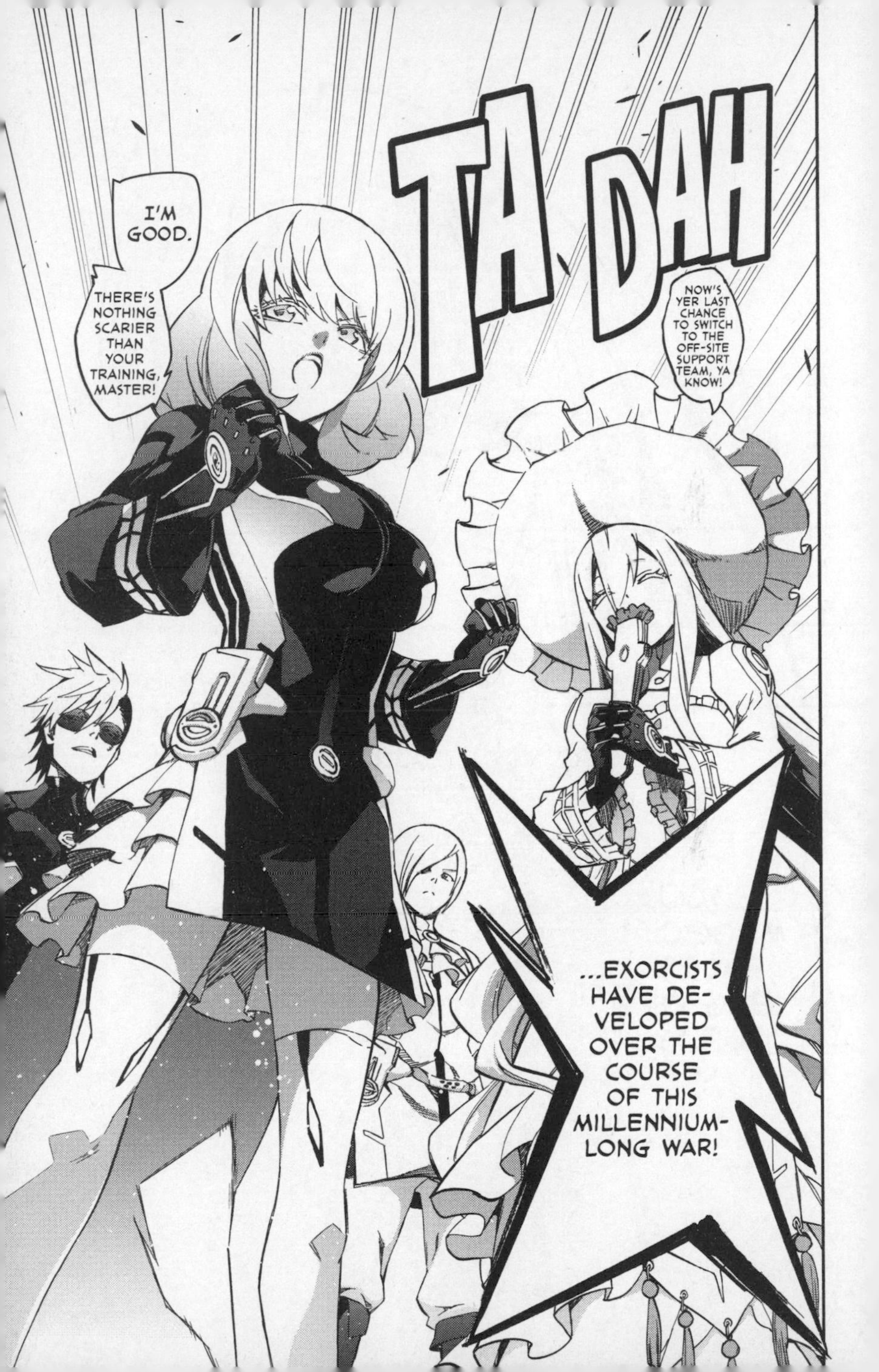
TA DAH
NOW'S YER LAST CHANCE TO SWITCH TO THE OFF-SITE SUPPORT TEAM, YA KNOW!
I'M GOOD.
THERE'S NOTHING SCARIER THAN YOUR TRAINING, MASTER!
...EXORCISTS HAVE DE-VELOPED OVER THE COURSE OF THIS MILLENNIUM-LONG WAR!

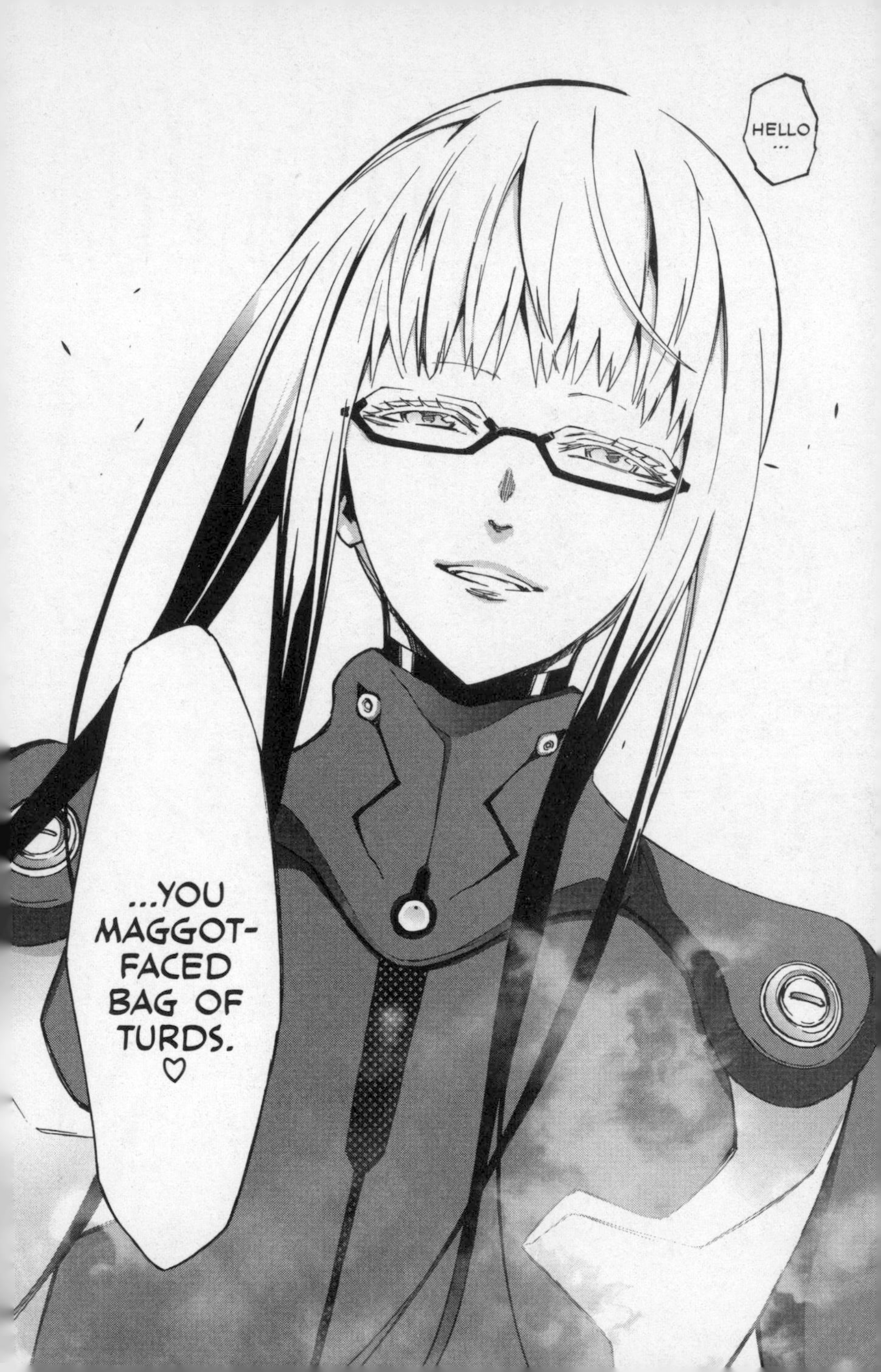
HELLO ...
...YOU MAGGOT-FACED BAG OF TURDS. ♡

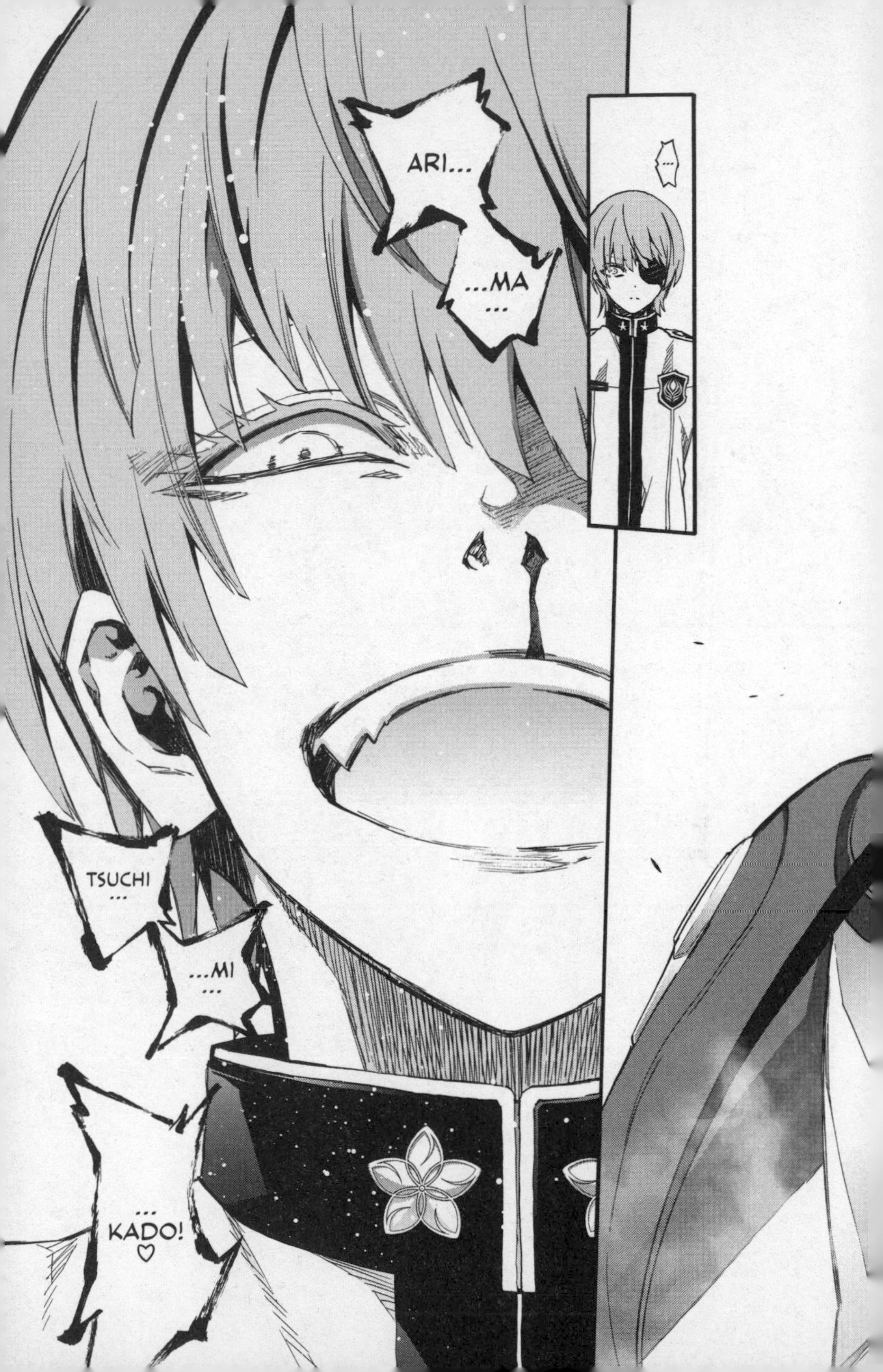
...
ARI...
...MA ...
TSUCHI ...
...MI ...
... KADO! ♡

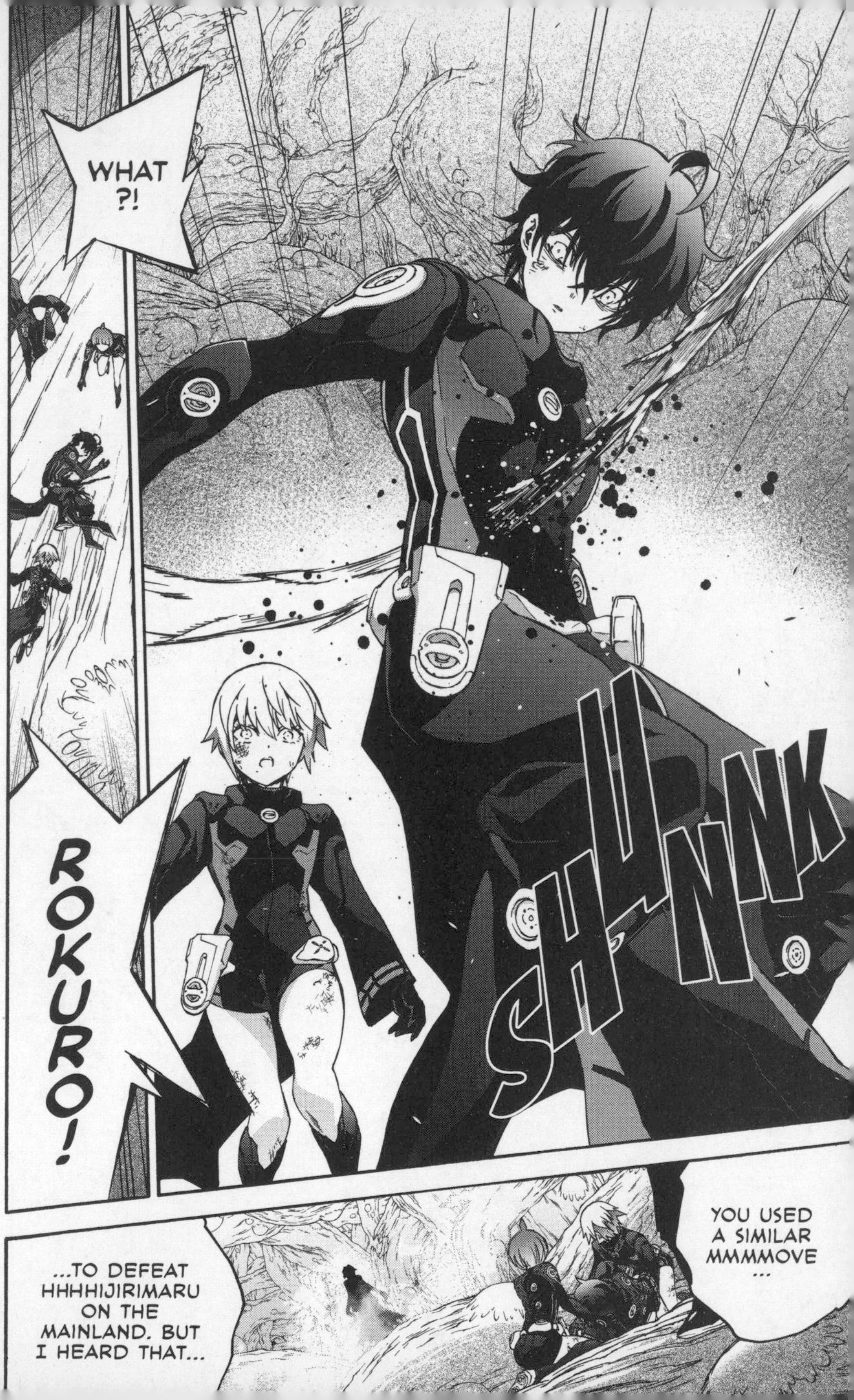
WHAT ?!
SHUNNK
ROKURO!
YOU USED A SIMILAR MMMMOVE ...
...TO DEFEAT HHHHIJIRIMARU ON THE MAINLAND. BUT I HEARD THAT...

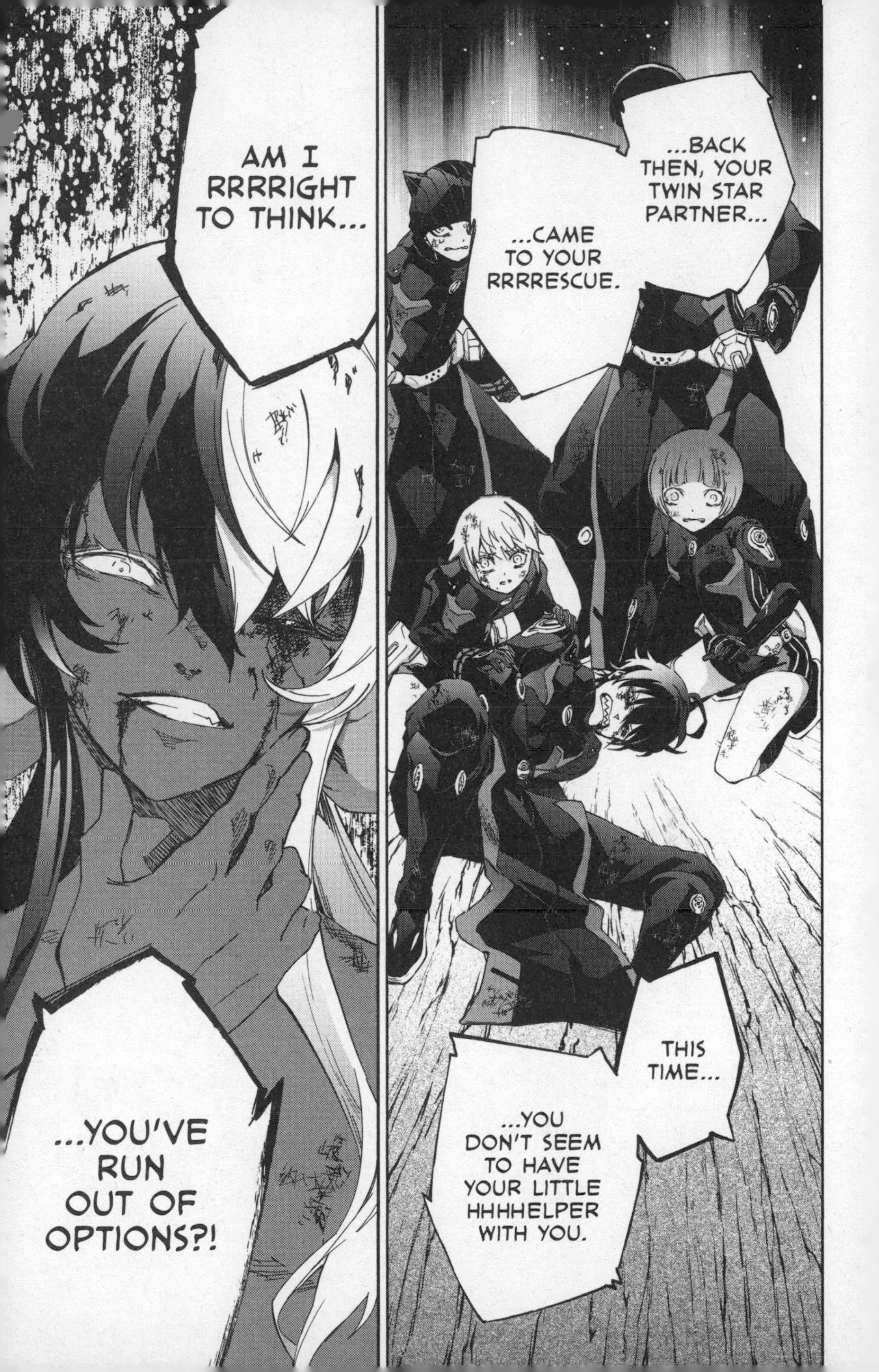
...BACK THEN, YOUR TWIN STAR PARTNER...
...CAME TO YOUR RRRRESCUE.
THIS TIME...
...YOU DON'T SEEM TO HAVE YOUR LITTLE HHHHELPER WITH YOU.
AM I RRRRIGHT TO THINK...
...YOU'VE RUN OUT OF OPTIONS?!

QQnyoritsuryo! Question Corner

Q Are the huge sickle-shaped enchantments and spells Sakura Sada uses in the anime different from the ones she uses in the manga? I really want to know! Please tell me! (From Meteor Lightning)

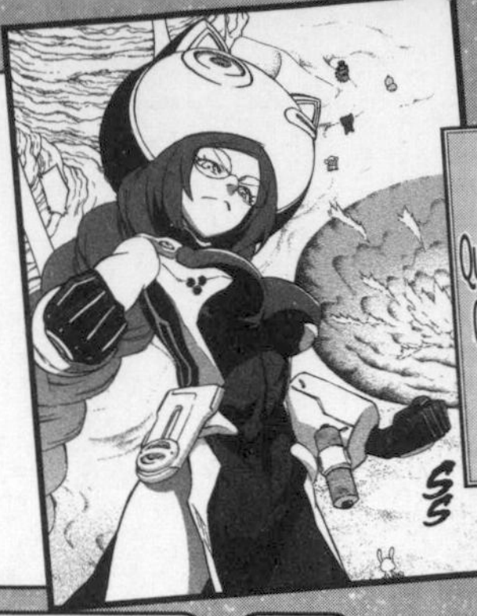

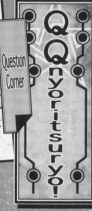

A They are different. Basically, consider the original manga and the anime as separate things.

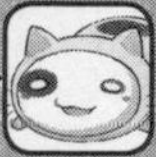

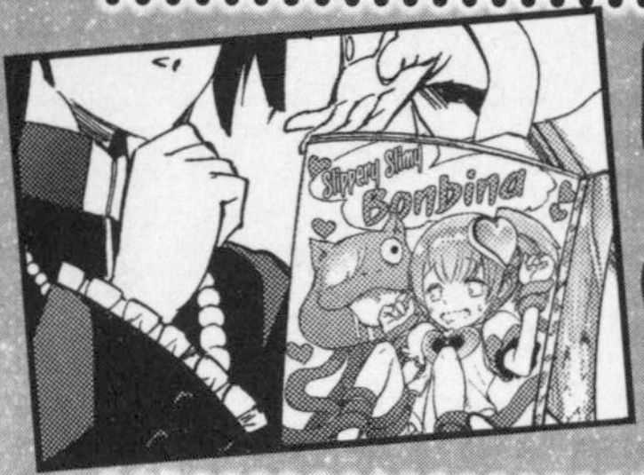

Slippery Slimy Bonbina

Q What is the story of Magic Girl Bon Bonbina like? (From Hexagon)

A An honor student (and boobalicious) girl transforms into a magic girl to fight evil. It's a coming-of-age story full of laughs, tears and fan service!

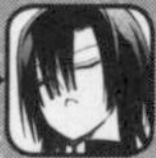

Request

R Here are the birthday requests I've received for each character. I wonder how old the Basara are...

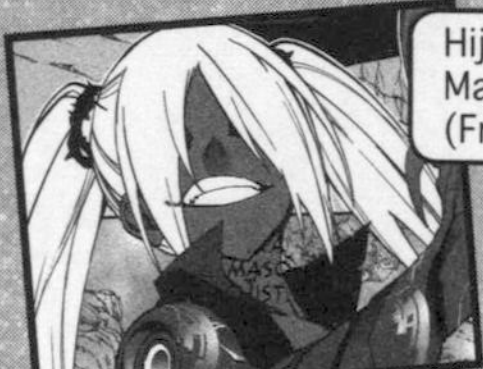

Hijirimaru: May 4 (From Mami)

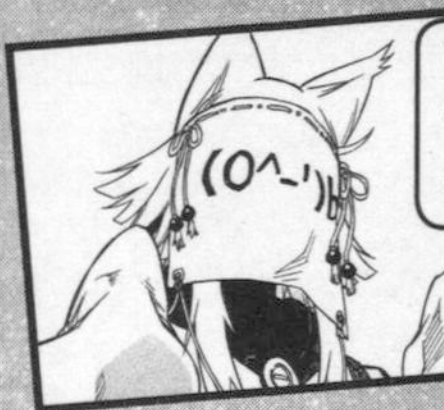

(O^_-)b

Tatara: April 19 (From Kimi the Bear)

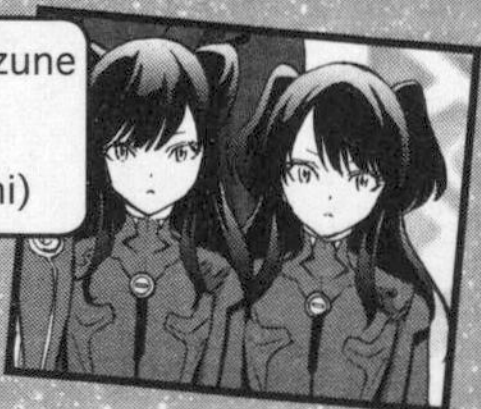

Suzuna & Suzune Unate: February 9 (From Nanami)

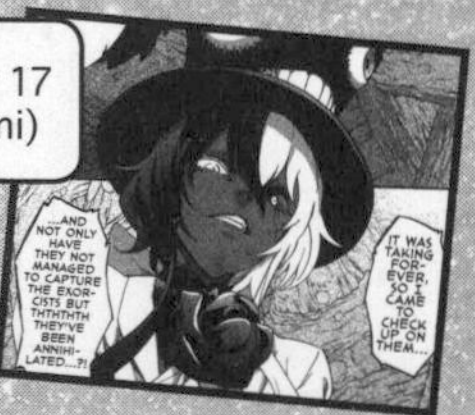

IT WAS TAKING FOR-EVER, SO I CAME TO CHECK UP ON THEM...
...AND NOT ONLY HAVE THEY NOT MANAGED TO CAPTURE THE EXOR-CISTS BUT THTHTHTH THEY'VE BEEN ANNIHI-LATED...?!

Shiromi: May 17 (From Megumi)

By the way, I received Hijirimaru's birthday request from a six-year-old girl. She has unusual taste. She's got a promising future ahead of her.

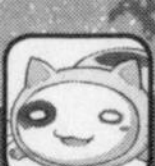

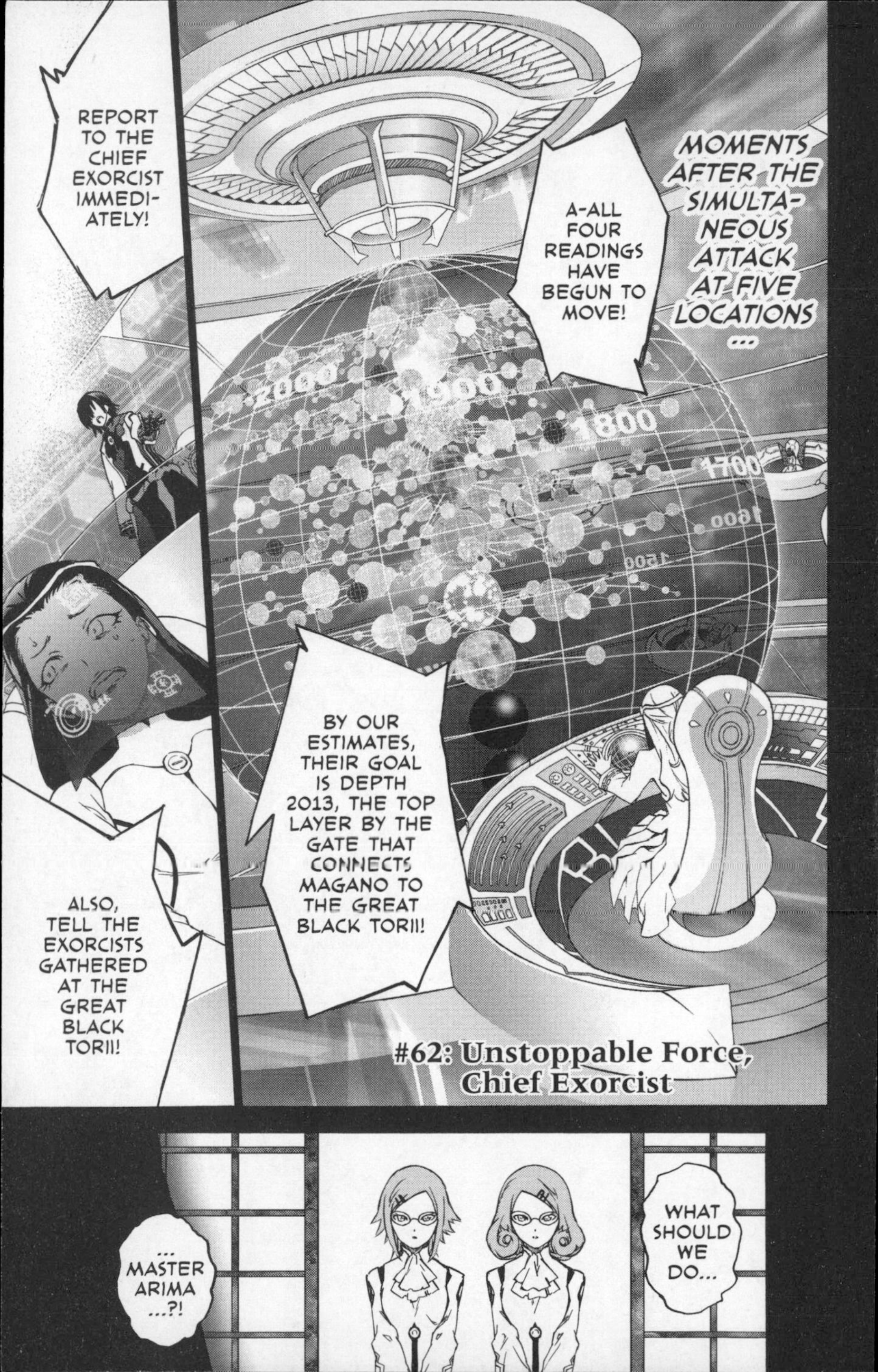
MOMENTS AFTER THE SIMULTANEOUS ATTACK AT FIVE LOCATIONS ...
A-ALL FOUR READINGS HAVE BEGUN TO MOVE!
2000
1900
1800
1700
1600
1500
BY OUR ESTIMATES, THEIR GOAL IS DEPTH 2013, THE TOP LAYER BY THE GATE THAT CONNECTS MAGANO TO THE GREAT BLACK TORII!
#62: Unstoppable Force, Chief Exorcist
REPORT TO THE CHIEF EXORCIST IMMEDIATELY!
ALSO, TELL THE EXORCISTS GATHERED AT THE GREAT BLACK TORII!
WHAT SHOULD WE DO...
... MASTER ARIMA ...?!

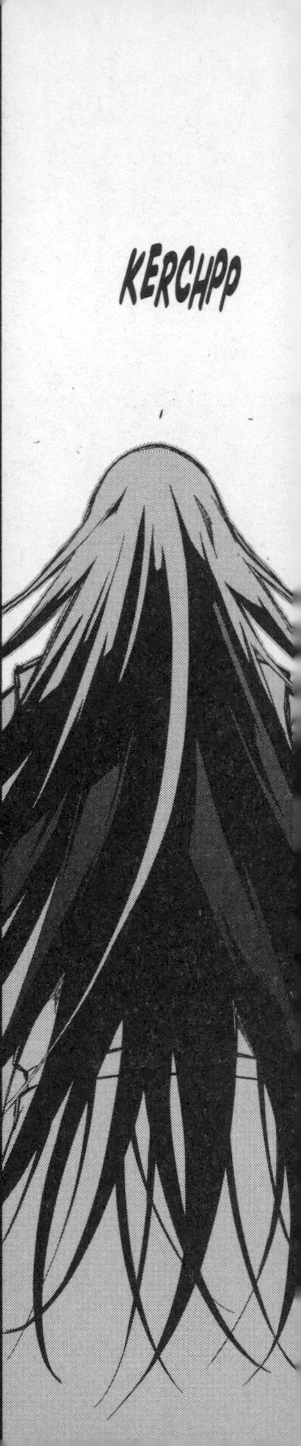
KERCHPP

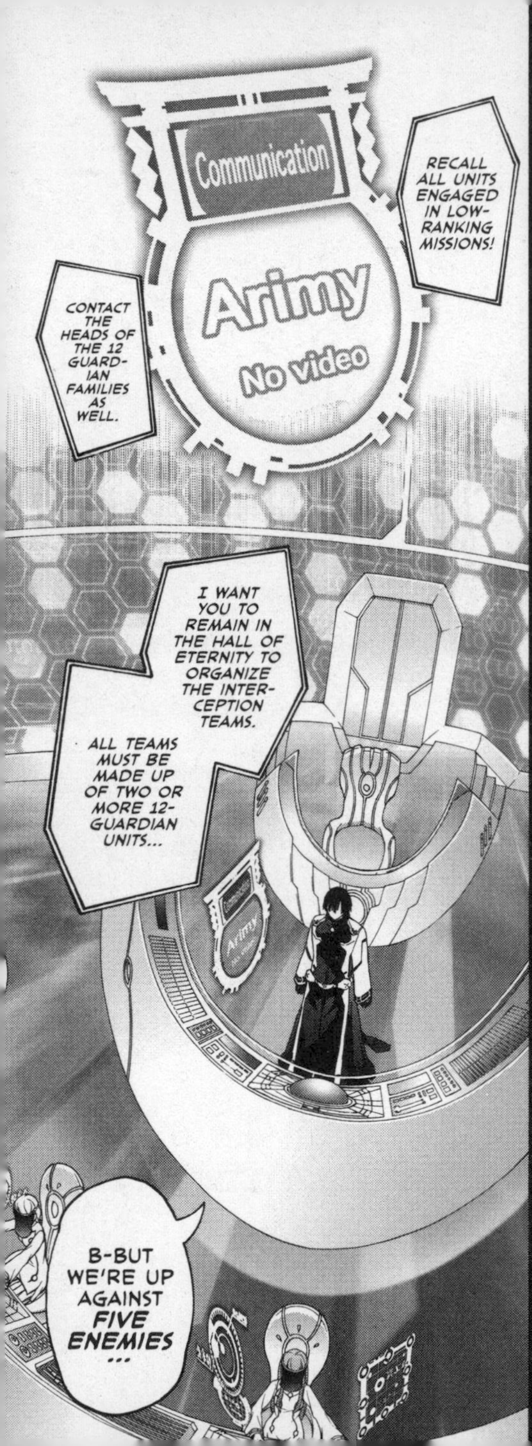
RECALL ALL UNITS ENGAGED IN LOW-RANKING MISSIONS!
Communication
Arimy
No video
CONTACT THE HEADS OF THE 12 GUARDIAN FAMILIES AS WELL.
I WANT YOU TO REMAIN IN THE HALL OF ETERNITY TO ORGANIZE THE INTERCEPTION TEAMS.
ALL TEAMS MUST BE MADE UP OF TWO OR MORE 12-GUARDIAN UNITS...
Arimy
B-BUT WE'RE UP AGAINST *FIVE ENEMIES*...

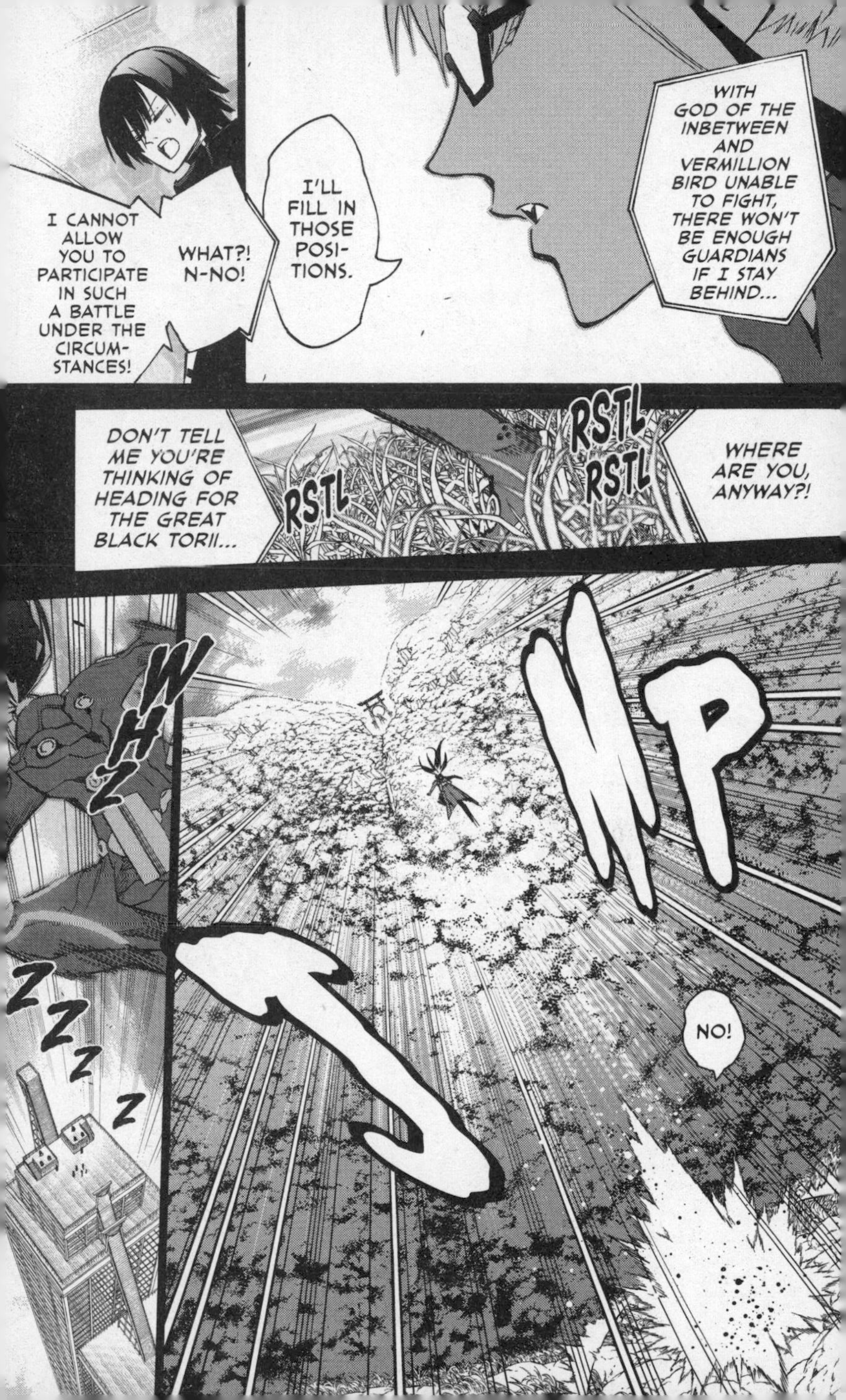
WITH GOD OF THE INBETWEEN AND VERMILLION BIRD UNABLE TO FIGHT, THERE WON'T BE ENOUGH GUARDIANS IF I STAY BEHIND...
I'LL FILL IN THOSE POSI-TIONS.
WHAT?! N-NO!
I CANNOT ALLOW YOU TO PARTICIPATE IN SUCH A BATTLE UNDER THE CIRCUM-STANCES!
WHERE ARE YOU, ANYWAY?!
RSTL RSTL
RSTL
DON'T TELL ME YOU'RE THINKING OF HEADING FOR THE GREAT BLACK TORII...
WHMP
NO!
WHZ
ZZZZ

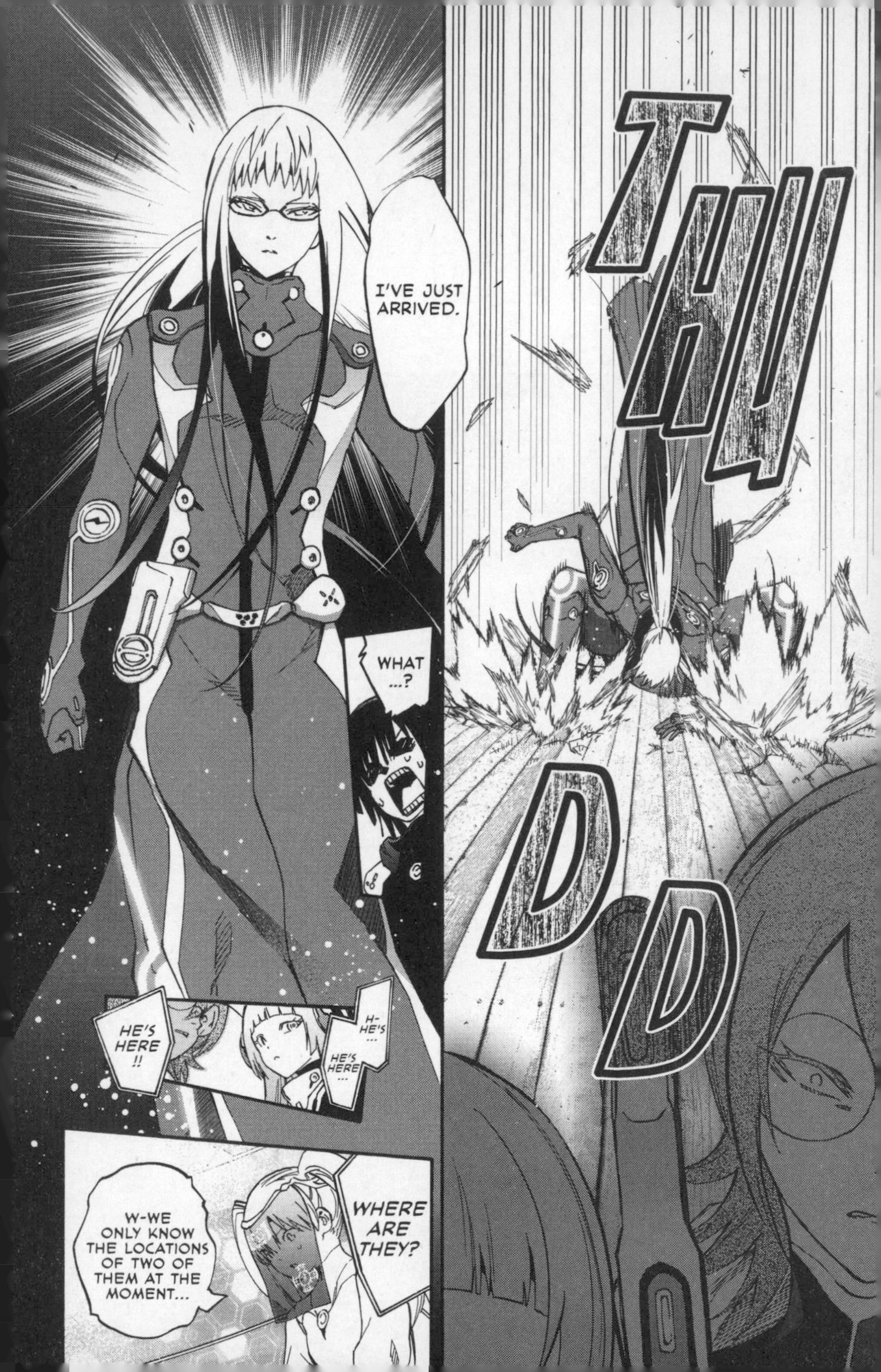
THUDD
I'VE JUST ARRIVED.
WHAT ...?
H-HE'S ... HE'S HERE ...
HE'S HERE !!
WHERE ARE THEY?
W-WE ONLY KNOW THE LOCATIONS OF TWO OF THEM AT THE MOMENT...

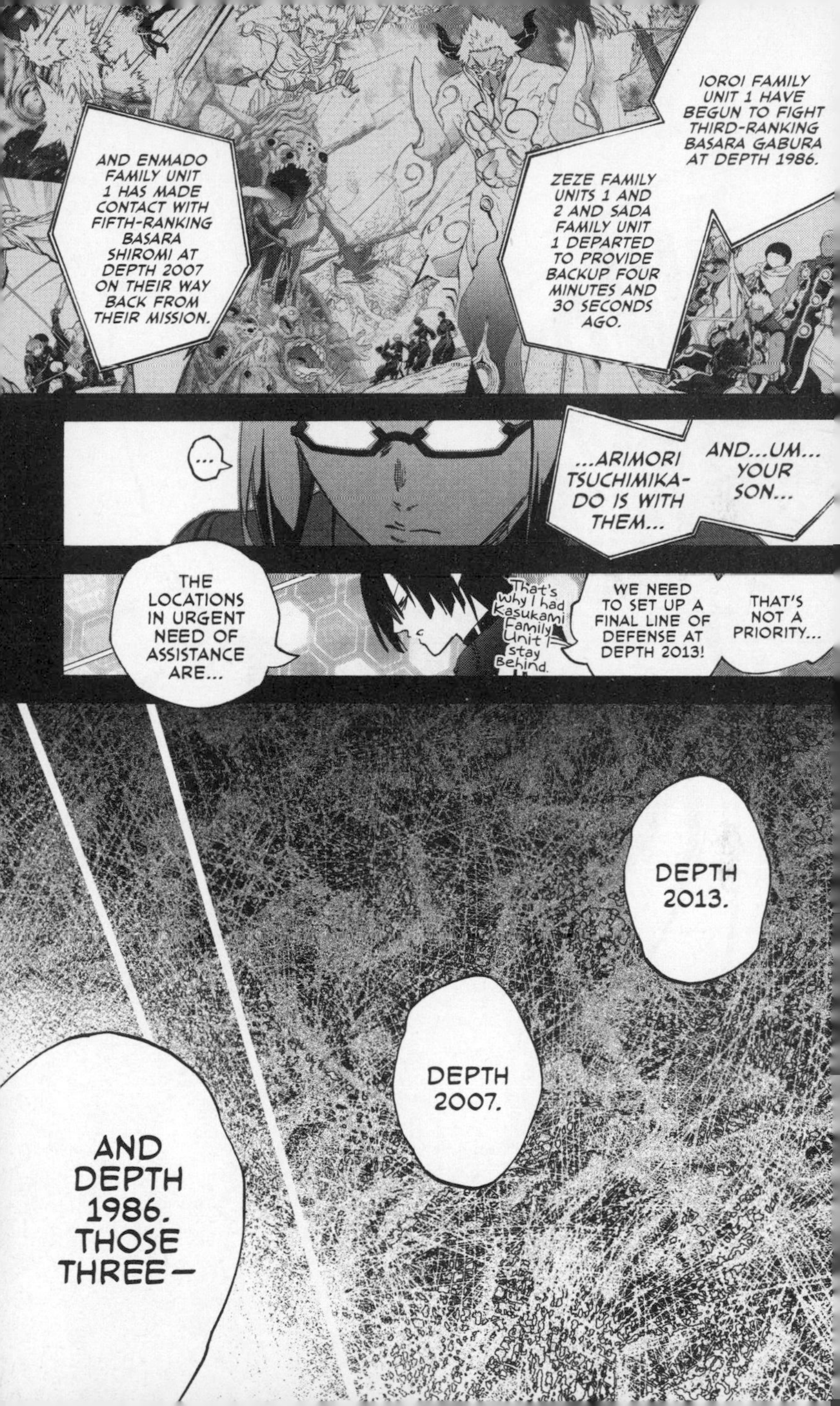
IOROI FAMILY UNIT 1 HAVE BEGUN TO FIGHT THIRD-RANKING BASARA GABURA AT DEPTH 1986.
ZEZE FAMILY UNITS 1 AND 2 AND SADA FAMILY UNIT 1 DEPARTED TO PROVIDE BACKUP FOUR MINUTES AND 30 SECONDS AGO.
AND ENMADO FAMILY UNIT 1 HAS MADE CONTACT WITH FIFTH-RANKING BASARA SHIROMI AT DEPTH 2007 ON THEIR WAY BACK FROM THEIR MISSION.
AND...UM... YOUR SON...
...ARIMORI TSUCHIMIKADO IS WITH THEM...
...
THAT'S NOT A PRIORITY...
WE NEED TO SET UP A FINAL LINE OF DEFENSE AT DEPTH 2013!
That's why I had Kasukami Family Unit 1 stay behind.
THE LOCATIONS IN URGENT NEED OF ASSISTANCE ARE...
DEPTH 2013.
DEPTH 2007.
AND DEPTH 1986. THOSE THREE—

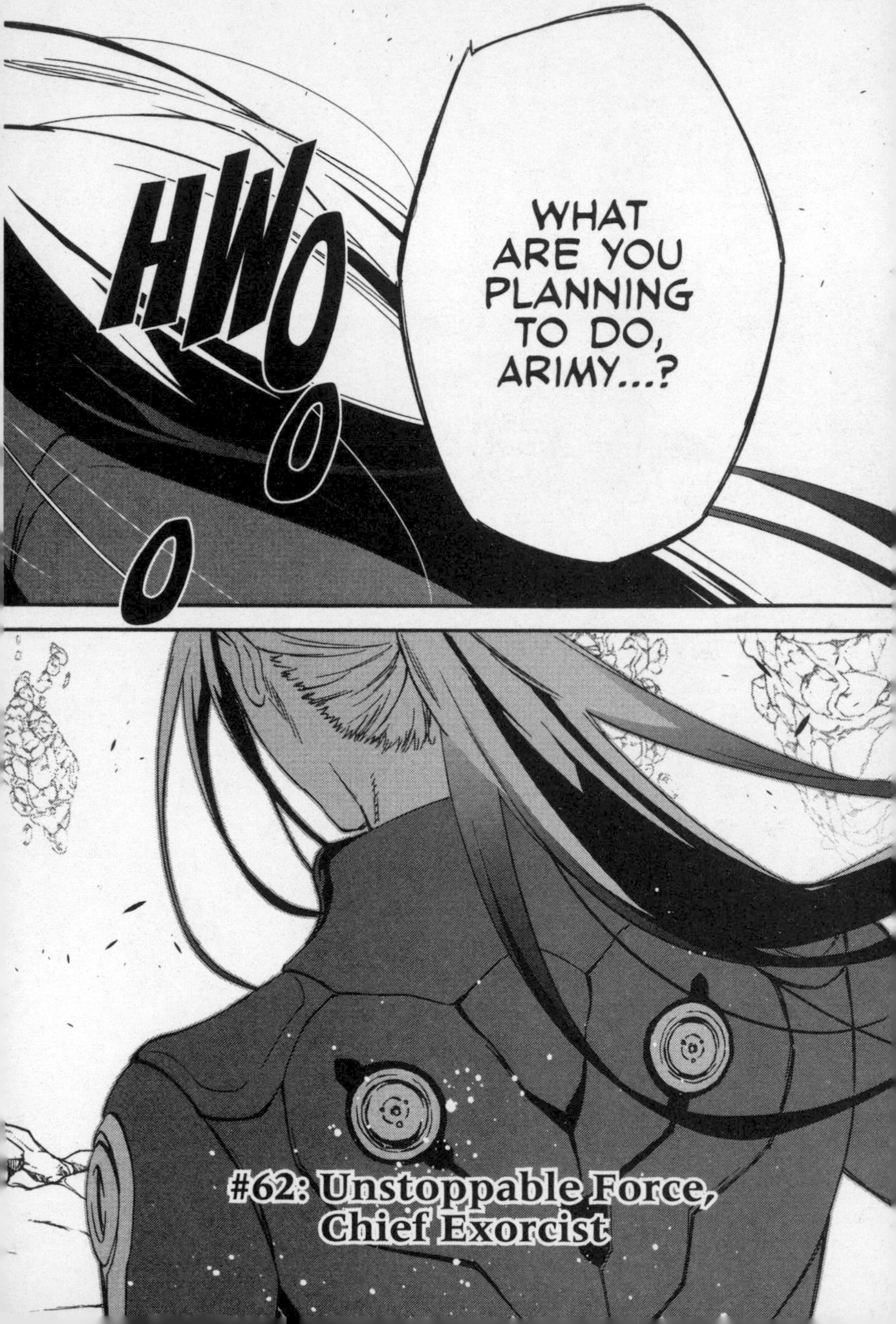
WHAT ARE YOU PLANNING TO DO, ARIMY...?
HWOOO
#62: Unstoppable Force, Chief Exorcist

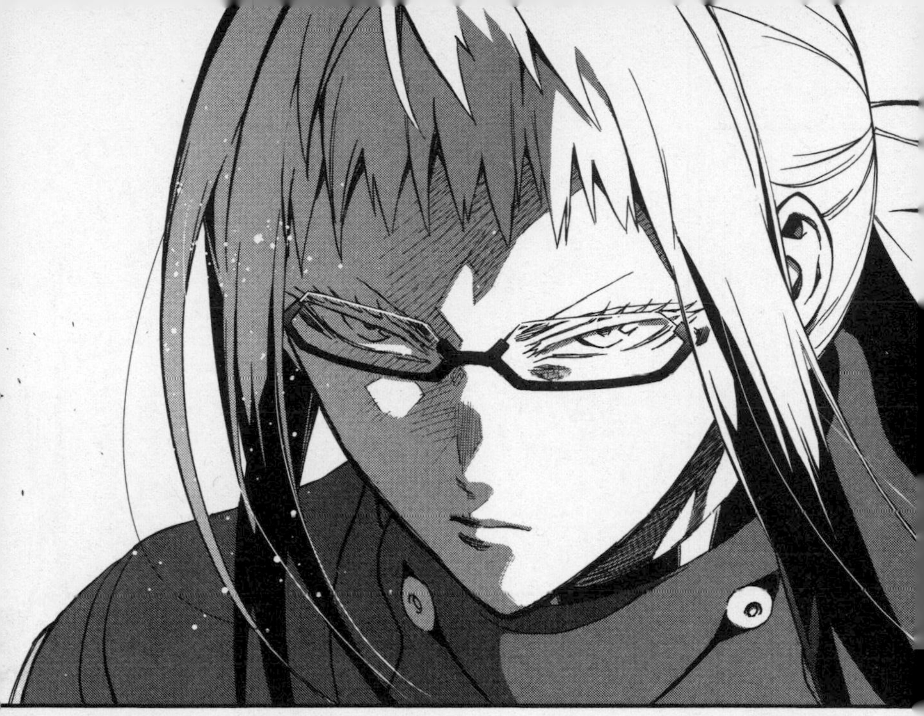

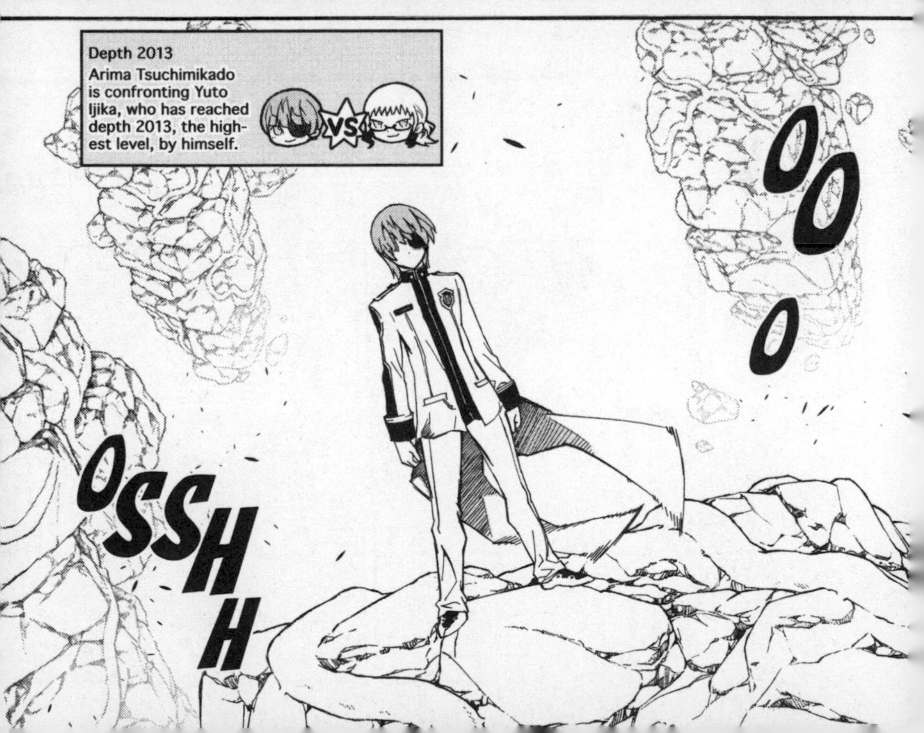
Depth 2013
Arima Tsuchimikado is confronting Yuto Ijika, who has reached depth 2013, the highest level, by himself.
VS
OOO
OSSHH

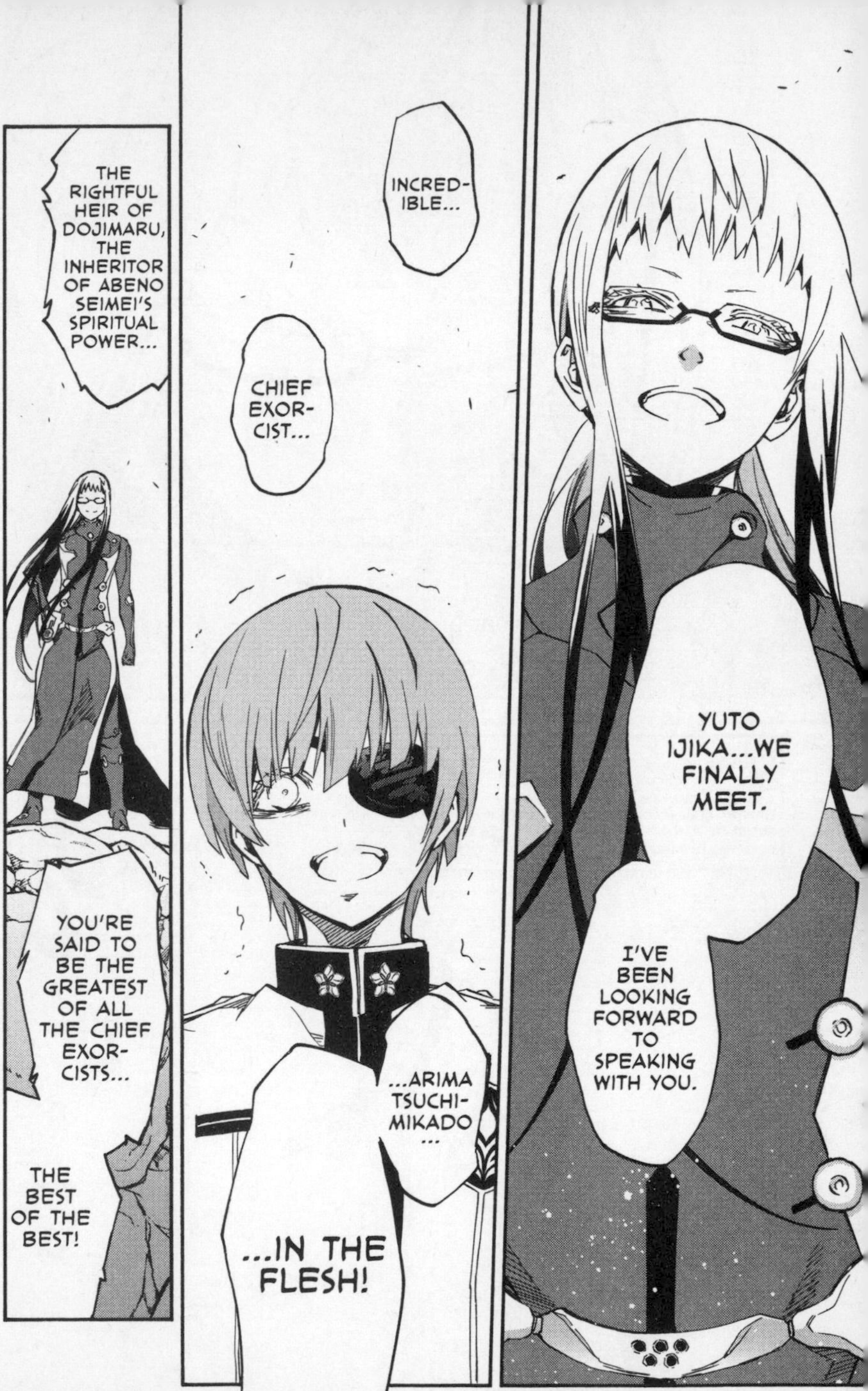
YUTO IJIKA...WE FINALLY MEET.
I'VE BEEN LOOKING FORWARD TO SPEAKING WITH YOU.
INCREDIBLE...
CHIEF EXORCIST...
...ARIMA TSUCHIMIKADO...
...IN THE FLESH!
THE RIGHTFUL HEIR OF DOJIMARU, THE INHERITOR OF ABENO SEIMEI'S SPIRITUAL POWER...
YOU'RE SAID TO BE THE GREATEST OF ALL THE CHIEF EXORCISTS...
THE BEST OF THE BEST!

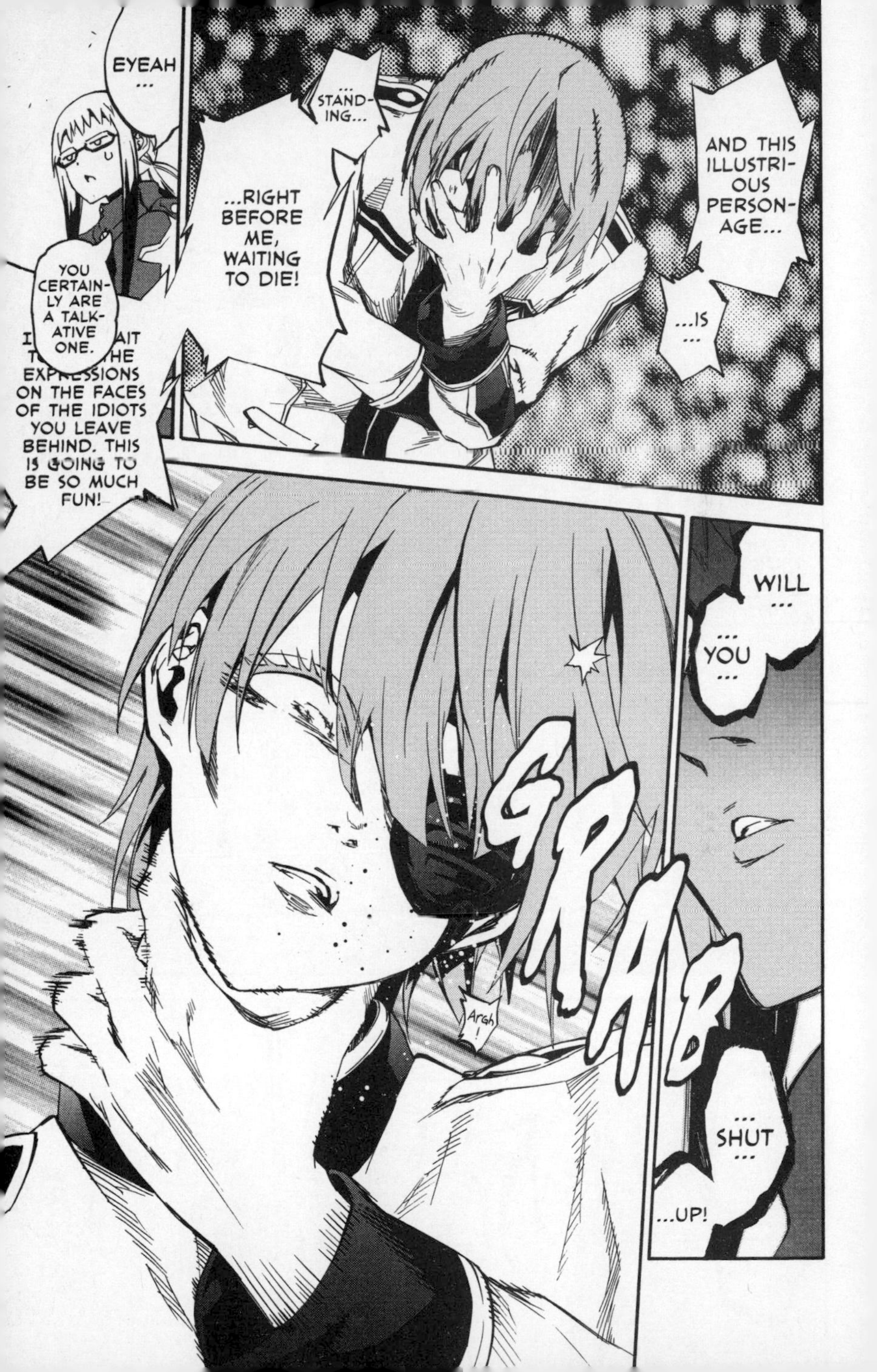
AND THIS ILLUSTRIOUS PERSONAGE...
...IS...
...STANDING...
...RIGHT BEFORE ME, WAITING TO DIE!
EYEAH...
YOU CERTAINLY ARE A TALKATIVE ONE.
I AIT T THE EXPRESSIONS ON THE FACES OF THE IDIOTS YOU LEAVE BEHIND. THIS IS GOING TO BE SO MUCH FUN!
WILL...
...YOU...
...SHUT...
...UP!
GRAB
Argh!

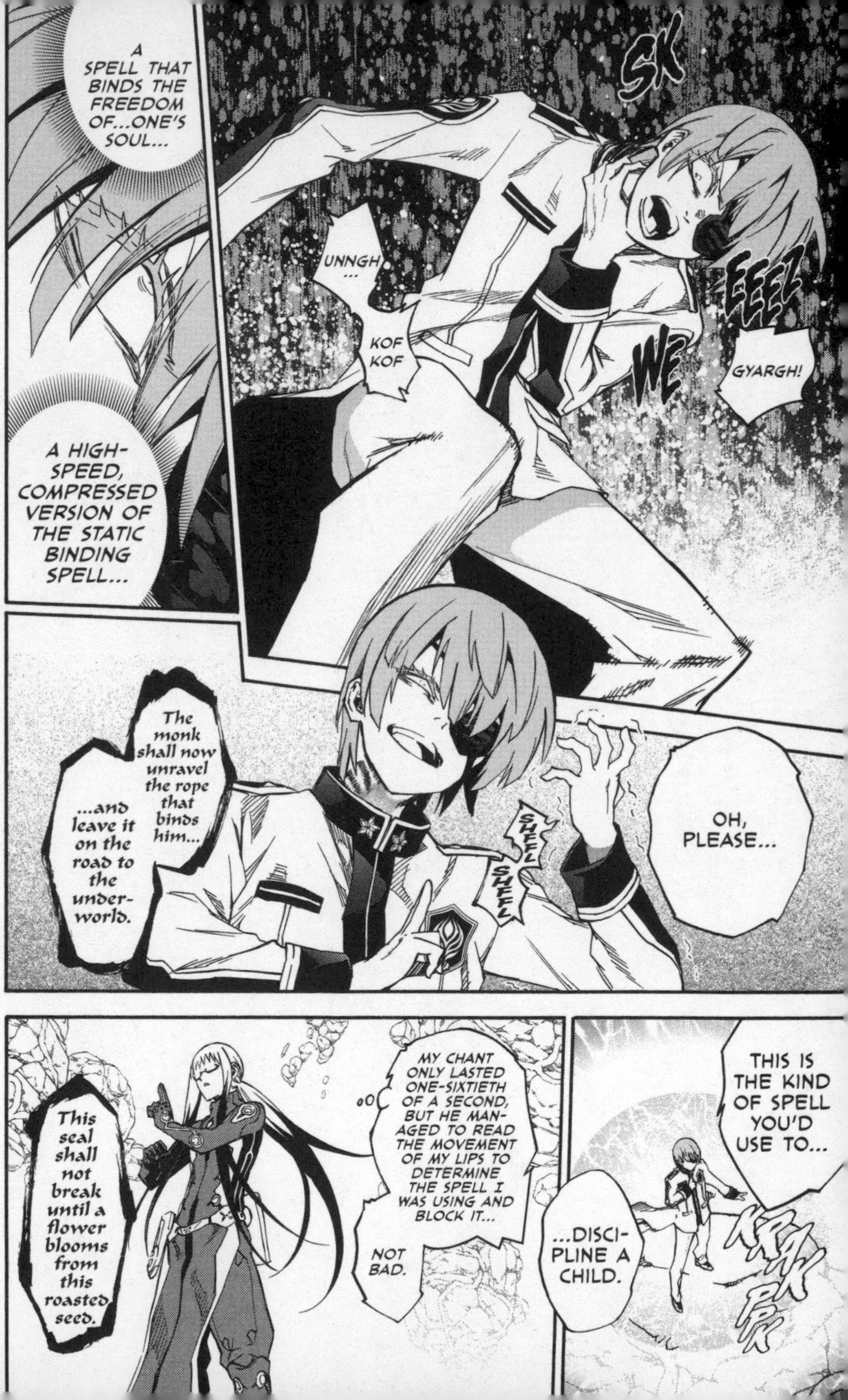
SK
UNNGH...
WE EEEZ
GYARGH!
KOF KOF
A SPELL THAT BINDS THE FREEDOM OF...ONE'S SOUL...
A HIGH-SPEED, COMPRESSED VERSION OF THE STATIC BINDING SPELL...
OH, PLEASE...
SHFFL SHFFL
The monk shall now unravel the rope that binds him...
...and leave it on the road to the underworld.
THIS IS THE KIND OF SPELL YOU'D USE TO...
KRAK PPK
...DISCIPLINE A CHILD.
MY CHANT ONLY LASTED ONE-SIXTIETH OF A SECOND, BUT HE MANAGED TO READ THE MOVEMENT OF MY LIPS TO DETERMINE THE SPELL I WAS USING AND BLOCK IT...
NOT BAD.
This seal shall not break until a flower blooms from this roasted seed.

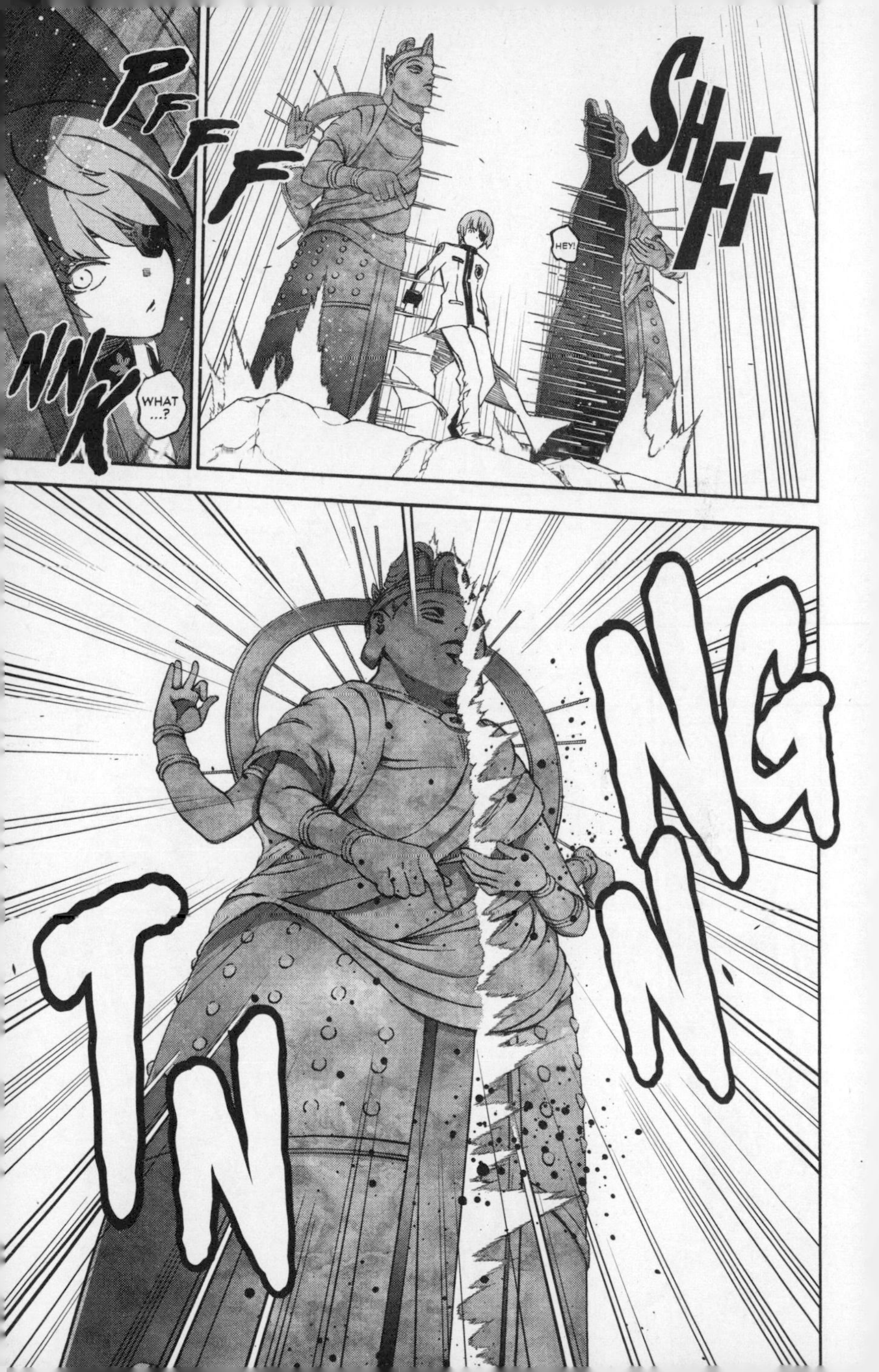
SHFF
HEY!
PFFF
NNK
WHAT ...?
TNNNG

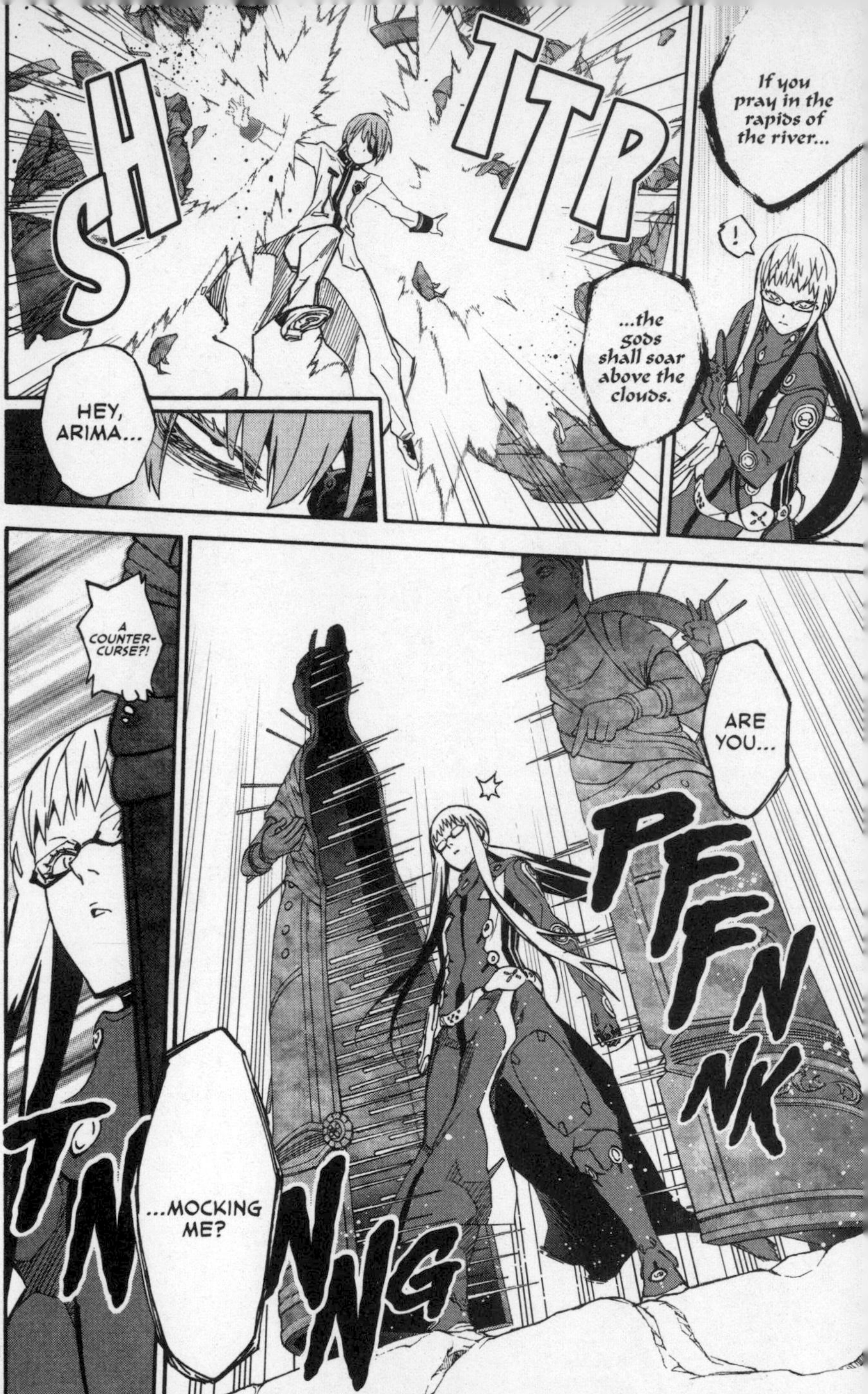
If you pray in the rapids of the river...
!
...the gods shall soar above the clouds.
SHTTR
HEY, ARIMA...
ARE YOU...
PFFNNK
...MOCKING ME?
TNNNG
A COUNTER-CURSE?!

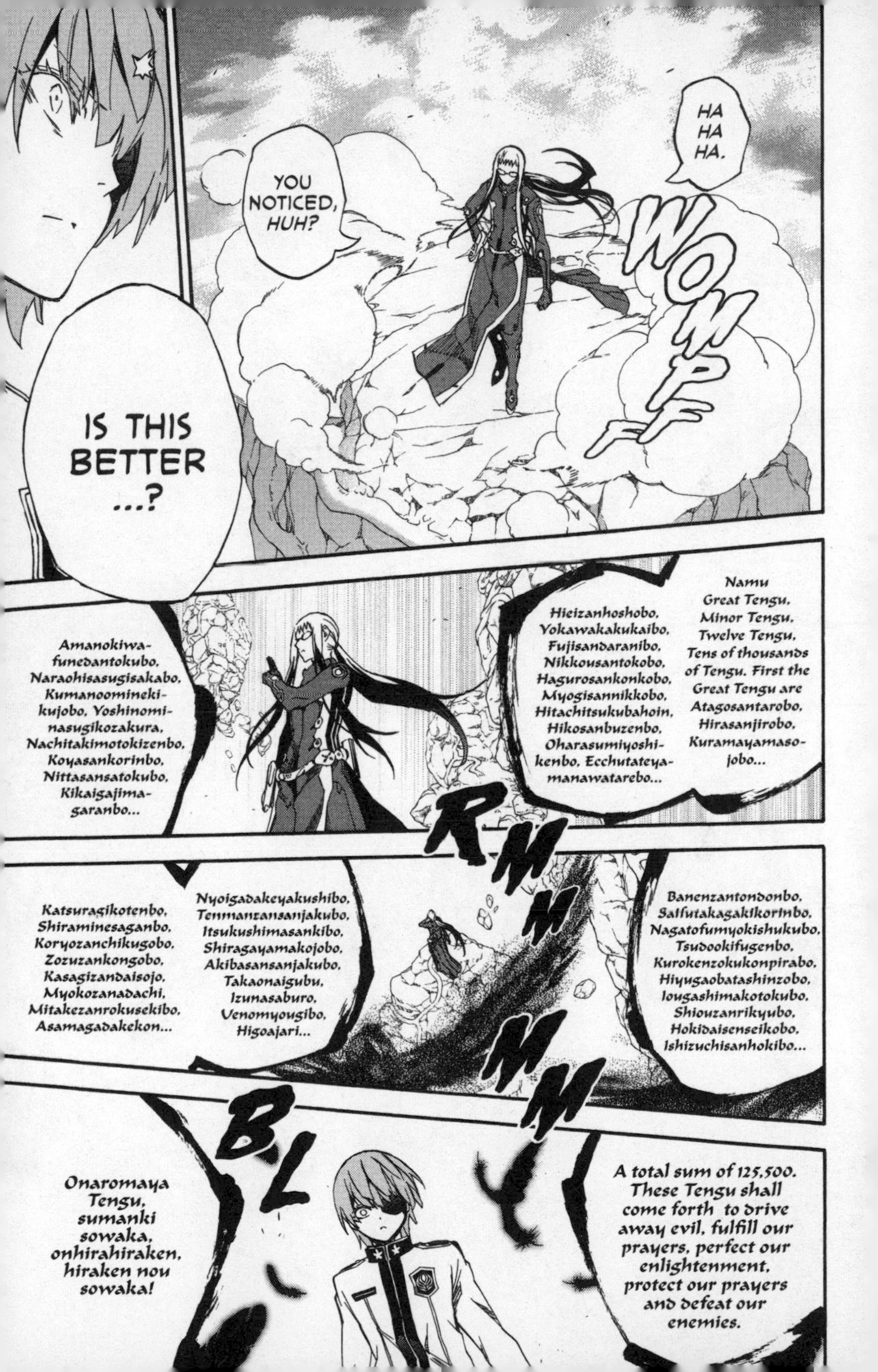
HA HA HA.
YOU NOTICED, HUH?
WOMPF
IS THIS BETTER ...?
Namu Great Tengu, Minor Tengu, Twelve Tengu, Tens of thousands of Tengu. First the Great Tengu are Atagosantarobo, Hirasanjirobo, Kuramayamasojobo...
Hieizanhoshobo, Yokawakakukaibo, Fujisandaranibo, Nikkousantokobo, Hagurosankonkobo, Myogisannikkobo, Hitachitsukubahoin, Hikosanbuzenbo, Oharasumiyoshikenbo, Ecchutateyamanawatarebo...
Amanokiwafunedantokubo, Naraohisasugisakabo, Kumanoominekikujobo, Yoshinominasugikozakura, Nachitakimotokizenbo, Koyasankorinbo, Nittasansatokubo, Kikaigajimagaranbo...
RMMMM
Banenzantondonbo, Saifutakagakikorinbo, Nagatofumyokishukubo, Tsudookifugenbo, Kurokenzokukonpirabo, Hiyugaobatashinzobo, Iougashimakotokubo, Shiouzanrikyubo, Hokidaisenseikobo, Ishizuchisanhokibo...
Nyoigadakeyakushibo, Tenmanzansanjakubo, Itsukushimasankibo, Shiragayamakojobo, Akibasansanjakubo, Takaonaigubu, Izunasaburo, Venomyougibo, Higoajari...
Katsuragikotenbo, Shiraminesaganbo, Koryozanchikugobo, Zozuzankongobo, Kasagizandaisojo, Myokozanadachi, Mitakezanrokusekibo, Asamagadakekon...
A total sum of 125,500. These Tengu shall come forth to drive away evil, fulfill our prayers, perfect our enlightenment, protect our prayers and defeat our enemies.
Onaromaya Tengu, sumanki sowaka, onhirahiraken, hiraken nou sowaka!
BL

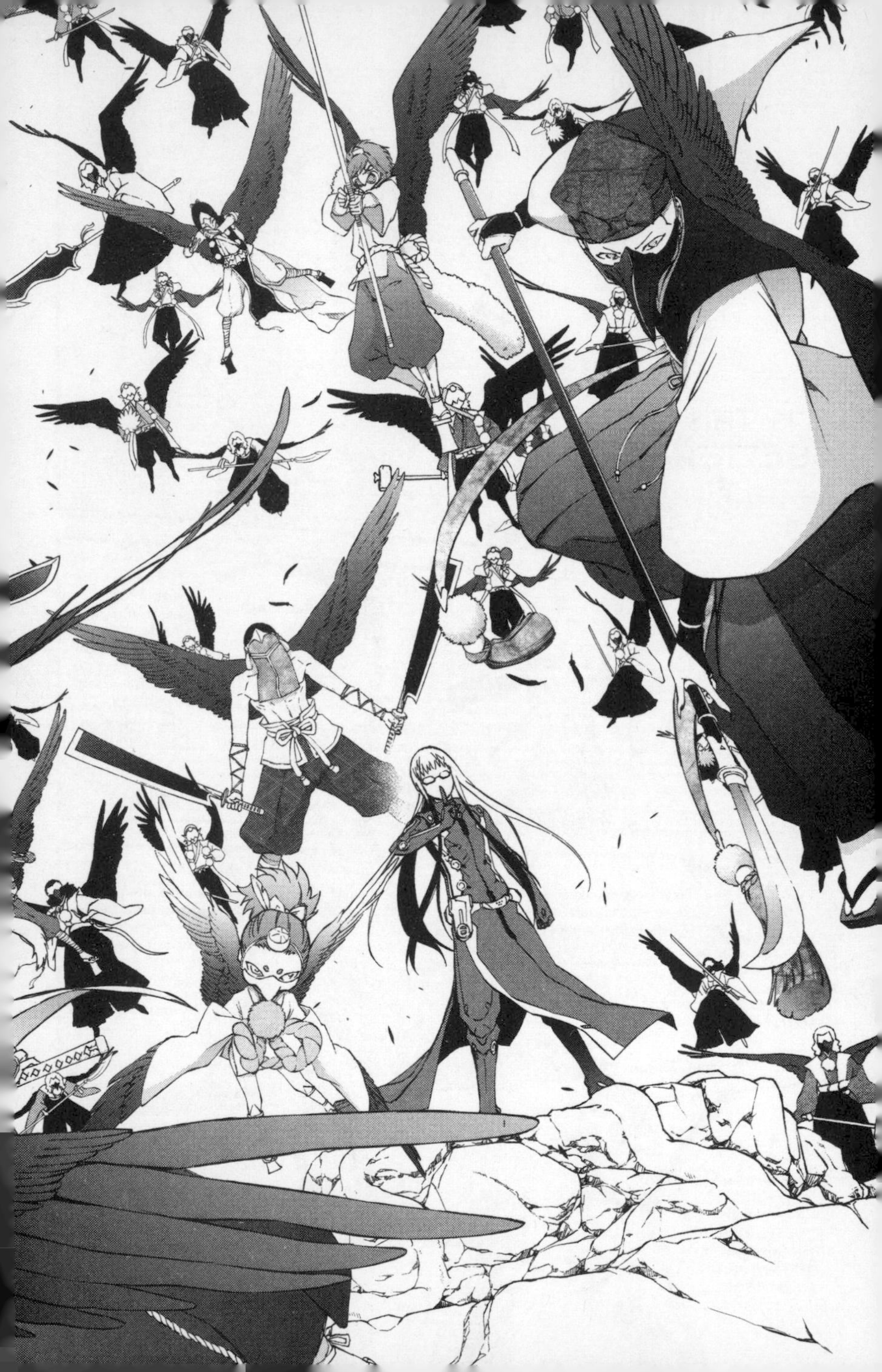

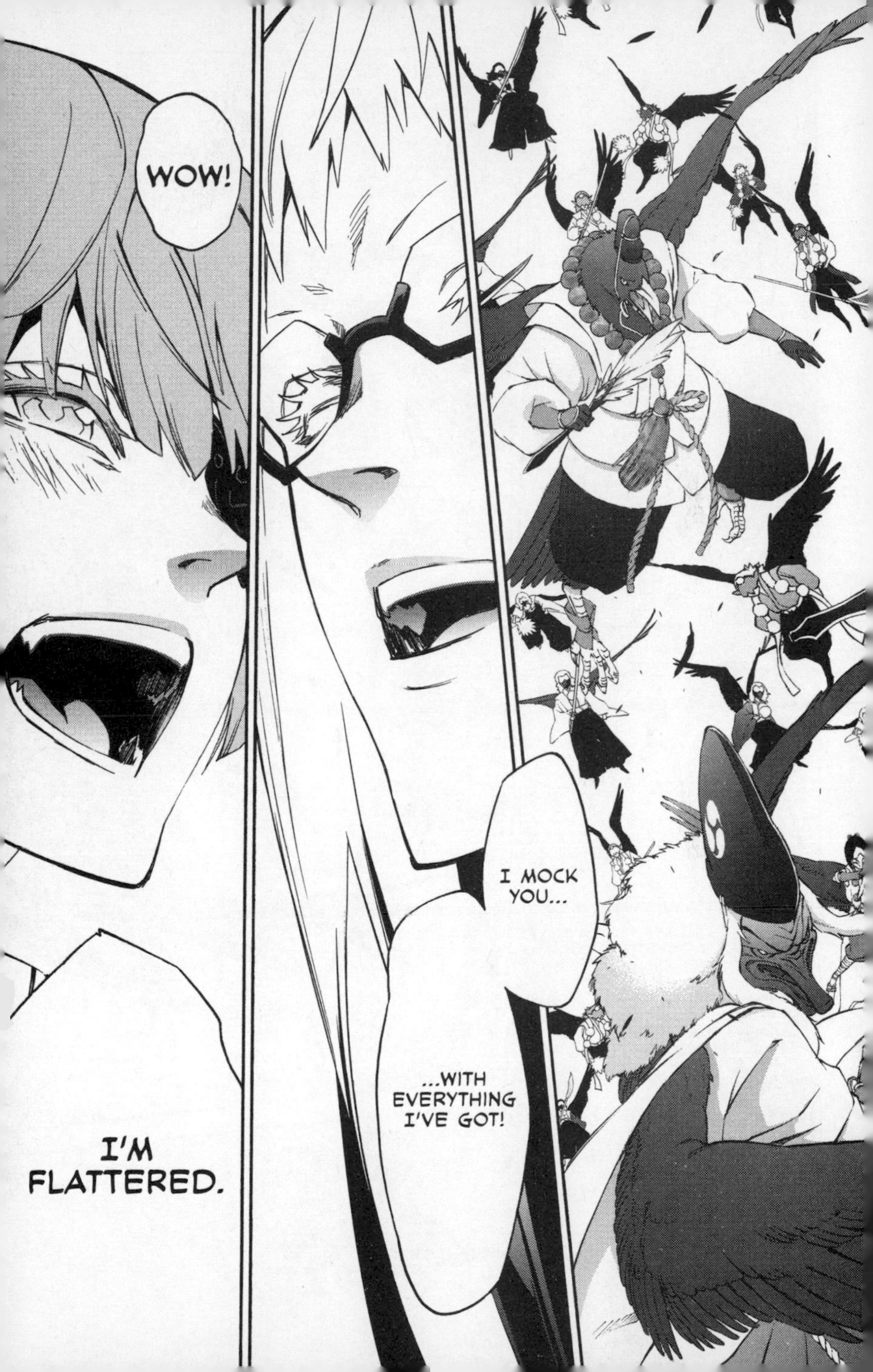
I MOCK YOU...
...WITH EVERYTHING I'VE GOT!
WOW!
I'M FLATTERED.

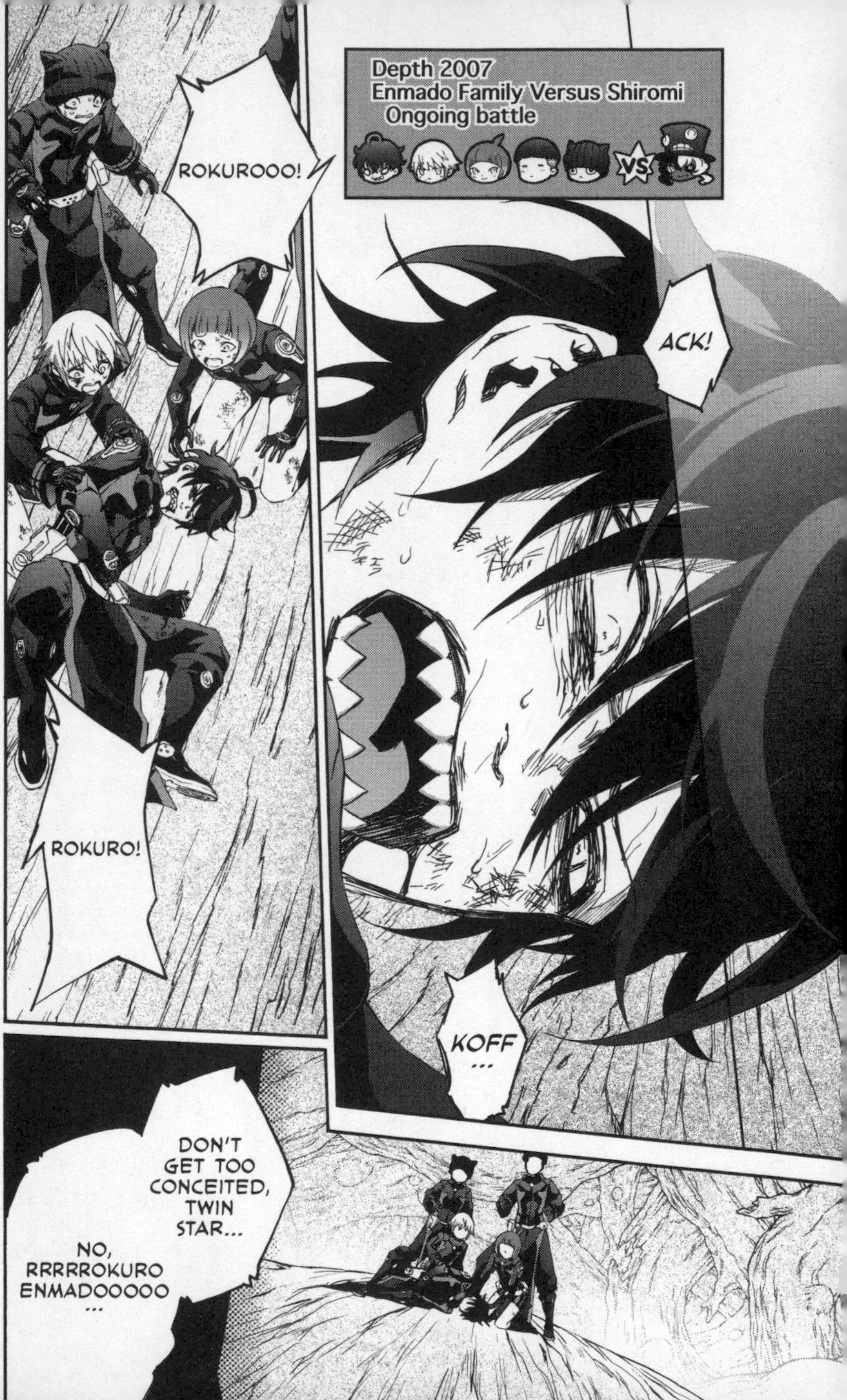
Depth 2007
Enmado Family Versus Shiromi
Ongoing battle
VS
ACK!
KOFF...
ROKUROOO!
ROKURO!
DON'T GET TOO CONCEITED, TWIN STAR...
NO, RRRRROKURO ENMADOOOOO...

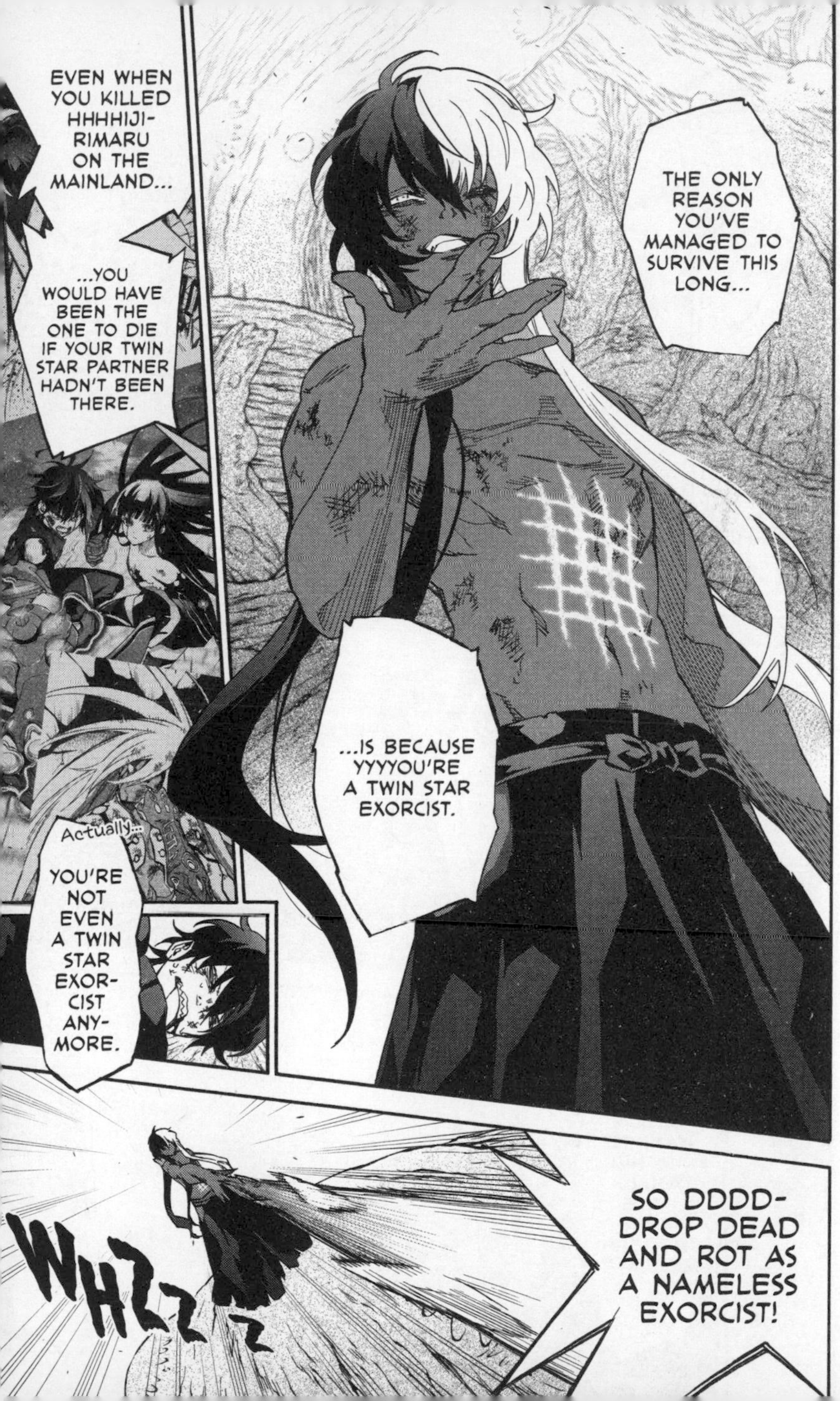
THE ONLY REASON YOU'VE MANAGED TO SURVIVE THIS LONG...
...IS BECAUSE YYYYOU'RE A TWIN STAR EXORCIST.
EVEN WHEN YOU KILLED HHHHIJI-RIMARU ON THE MAINLAND...
...YOU WOULD HAVE BEEN THE ONE TO DIE IF YOUR TWIN STAR PARTNER HADN'T BEEN THERE.
Actually...
YOU'RE NOT EVEN A TWIN STAR EXOR-CIST ANY-MORE.
SO DDDD-DROP DEAD AND ROT AS A NAMELESS EXORCIST!
WHZZZ

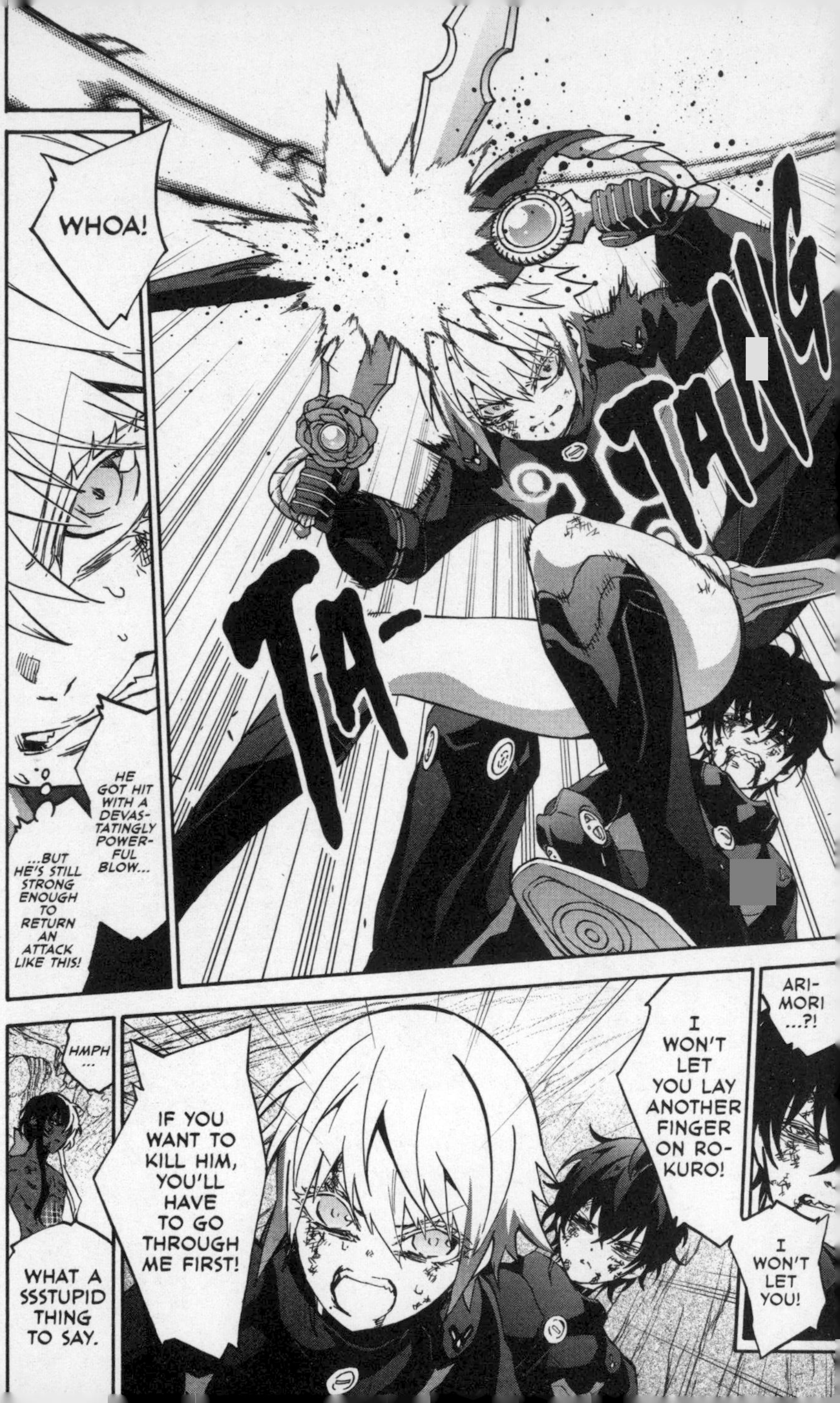
TA-
TANG
WHOA!
HE GOT HIT WITH A DEVASTATINGLY POWERFUL BLOW...
...BUT HE'S STILL STRONG ENOUGH TO RETURN AN ATTACK LIKE THIS!
ARIMORI ...?!
I WON'T LET YOU LAY ANOTHER FINGER ON ROKURO!
IF YOU WANT TO KILL HIM, YOU'LL HAVE TO GO THROUGH ME FIRST!
I WON'T LET YOU!
HMPH ...
WHAT A SSSTUPID THING TO SAY.

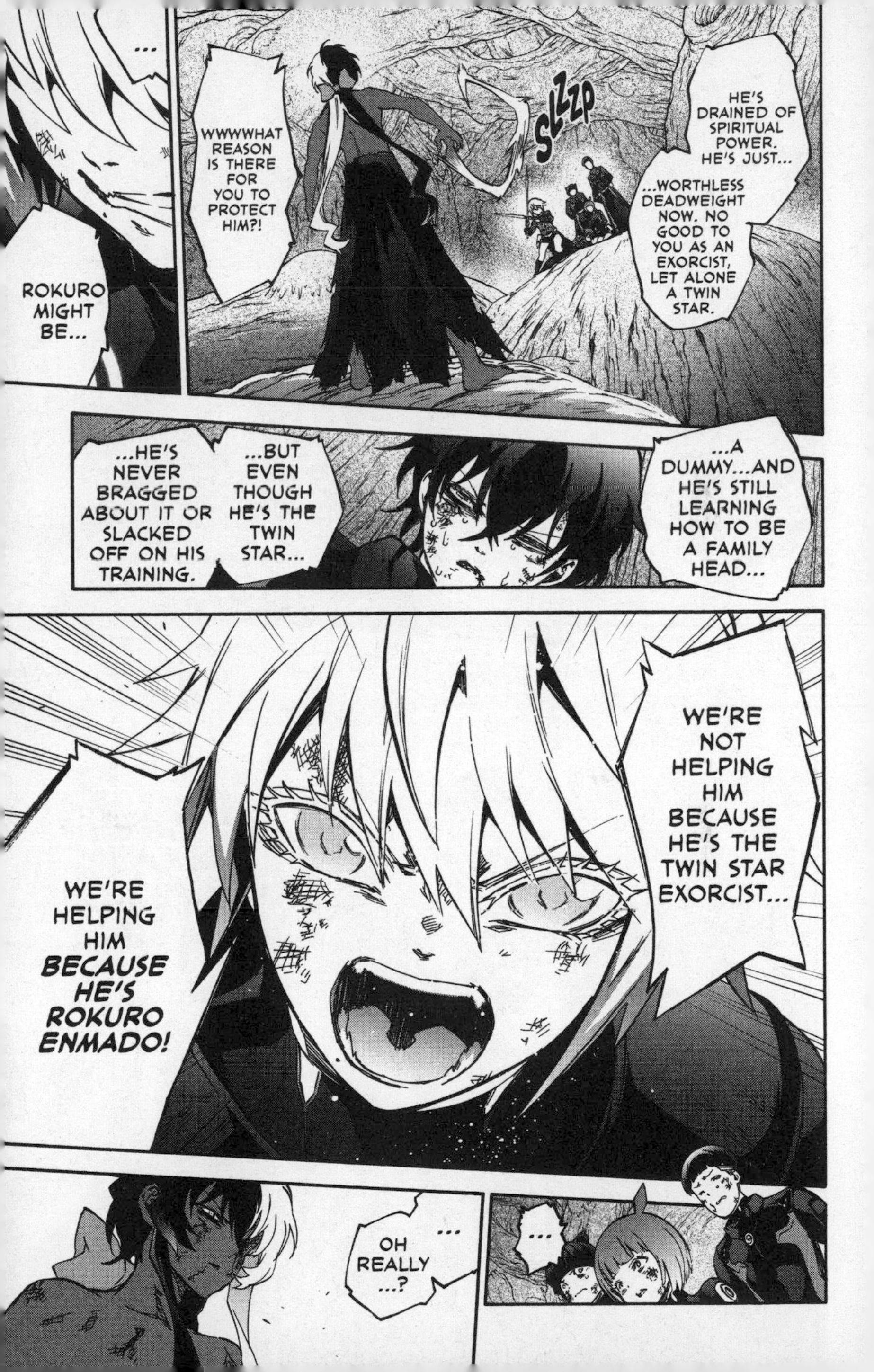
HE'S DRAINED OF SPIRITUAL POWER. HE'S JUST...
...WORTHLESS DEADWEIGHT NOW. NO GOOD TO YOU AS AN EXORCIST, LET ALONE A TWIN STAR.
SLZZP
WWWWHAT REASON IS THERE FOR YOU TO PROTECT HIM?!
...
ROKURO MIGHT BE...
...A DUMMY...AND HE'S STILL LEARNING HOW TO BE A FAMILY HEAD...
...BUT EVEN THOUGH HE'S THE TWIN STAR...
...HE'S NEVER BRAGGED ABOUT IT OR SLACKED OFF ON HIS TRAINING.
WE'RE NOT HELPING HIM BECAUSE HE'S THE TWIN STAR EXORCIST...
WE'RE HELPING HIM *BECAUSE HE'S ROKURO ENMADO!*
...
...
OH REALLY ...?

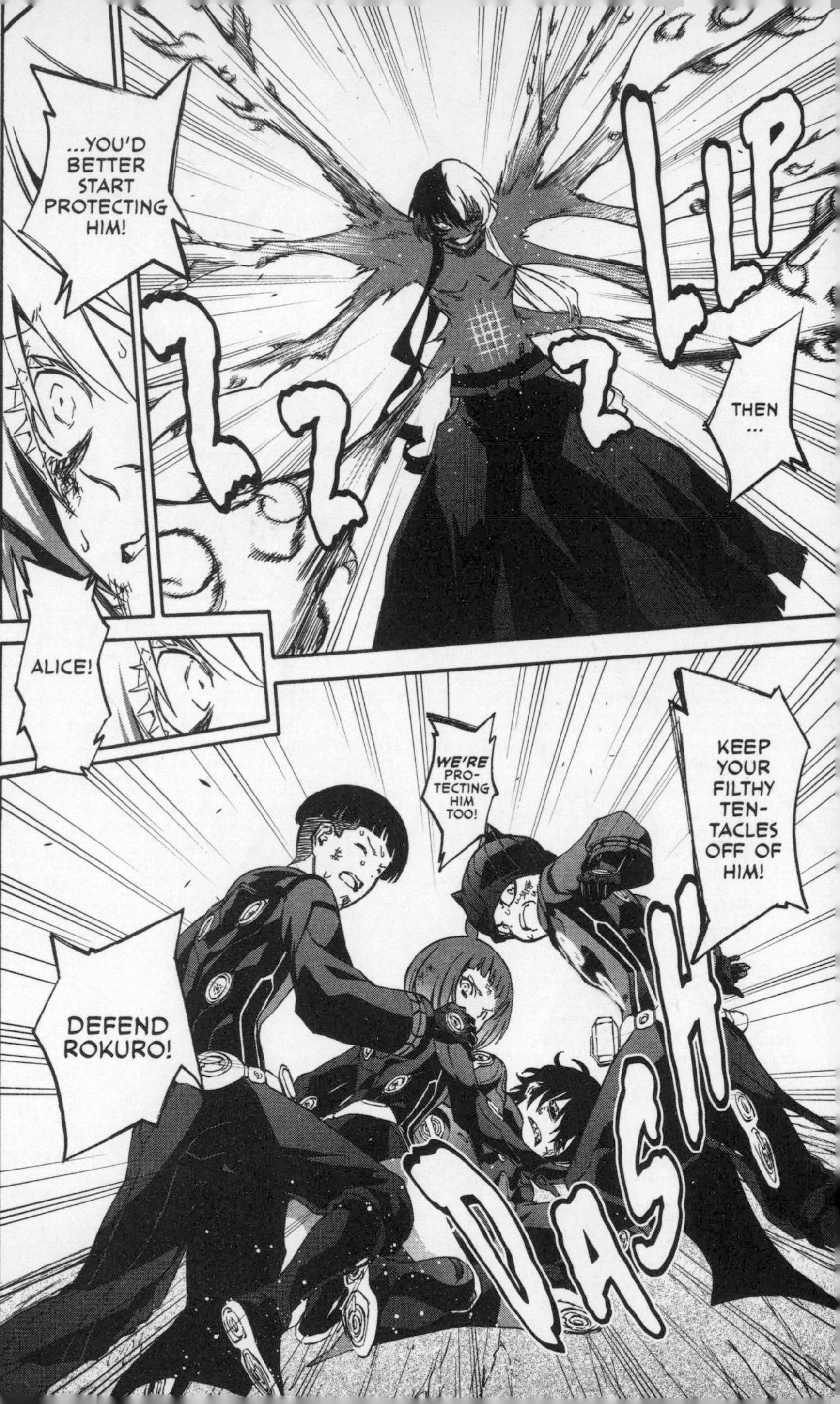
THEN...
...YOU'D BETTER START PROTECTING HIM!
ALICE!
KEEP YOUR FILTHY TEN-TACLES OFF OF HIM!
WE'RE PRO-TECTING HIM TOO!
DEFEND ROKURO!
DASH

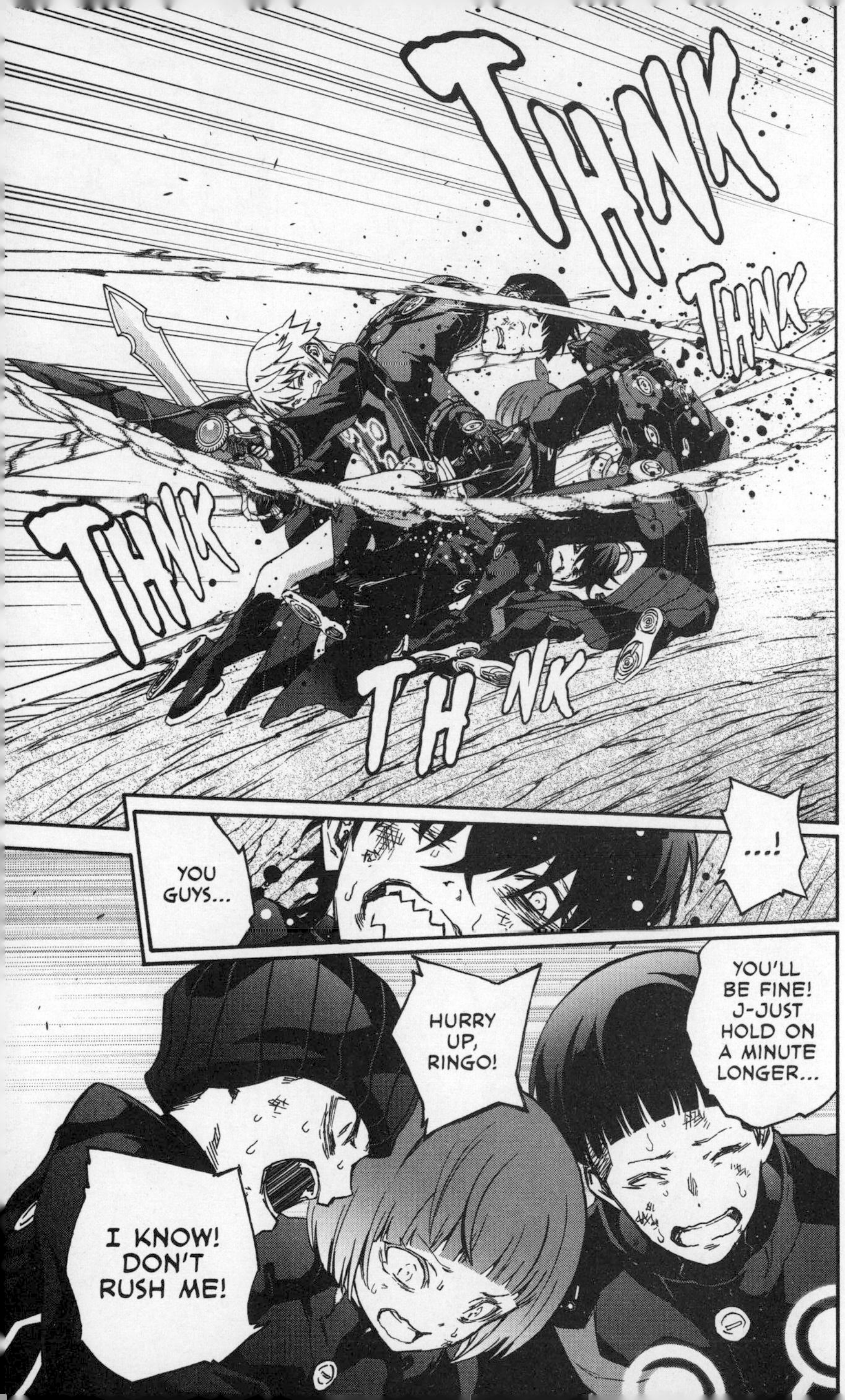
THNK
THNK
THNK
TH NK
...!
YOU GUYS...
YOU'LL BE FINE! J-JUST HOLD ON A MINUTE LONGER...
HURRY UP, RINGO!
I KNOW! DON'T RUSH ME!

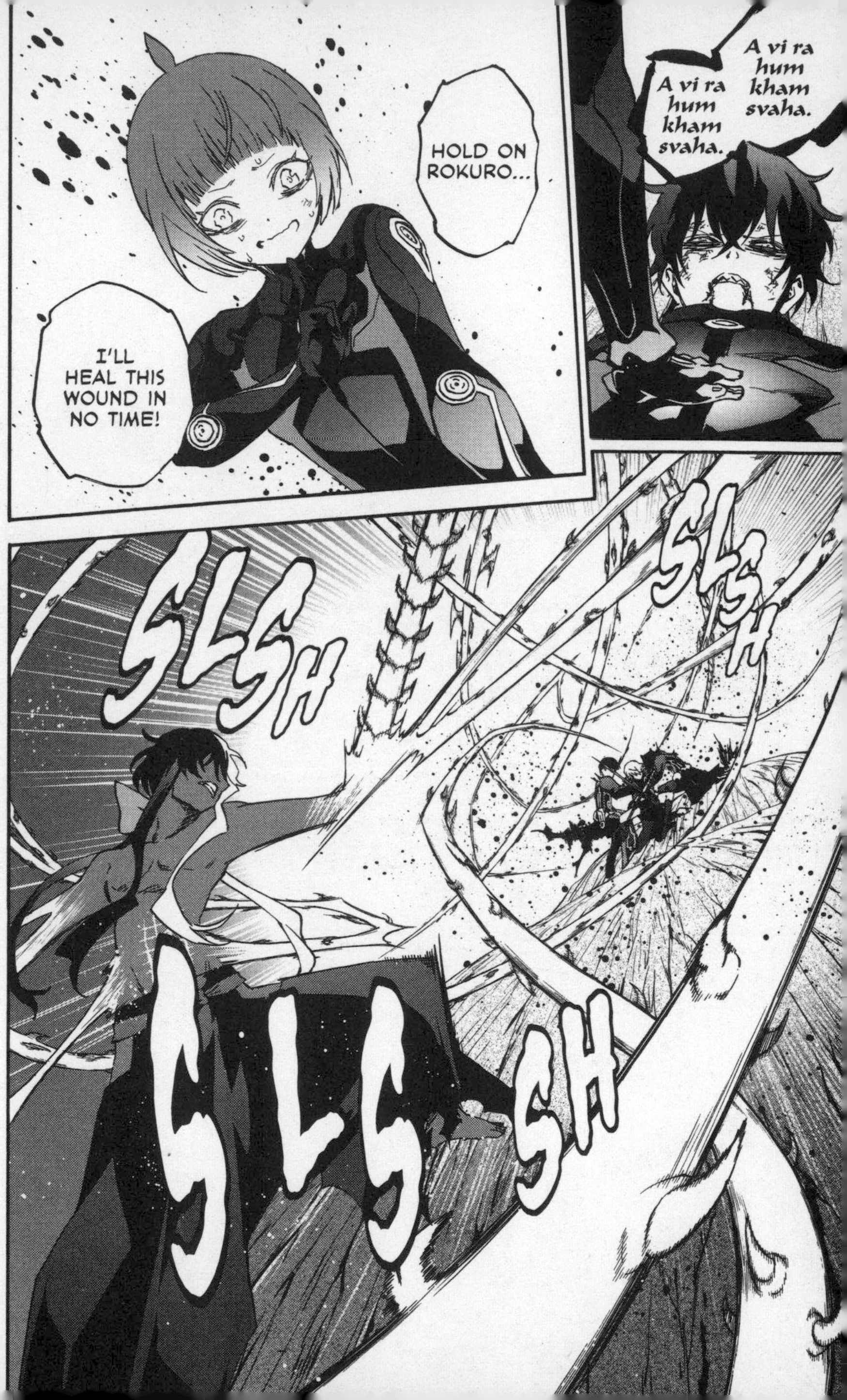
A vi ra hum kham svaha.
A vi ra hum kham svaha.
HOLD ON ROKURO...
I'LL HEAL THIS WOUND IN NO TIME!
SLSH
SLSH
SLSSH

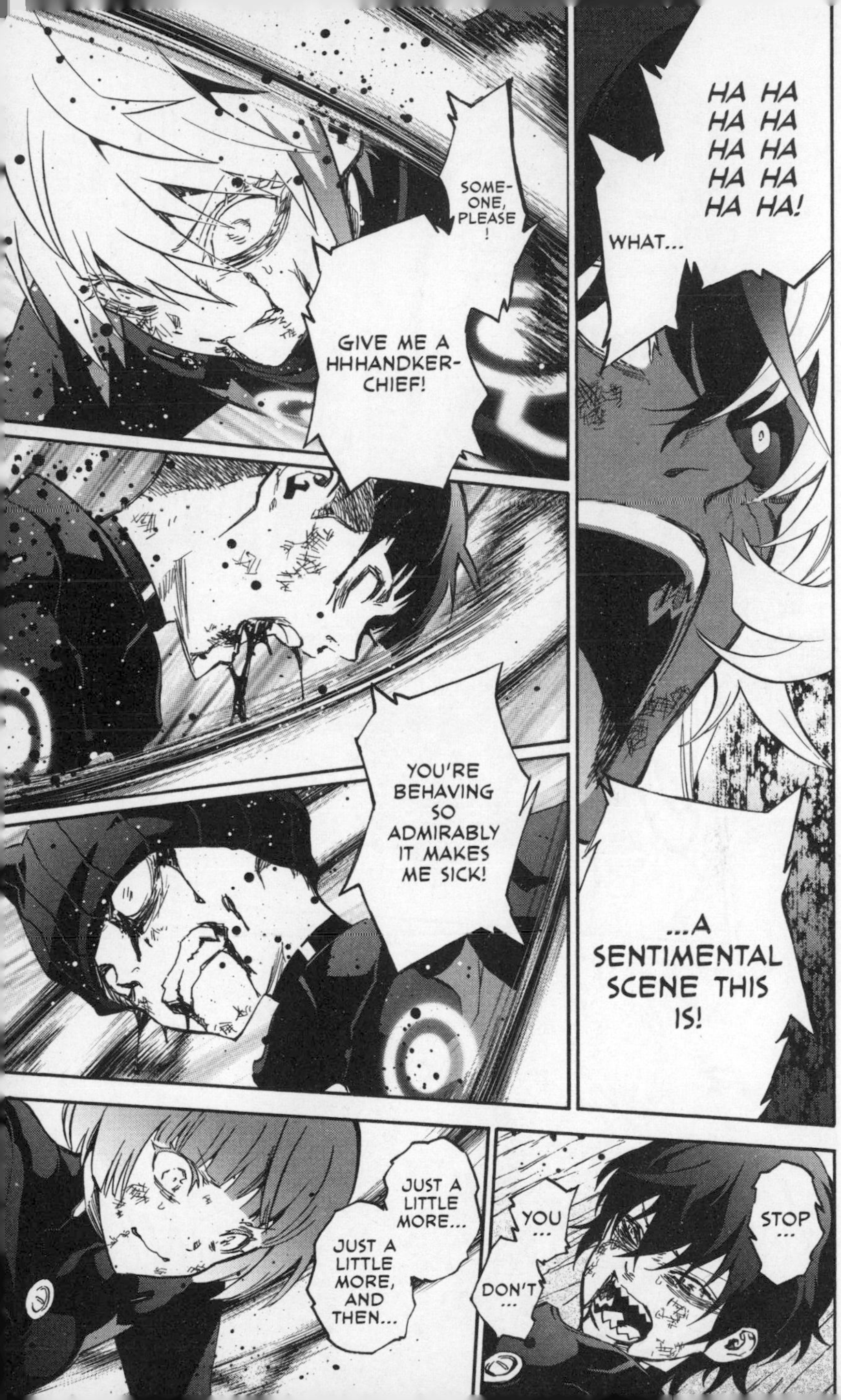
HA HA HA HA HA HA HA HA HA HA!
WHAT...
...A SENTIMENTAL SCENE THIS IS!
SOME-ONE, PLEASE!
GIVE ME A HHHANDKER-CHIEF!
YOU'RE BEHAVING SO ADMIRABLY IT MAKES ME SICK!
STOP...
YOU... DON'T...
JUST A LITTLE MORE...
JUST A LITTLE MORE, AND THEN...

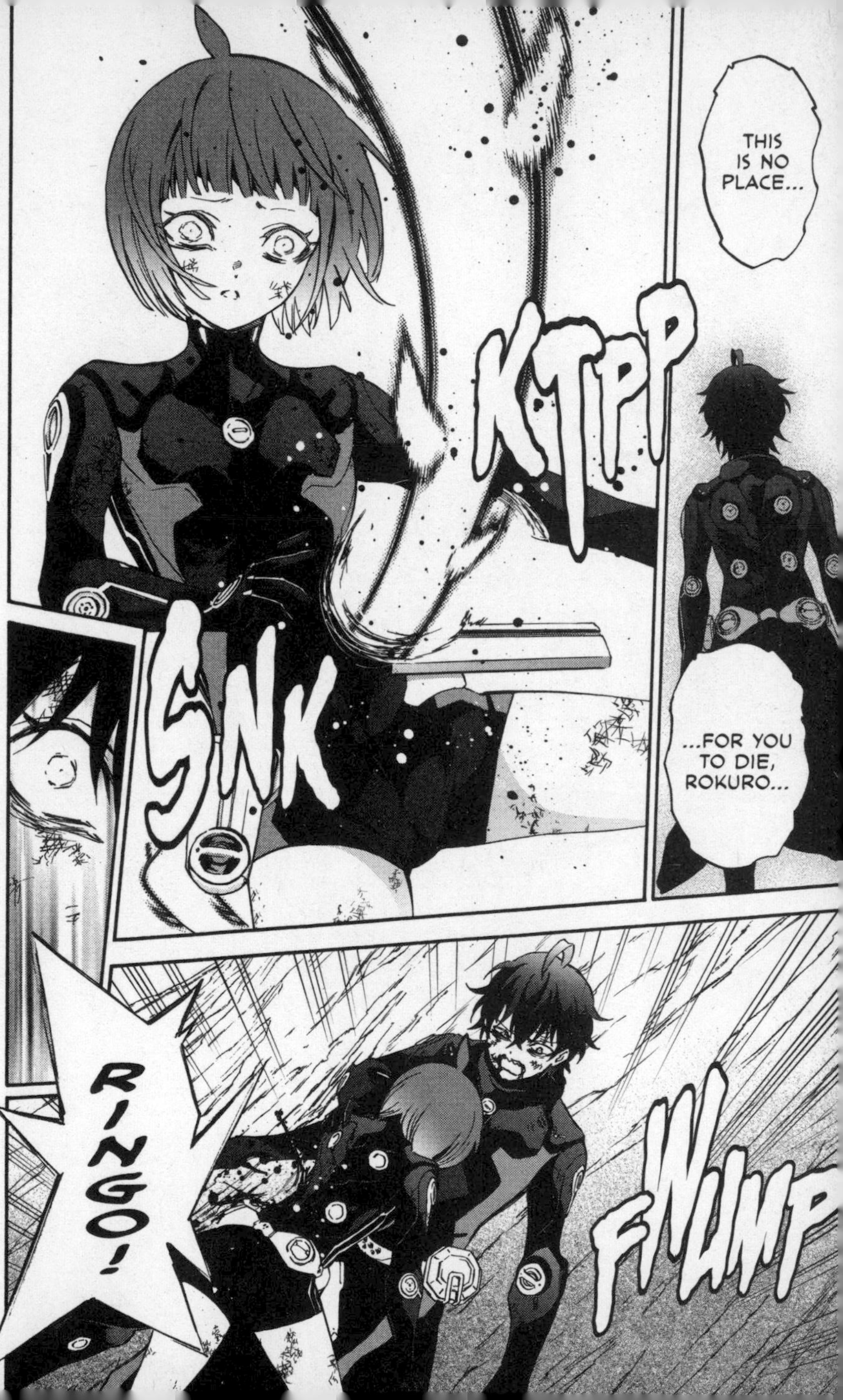
THIS IS NO PLACE...
...FOR YOU TO DIE, ROKURO...
KTPP
SNK
FWUMP
RINGO!

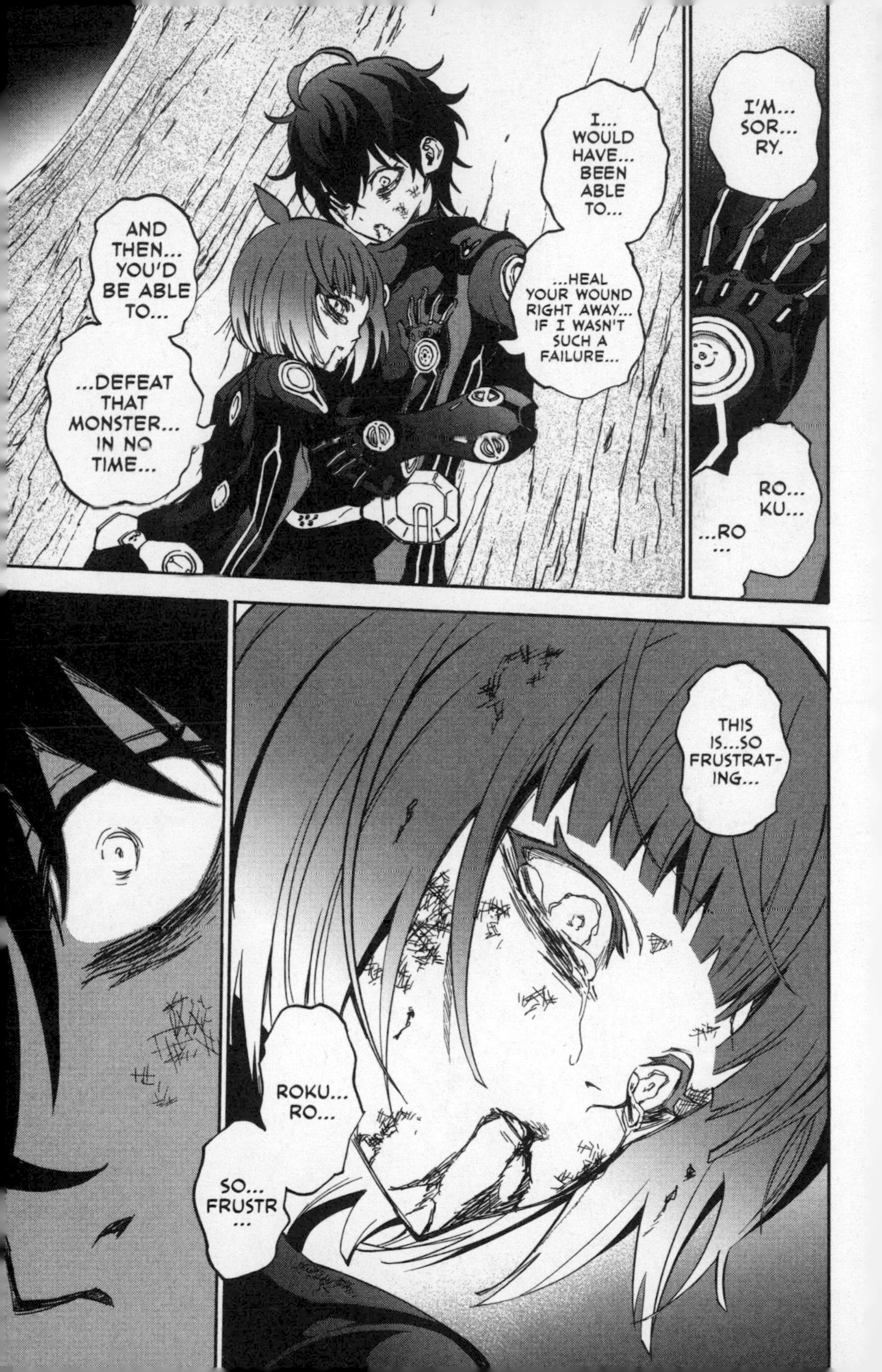
I'M... SOR... RY.
RO... KU... ...RO ...
I... WOULD HAVE... BEEN ABLE TO...
...HEAL YOUR WOUND RIGHT AWAY... IF I WASN'T SUCH A FAILURE...
AND THEN... YOU'D BE ABLE TO...
...DEFEAT THAT MONSTER... IN NO TIME...
THIS IS...SO FRUSTRAT-ING...
ROKU... RO...
SO... FRUSTR ...

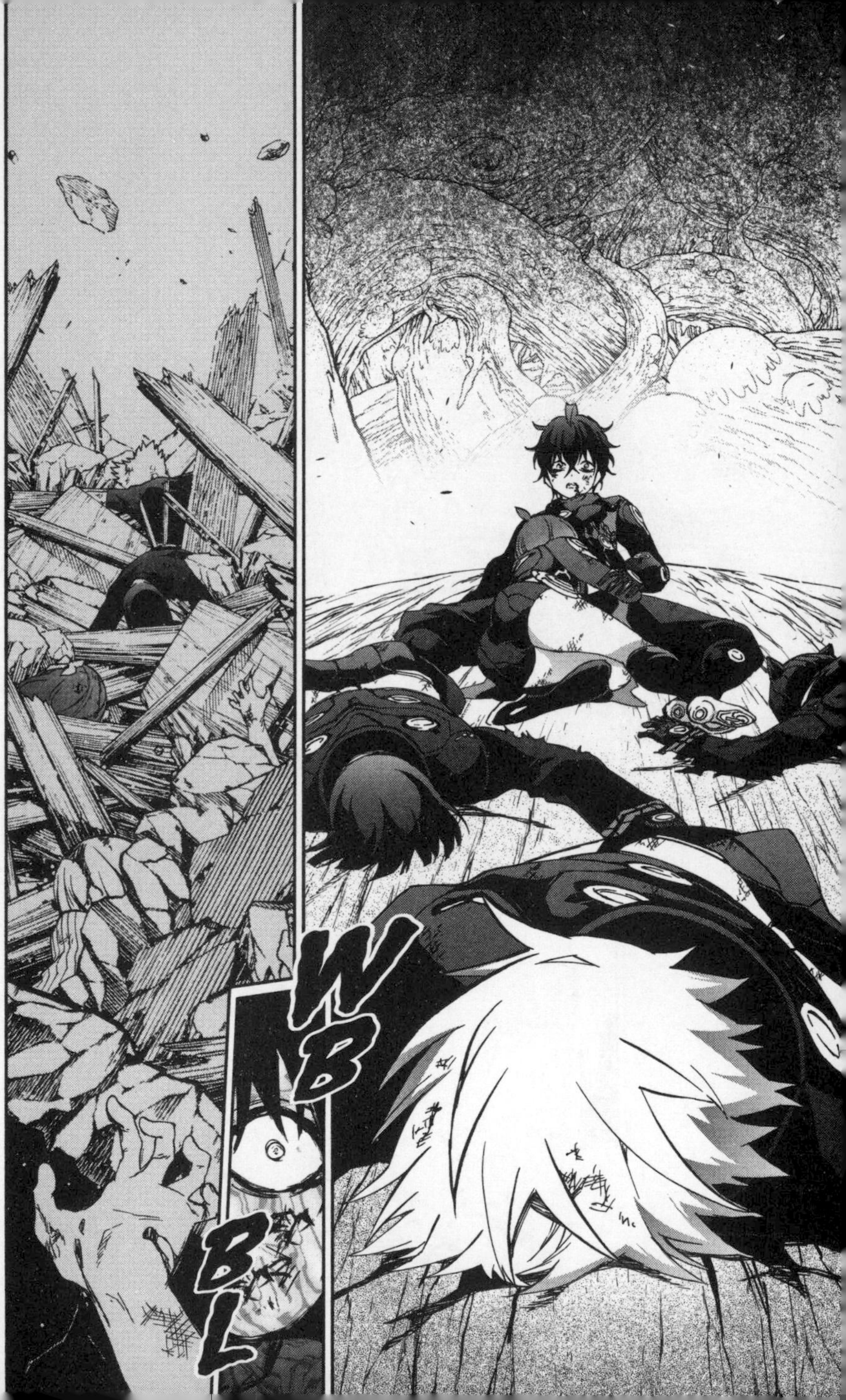
WB
BL

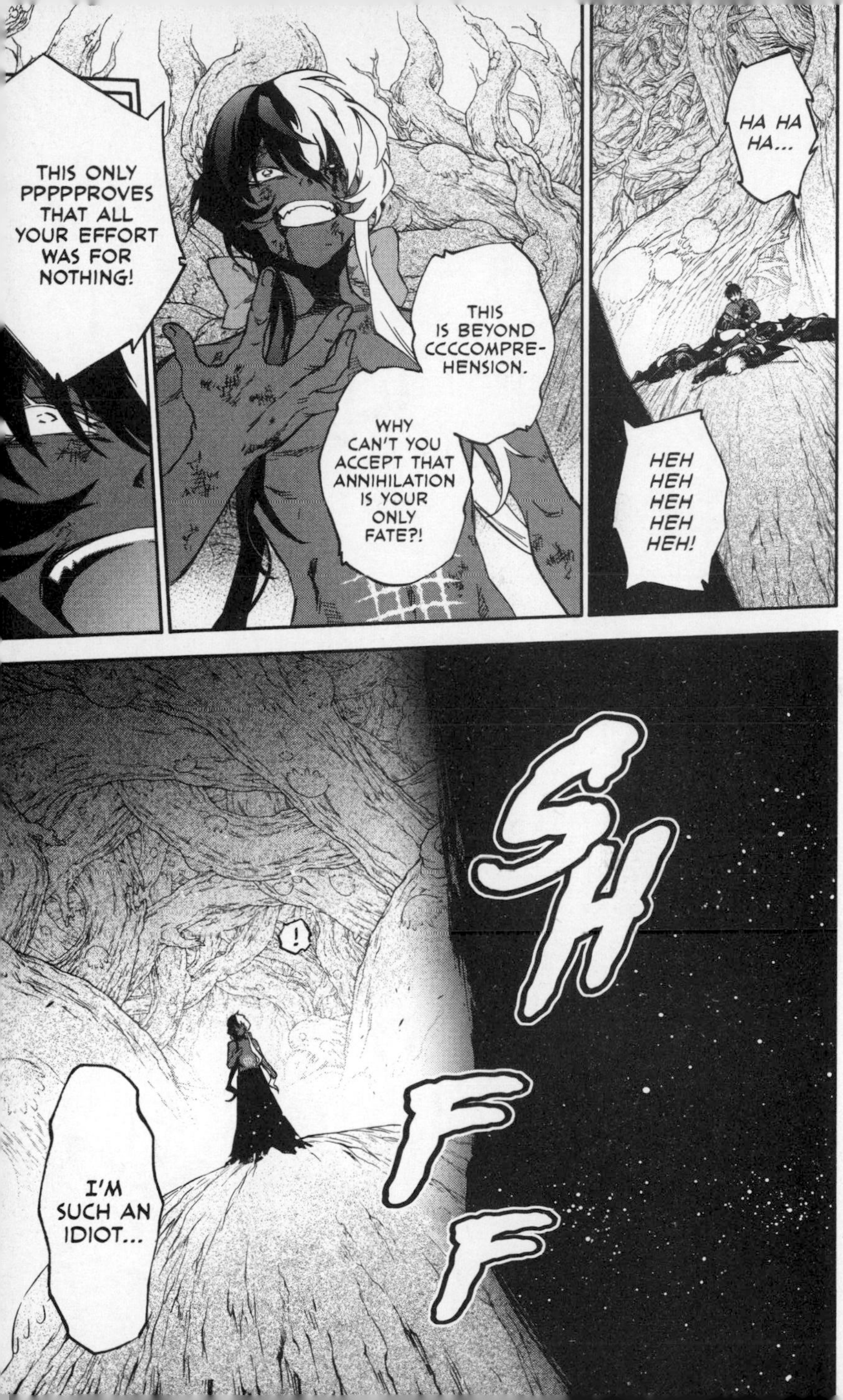
HA HA HA...
HEH HEH HEH HEH HEH!
THIS IS BEYOND CCCCOMPRE-HENSION.
WHY CAN'T YOU ACCEPT THAT ANNIHILATION IS YOUR ONLY FATE?!
THIS ONLY PPPPPROVES THAT ALL YOUR EFFORT WAS FOR NOTHING!
SHFFF
!
I'M SUCH AN IDIOT...

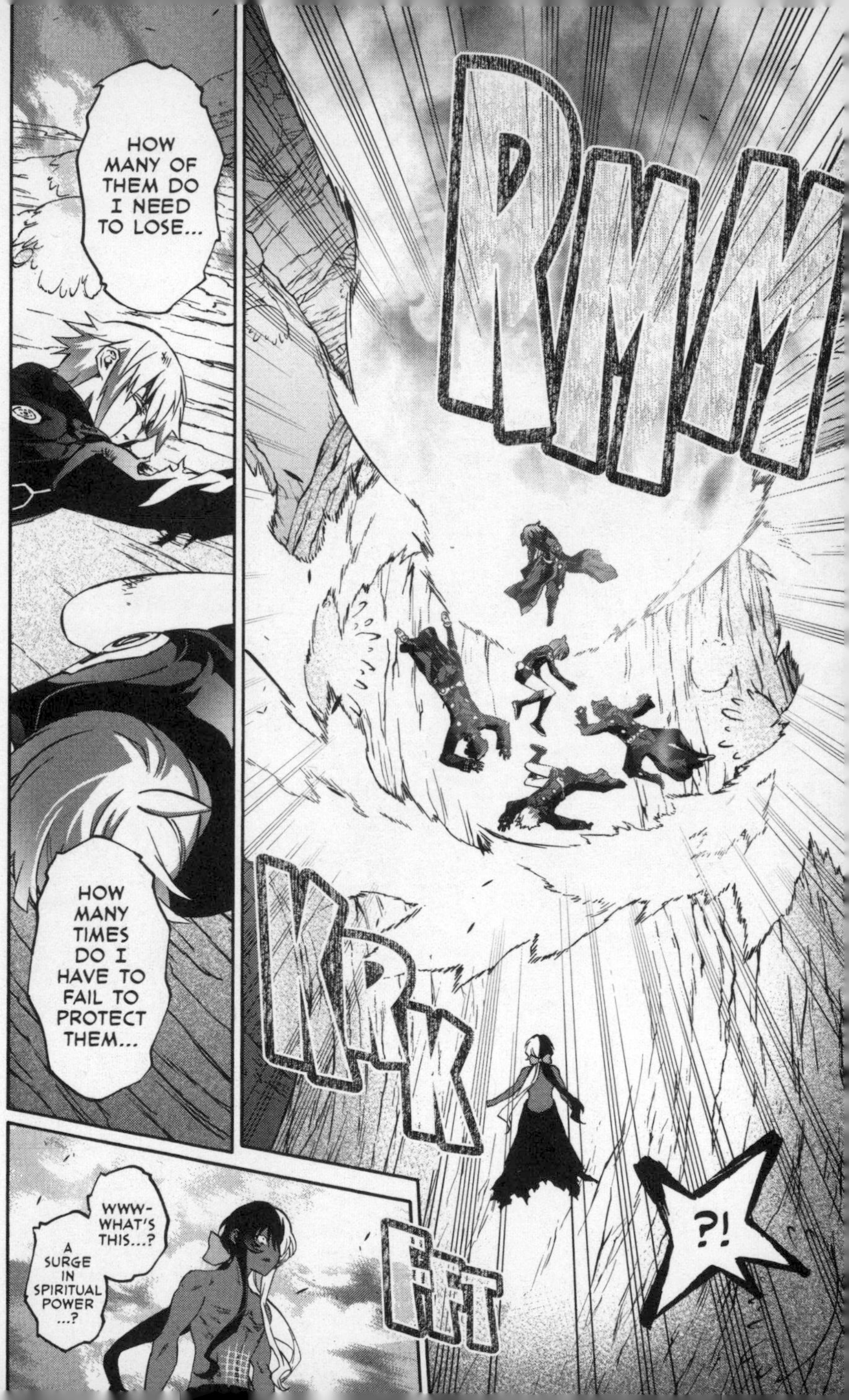
RMM
KRK
?!
HOW MANY OF THEM DO I NEED TO LOSE...
HOW MANY TIMES DO I HAVE TO FAIL TO PROTECT THEM...
WWW-WHAT'S THIS...?
A SURGE IN SPIRITUAL POWER ...?

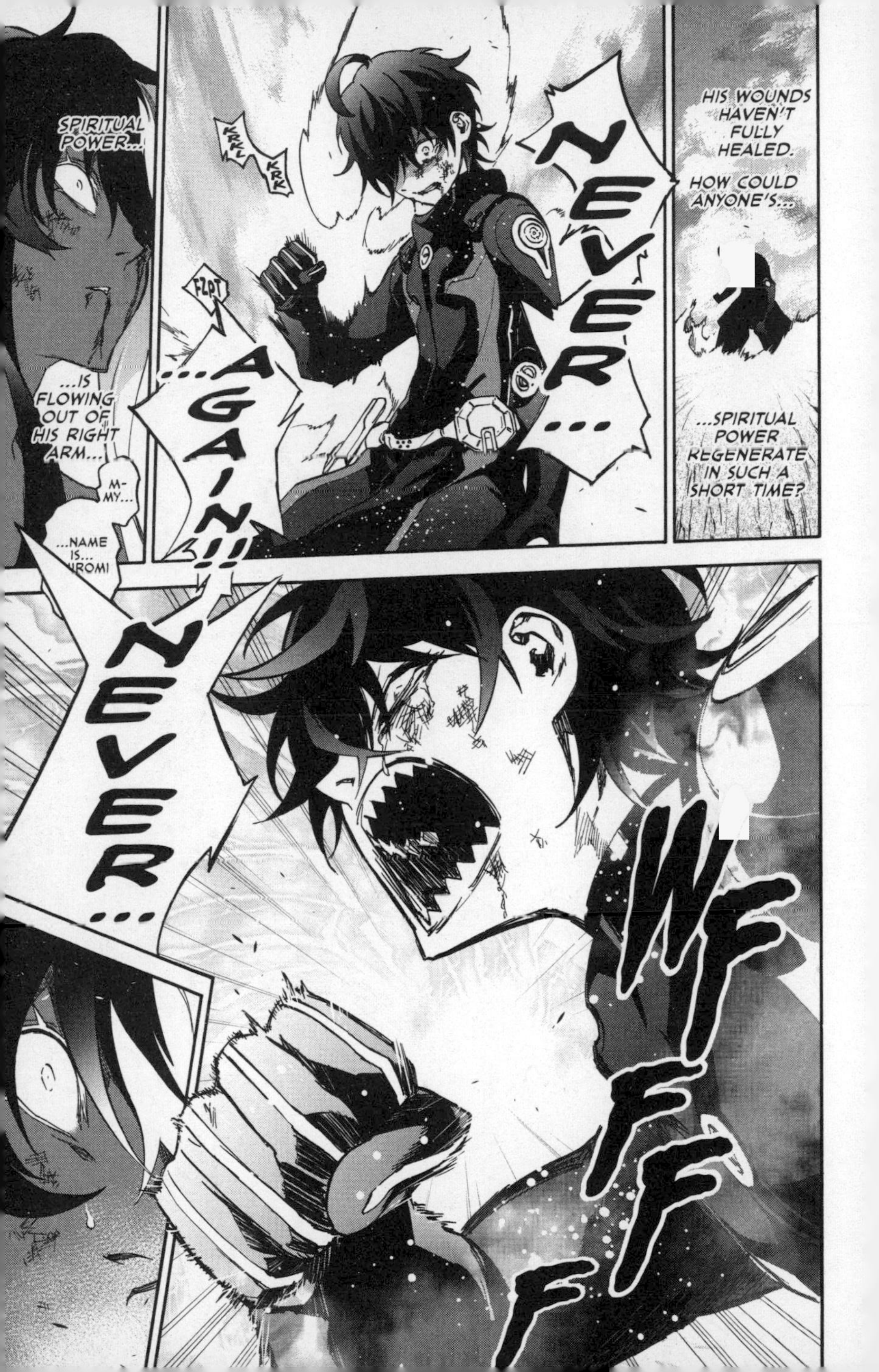
HIS WOUNDS HAVEN'T FULLY HEALED.
HOW COULD ANYONE'S...
...SPIRITUAL POWER REGENERATE IN SUCH A SHORT TIME?
NEVER...
KRKL
KRK
FZPT
...AGAIN!!
SPIRITUAL POWER...
...IS FLOWING OUT OF HIS RIGHT ARM...
M-MY...
...NAME IS...
NEVER...
WFFF

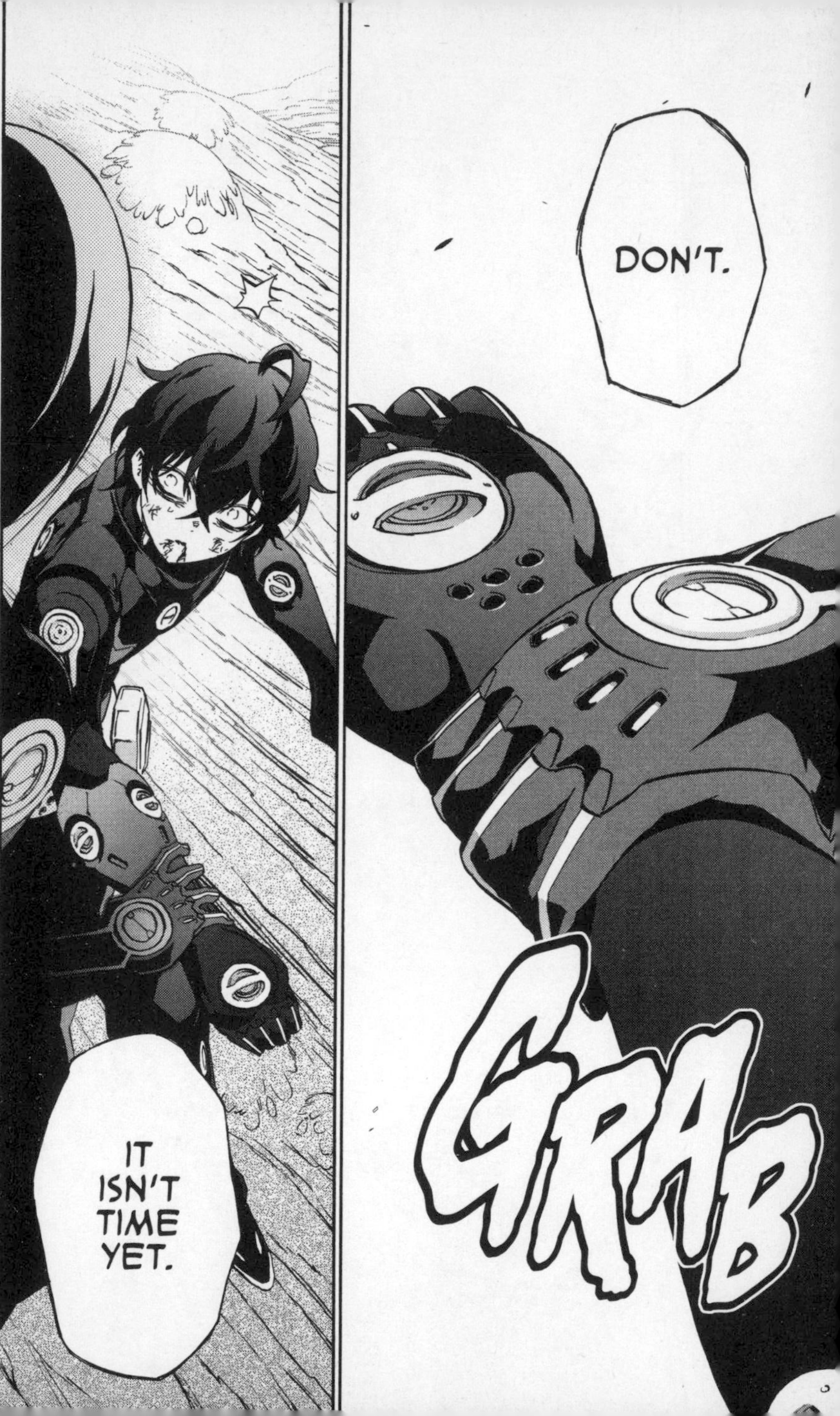
DON'T.
GRAB
IT ISN'T TIME YET.

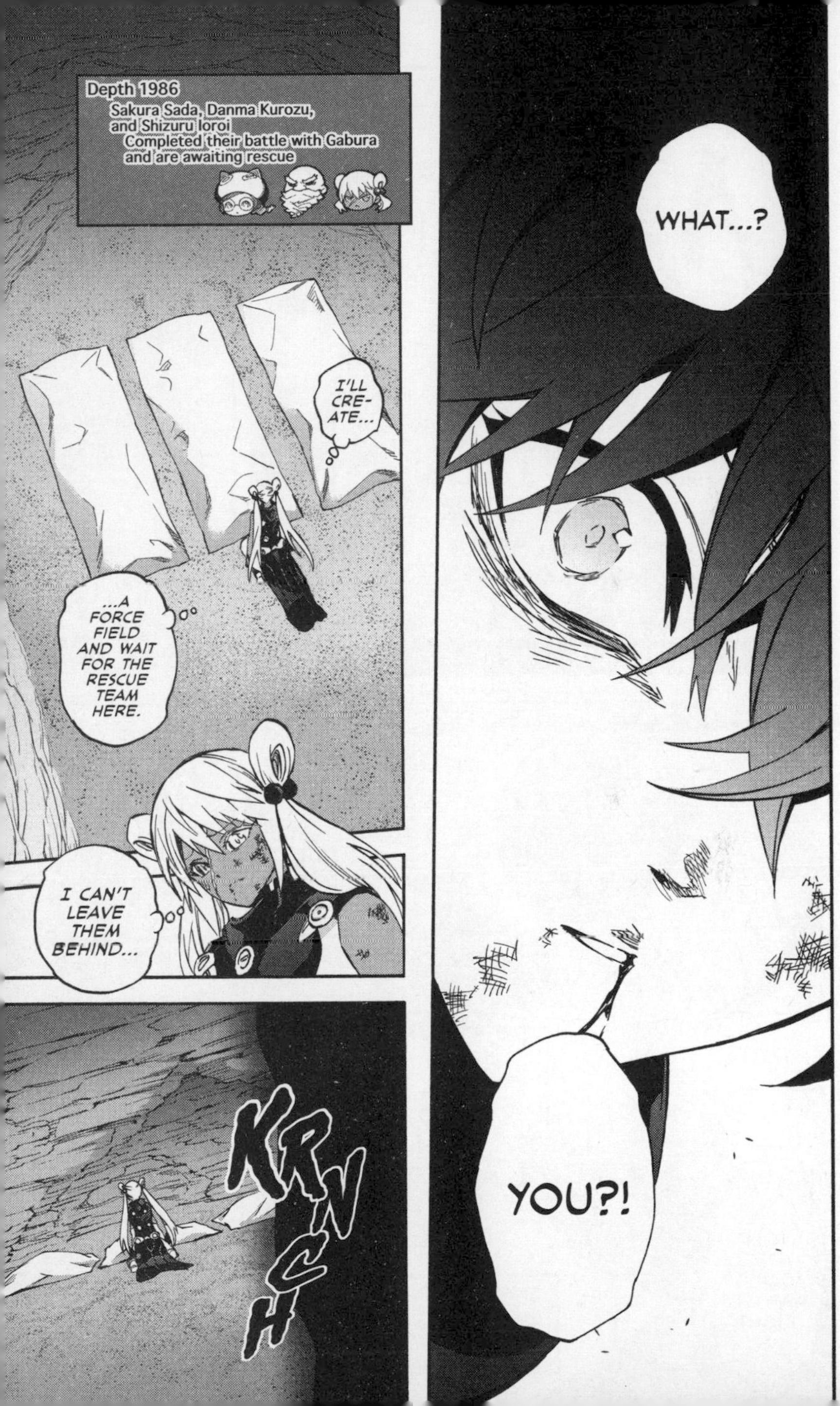
WHAT...?
YOU?!
Depth 1986
Sakura Sada, Danma Kurozu, and Shizuru Ioroi
Completed their battle with Gabura and are awaiting rescue
I'LL CREATE...
...A FORCE FIELD AND WAIT FOR THE RESCUE TEAM HERE.
I CAN'T LEAVE THEM BEHIND...
KRNCH

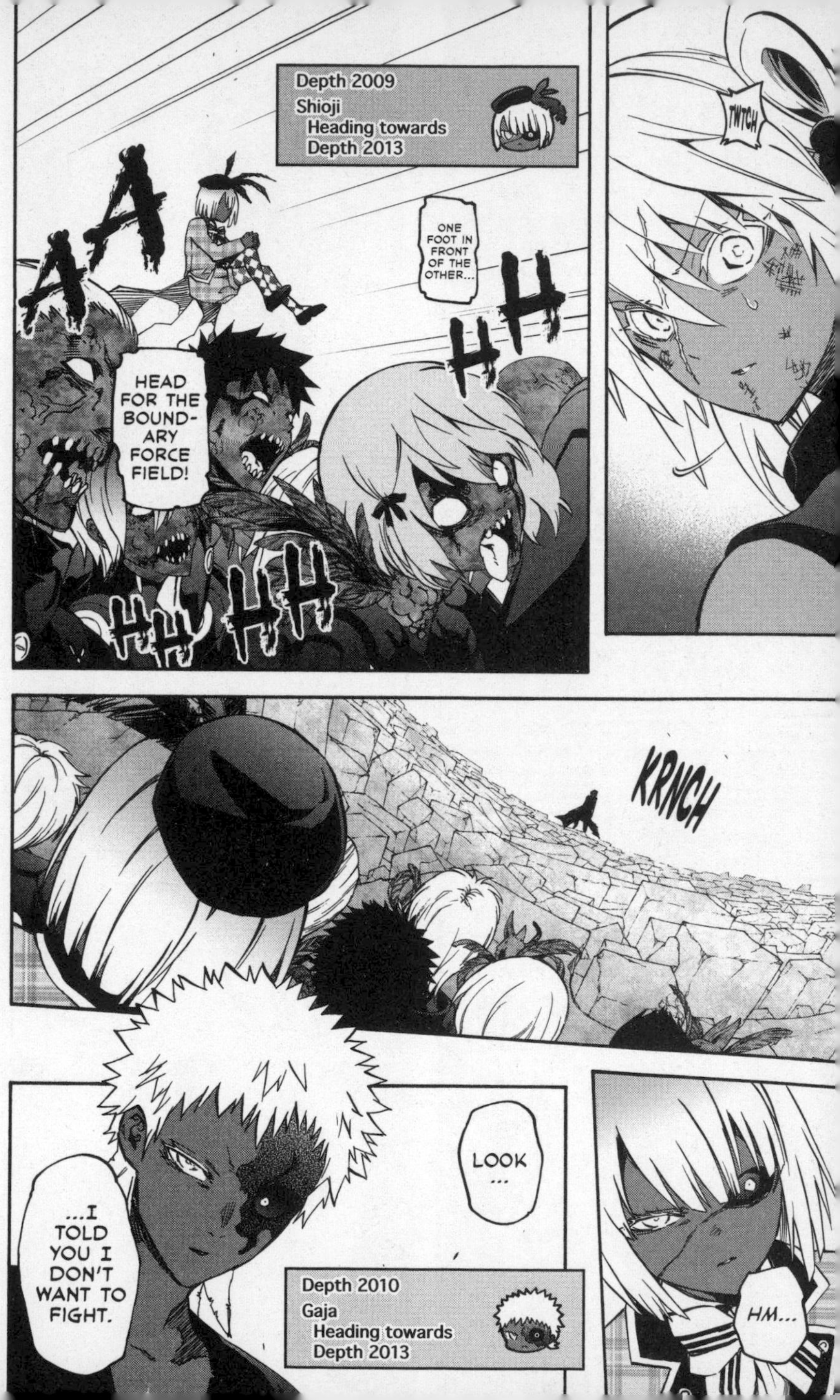
TWTCH
Depth 2009
Shioji
Heading towards
Depth 2013
ONE FOOT IN FRONT OF THE OTHER...
HH
AA
HEAD FOR THE BOUNDARY FORCE FIELD!
HH HH
KRNCH
HM...
LOOK...
...I TOLD YOU I DON'T WANT TO FIGHT.
Depth 2010
Gaja
Heading towards
Depth 2013

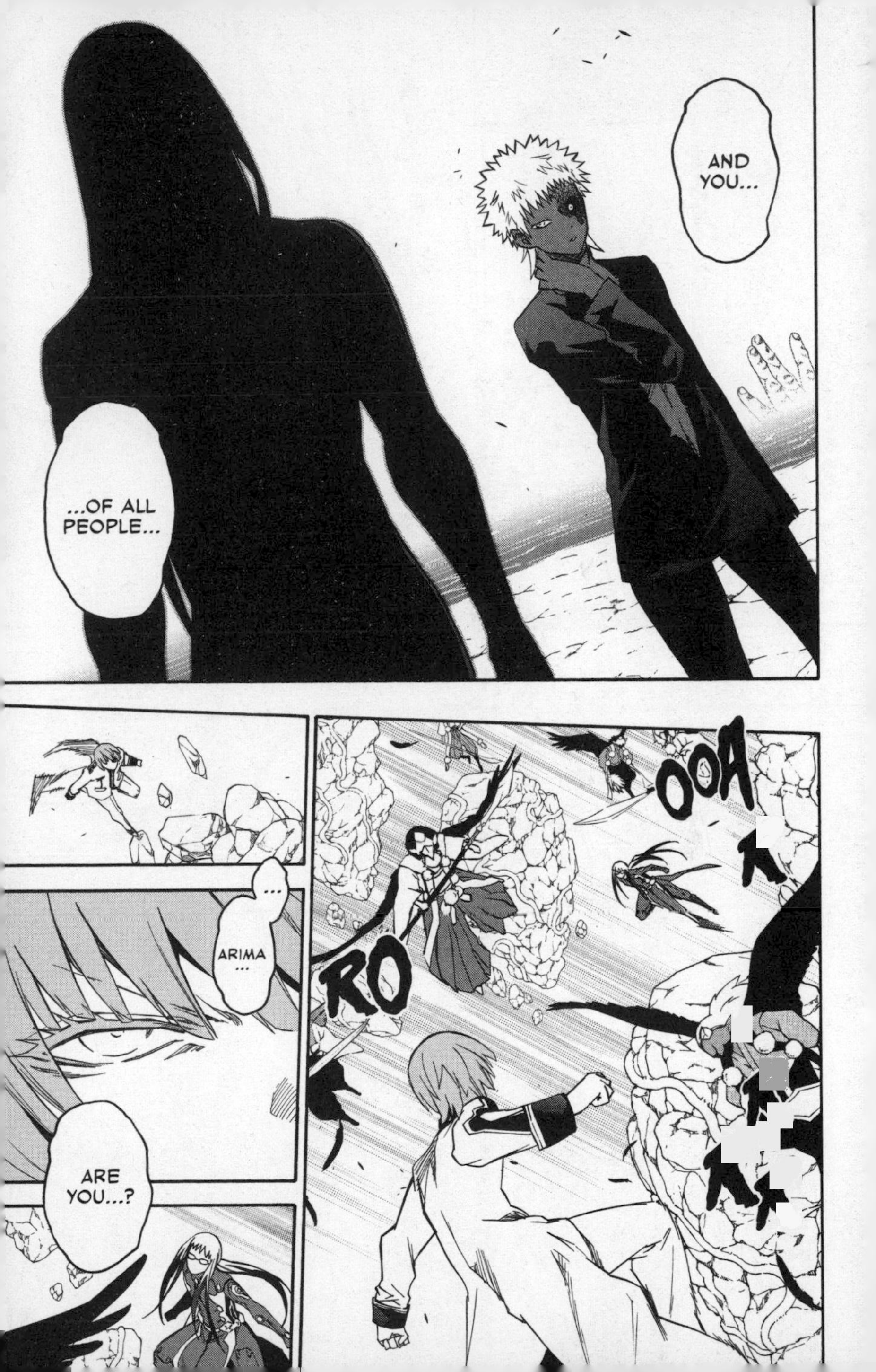
AND YOU...
...OF ALL PEOPLE...
RO OOA
...
ARIMA ...
ARE YOU...?

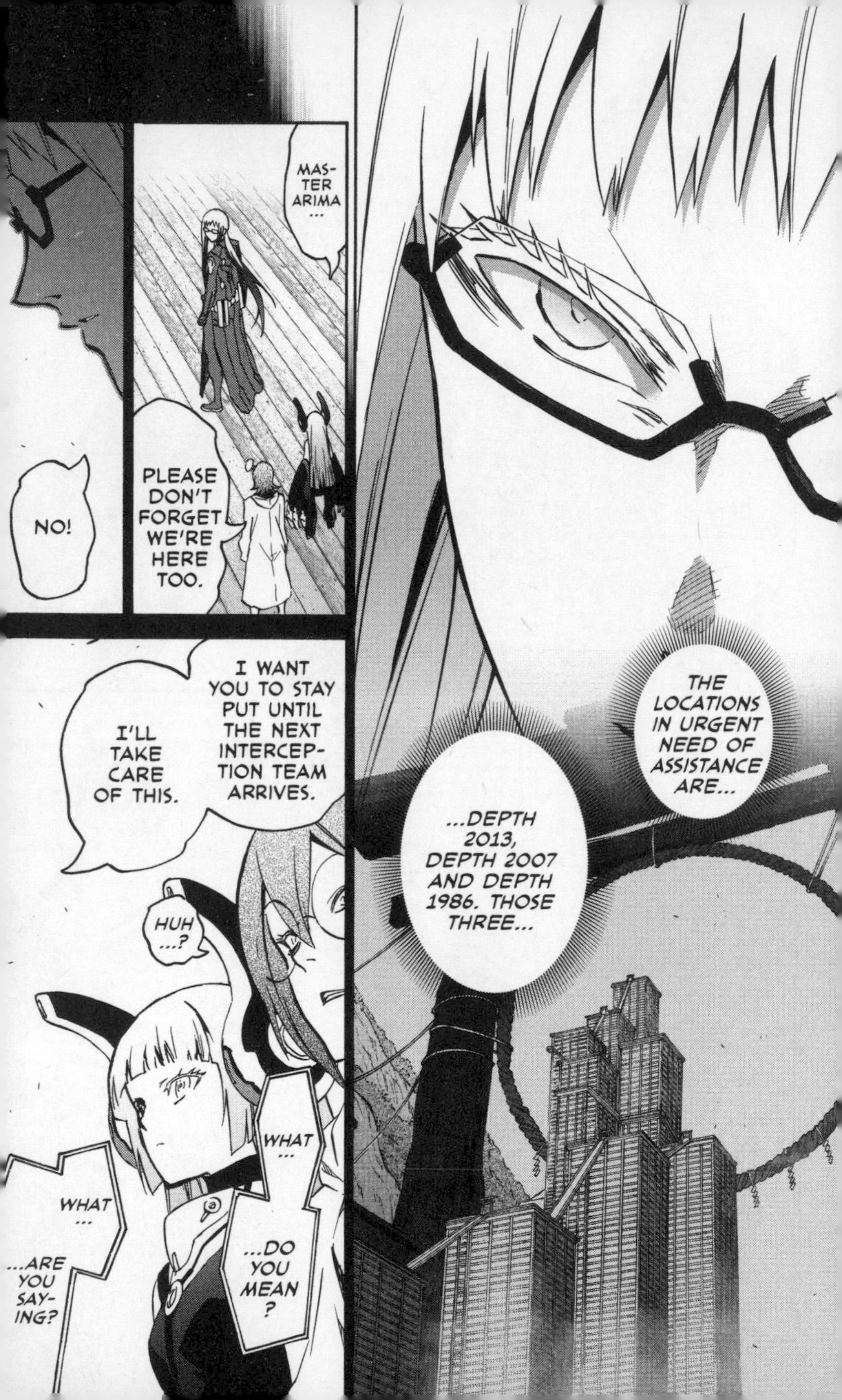
THE LOCATIONS IN URGENT NEED OF ASSISTANCE ARE...
...DEPTH 2013, DEPTH 2007 AND DEPTH 1986. THOSE THREE...
MAS-TER ARIMA...
PLEASE DON'T FORGET WE'RE HERE TOO.
NO!
I WANT YOU TO STAY PUT UNTIL THE NEXT INTERCEP-TION TEAM ARRIVES.
I'LL TAKE CARE OF THIS.
HUH...?
WHAT...
...DO YOU MEAN?
WHAT...
...ARE YOU SAY-ING?

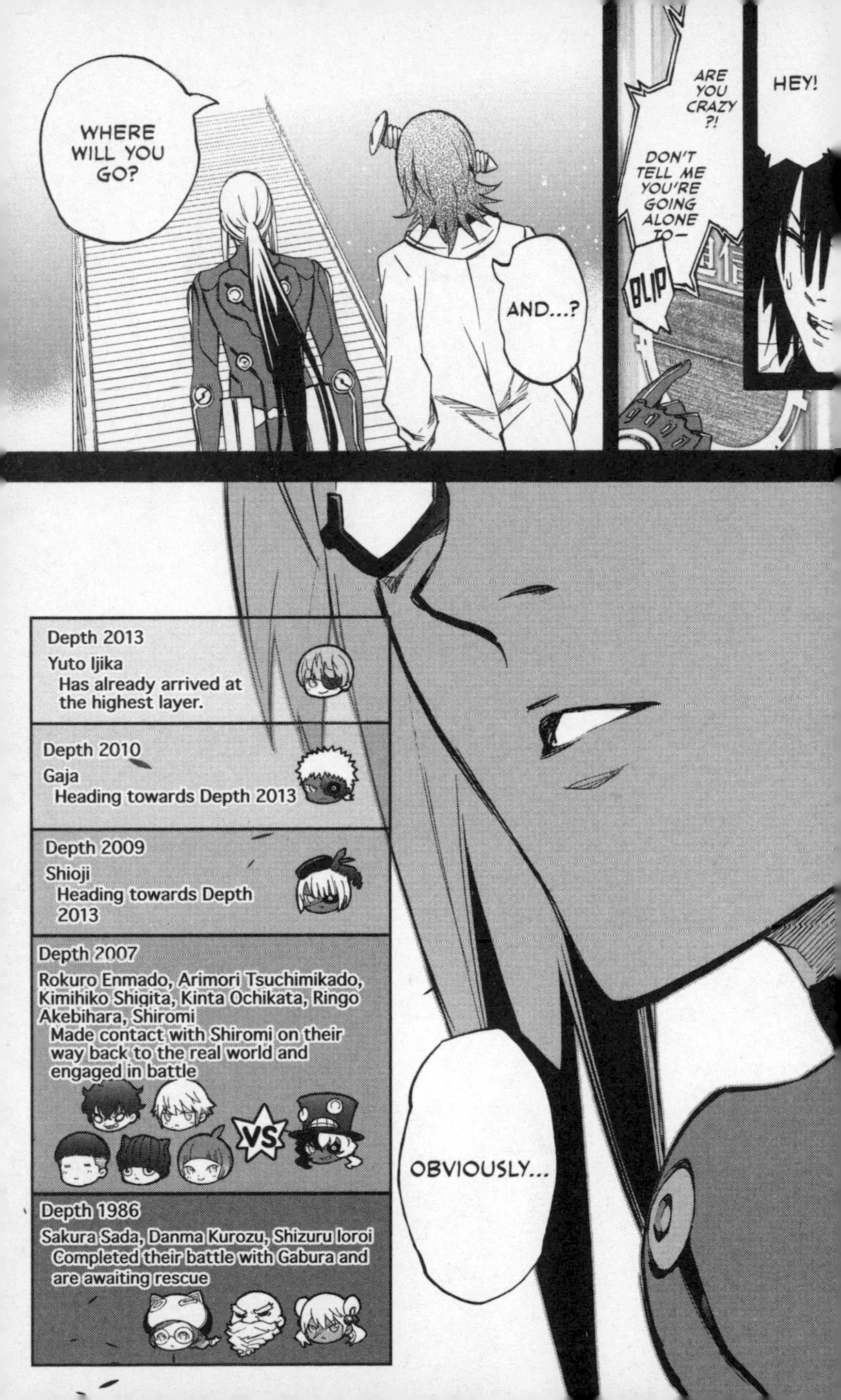
HEY!
ARE YOU CRAZY?!
DON'T TELL ME YOU'RE GOING ALONE TO—
BLIP
WHERE WILL YOU GO?
AND...?
Depth 2013
Yuto Ijika
Has already arrived at the highest layer.
Depth 2010
Gaja
Heading towards Depth 2013
Depth 2009
Shioji
Heading towards Depth 2013
Depth 2007
Rokuro Enmado, Arimori Tsuchimikado, Kimihiko Shigita, Kinta Ochikata, Ringo Akebihara, Shiromi
Made contact with Shiromi on their way back to the real world and engaged in battle
VS
Depth 1986
Sakura Sada, Danma Kurozu, Shizuru Ioroi
Completed their battle with Gabura and are awaiting rescue
OBVIOUSLY...

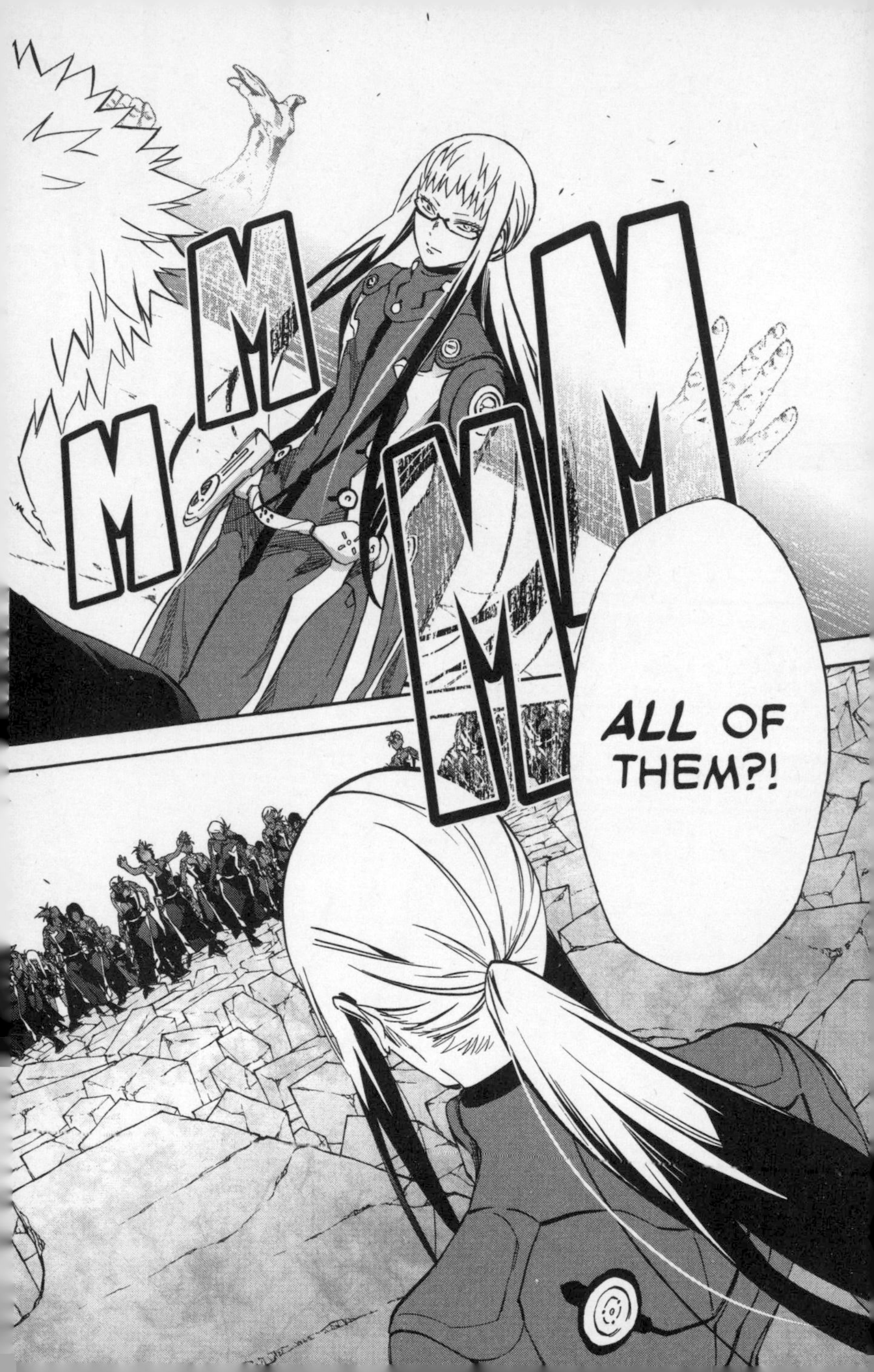
MMMMM
ALL OF THEM?!

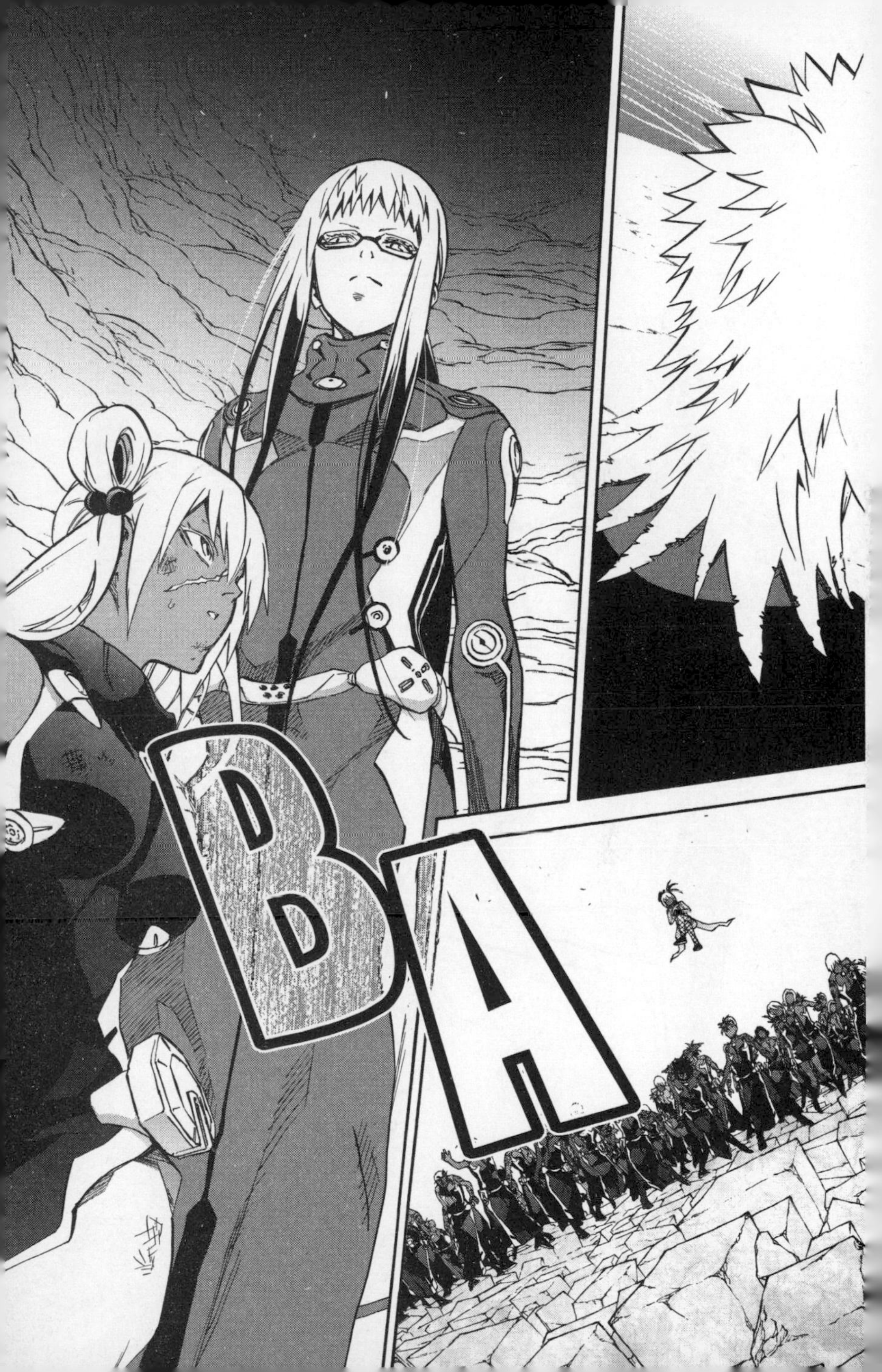
BA

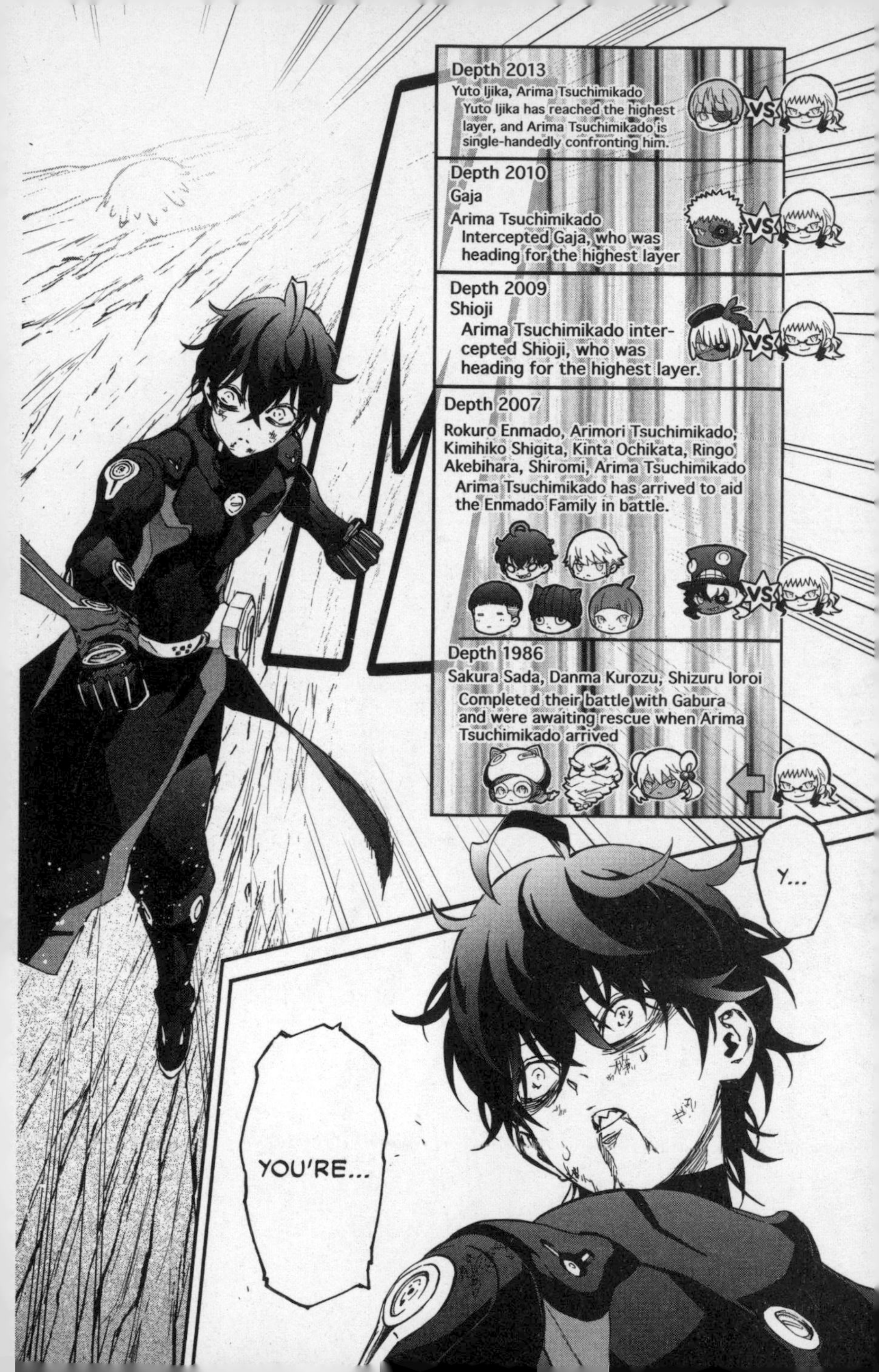
Depth 2013
Yuto Ijika, Arima Tsuchimikado
Yuto Ijika has reached the highest layer, and Arima Tsuchimikado is single-handedly confronting him.
VS
Depth 2010
Gaja
Arima Tsuchimikado
Intercepted Gaja, who was heading for the highest layer
VS
Depth 2009
Shioji
Arima Tsuchimikado intercepted Shioji, who was heading for the highest layer.
VS
Depth 2007
Rokuro Enmado, Arimori Tsuchimikado, Kimihiko Shigita, Kinta Ochikata, Ringo Akebihara, Shiromi, Arima Tsuchimikado
Arima Tsuchimikado has arrived to aid the Enmado Family in battle.
VS
Depth 1986
Sakura Sada, Danma Kurozu, Shizuru Ioroi
Completed their battle with Gabura and were awaiting rescue when Arima Tsuchimikado arrived
Y...
YOU'RE...

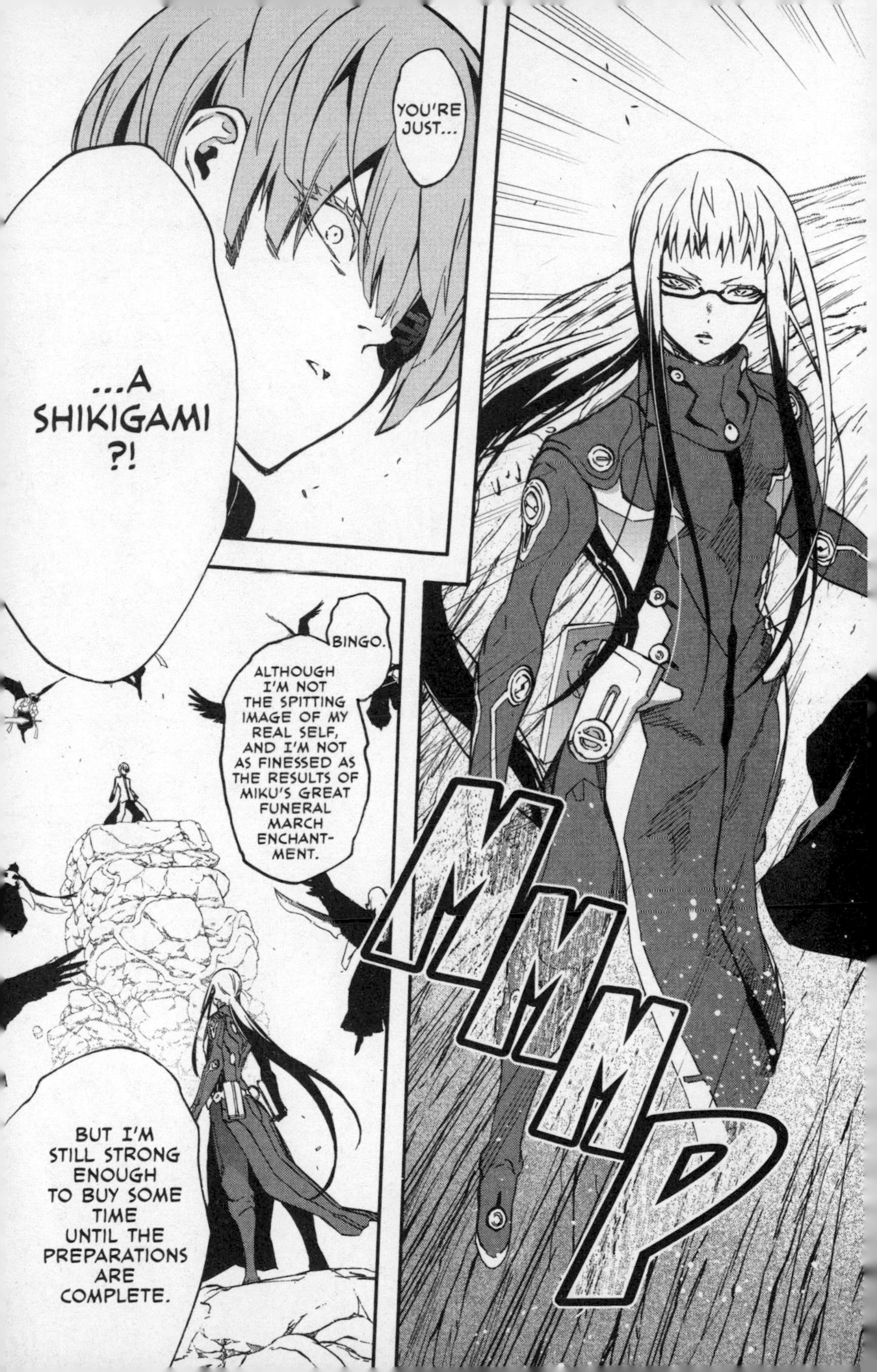
MMMP
YOU'RE JUST...
...A SHIKIGAMI ?!
BINGO.
ALTHOUGH I'M NOT THE SPITTING IMAGE OF MY REAL SELF, AND I'M NOT AS FINESSED AS THE RESULTS OF MIKU'S GREAT FUNERAL MARCH ENCHANT- MENT.
BUT I'M STILL STRONG ENOUGH TO BUY SOME TIME UNTIL THE PREPARATIONS ARE COMPLETE.

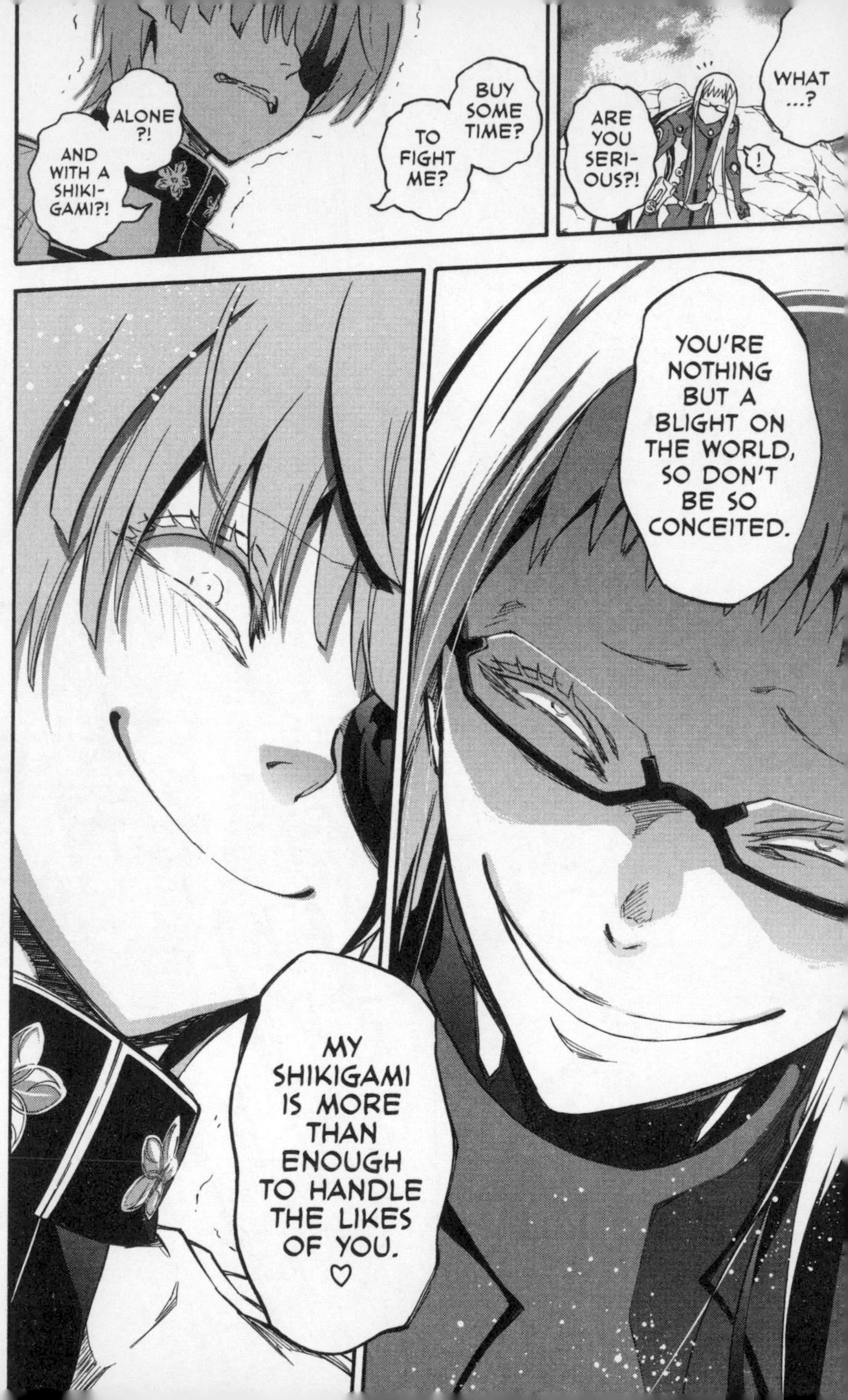
WHAT ...?
!
ARE YOU SERIOUS?!
BUY SOME TIME?
TO FIGHT ME?
ALONE?!
AND WITH A SHIKIGAMI?!
YOU'RE NOTHING BUT A BLIGHT ON THE WORLD, SO DON'T BE SO CONCEITED.
MY SHIKIGAMI IS MORE THAN ENOUGH TO HANDLE THE LIKES OF YOU. ♡

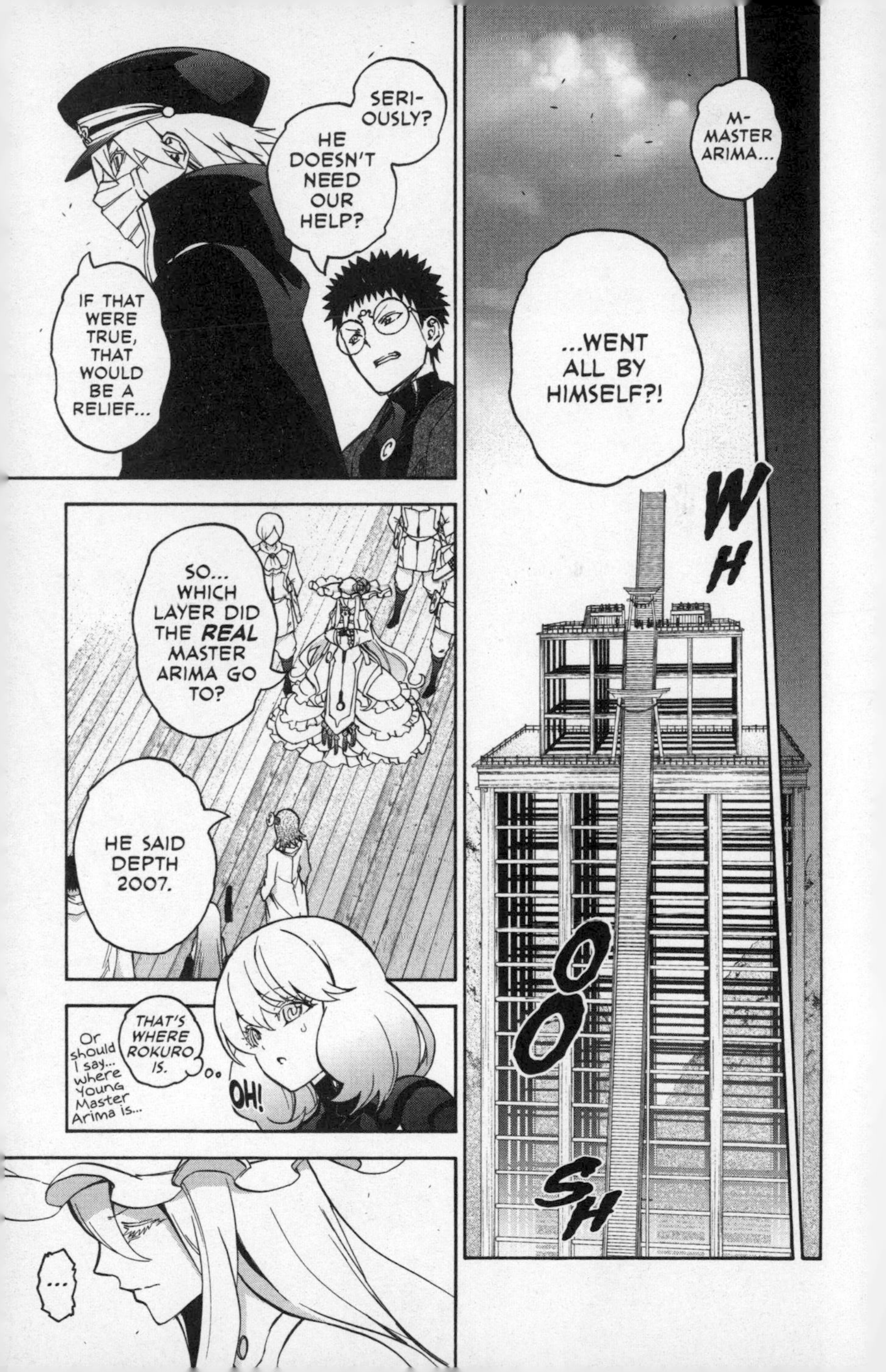
M-MASTER ARIMA...
...WENT ALL BY HIMSELF?!
WHOOSH
SERI-OUSLY? HE DOESN'T NEED OUR HELP?
IF THAT WERE TRUE, THAT WOULD BE A RELIEF...
SO... WHICH LAYER DID THE *REAL* MASTER ARIMA GO TO?
HE SAID DEPTH 2007.
THAT'S WHERE ROKURO IS.
Or should I say... where Young Master Arima is...
OH!
...

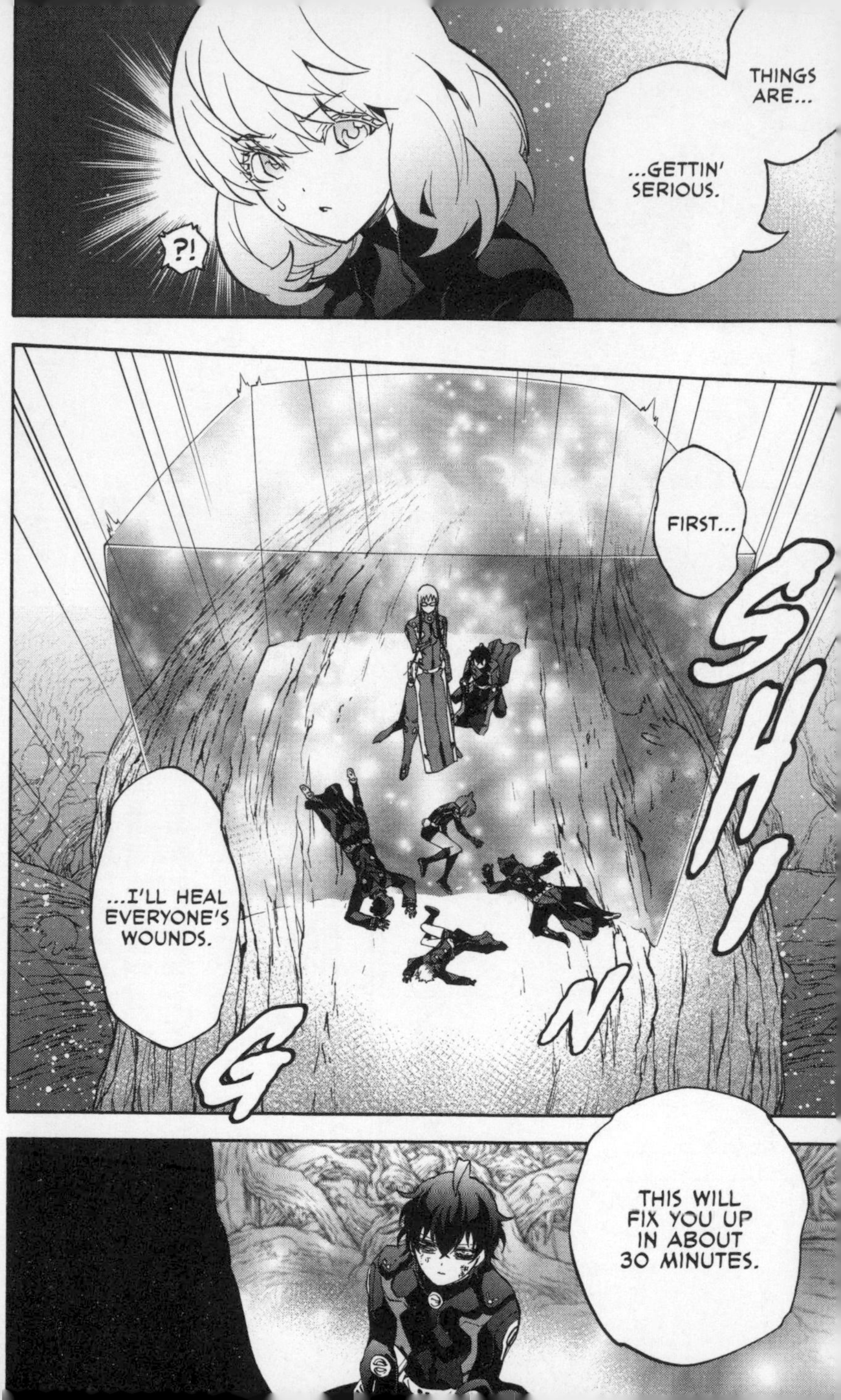
THINGS ARE...
...GETTIN' SERIOUS.
?!
FIRST...
SHIING
...I'LL HEAL EVERYONE'S WOUNDS.
THIS WILL FIX YOU UP IN ABOUT 30 MINUTES.

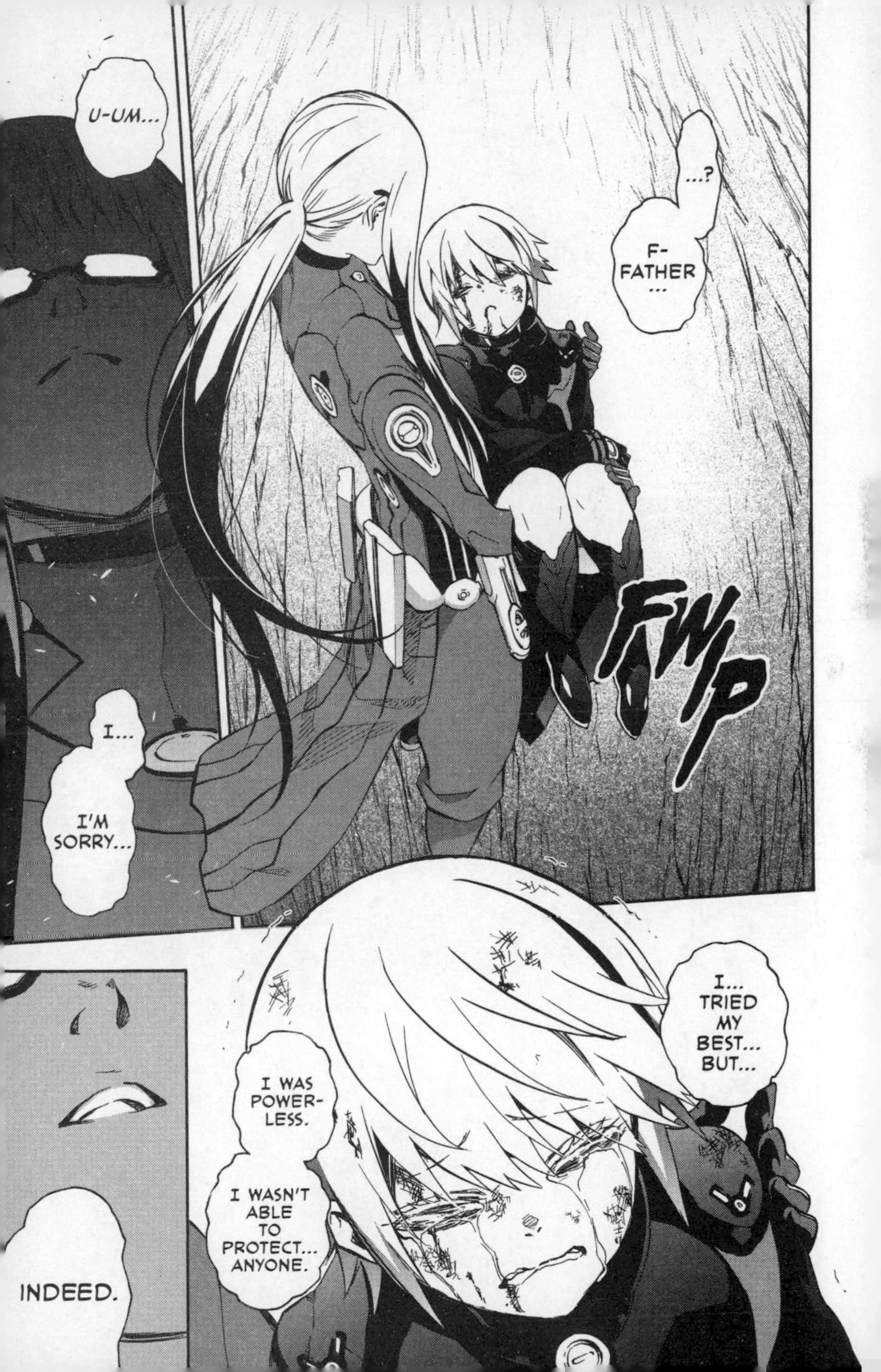
...?
F-FATHER...
FWP
U-UM...
I...
I'M SORRY...
I... TRIED MY BEST... BUT...
I WAS POWER-LESS.
I WASN'T ABLE TO PROTECT... ANYONE.
INDEED.

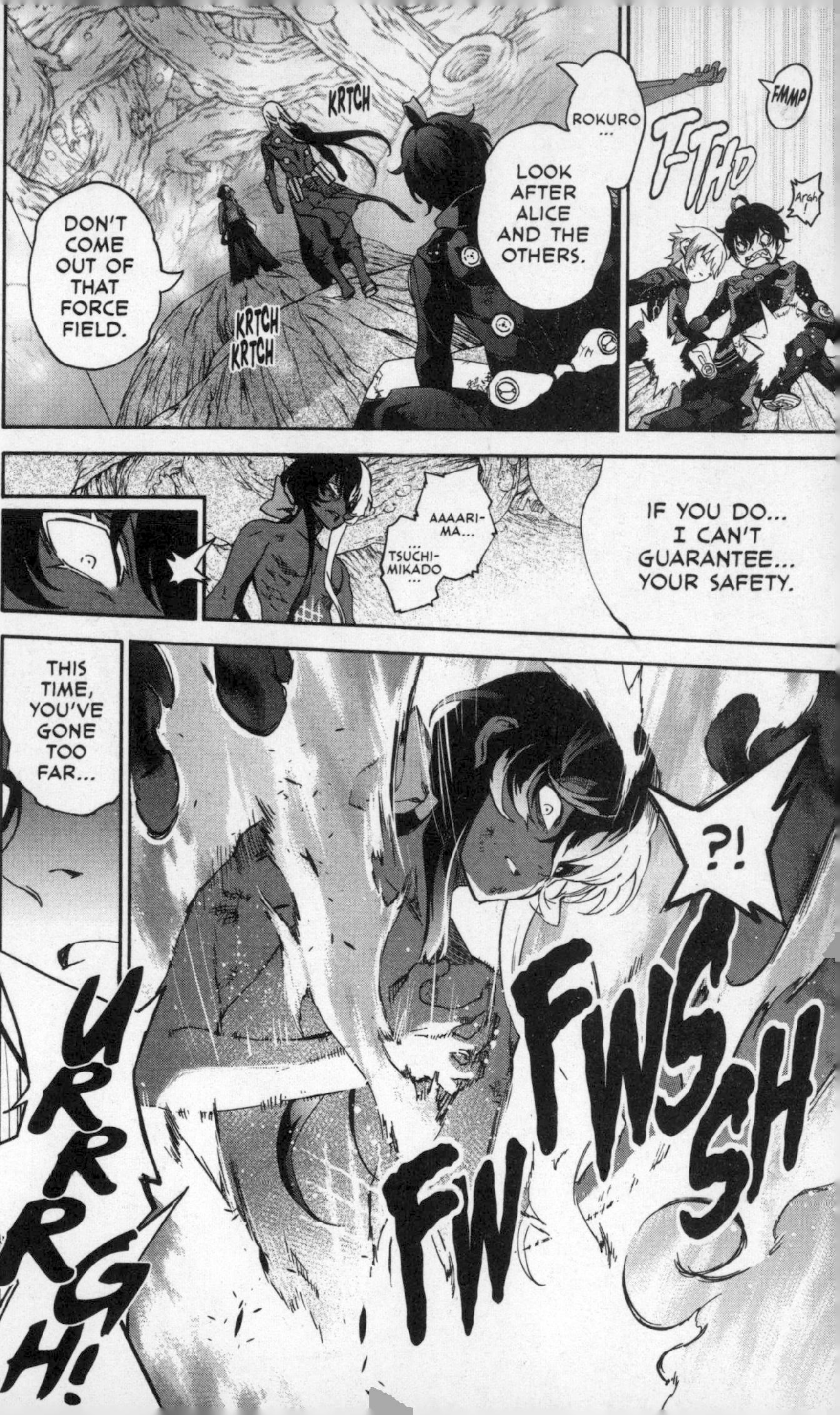
FMMP
F-THD
Argh!
ROKURO ...
LOOK AFTER ALICE AND THE OTHERS.
KRTCH
DON'T COME OUT OF THAT FORCE FIELD.
KRTCH KRTCH
IF YOU DO... I CAN'T GUARANTEE... YOUR SAFETY.
AAAARI-MA...
TSUCHI-MIKADO ...
THIS TIME, YOU'VE GONE TOO FAR...
?!
FWSSH
FW
URRRGH!

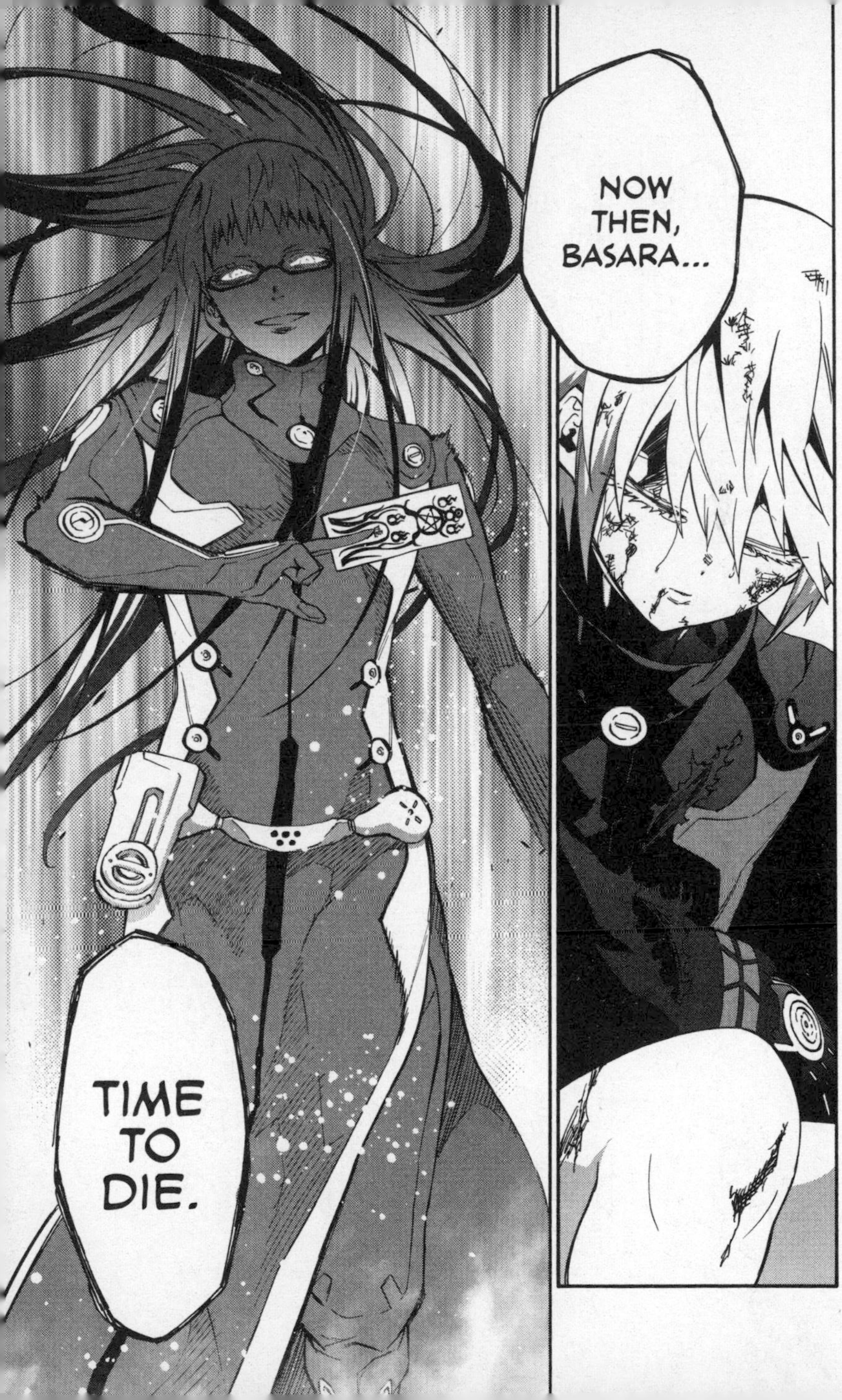
NOW THEN, BASARA...
TIME TO DIE.

Twelve Guardian Talismans

Hijirimaru
Shapeless Blade
of Debris

Gabura
Raging Cannon
of Evil

Sakanashi
Puppets of
Ultimate Darkness

**Basara Paper
Talisman**
Chinu
???

Shioji
Underworld
Controller

Gajae
Magnetic Corpse

Kaguya
Murky Blue Princess
of Hatred

Shiromi
Spiraling Grief

Kamui
Dark Razor That
Cuts the Gods

Yuzuriha
Eyes of Death

Higano
Pain of Lightning

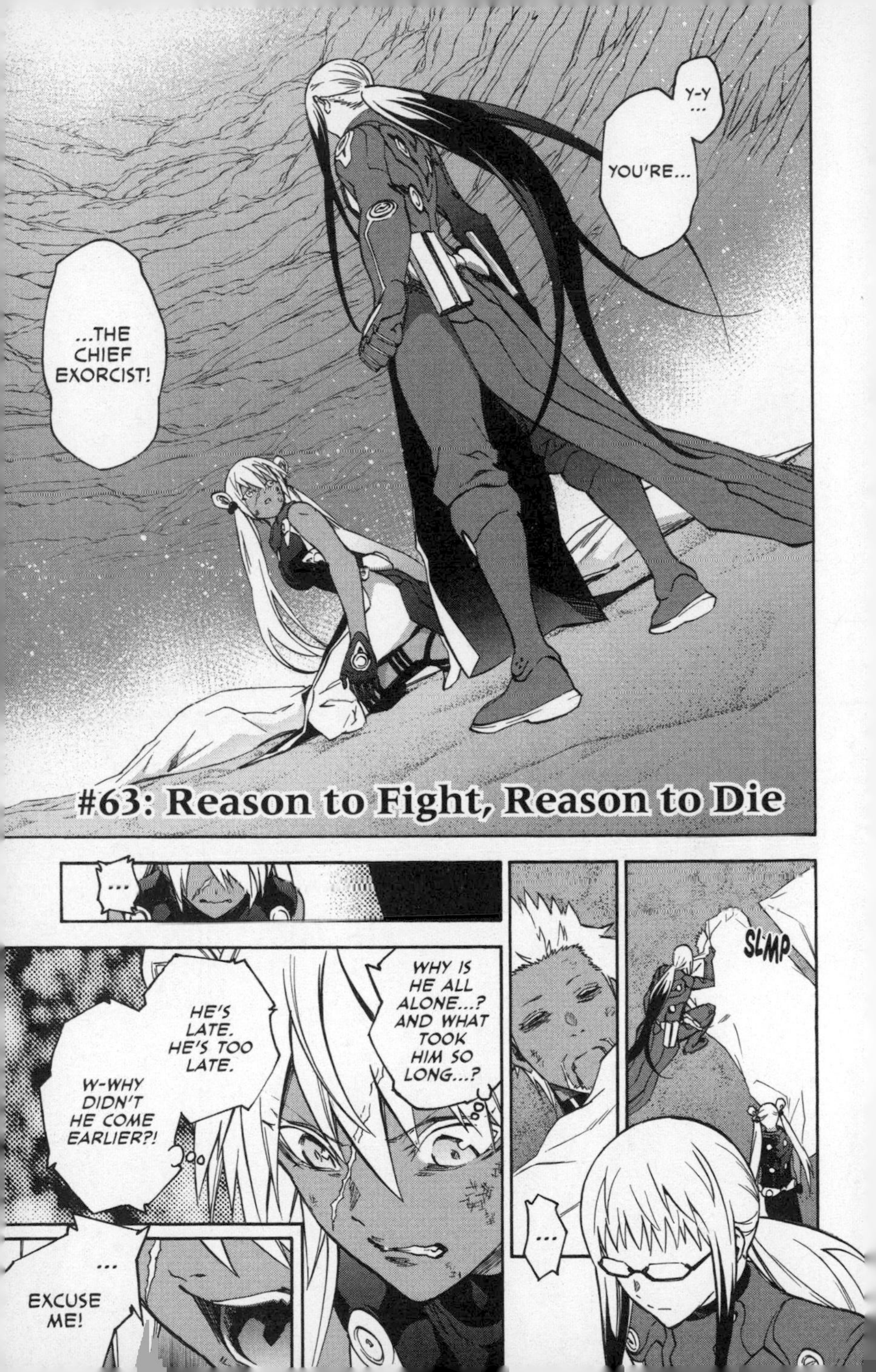
Y-Y ...
YOU'RE...
...THE CHIEF EXORCIST!
#63: Reason to Fight, Reason to Die
SLMP
...
...
WHY IS HE ALL ALONE...? AND WHAT TOOK HIM SO LONG...?
HE'S LATE. HE'S TOO LATE.
W-WHY DIDN'T HE COME EARLIER?!
...
EXCUSE ME!

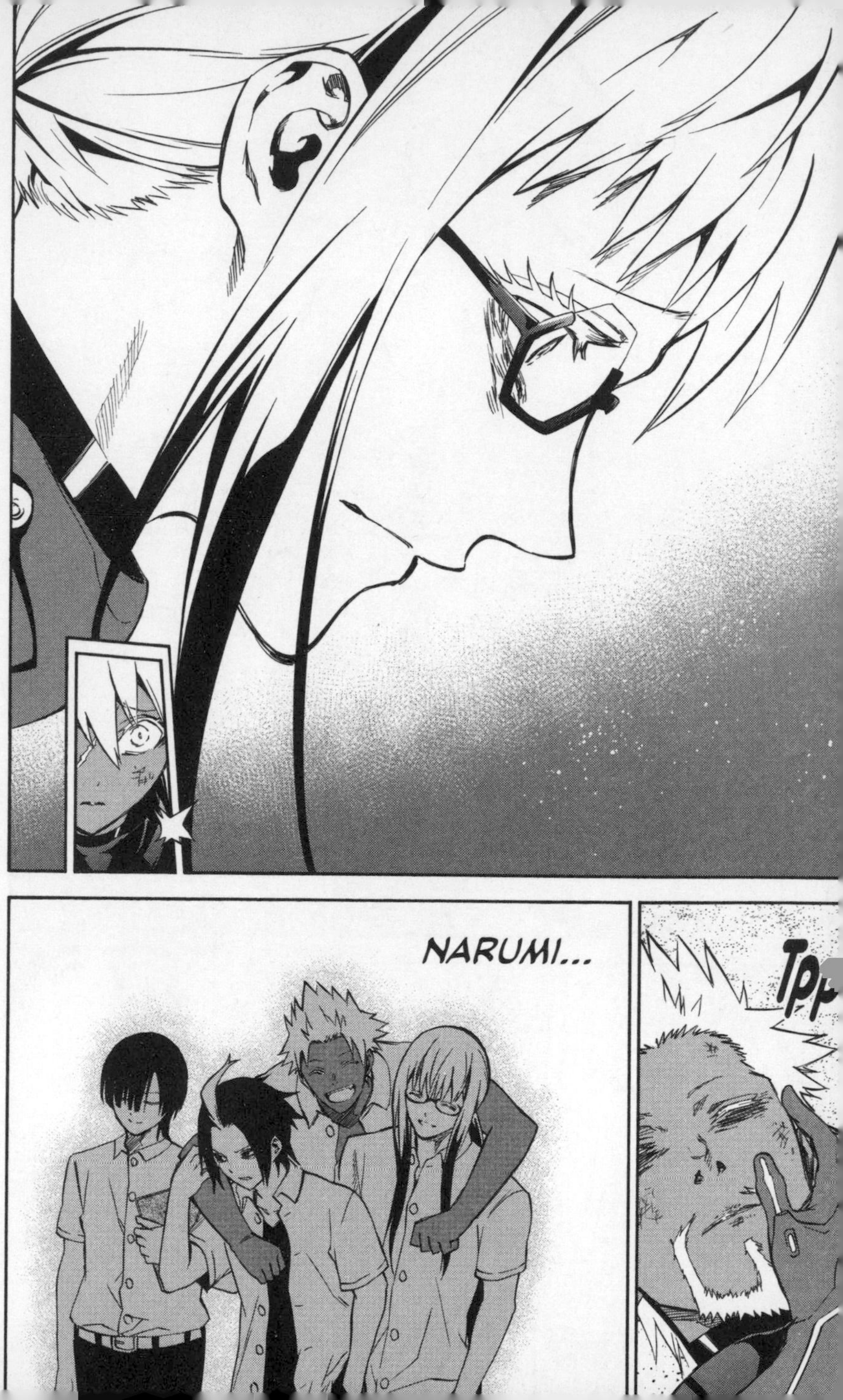
Tpp
NARUMI...

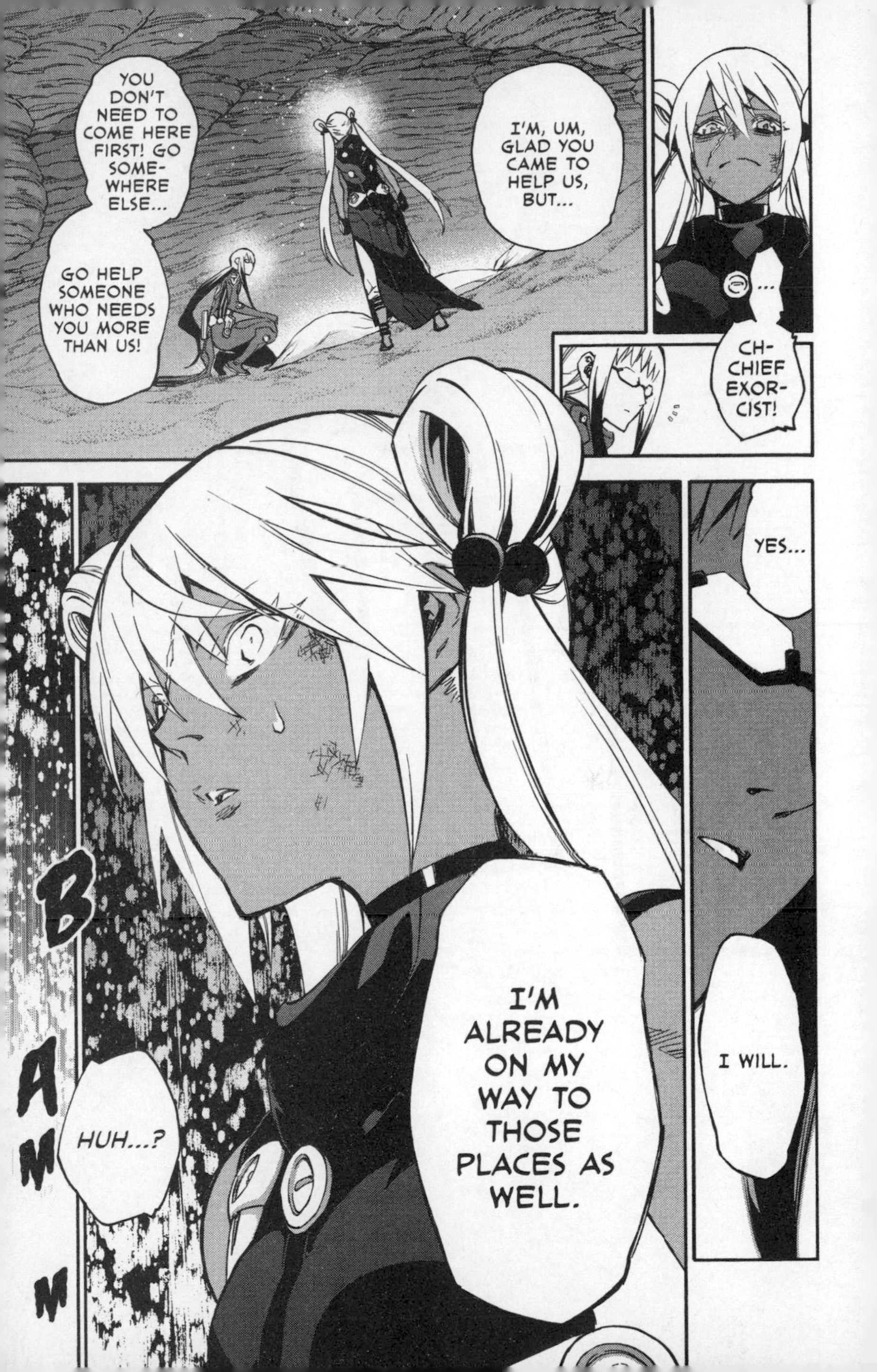
...
CH-CHIEF EXORCIST!
I'M, UM, GLAD YOU CAME TO HELP US, BUT...
YOU DON'T NEED TO COME HERE FIRST! GO SOME-WHERE ELSE...
GO HELP SOMEONE WHO NEEDS YOU MORE THAN US!
YES...
I WILL.
I'M ALREADY ON MY WAY TO THOSE PLACES AS WELL.
HUH...?
BAMM

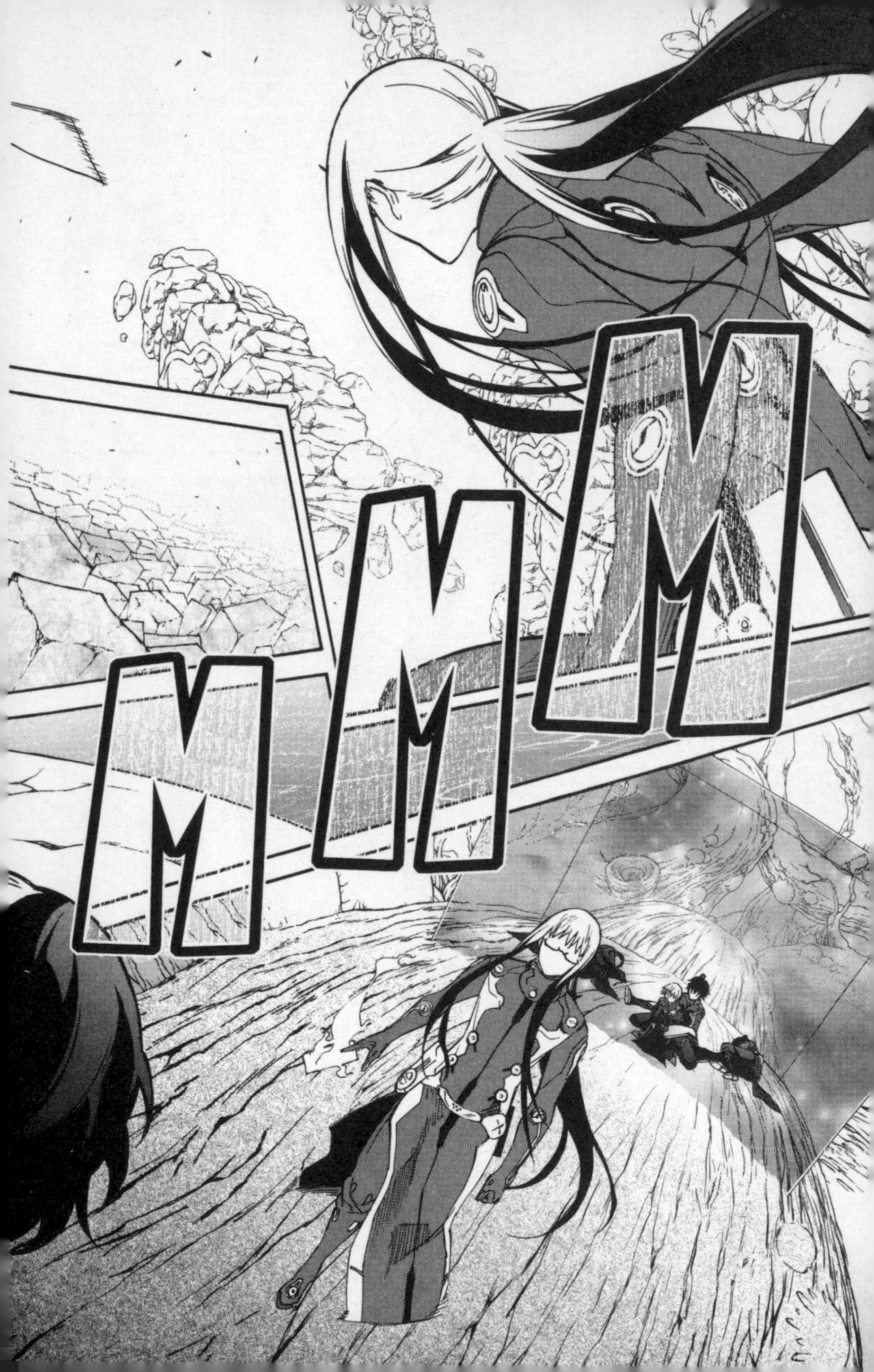
MMMM

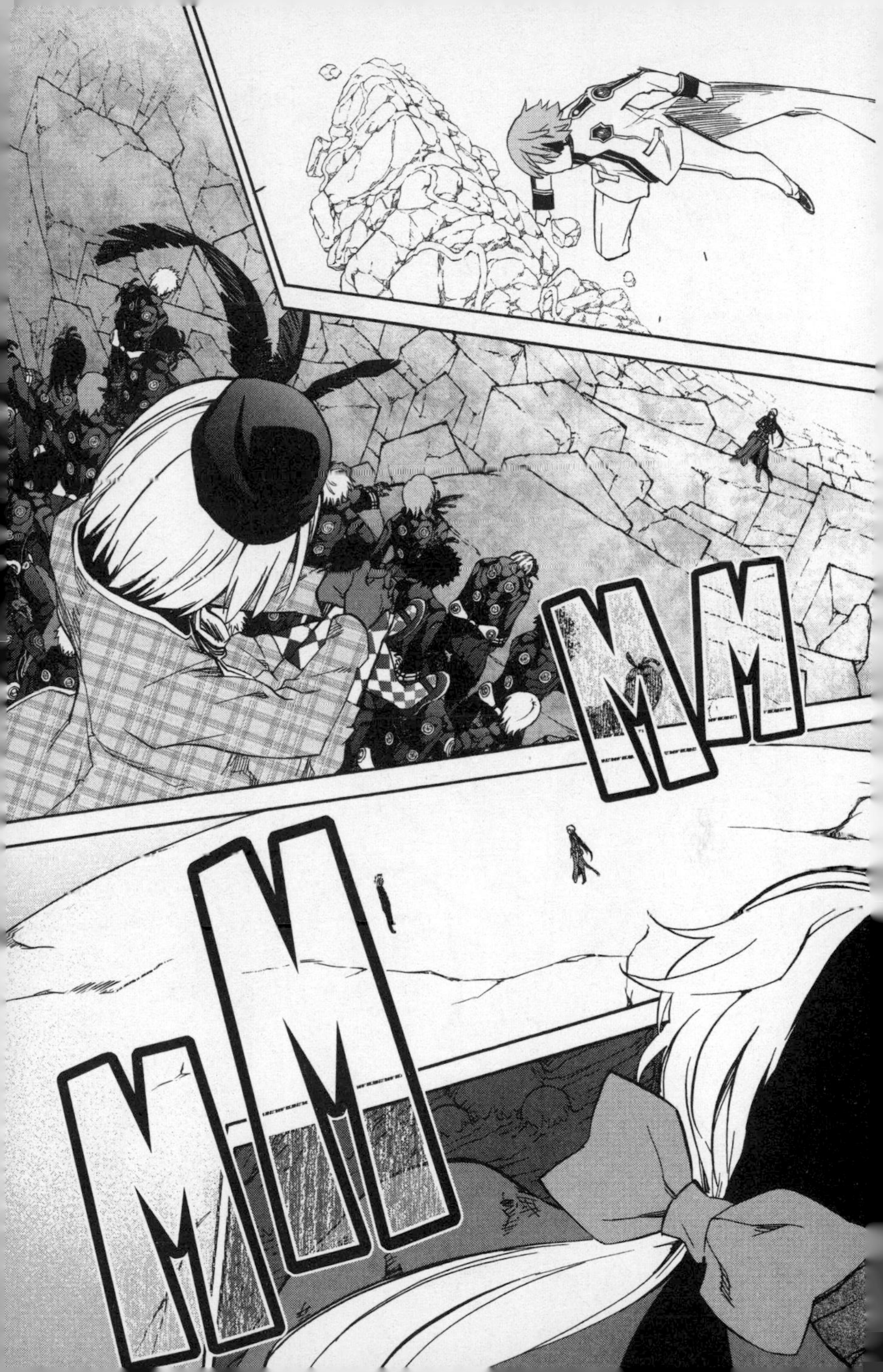
MM
MMM

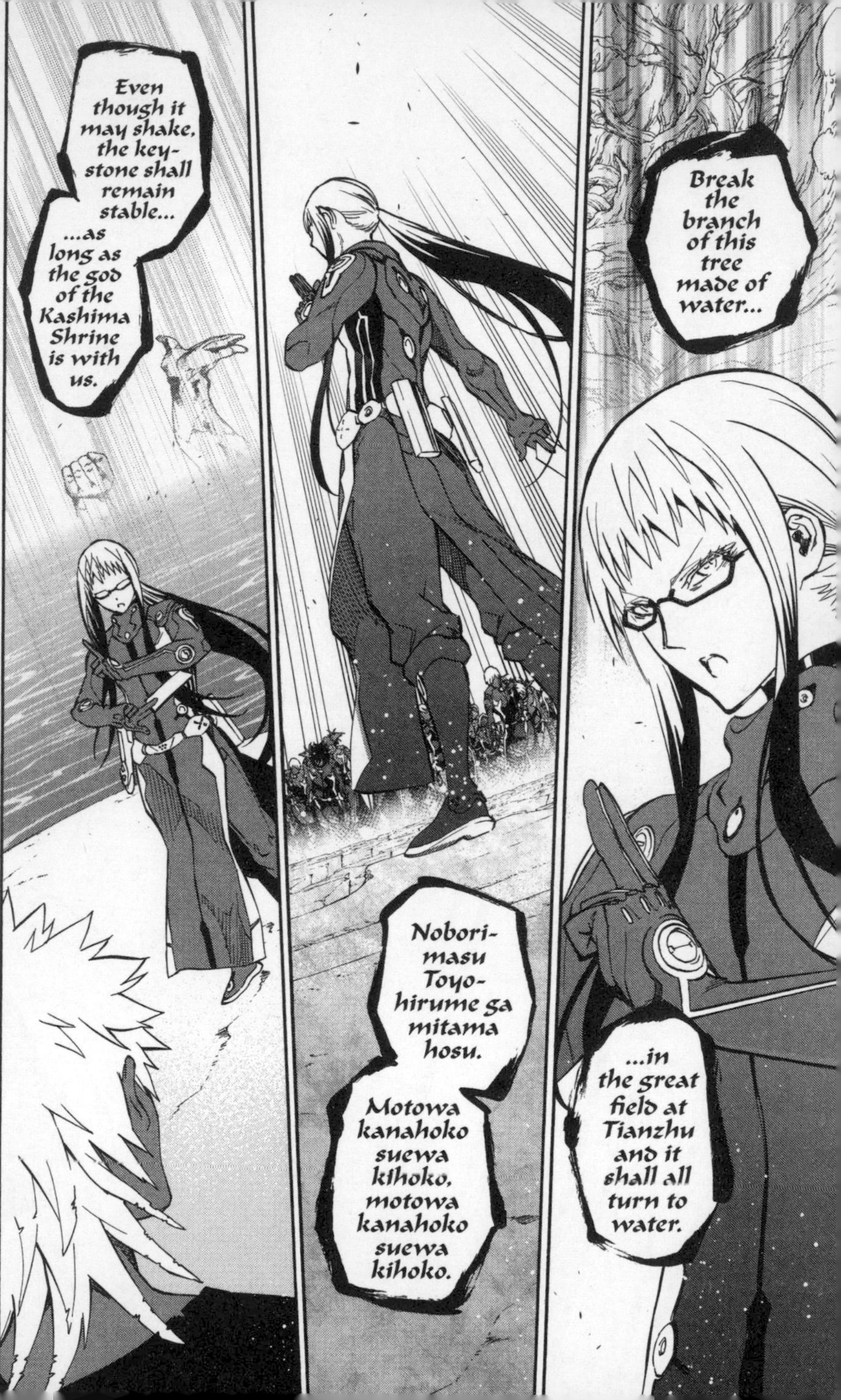
Break the branch of this tree made of water...
...in the great field at Tianzhu and it shall all turn to water.
Noborimasu Toyohirume ga mitama hosu.
Motowa kanahoko suewa kihoko, motowa kanahoko suewa kihoko.
Even though it may shake, the keystone shall remain stable...
...as long as the god of the Kashima Shrine is with us.

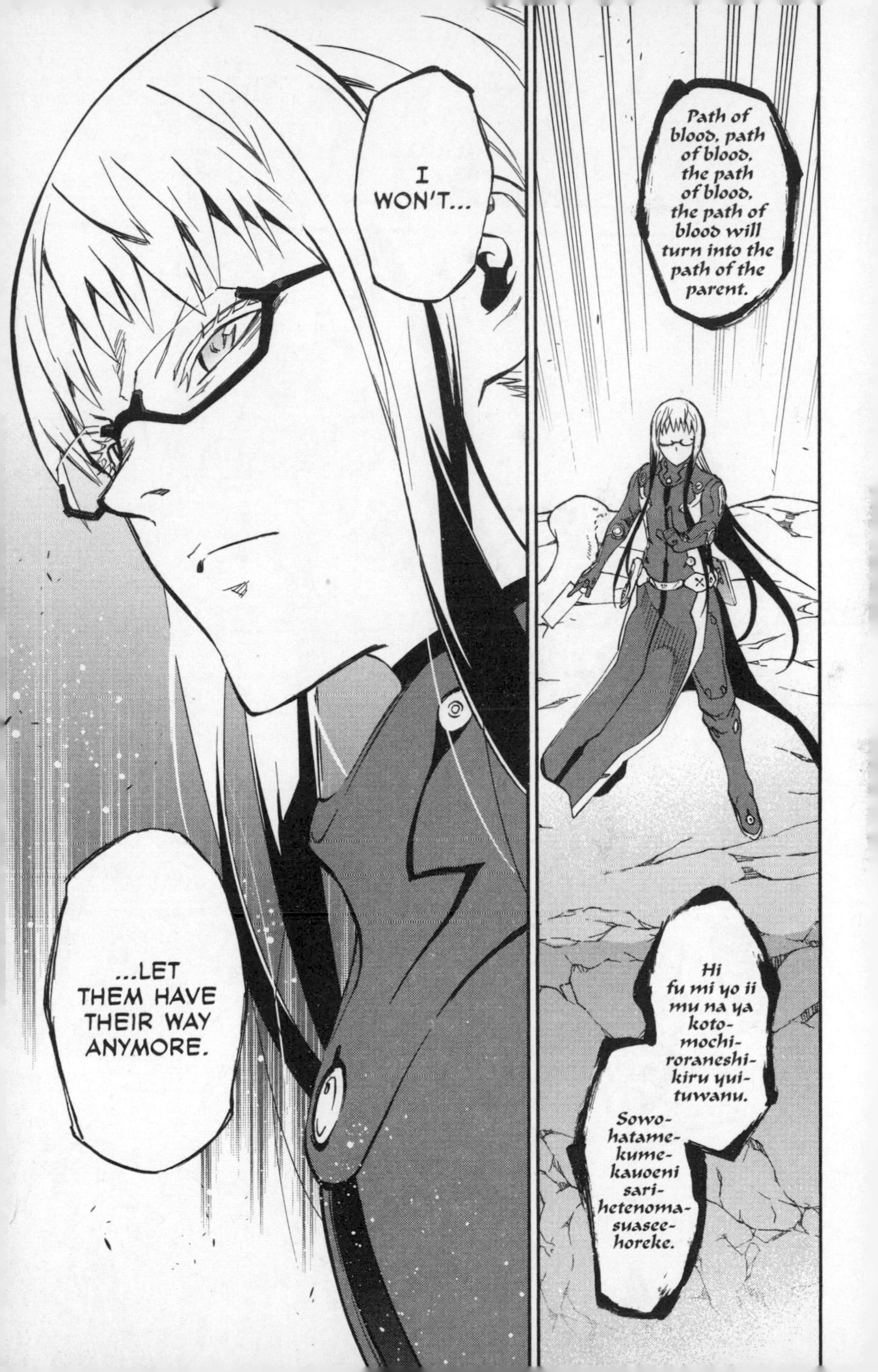
Path of blood, path of blood, the path of blood, the path of blood will turn into the path of the parent.
Hi fu mi yo ii mu na ya koto-mochi-roraneshi-kiru yui-tuwanu. Sowo-hatame-kume-kauoeni sari-hetenoma-suasee-horeke.
I WON'T...
...LET THEM HAVE THEIR WAY ANYMORE.

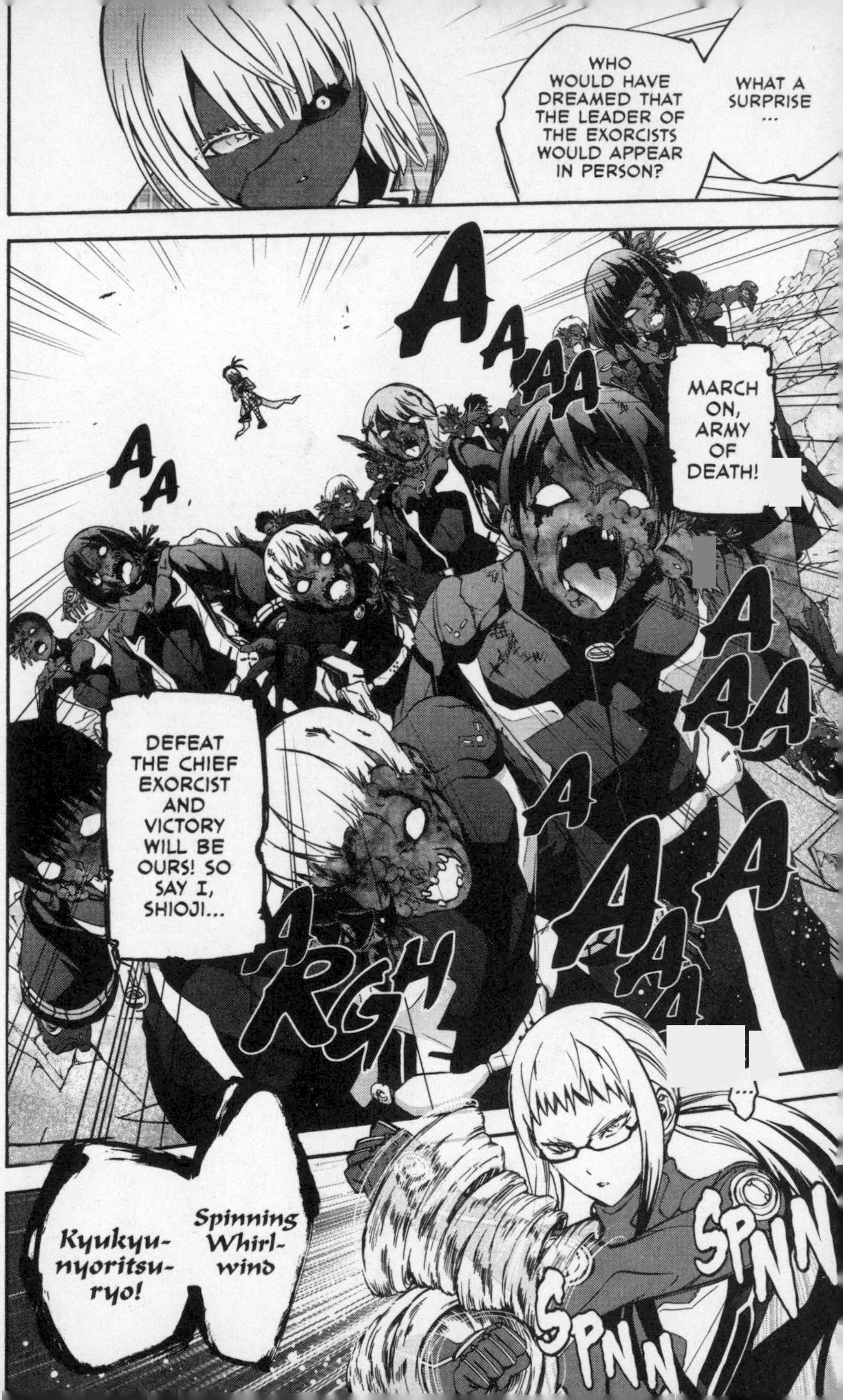
WHAT A SURPRISE ...
WHO WOULD HAVE DREAMED THAT THE LEADER OF THE EXORCISTS WOULD APPEAR IN PERSON?
MARCH ON, ARMY OF DEATH!
AAAAA
AA
AAAAA
DEFEAT THE CHIEF EXORCIST AND VICTORY WILL BE OURS! SO SAY I, SHIOJI...
AAAAA
ARGH
...
Spinning Whirlwind
Kyukyu-nyoritsu-ryo!
SPNN
SPNN

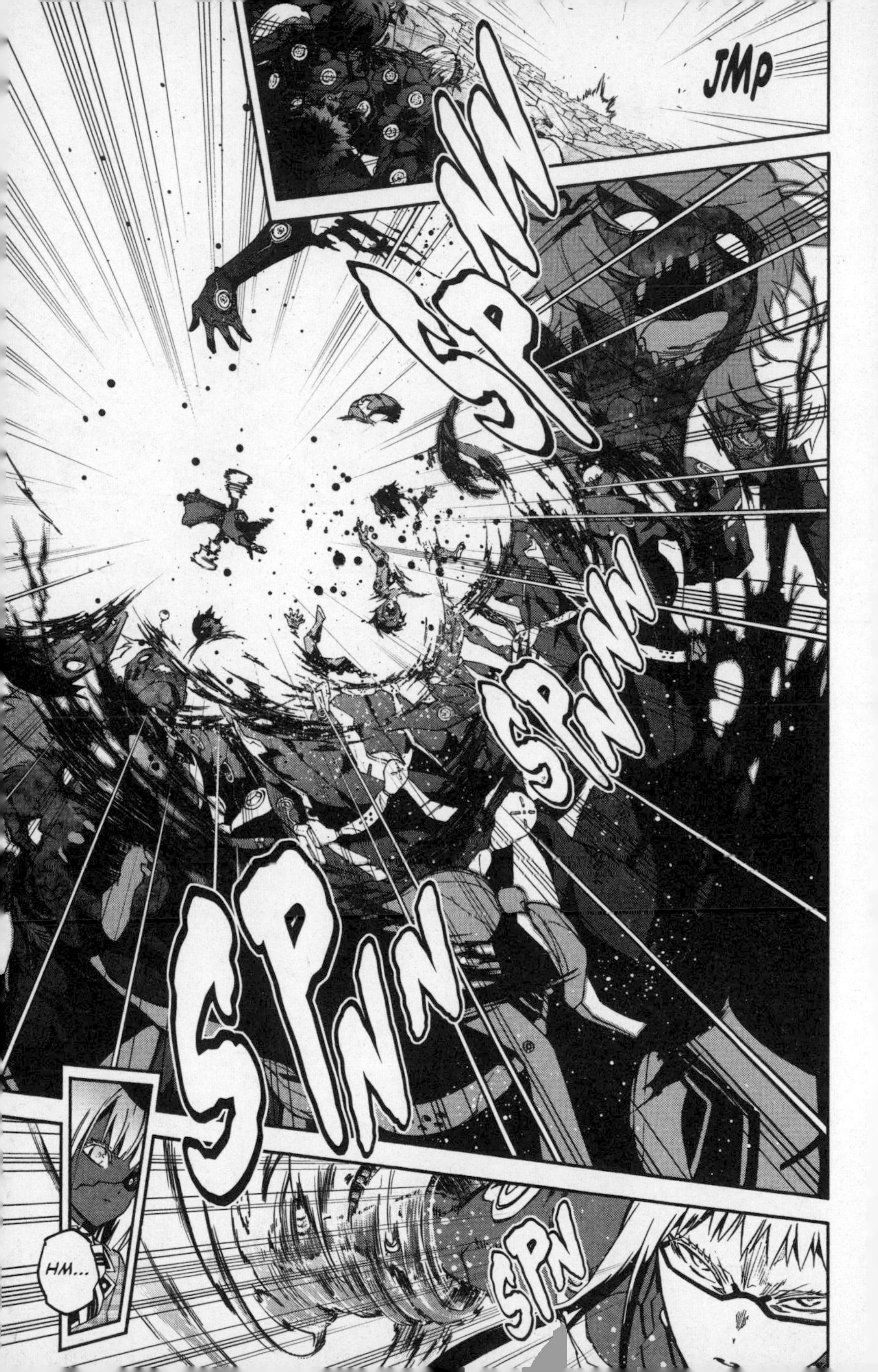
JMP
SPNN
SPNN
SPNN
SPN
HM...

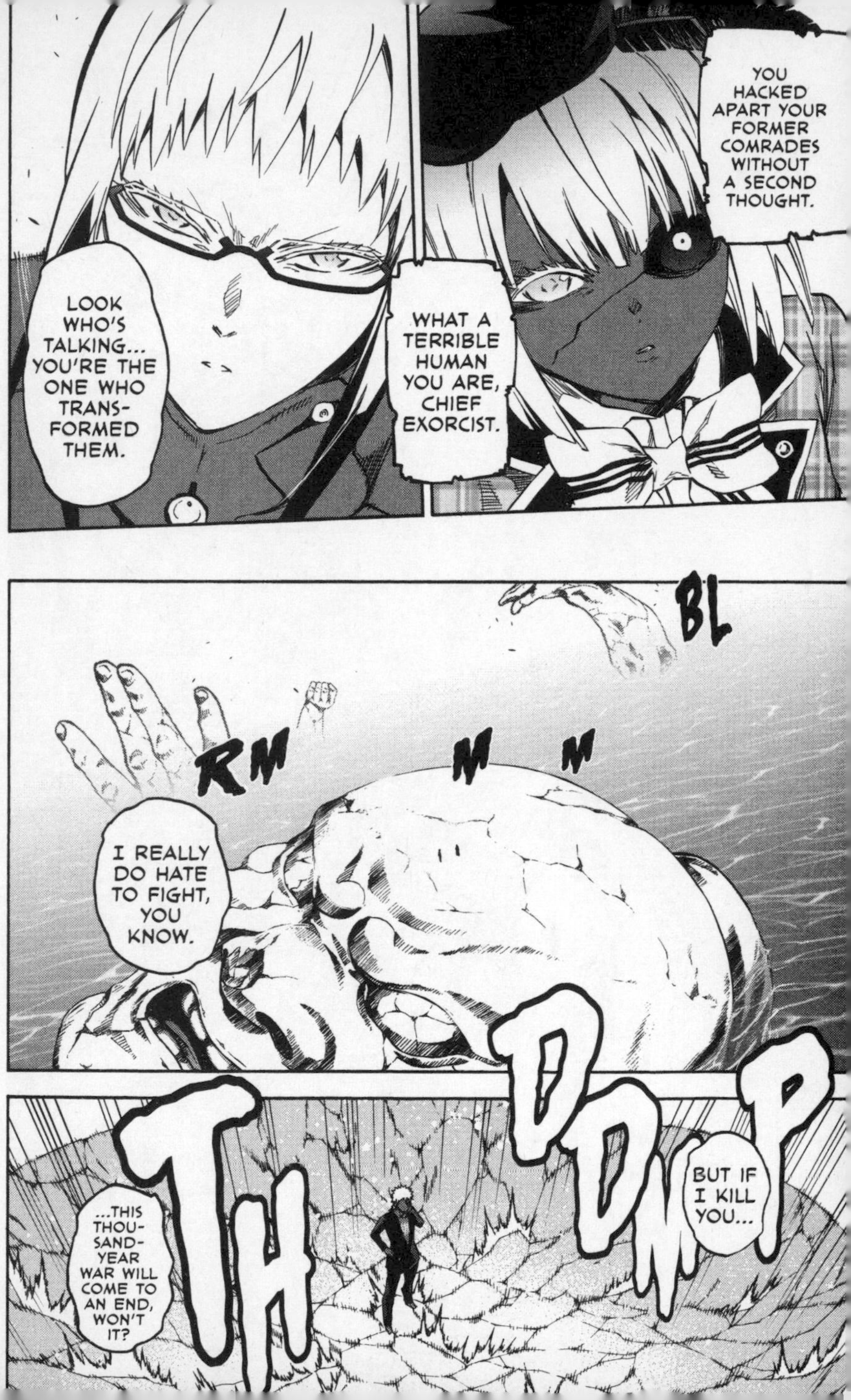
YOU HACKED APART YOUR FORMER COMRADES WITHOUT A SECOND THOUGHT.
WHAT A TERRIBLE HUMAN YOU ARE, CHIEF EXORCIST.
LOOK WHO'S TALKING... YOU'RE THE ONE WHO TRANS-FORMED THEM.
BL
RMMM
I REALLY DO HATE TO FIGHT, YOU KNOW.
THDOMP
BUT IF I KILL YOU...
...THIS THOUSAND-YEAR WAR WILL COME TO AN END, WON'T IT?

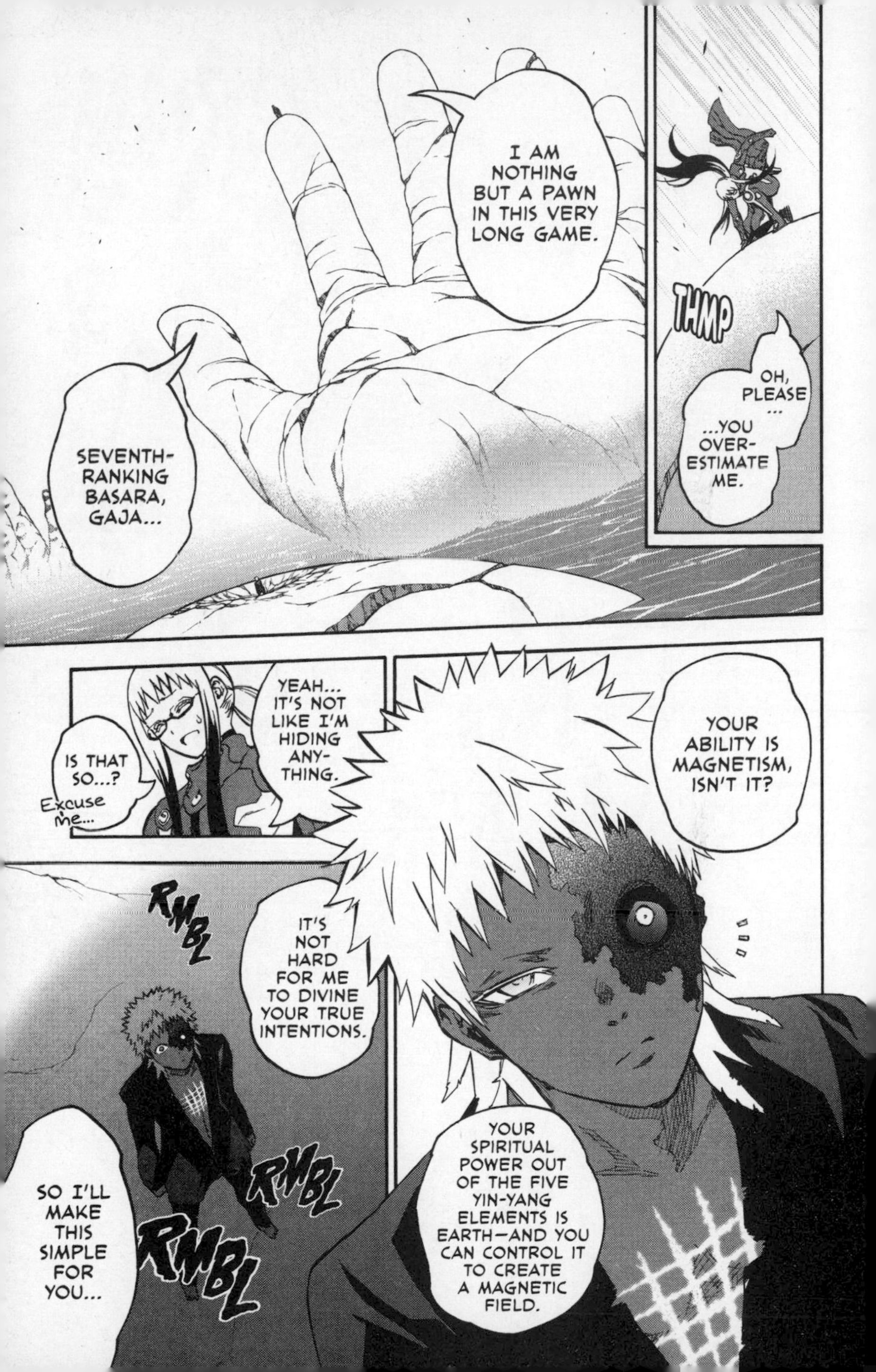
THMP
OH, PLEASE... ...YOU OVER-ESTIMATE ME.
I AM NOTHING BUT A PAWN IN THIS VERY LONG GAME.
SEVENTH-RANKING BASARA, GAJA...
YOUR ABILITY IS MAGNETISM, ISN'T IT?
YEAH... IT'S NOT LIKE I'M HIDING ANYTHING.
IS THAT SO...?
Excuse me...
IT'S NOT HARD FOR ME TO DIVINE YOUR TRUE INTENTIONS.
YOUR SPIRITUAL POWER OUT OF THE FIVE YIN-YANG ELEMENTS IS EARTH—AND YOU CAN CONTROL IT TO CREATE A MAGNETIC FIELD.
RMBL
RMBL
RMBL
SO I'LL MAKE THIS SIMPLE FOR YOU...

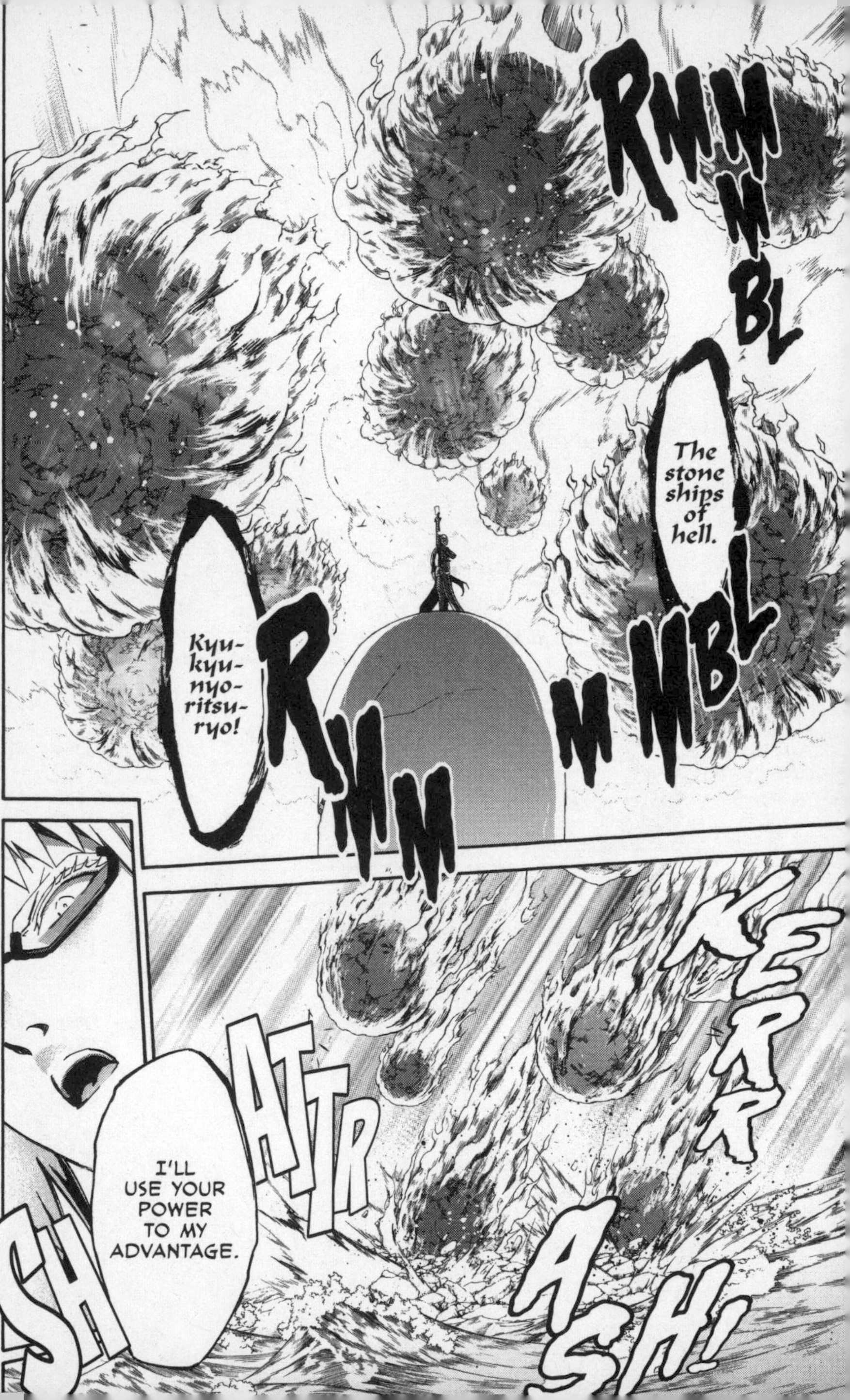
RMMMMBL
The stone ships of hell.
Kyu-kyu-nyo-ritsu-ryo!
RMMM M MBL
KERRASH!
SHATTR
I'LL USE YOUR POWER TO MY ADVANTAGE.

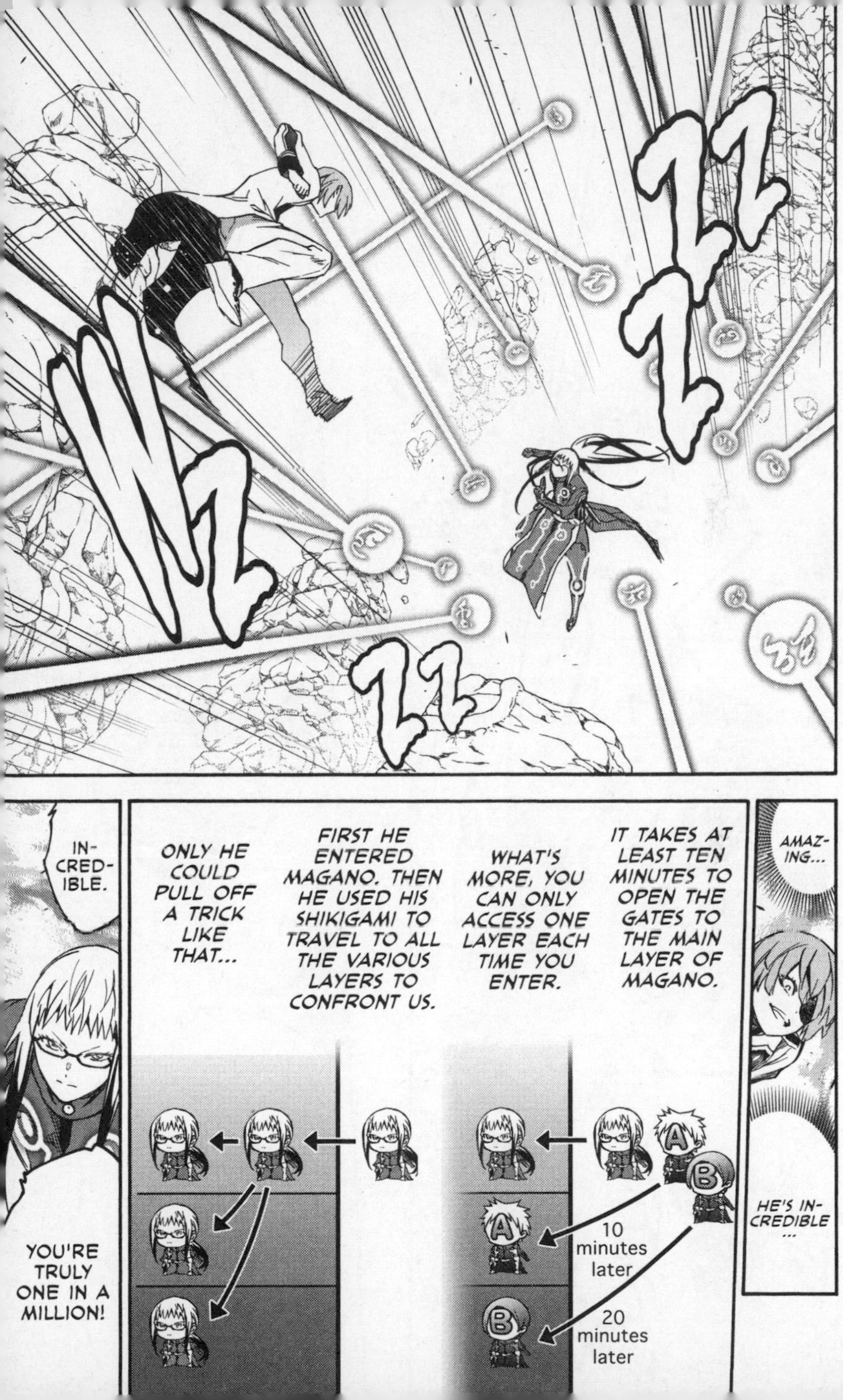
AMAZ-ING...
HE'S IN-CREDIBLE ...
IT TAKES AT LEAST TEN MINUTES TO OPEN THE GATES TO THE MAIN LAYER OF MAGANO.
WHAT'S MORE, YOU CAN ONLY ACCESS ONE LAYER EACH TIME YOU ENTER.
FIRST HE ENTERED MAGANO. THEN HE USED HIS SHIKIGAMI TO TRAVEL TO ALL THE VARIOUS LAYERS TO CONFRONT US.
ONLY HE COULD PULL OFF A TRICK LIKE THAT...
A
B
A
10 minutes later
B
20 minutes later
IN-CRED-IBLE.
YOU'RE TRULY ONE IN A MILLION!

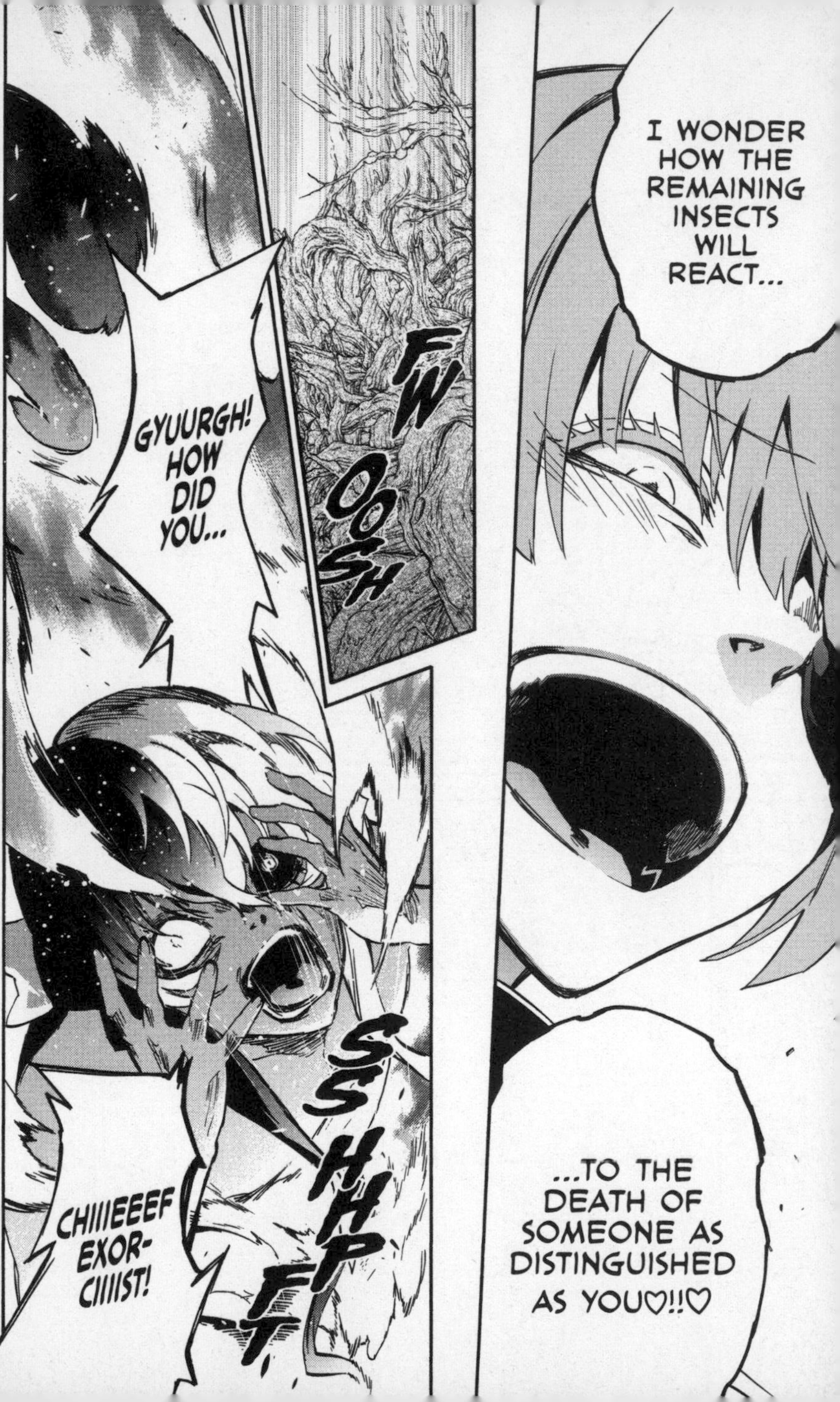
I WONDER HOW THE REMAINING INSECTS WILL REACT...
...TO THE DEATH OF SOMEONE AS DISTINGUISHED AS YOU♡!!♡
FWOOSH
GYUURGH! HOW DID YOU...
SSHHPFFT
CHIIIEEEF EXOR-CIIIIST!

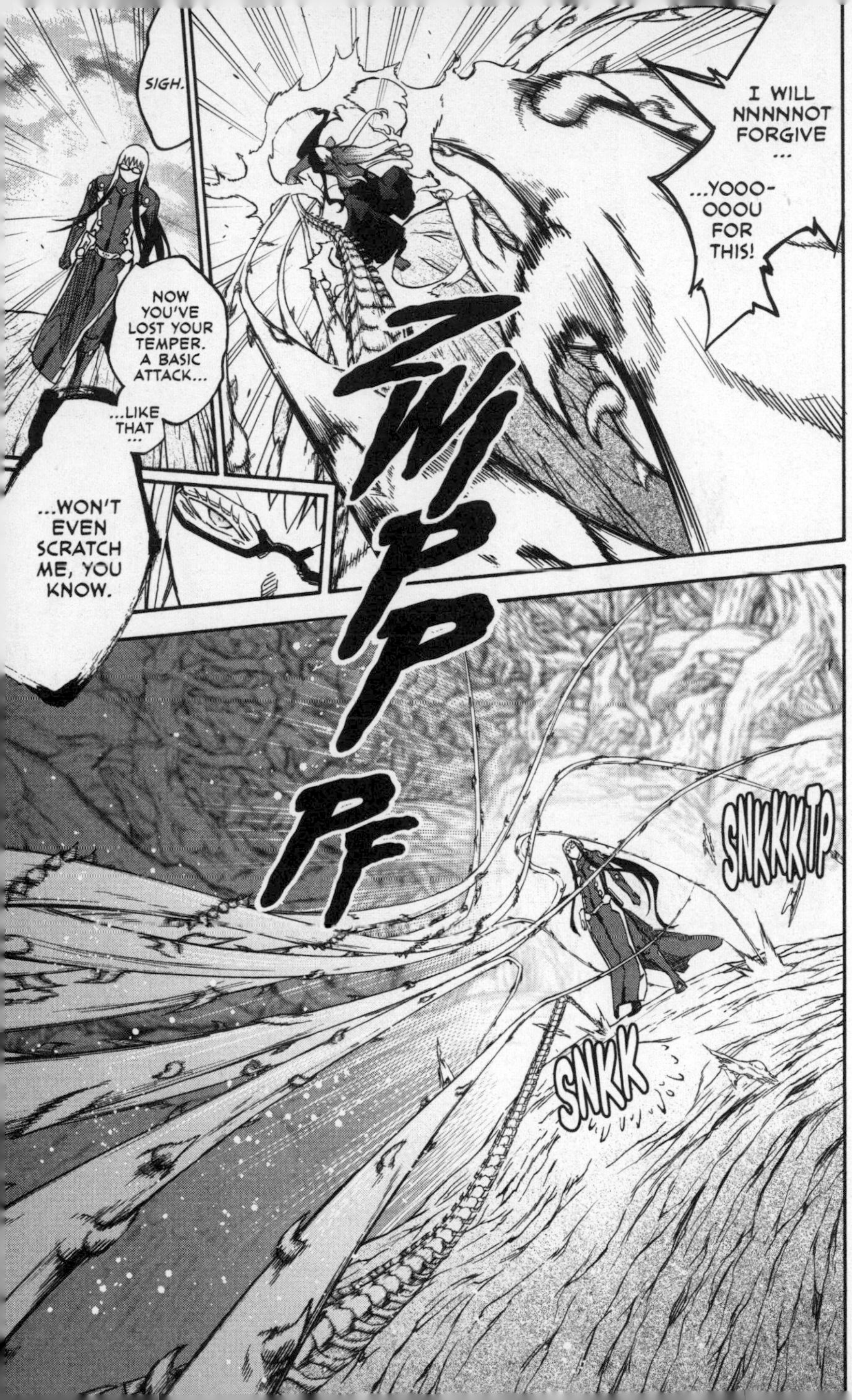
I WILL NNNNNOT FORGIVE ...
...YOOO-OOOU FOR THIS!
ZWPPPF
SIGH.
NOW YOU'VE LOST YOUR TEMPER. A BASIC ATTACK...
...LIKE THAT ...
...WON'T EVEN SCRATCH ME, YOU KNOW.
SNKKKTP
SNKK

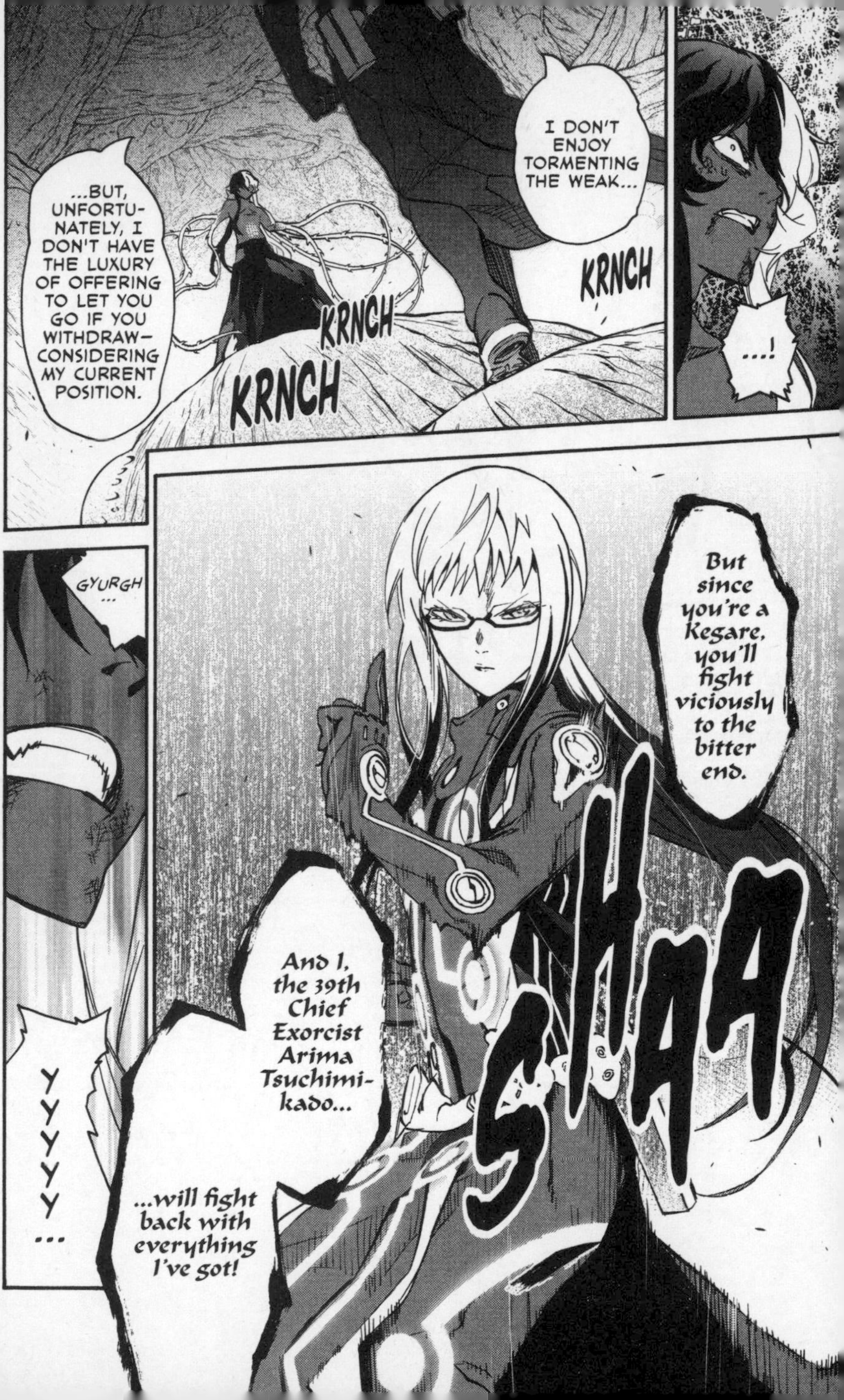
...!
I DON'T ENJOY TORMENTING THE WEAK...
KRNCH
KRNCH
KRNCH
...BUT, UNFORTUNATELY, I DON'T HAVE THE LUXURY OF OFFERING TO LET YOU GO IF YOU WITHDRAW—CONSIDERING MY CURRENT POSITION.
But since you're a Kegare, you'll fight viciously to the bitter end.
SHAA
And I, the 39th Chief Exorcist Arima Tsuchimikado...
...will fight back with everything I've got!
GYURGH...
YYYYY...

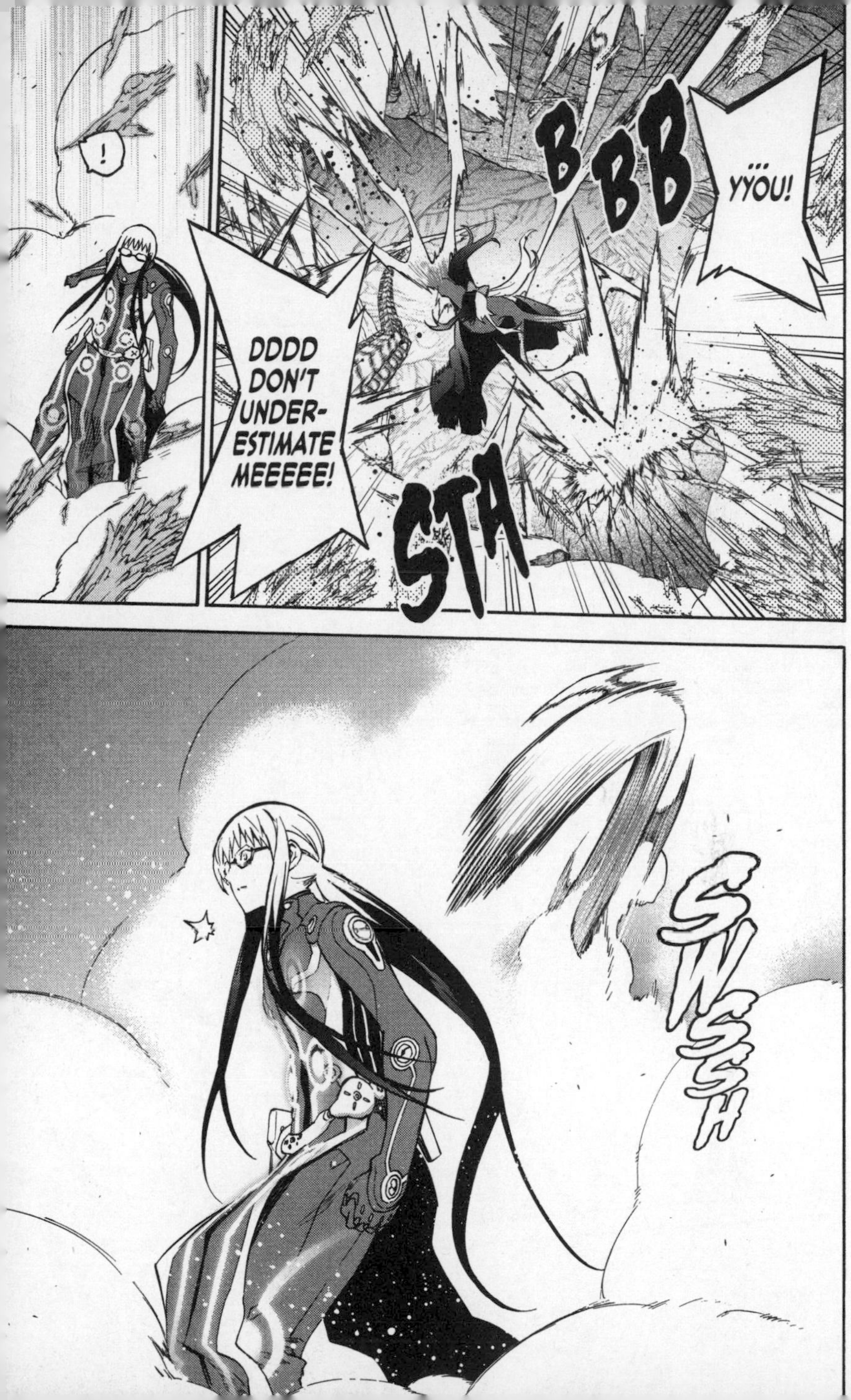
BBB
...YYÖU!
DDDD DON'T UNDER-ESTIMATE MEEEEE!
STA
!
SWISH

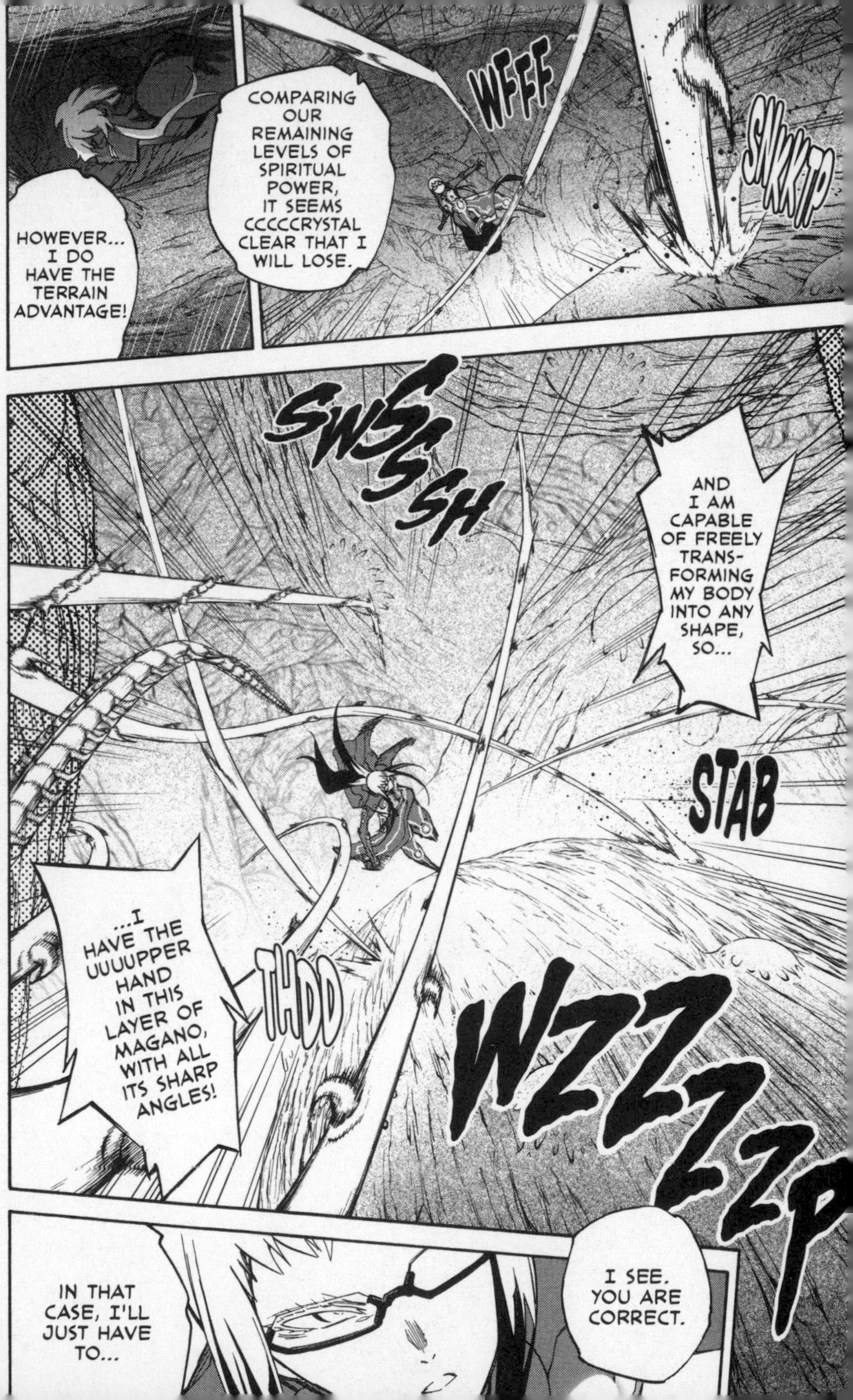
SNKKTP
WFFF
COMPARING OUR REMAINING LEVELS OF SPIRITUAL POWER, IT SEEMS CCCCCRYSTAL CLEAR THAT I WILL LOSE.
HOWEVER... I DO HAVE THE TERRAIN ADVANTAGE!
SWSSSH
AND I AM CAPABLE OF FREELY TRANS-FORMING MY BODY INTO ANY SHAPE, SO...
STAB
WZZZZP
THDD
...I HAVE THE UUUUPPER HAND IN THIS LAYER OF MAGANO, WITH ALL ITS SHARP ANGLES!
I SEE. YOU ARE CORRECT.
IN THAT CASE, I'LL JUST HAVE TO...

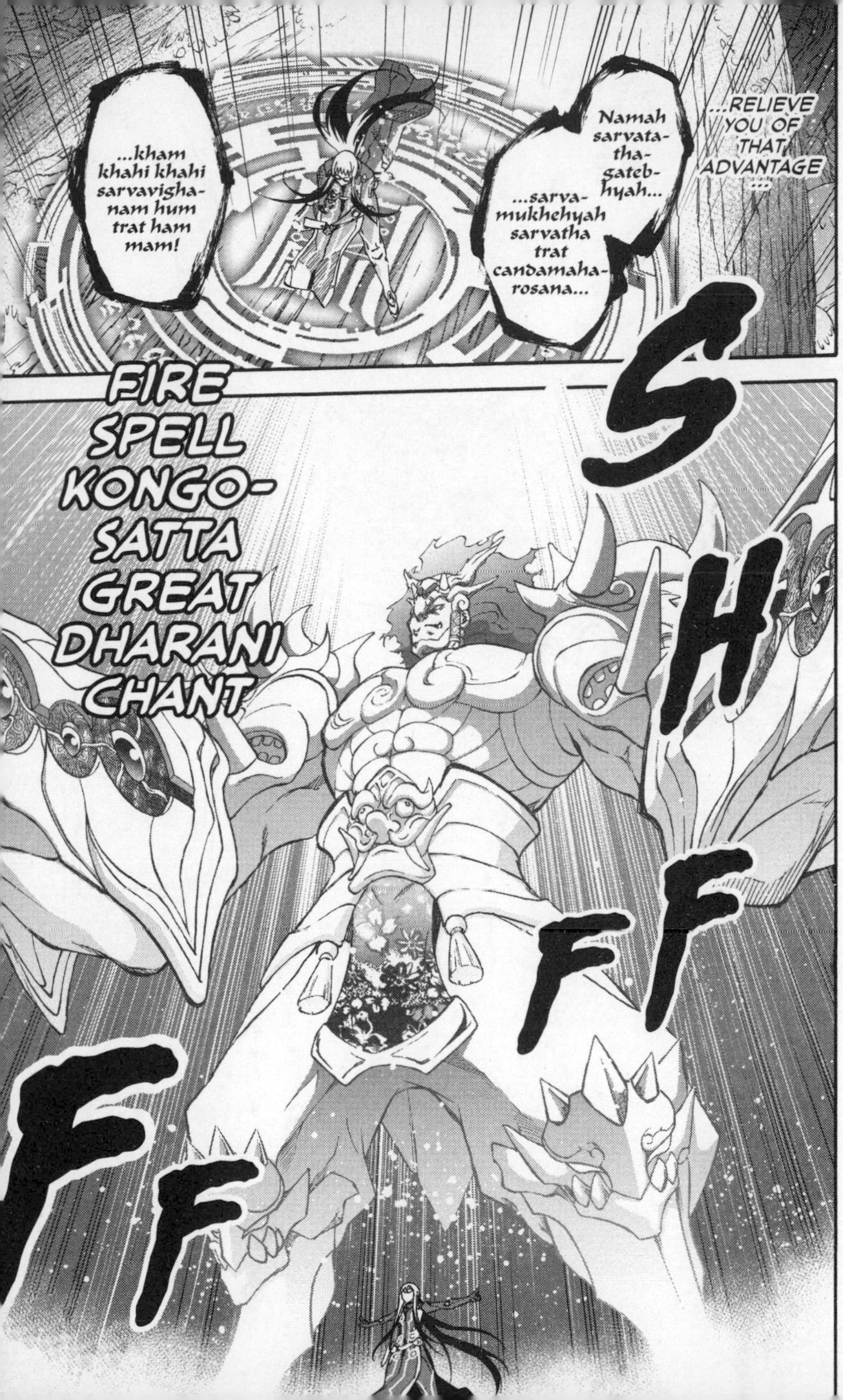
...RELIEVE YOU OF THAT ADVANTAGE...
Namah sarvata-tha-gateb-hyah...
...sarva-mukhehyah sarvatha trat candamaha-rosana...
...kham khahi khahi sarvavigha-nam hum trat ham mam!
SHFF
FIRE SPELL KONGO-SATTA GREAT DHARANI CHANT
FF

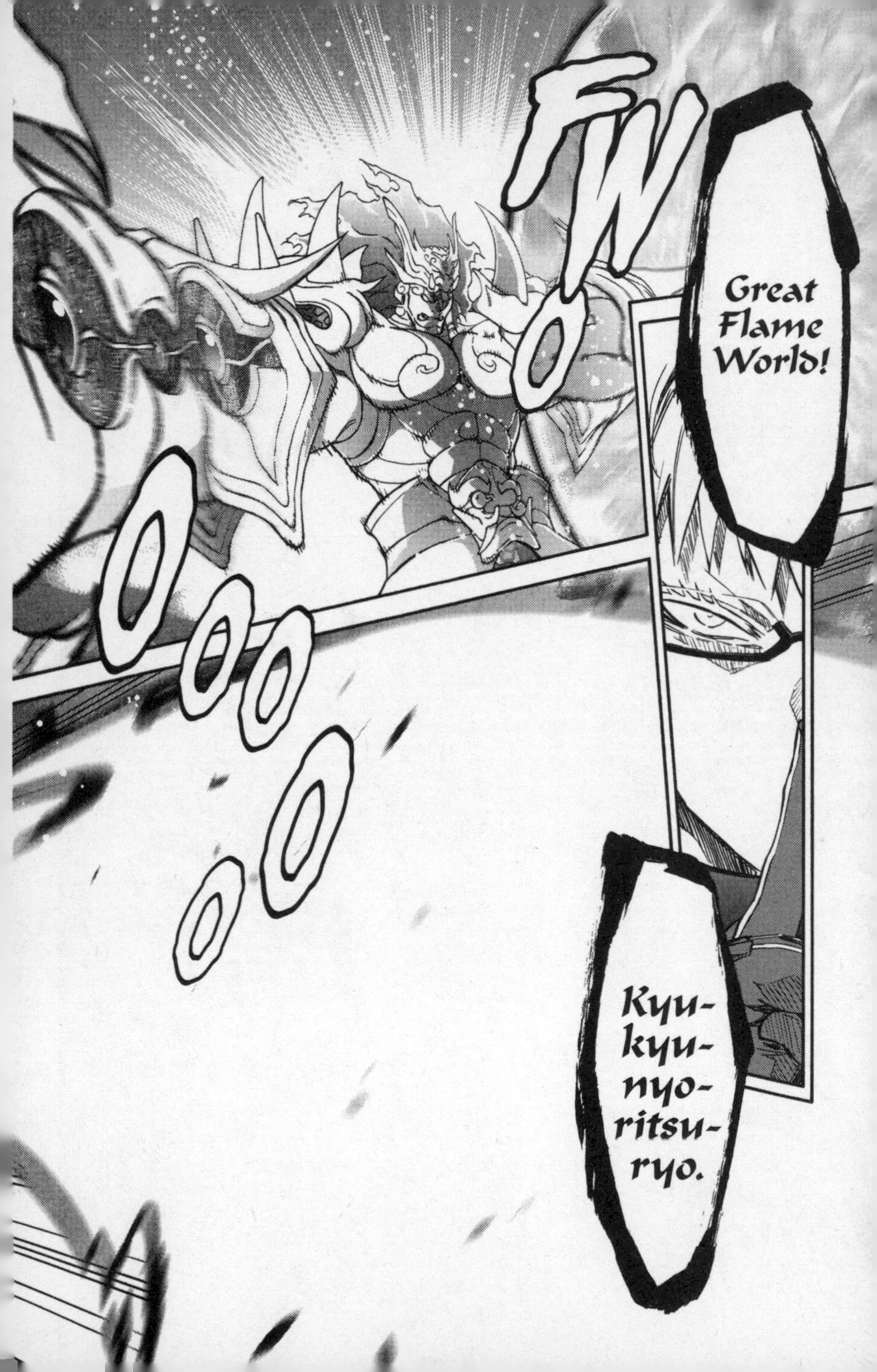
FWOOOOOO
Great Flame World!
Kyu-kyu-nyo-ritsu-ryo.

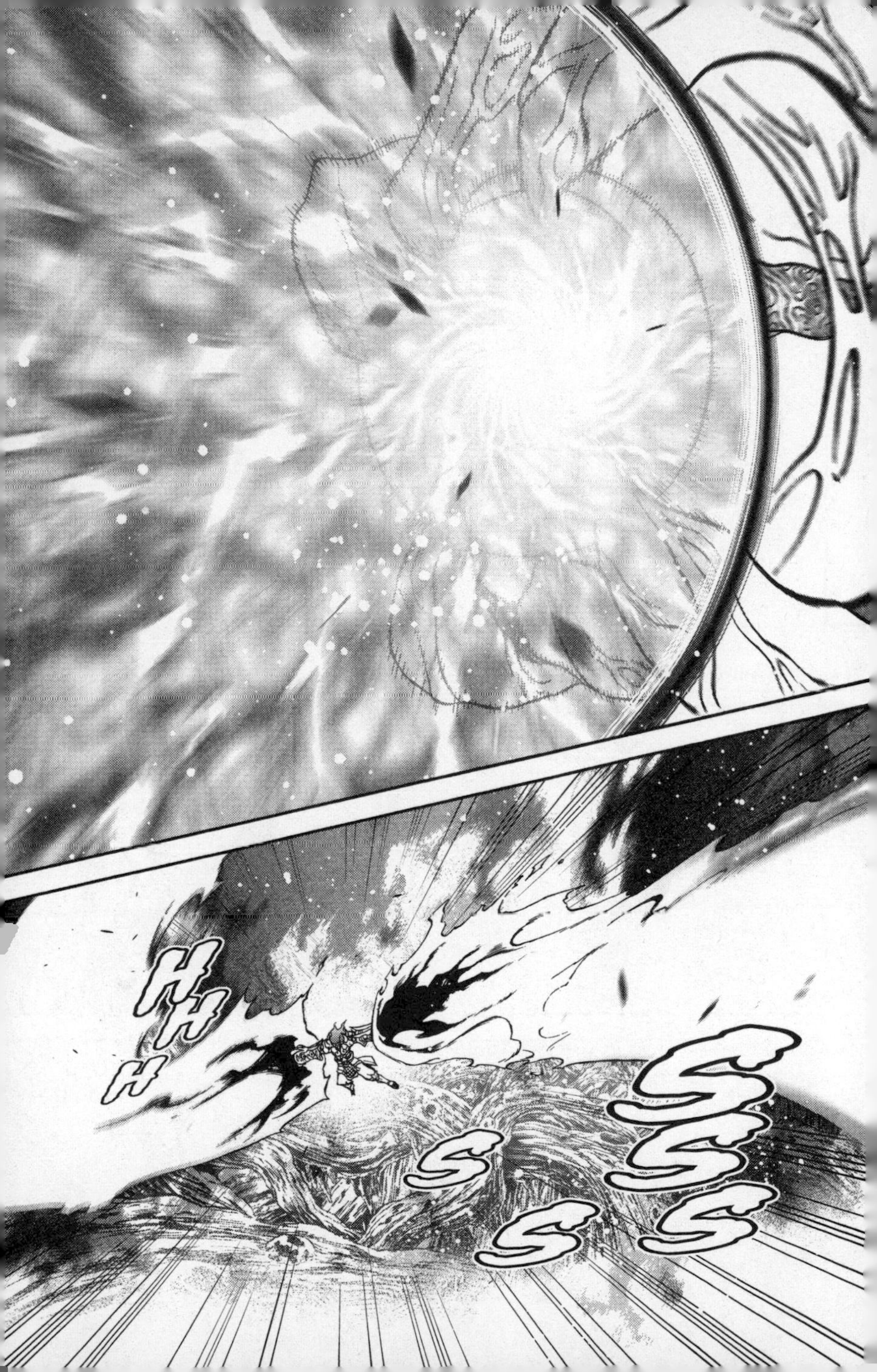
SSSSSS
HHH

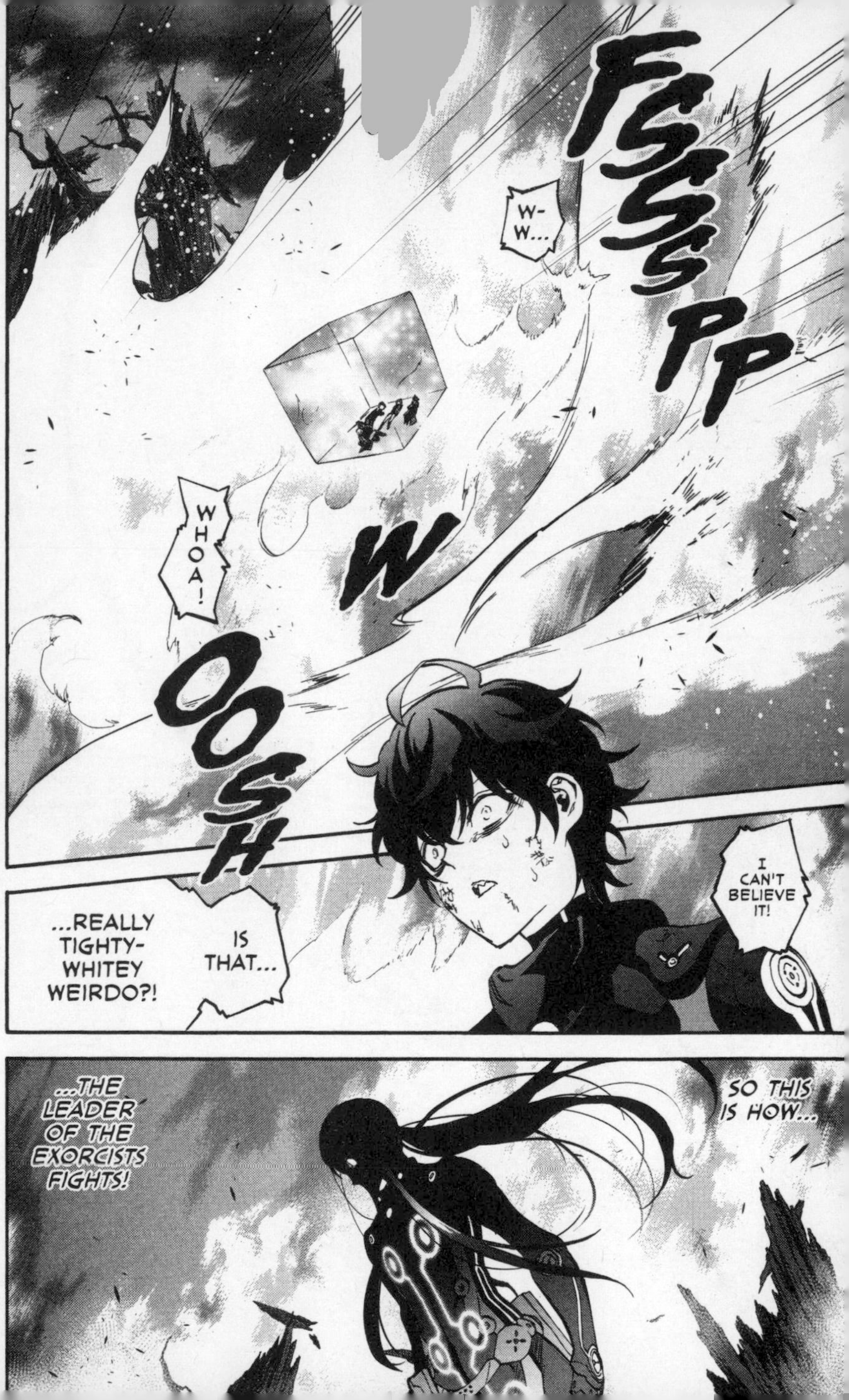
FSSSPP
W-W...
WHOA!
WOOSH
I CAN'T BELIEVE IT!
IS THAT...
...REALLY TIGHTY-WHITEY WEIRDO?!
SO THIS IS HOW...
...THE LEADER OF THE EXORCISTS FIGHTS!

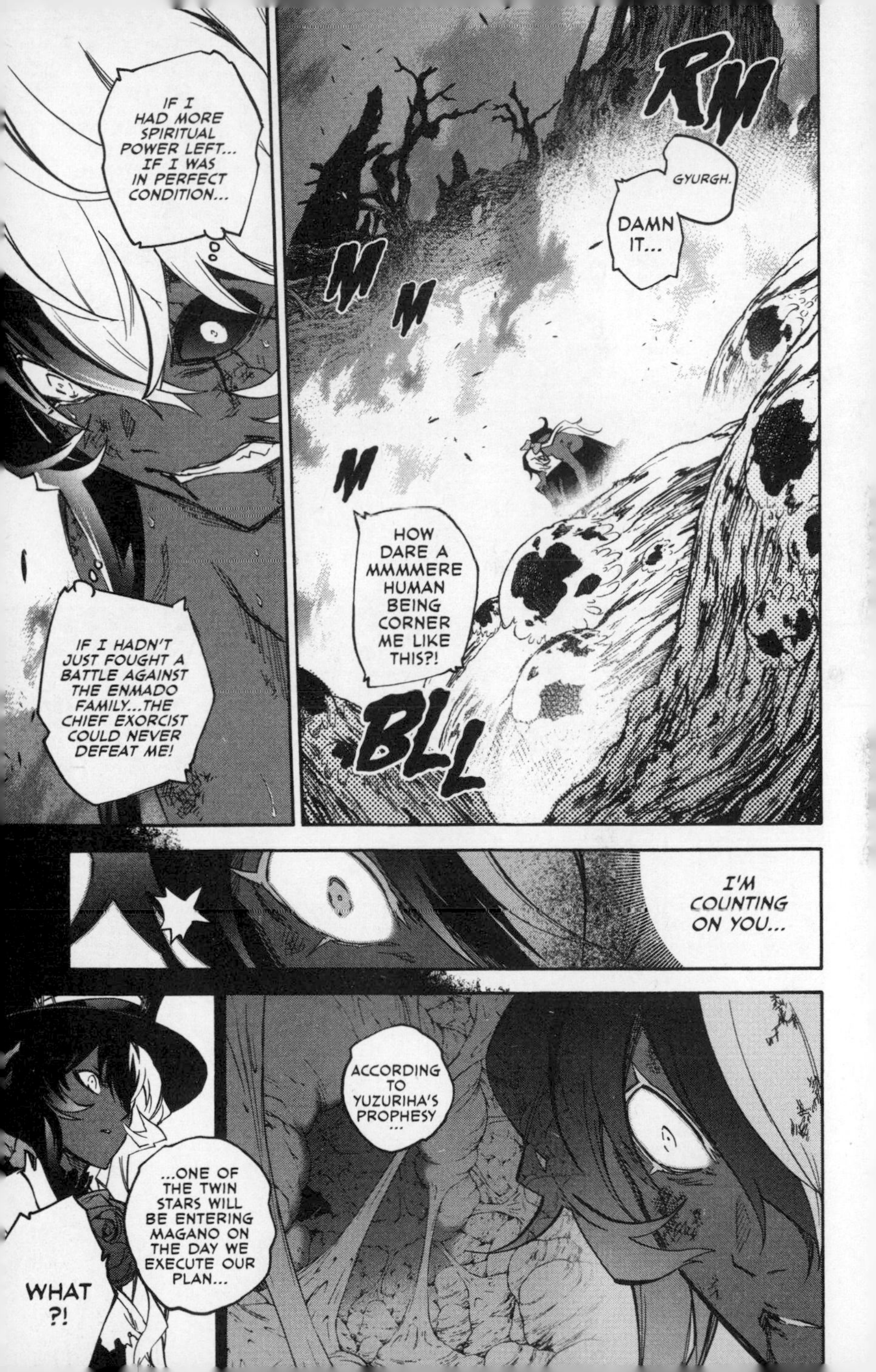
RM
GYURGH.
DAMN IT...
M M M
HOW DARE A MMMMERE HUMAN BEING CORNER ME LIKE THIS?!
BLL
IF I HAD MORE SPIRITUAL POWER LEFT... IF I WAS IN PERFECT CONDITION...
IF I HADN'T JUST FOUGHT A BATTLE AGAINST THE ENMADO FAMILY...THE CHIEF EXORCIST COULD NEVER DEFEAT ME!
I'M COUNTING ON YOU...
ACCORDING TO YUZURIHA'S PROPHESY ...
...ONE OF THE TWIN STARS WILL BE ENTERING MAGANO ON THE DAY WE EXECUTE OUR PLAN...
WHAT ?!

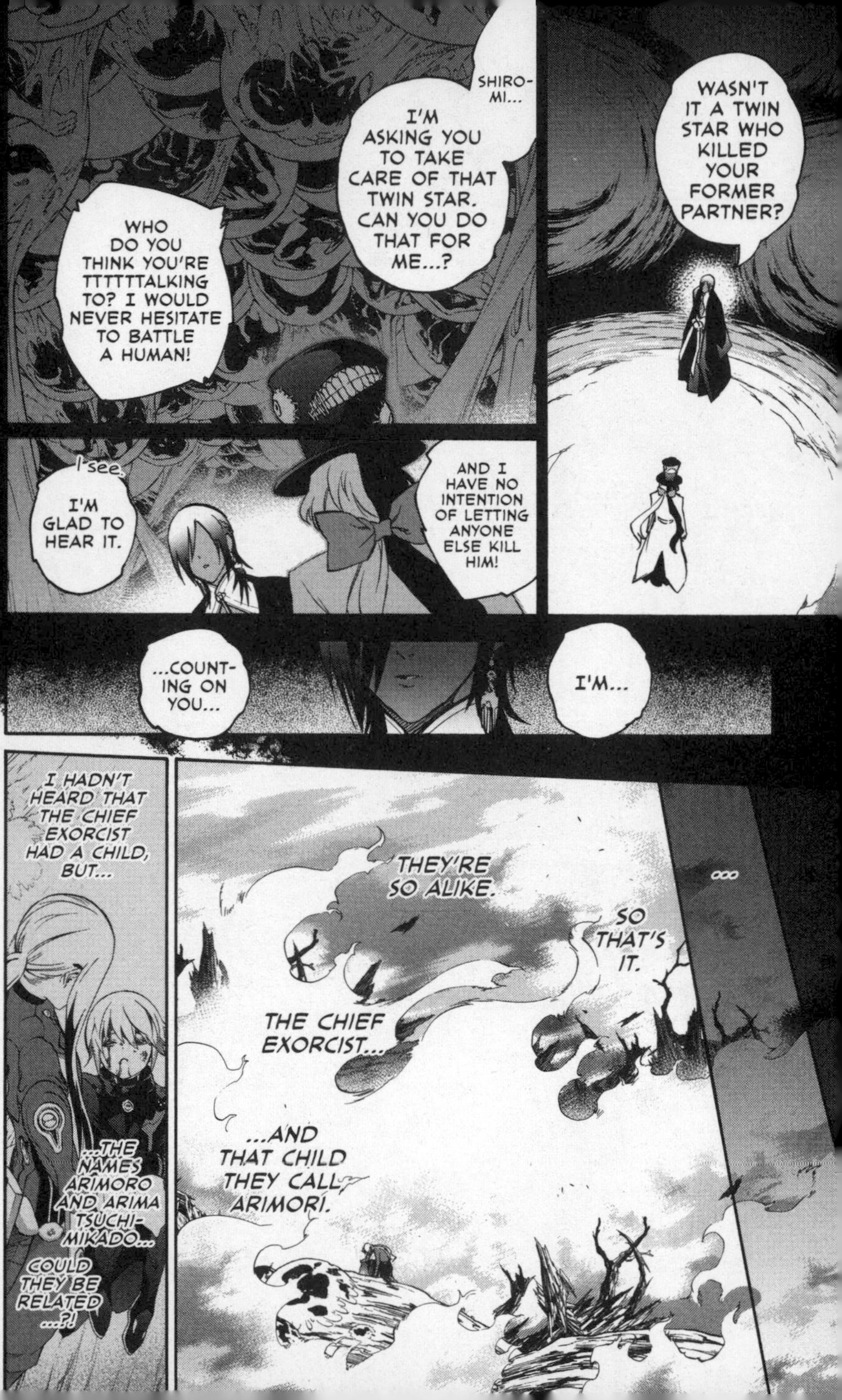
WASN'T IT A TWIN STAR WHO KILLED YOUR FORMER PARTNER?
SHIRO-MI...
I'M ASKING YOU TO TAKE CARE OF THAT TWIN STAR. CAN YOU DO THAT FOR ME...?
WHO DO YOU THINK YOU'RE TTTTTTALKING TO? I WOULD NEVER HESITATE TO BATTLE A HUMAN!
AND I HAVE NO INTENTION OF LETTING ANYONE ELSE KILL HIM!
I see.
I'M GLAD TO HEAR IT.
I'M...
...COUNTING ON YOU...
...
SO THAT'S IT.
THEY'RE SO ALIKE.
THE CHIEF EXORCIST...
...AND THAT CHILD THEY CALL ARIMORI.
I HADN'T HEARD THAT THE CHIEF EXORCIST HAD A CHILD, BUT...
...THE NAMES ARIMORO AND ARIMA TSUCHI-MIKADO...
COULD THEY BE RELATED ...?!

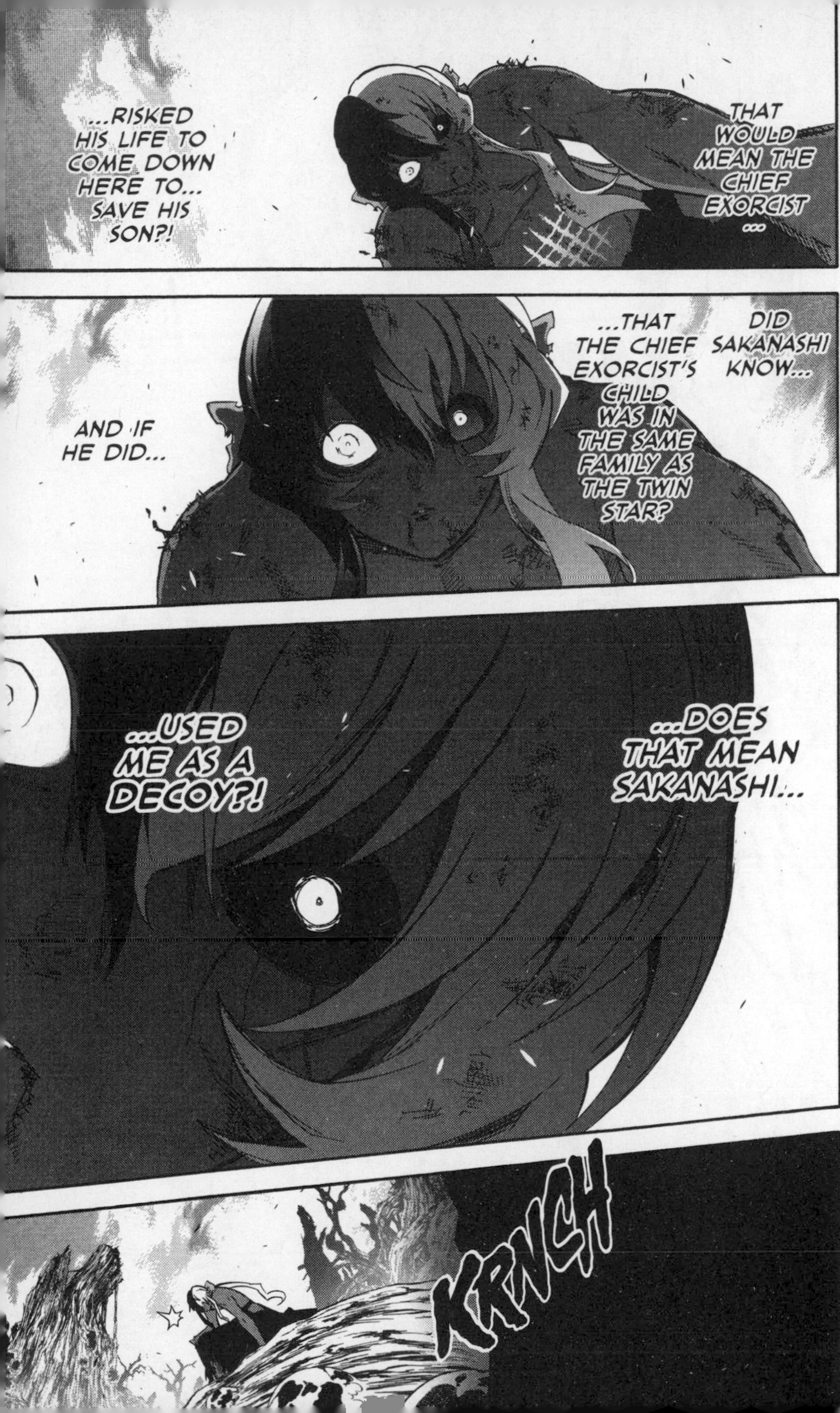
THAT WOULD MEAN THE CHIEF EXORCIST...
...RISKED HIS LIFE TO COME DOWN HERE TO... SAVE HIS SON?!
DID SAKANASHI KNOW...
...THAT THE CHIEF EXORCIST'S CHILD WAS IN THE SAME FAMILY AS THE TWIN STAR?
AND IF HE DID...
...DOES THAT MEAN SAKANASHI...
...USED ME AS A DECOY?!
KRNCH

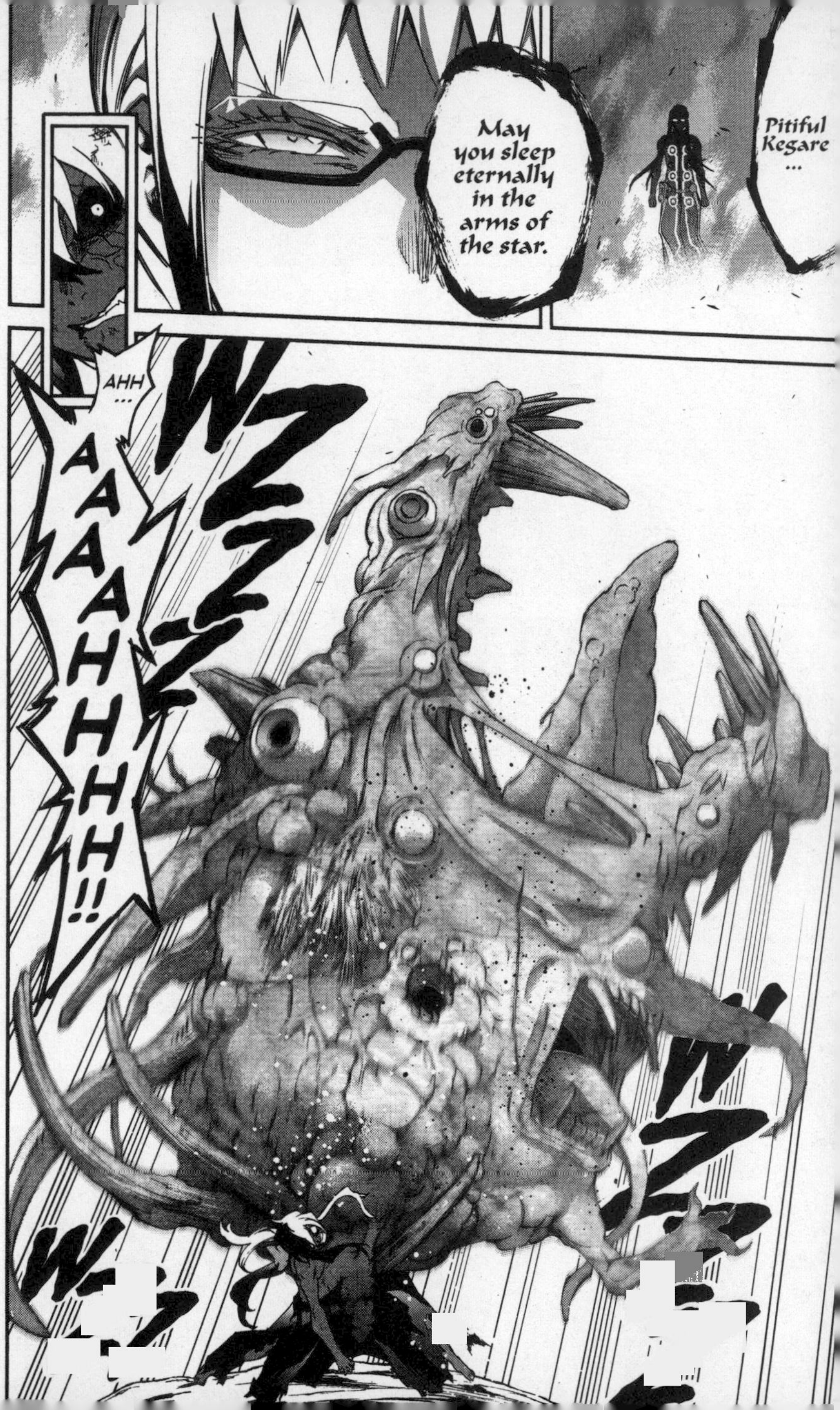
Pitiful Kegare ...
May you sleep eternally in the arms of the star.
AHH ...
AAAAHHHHH!!

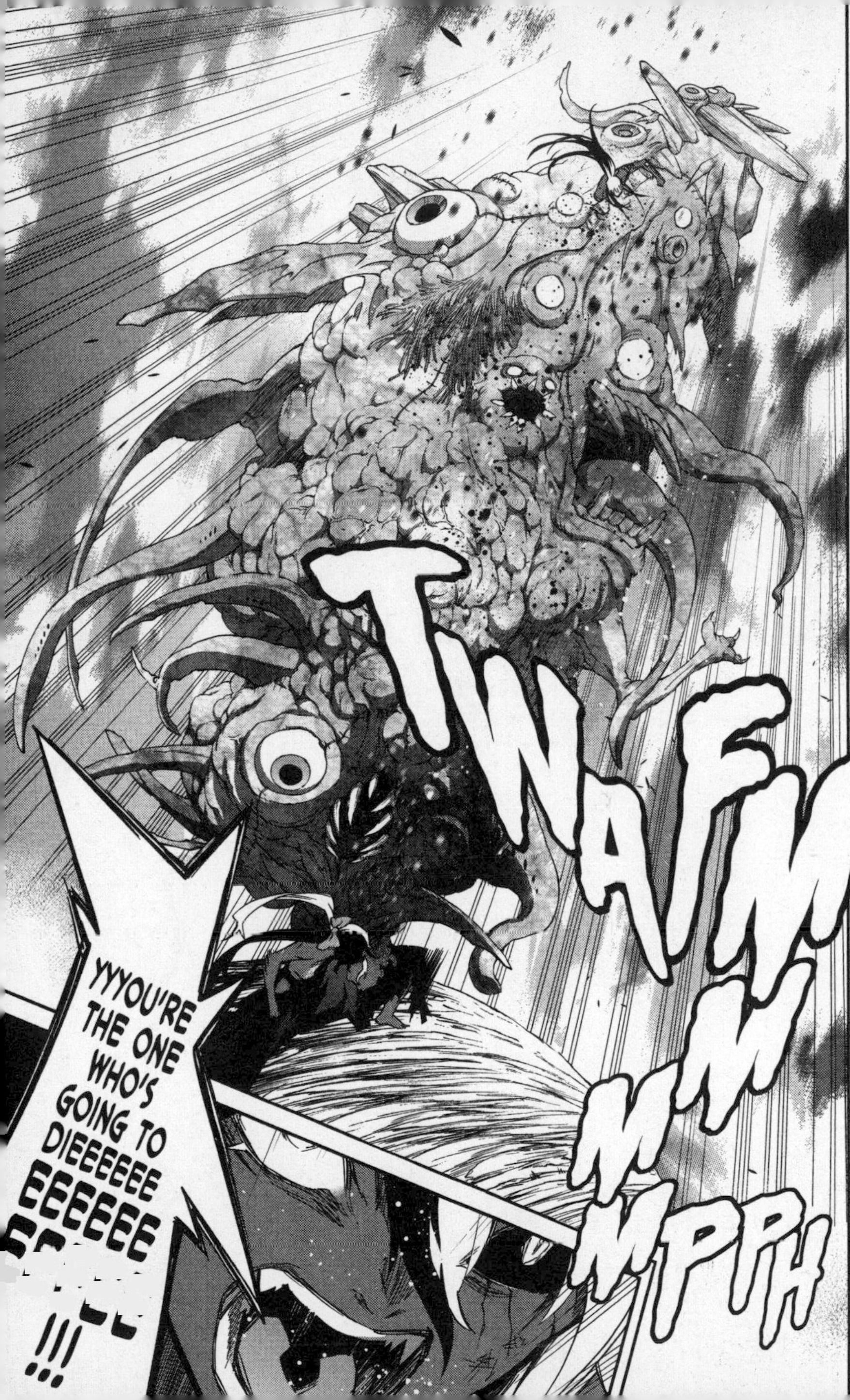
TWAFMMMMPH
YYYOU'RE THE ONE WHO'S GOING TO DIEEEEEEE EEEEEEE
!!!

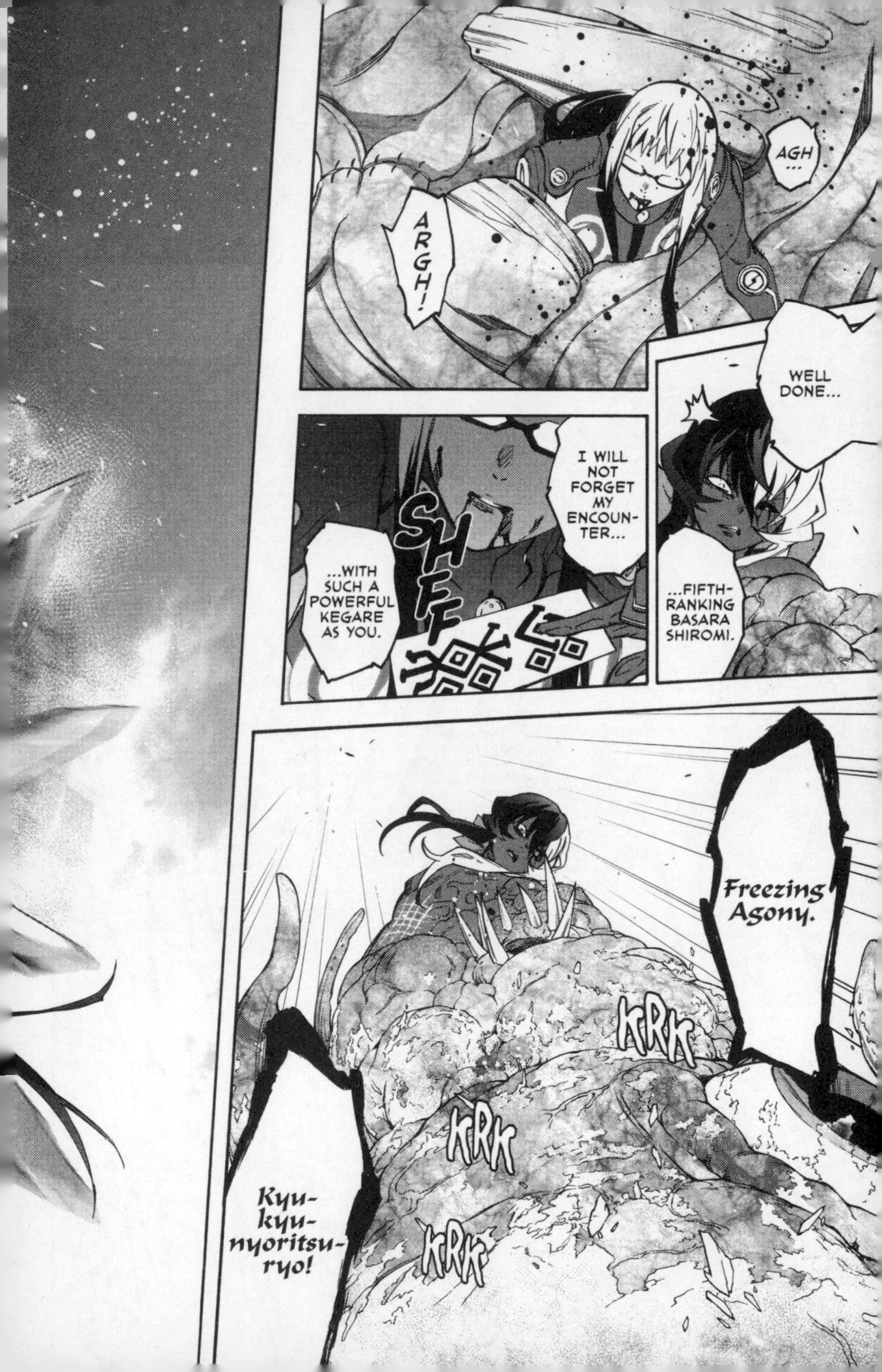
AGH...
ARGH!
WELL DONE...
...FIFTH-RANKING BASARA SHIROMI.
I WILL NOT FORGET MY ENCOUNTER...
SHFF
...WITH SUCH A POWERFUL KEGARE AS YOU.
Freezing Agony.
KRK
KRK
KRK
Kyu-kyu-nyoritsu-ryo!

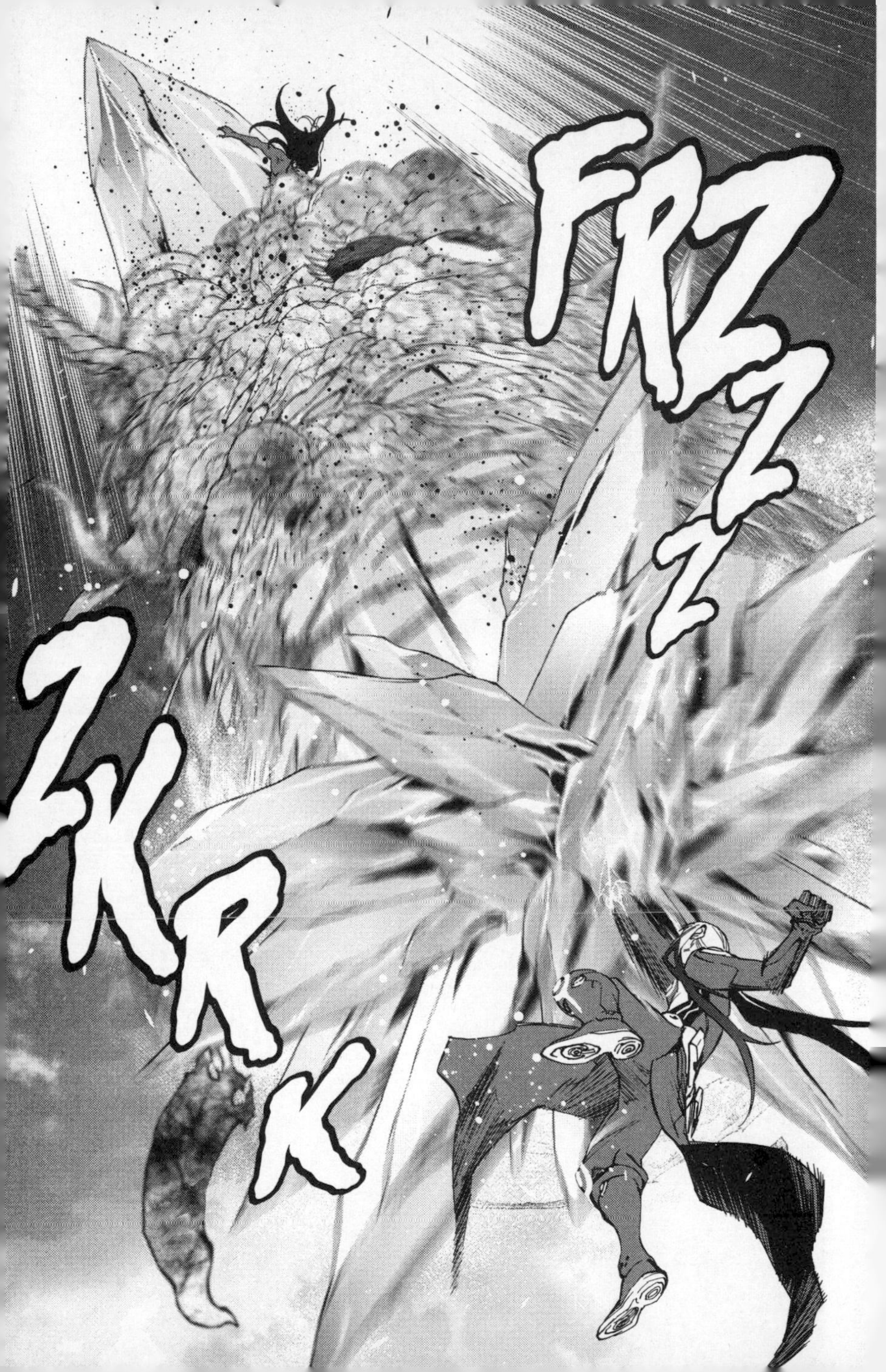
FRZZZ
ZKRK

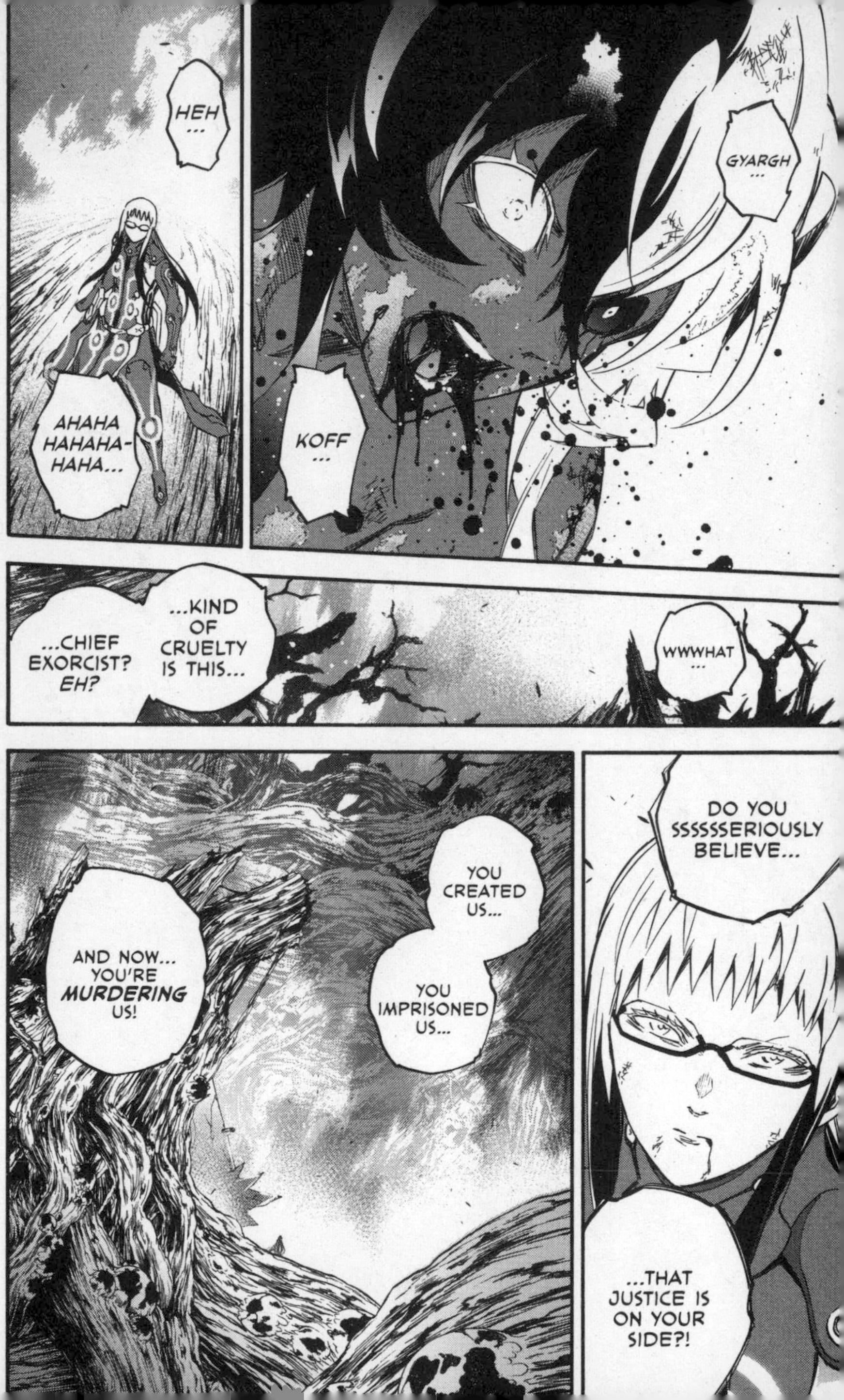
GYARGH...
KOFF...
HEH...
AHAHA HAHAHA-HAHA...
WWWHAT...
...KIND OF CRUELTY IS THIS...
...CHIEF EXORCIST? EH?
DO YOU SSSSSSERIOUSLY BELIEVE...
...THAT JUSTICE IS ON YOUR SIDE?!
YOU CREATED US...
YOU IMPRISONED US...
AND NOW... YOU'RE MURDERING US!

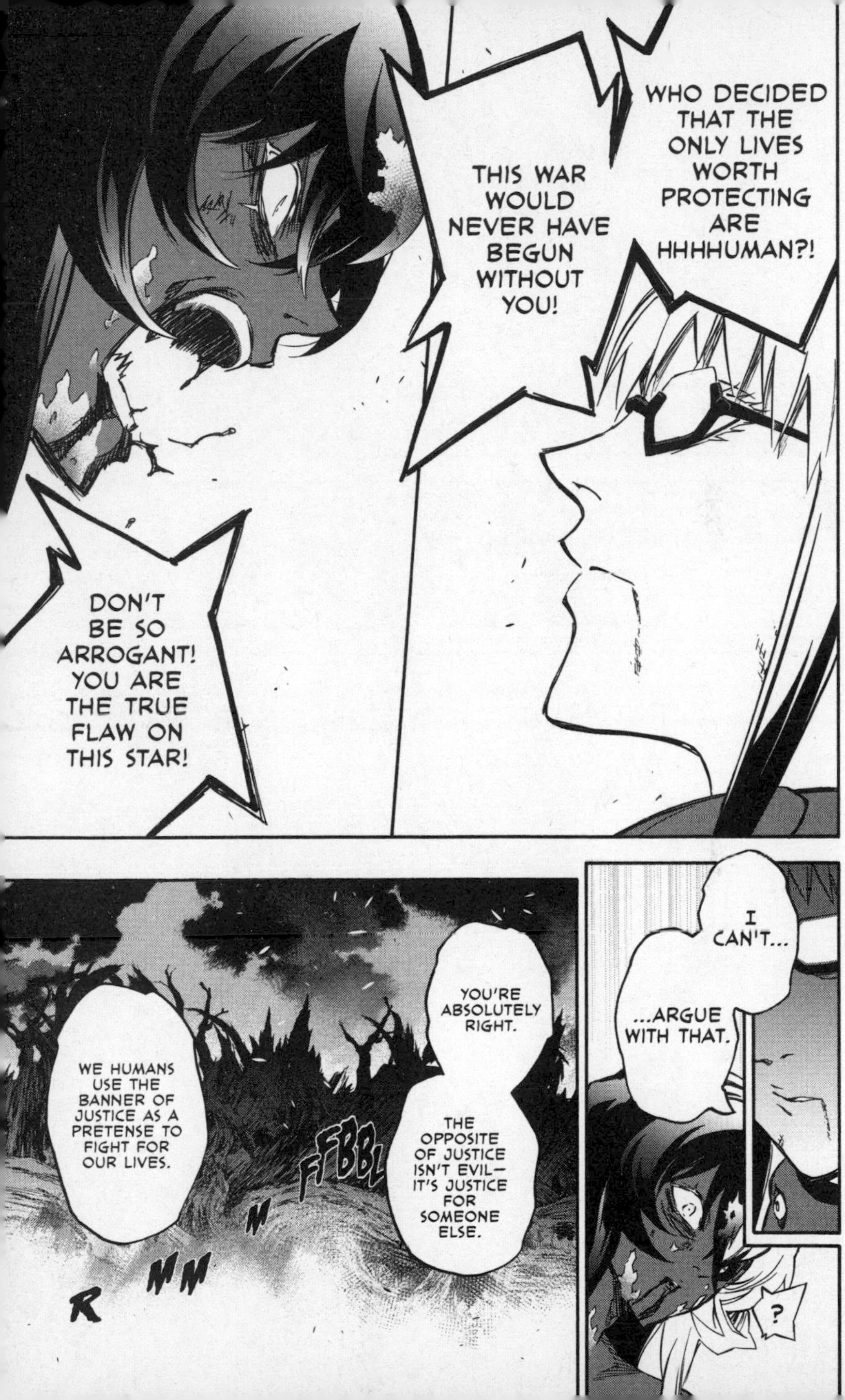
WHO DECIDED THAT THE ONLY LIVES WORTH PROTECTING ARE HHHHUMAN?!
THIS WAR WOULD NEVER HAVE BEGUN WITHOUT YOU!
DON'T BE SO ARROGANT! YOU ARE THE TRUE FLAW ON THIS STAR!
I CAN'T...
...ARGUE WITH THAT.
?
YOU'RE ABSOLUTELY RIGHT.
THE OPPOSITE OF JUSTICE ISN'T EVIL—IT'S JUSTICE FOR SOMEONE ELSE.
WE HUMANS USE THE BANNER OF JUSTICE AS A PRETENSE TO FIGHT FOR OUR LIVES.
FFBBL
RMMMM

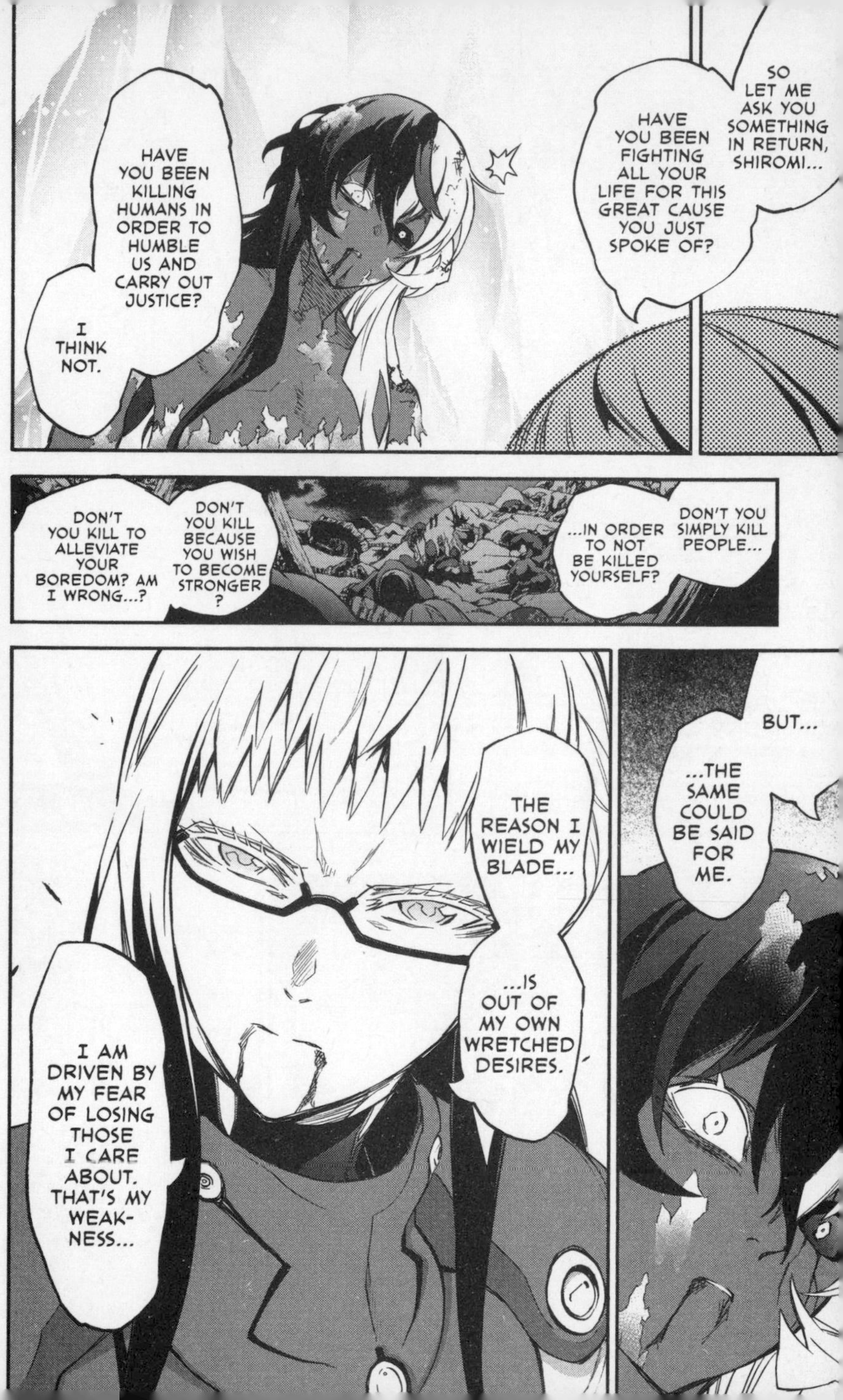
SO LET ME ASK YOU SOMETHING IN RETURN, SHIROMI...
HAVE YOU BEEN FIGHTING ALL YOUR LIFE FOR THIS GREAT CAUSE YOU JUST SPOKE OF?
HAVE YOU BEEN KILLING HUMANS IN ORDER TO HUMBLE US AND CARRY OUT JUSTICE?
I THINK NOT.
DON'T YOU SIMPLY KILL PEOPLE...
...IN ORDER TO NOT BE KILLED YOURSELF?
DON'T YOU KILL BECAUSE YOU WISH TO BECOME STRONGER?
DON'T YOU KILL TO ALLEVIATE YOUR BOREDOM? AM I WRONG...?
BUT...
...THE SAME COULD BE SAID FOR ME.
THE REASON I WIELD MY BLADE...
...IS OUT OF MY OWN WRETCHED DESIRES.
I AM DRIVEN BY MY FEAR OF LOSING THOSE I CARE ABOUT. THAT'S MY WEAKNESS...

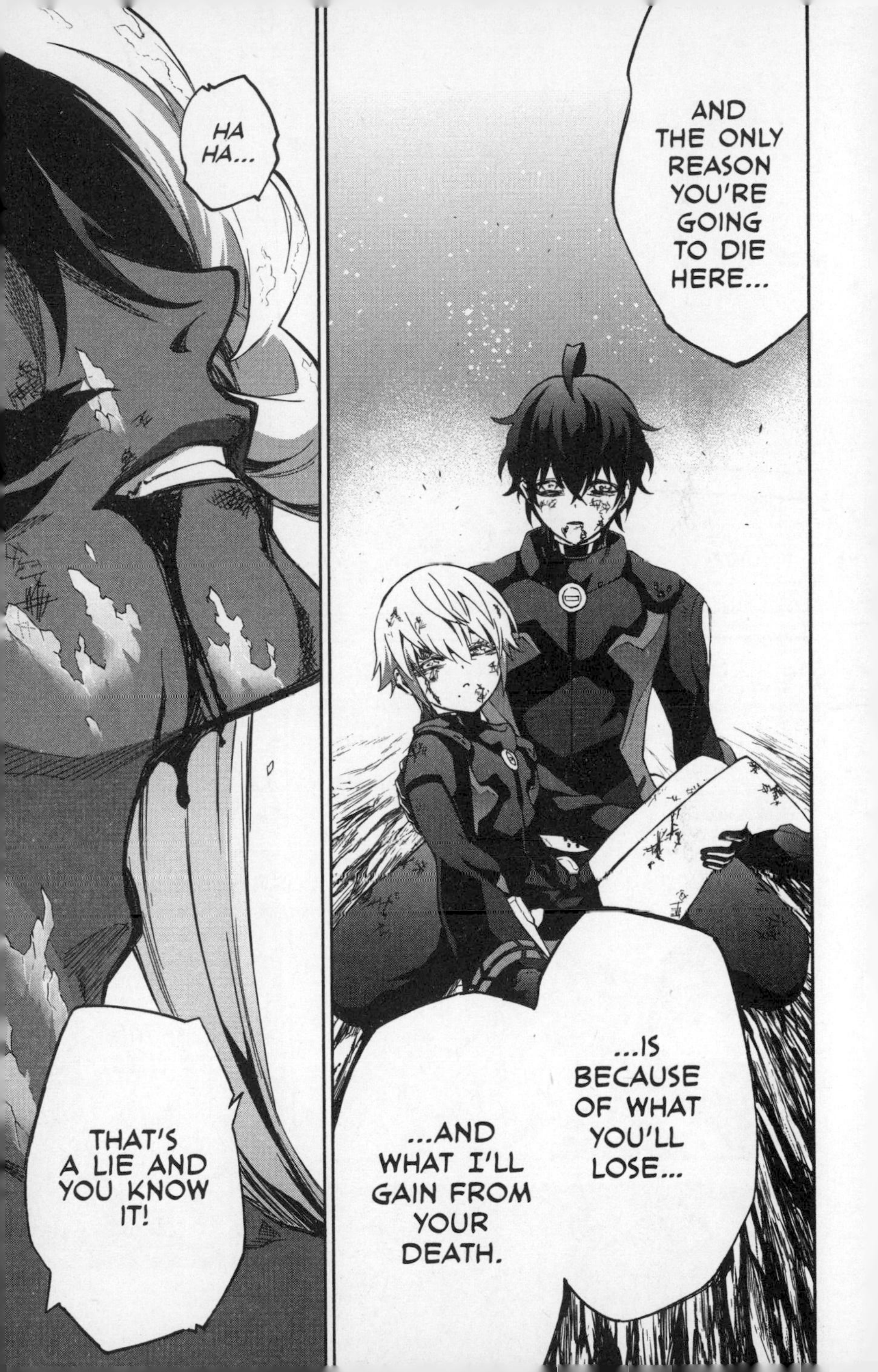
AND THE ONLY REASON YOU'RE GOING TO DIE HERE...
...IS BECAUSE OF WHAT YOU'LL LOSE...
...AND WHAT I'LL GAIN FROM YOUR DEATH.
HA HA...
THAT'S A LIE AND YOU KNOW IT!

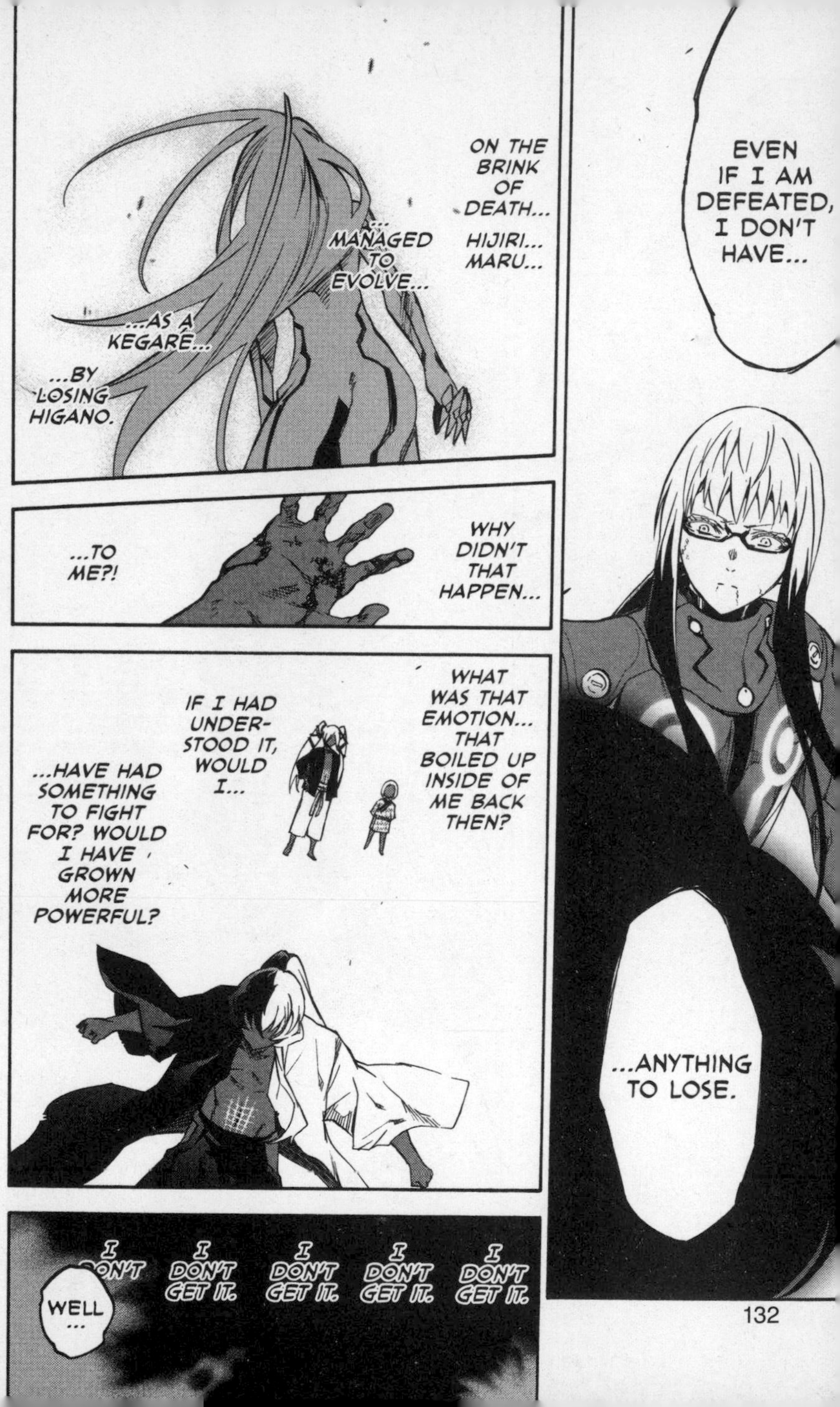
EVEN IF I AM DEFEATED, I DON'T HAVE...
...ANYTHING TO LOSE.
ON THE BRINK OF DEATH...
HIJIRI... MARU...
...MANAGED TO EVOLVE...
...AS A KEGARE...
...BY LOSING HIGANO.
WHY DIDN'T THAT HAPPEN...
...TO ME?!
WHAT WAS THAT EMOTION... THAT BOILED UP INSIDE OF ME BACK THEN?
IF I HAD UNDER-STOOD IT, WOULD I...
...HAVE HAD SOMETHING TO FIGHT FOR? WOULD I HAVE GROWN MORE POWERFUL?
I DON'T GET IT.
I DON'T GET IT.
I DON'T GET IT.
I DON'T GET IT.
I DON'T GET IT.
WELL...

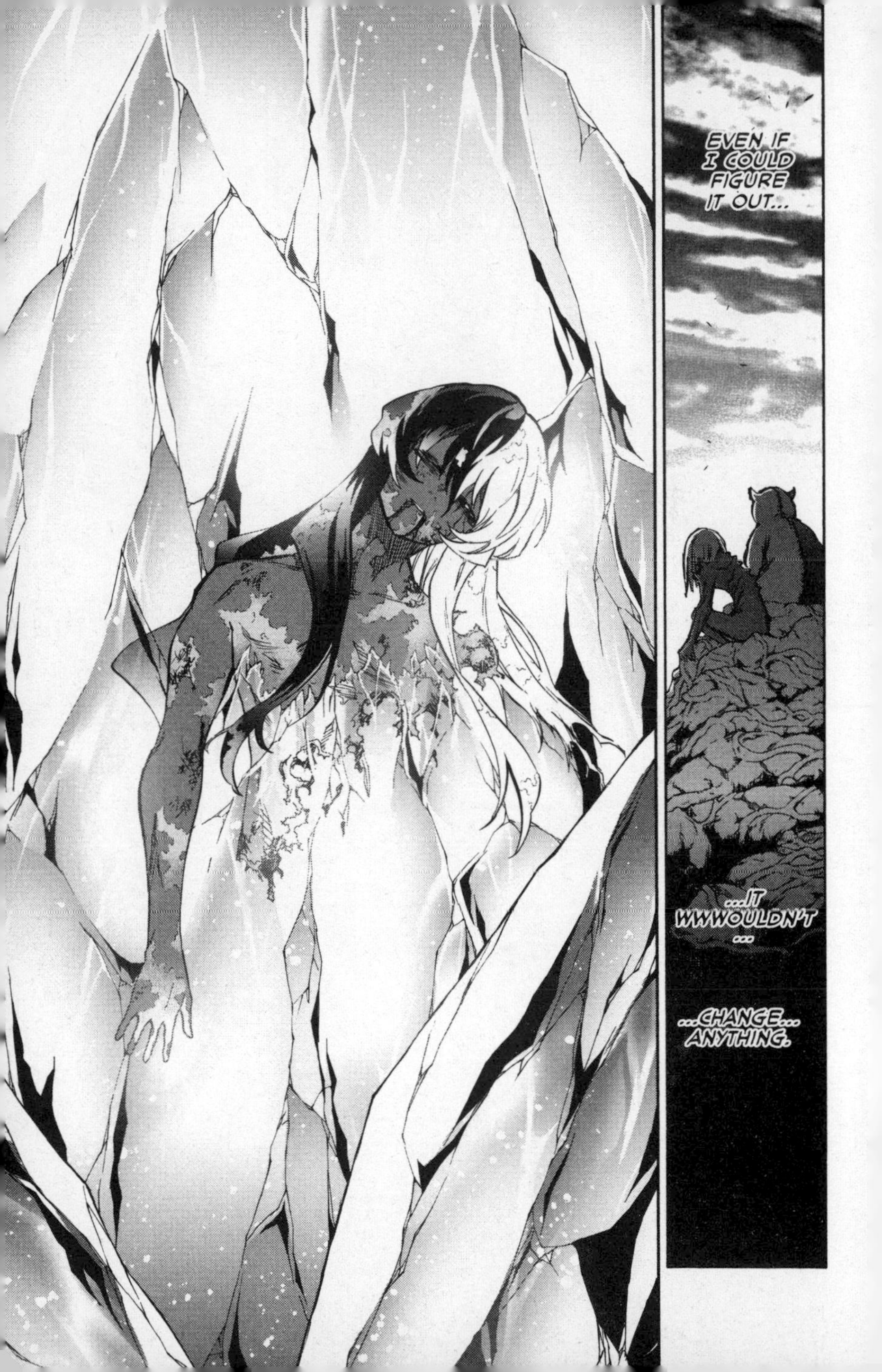
EVEN IF I COULD FIGURE IT OUT...
...IT WWWOULDN'T ...
...CHANGE... ANYTHING.

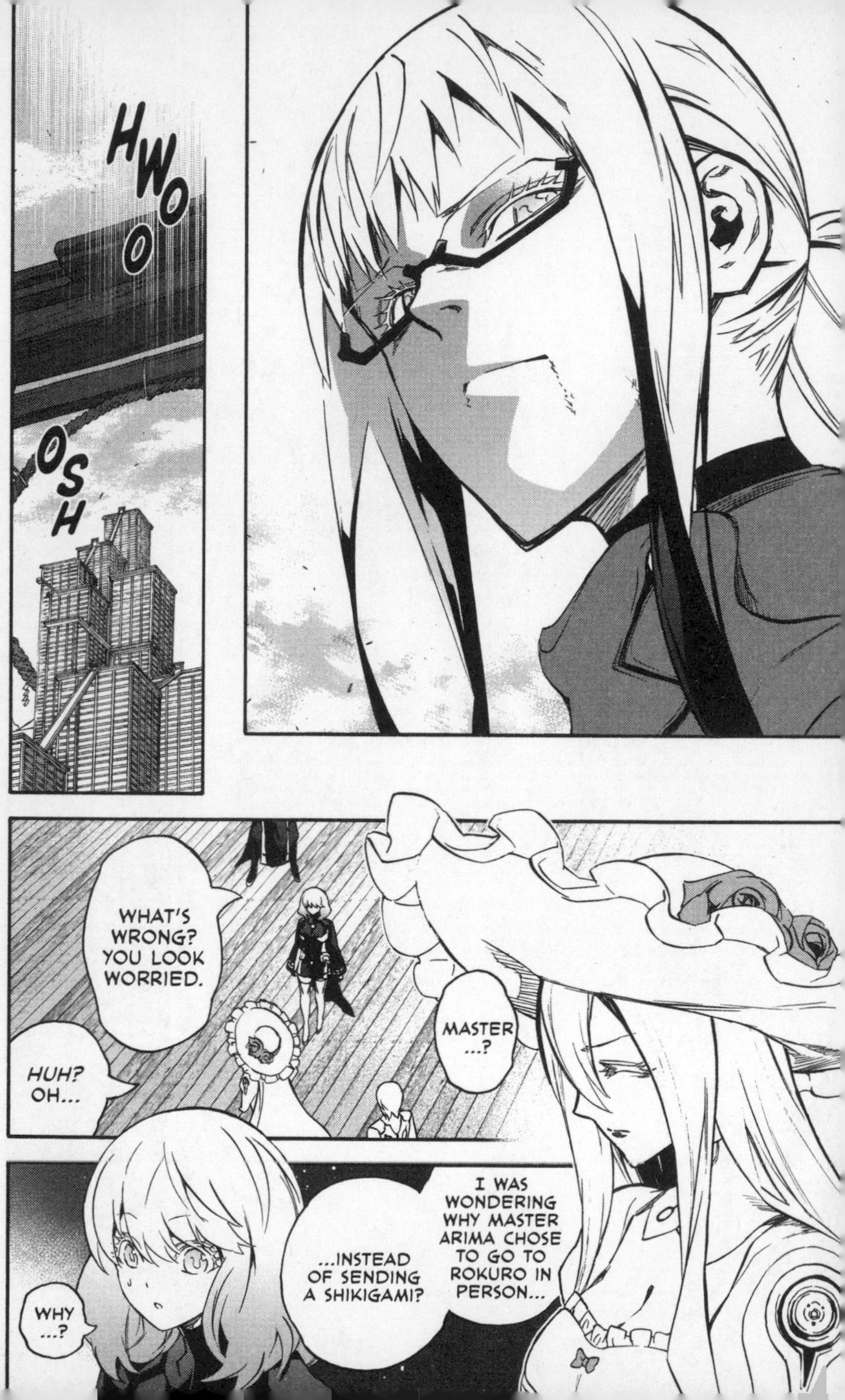
HWOOOSH
MASTER ...?
WHAT'S WRONG? YOU LOOK WORRIED.
HUH? OH...
I WAS WONDERING WHY MASTER ARIMA CHOSE TO GO TO ROKURO IN PERSON...
...INSTEAD OF SENDING A SHIKIGAMI?
WHY ...?

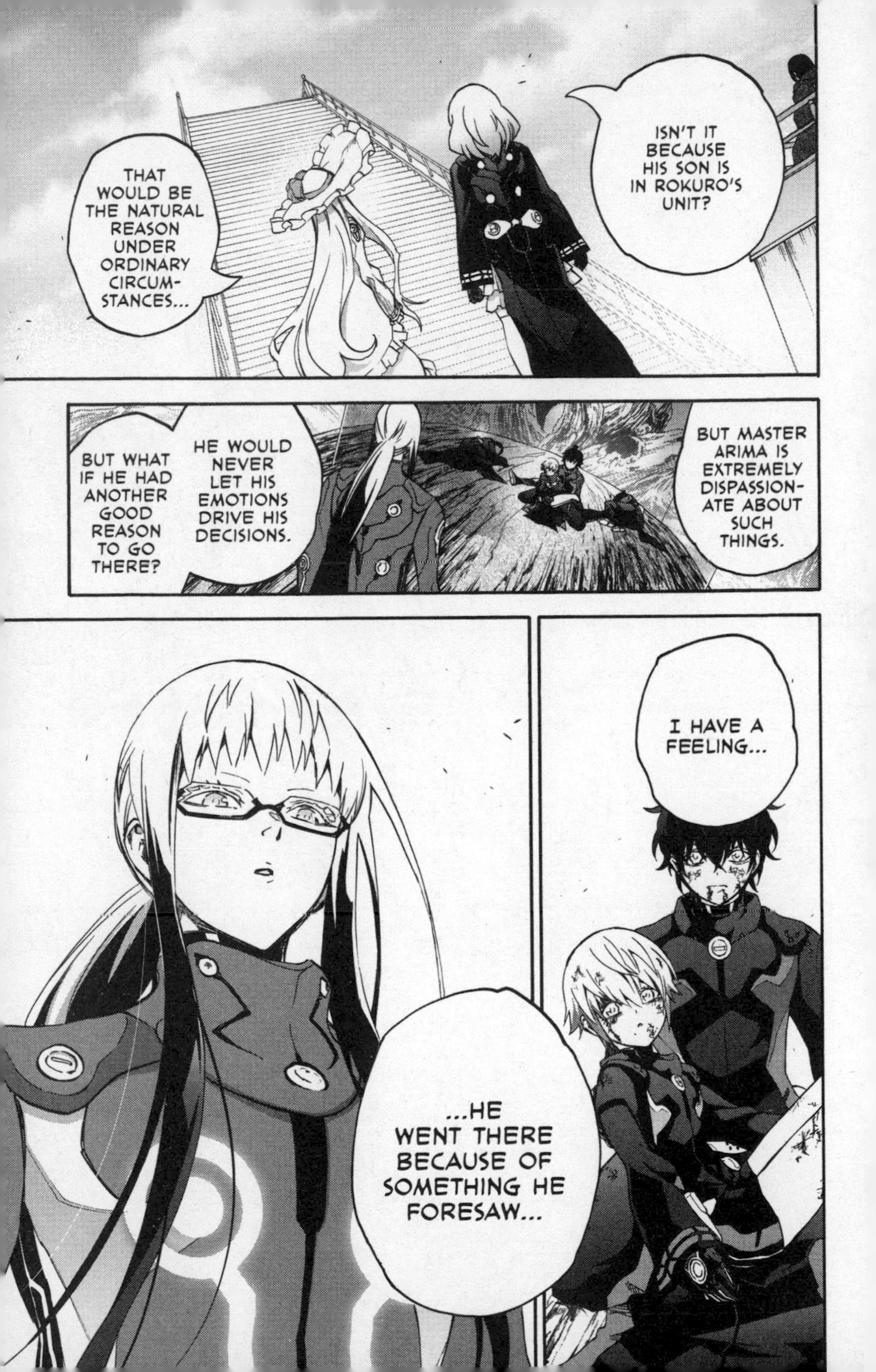
ISN'T IT BECAUSE HIS SON IS IN ROKURO'S UNIT?
THAT WOULD BE THE NATURAL REASON UNDER ORDINARY CIRCUM-STANCES...
BUT MASTER ARIMA IS EXTREMELY DISPASSION-ATE ABOUT SUCH THINGS.
HE WOULD NEVER LET HIS EMOTIONS DRIVE HIS DECISIONS.
BUT WHAT IF HE HAD ANOTHER GOOD REASON TO GO THERE?
I HAVE A FEELING...
...HE WENT THERE BECAUSE OF SOMETHING HE FORESAW...

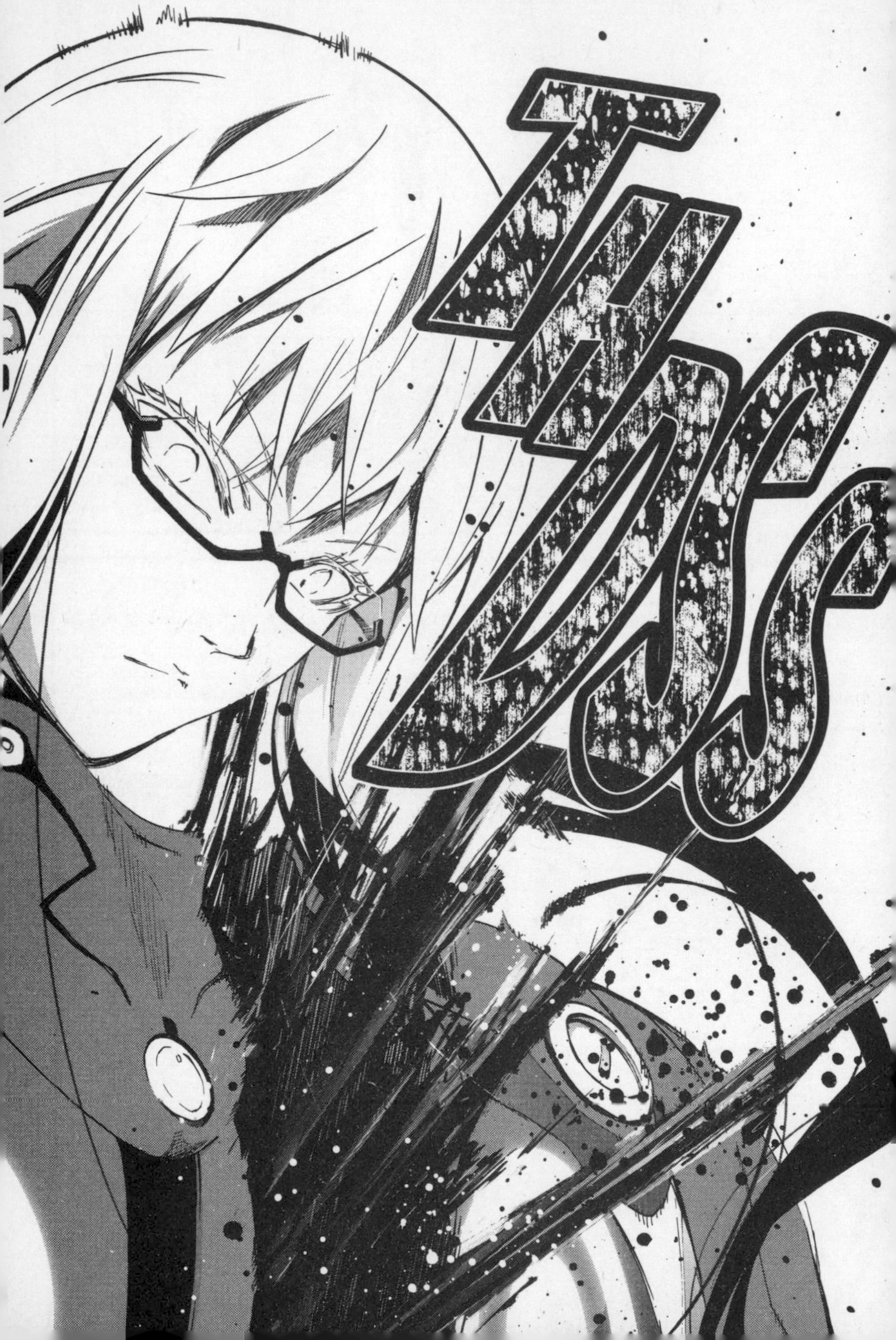

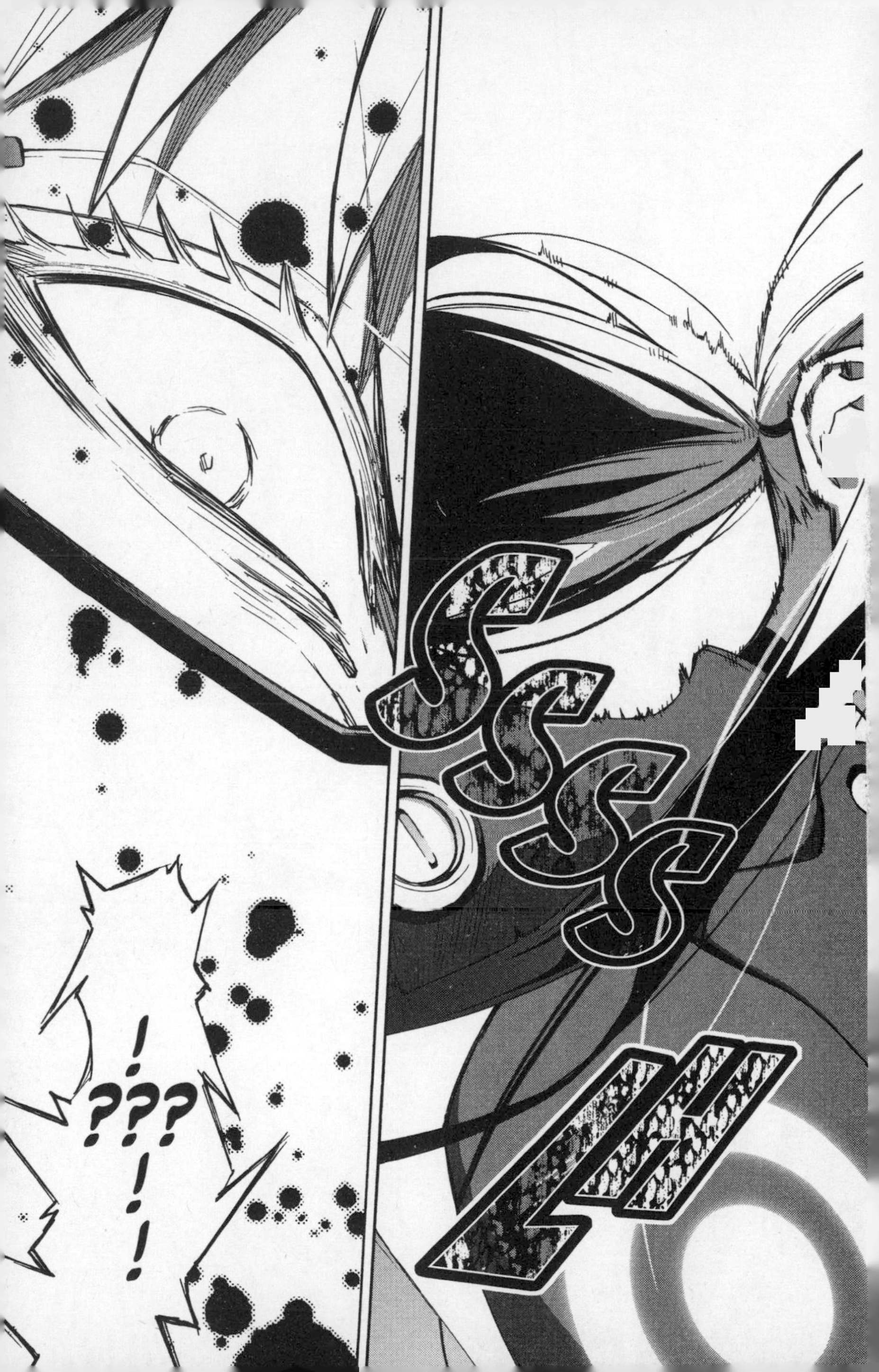
SSSSH
!???!!

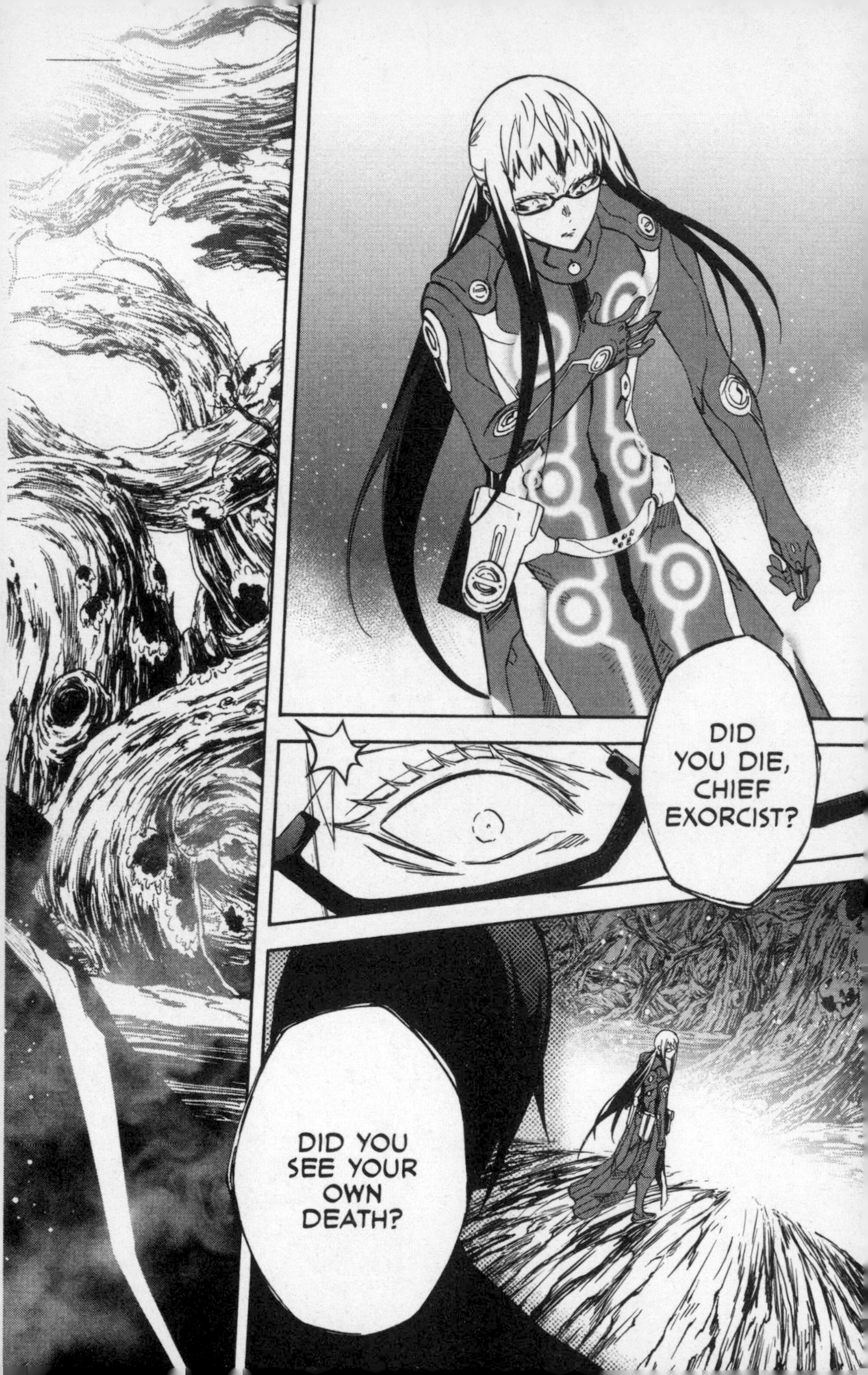
DID YOU DIE, CHIEF EXORCIST?
DID YOU SEE YOUR OWN DEATH?

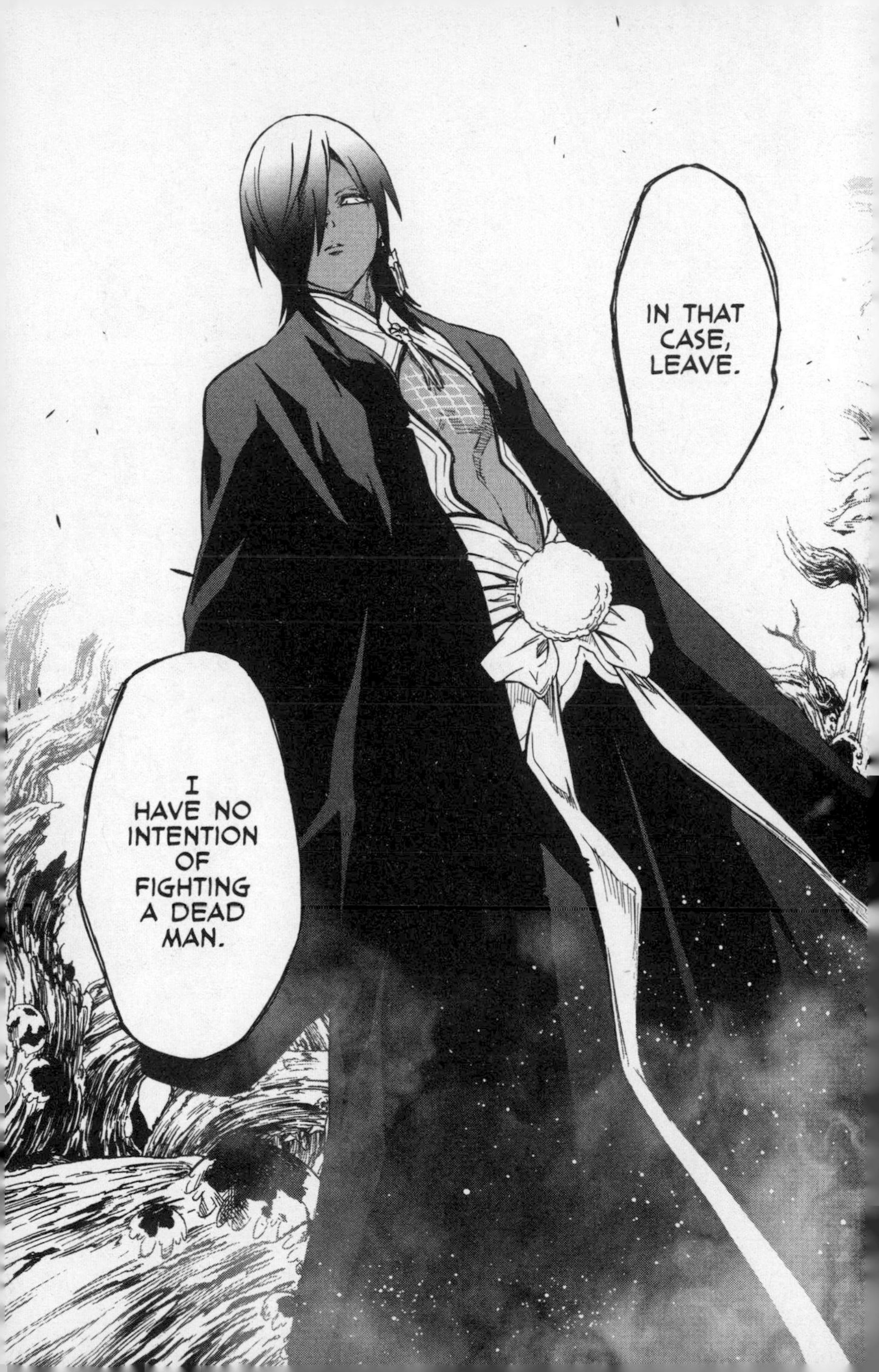
IN THAT CASE, LEAVE.
I HAVE NO INTENTION OF FIGHTING A DEAD MAN.

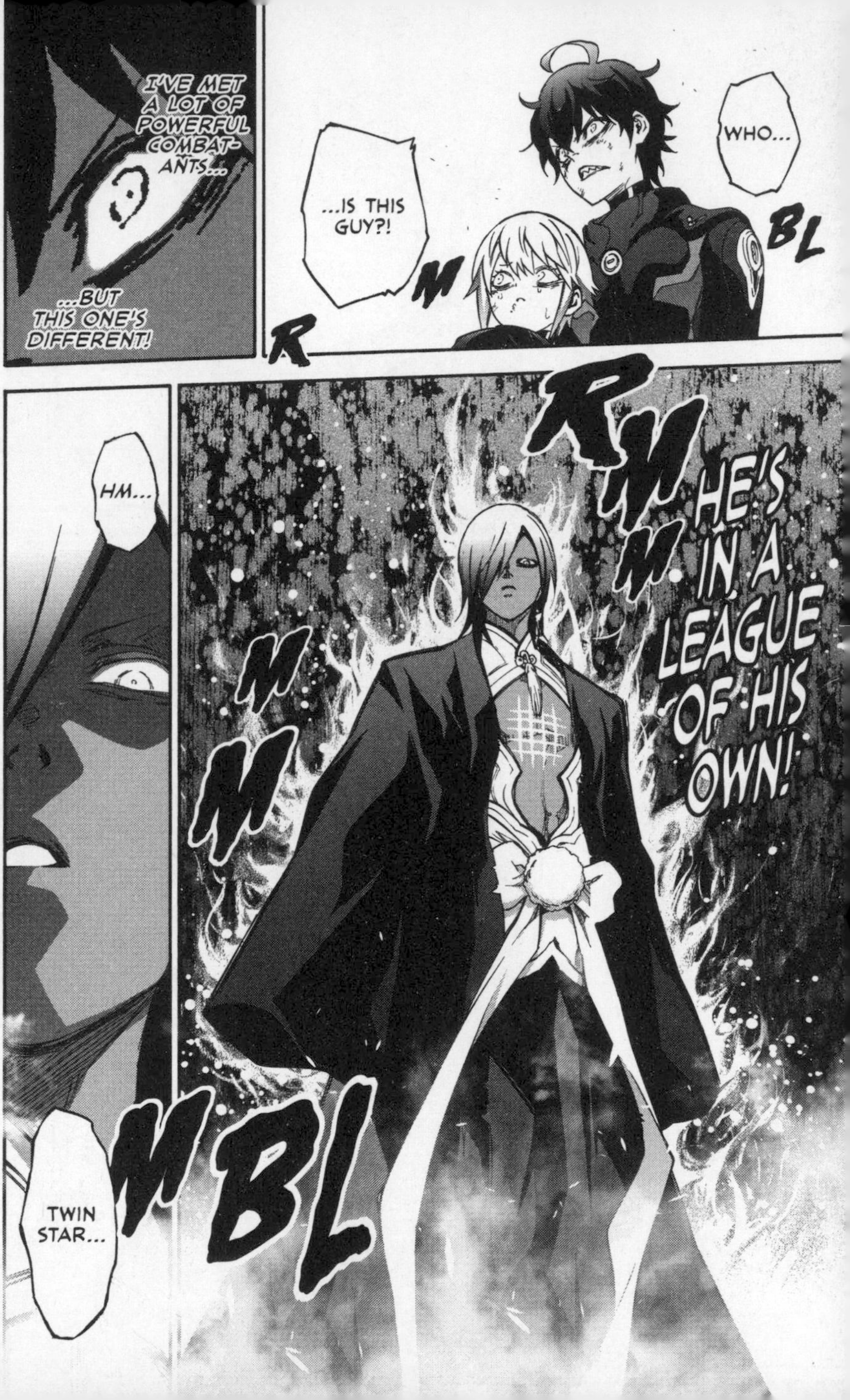
WHO...
...IS THIS GUY?!
R M BL
I'VE MET A LOT OF POWERFUL COMBAT-ANTS...
...BUT THIS ONE'S DIFFERENT!
RMMM
HE'S IN A LEAGUE OF HIS OWN!
MMMBL
HM...
TWIN STAR...

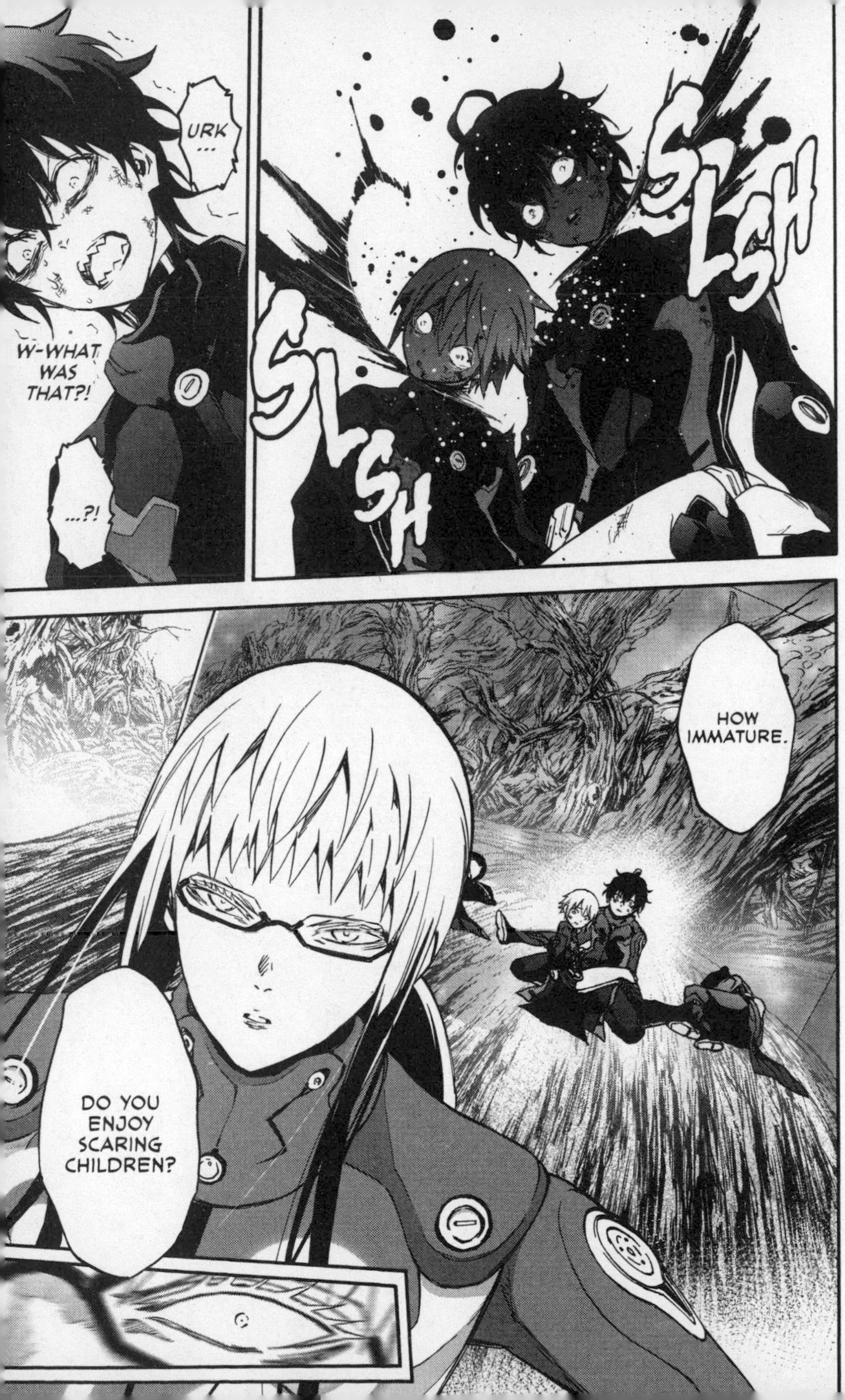
SLSH
SLSH
URK...
W-WHAT WAS THAT?!
...?!
HOW IMMATURE.
DO YOU ENJOY SCARING CHILDREN?

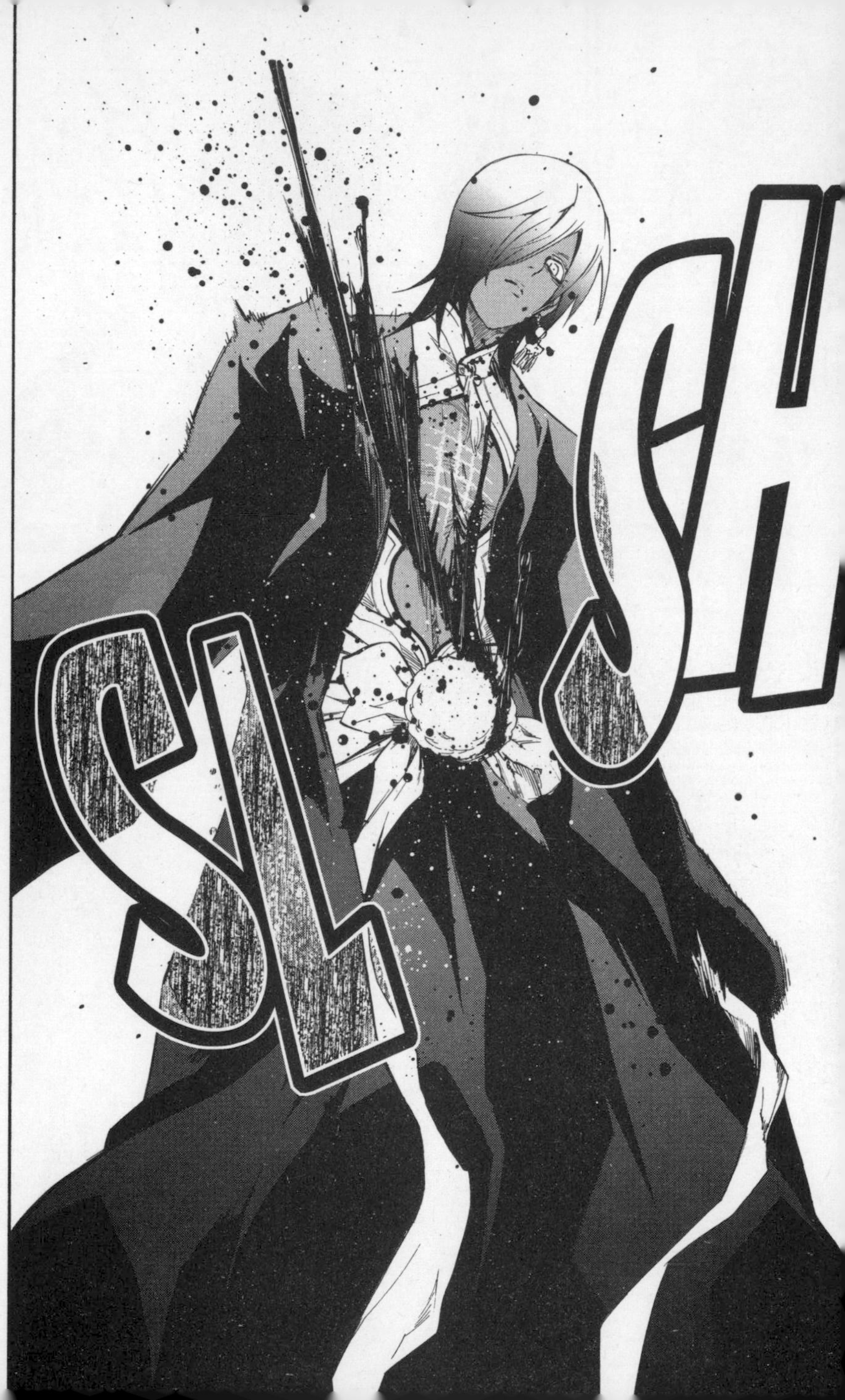
SL SH

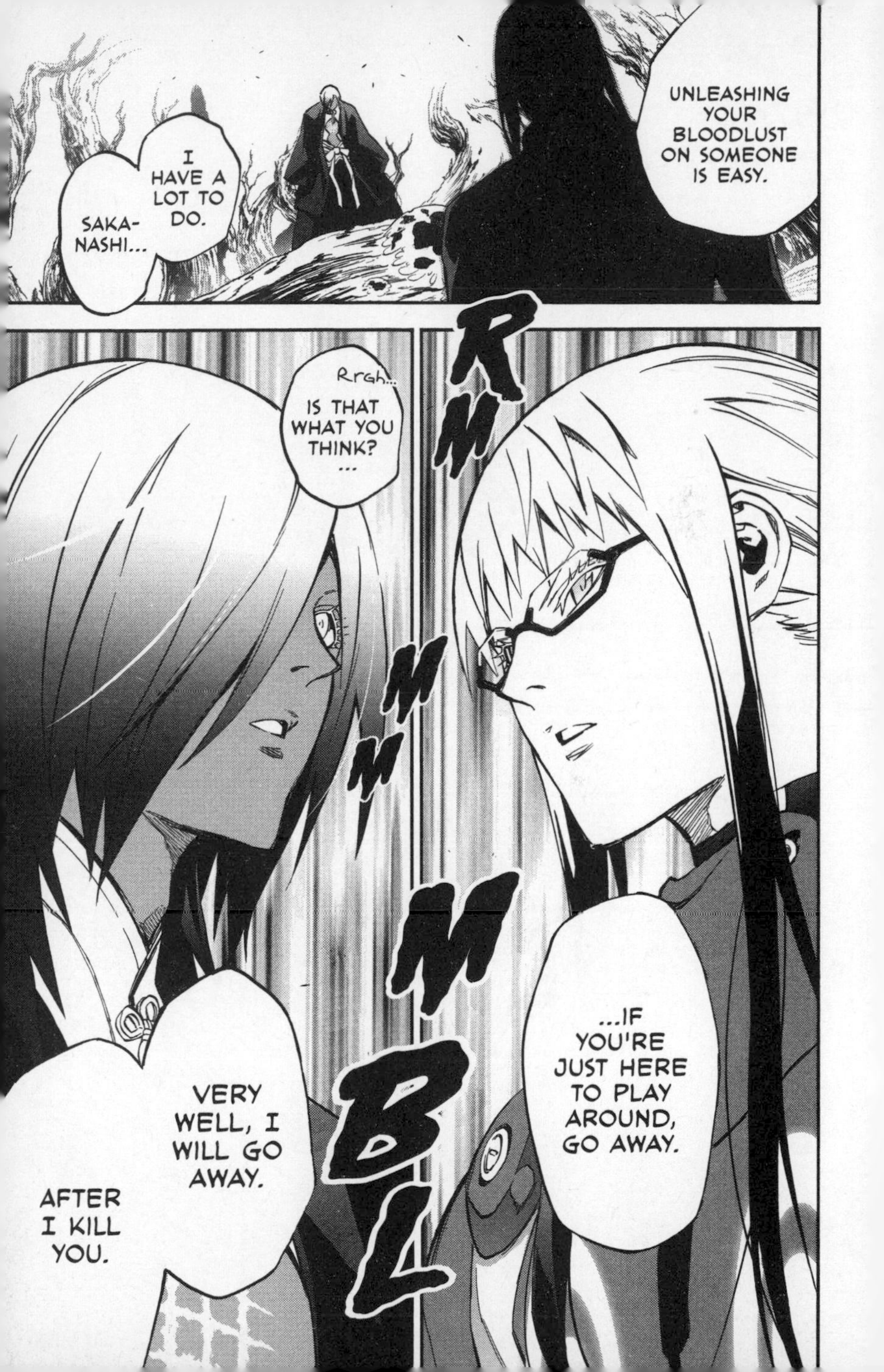
UNLEASHING YOUR BLOODLUST ON SOMEONE IS EASY.
I HAVE A LOT TO DO.
SAKA-NASHI...
...IF YOU'RE JUST HERE TO PLAY AROUND, GO AWAY.
RMMMMBL
Rrgh...
IS THAT WHAT YOU THINK? ...
VERY WELL, I WILL GO AWAY.
AFTER I KILL YOU.

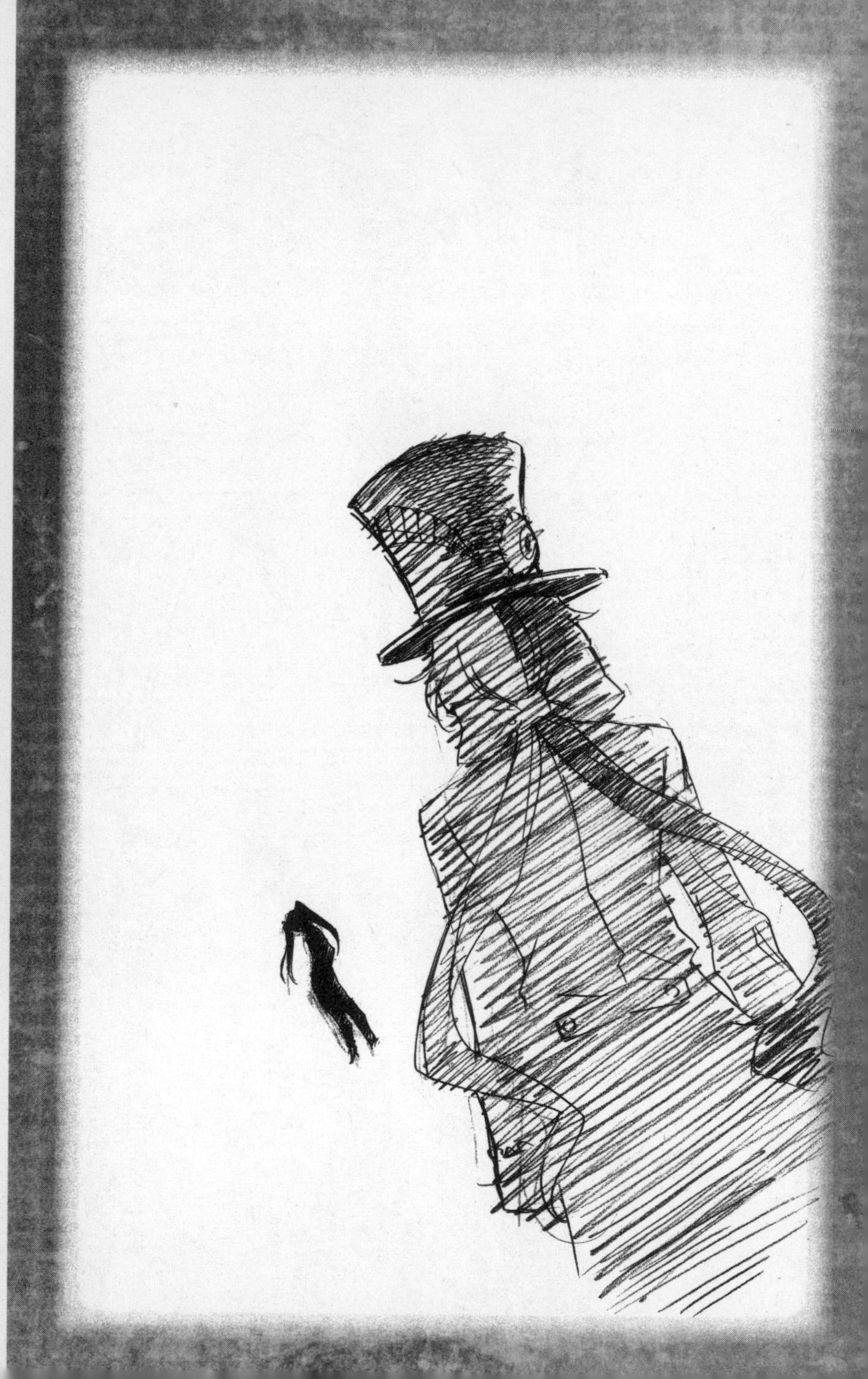

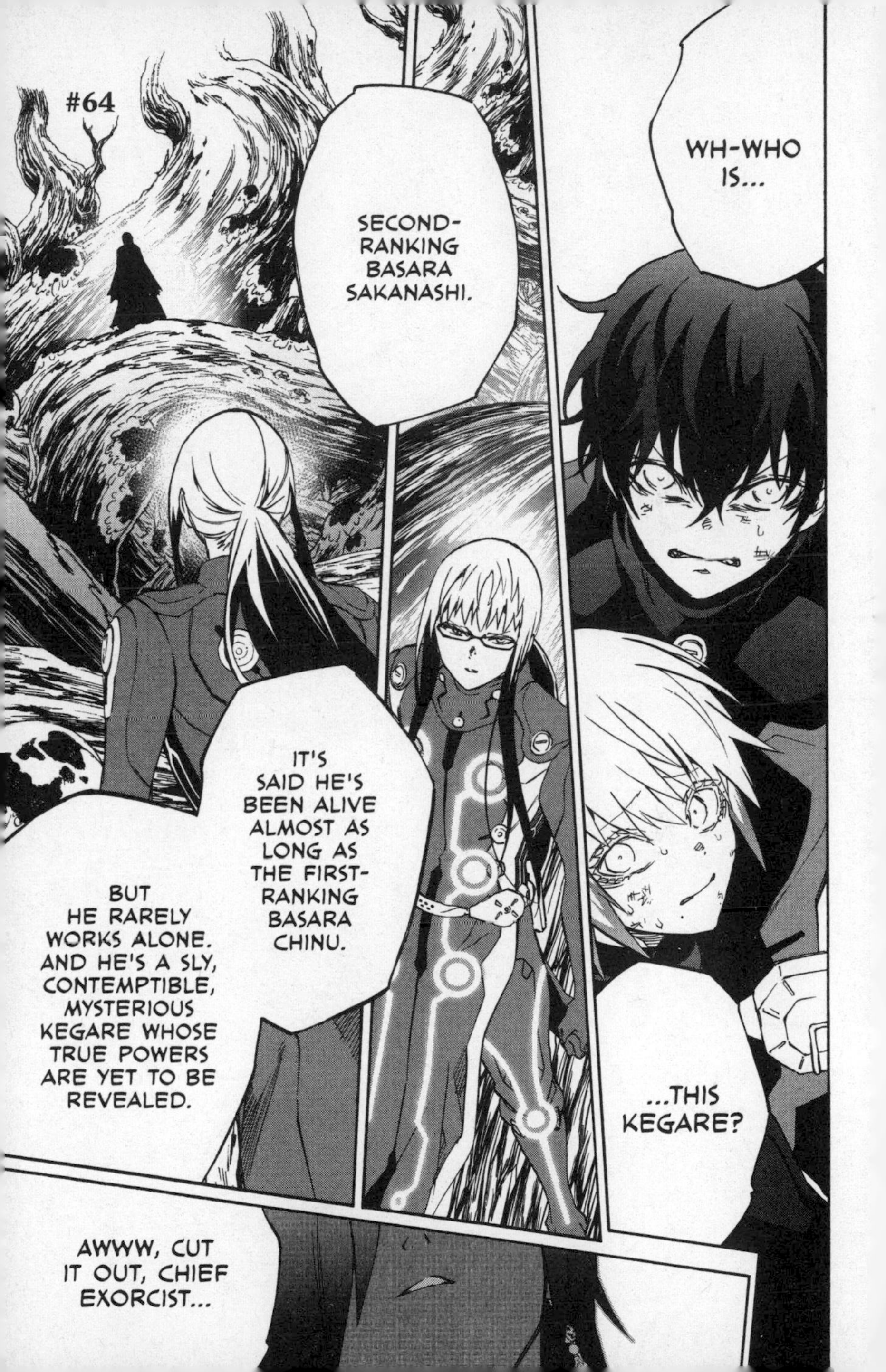
WH-WHO IS...
...THIS KEGARE?
SECOND-RANKING BASARA SAKANASHI.
IT'S SAID HE'S BEEN ALIVE ALMOST AS LONG AS THE FIRST-RANKING BASARA CHINU.
#64
BUT HE RARELY WORKS ALONE. AND HE'S A SLY, CONTEMPTIBLE, MYSTERIOUS KEGARE WHOSE TRUE POWERS ARE YET TO BE REVEALED.
AWWW, CUT IT OUT, CHIEF EXORCIST...

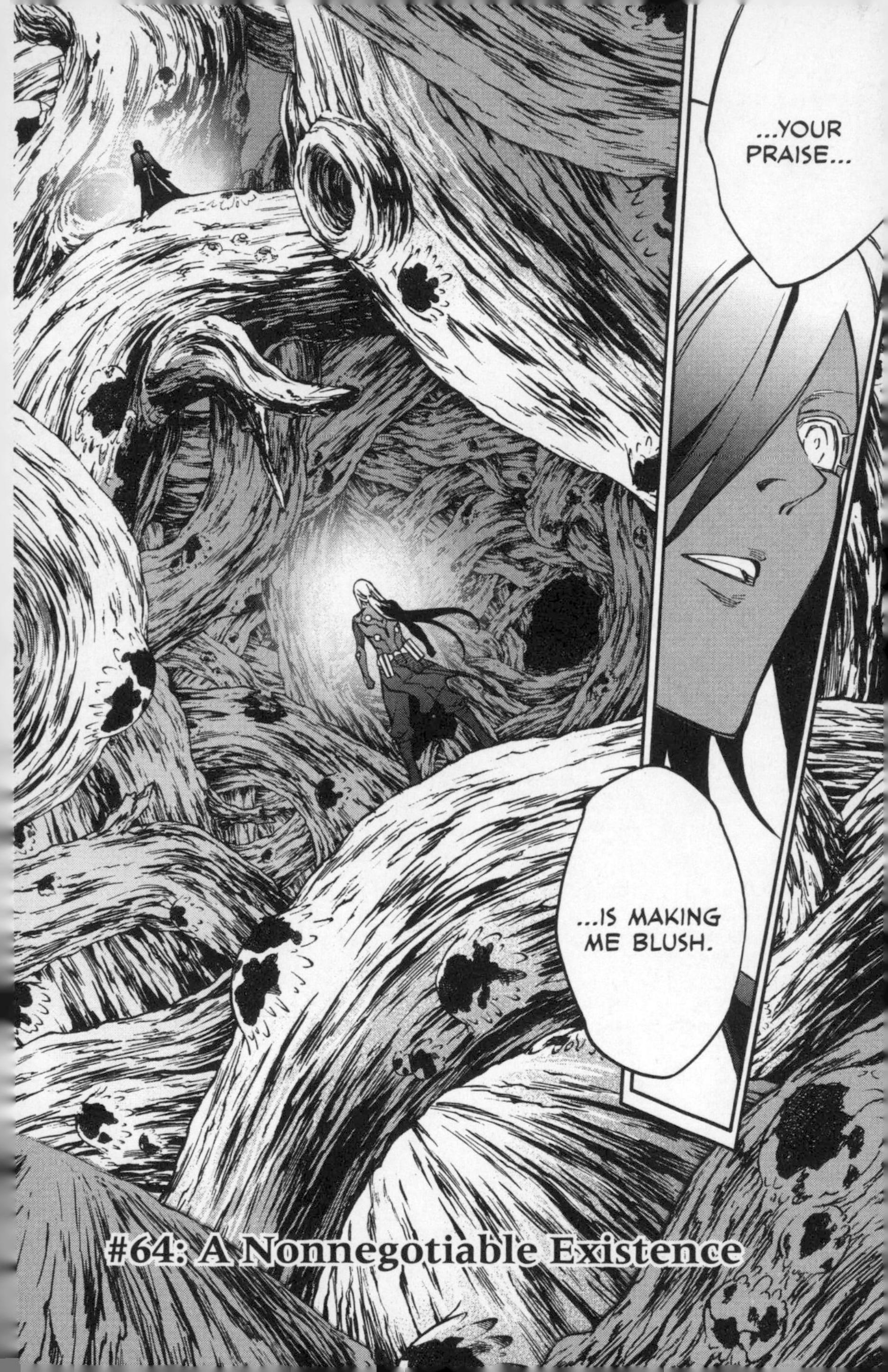
...YOUR PRAISE...
...IS MAKING ME BLUSH.
#64: A Nonnegotiable Existence

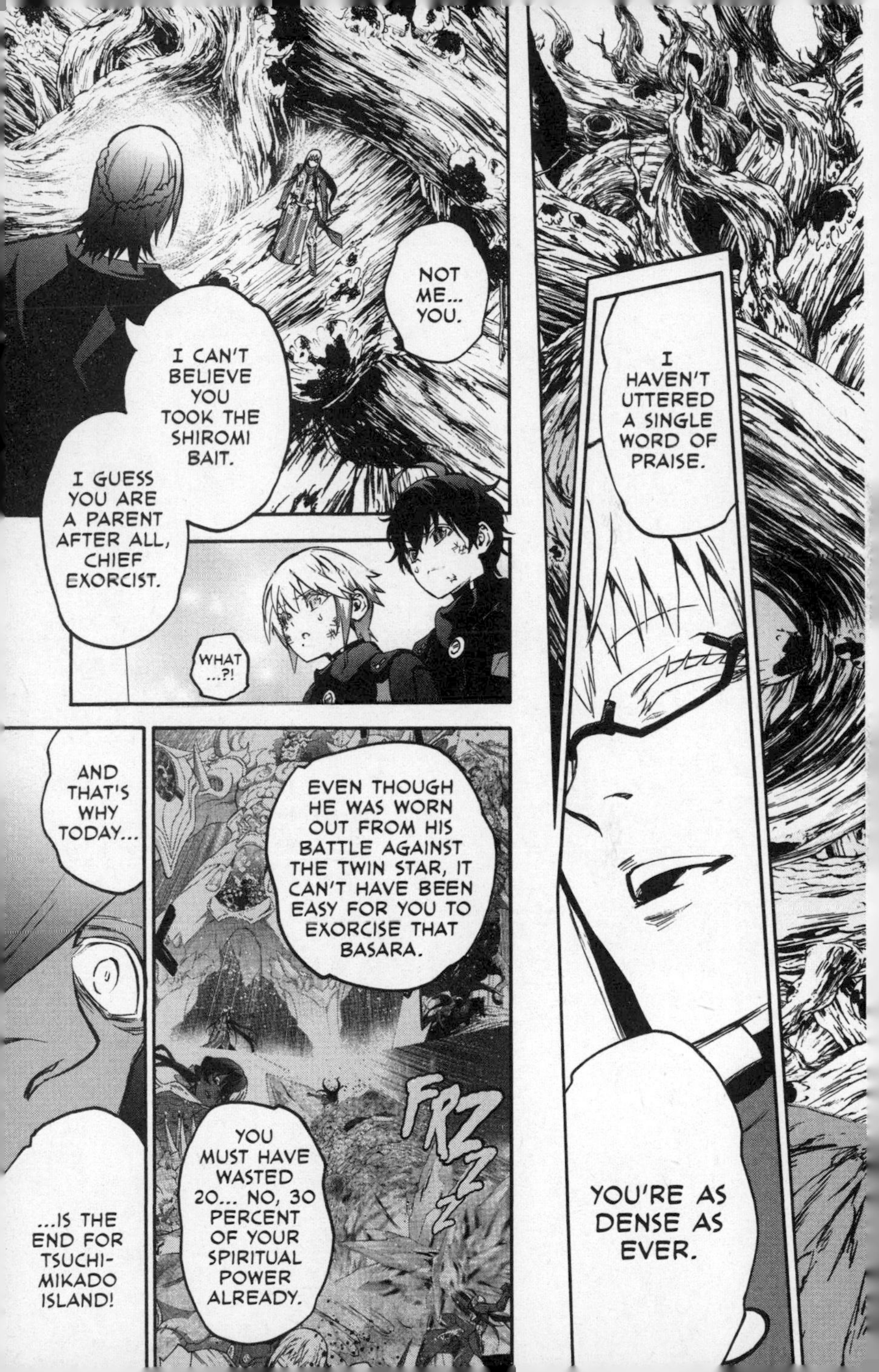
I HAVEN'T UTTERED A SINGLE WORD OF PRAISE.
YOU'RE AS DENSE AS EVER.
NOT ME... YOU.
I CAN'T BELIEVE YOU TOOK THE SHIROMI BAIT.
I GUESS YOU ARE A PARENT AFTER ALL, CHIEF EXORCIST.
WHAT ...?!
EVEN THOUGH HE WAS WORN OUT FROM HIS BATTLE AGAINST THE TWIN STAR, IT CAN'T HAVE BEEN EASY FOR YOU TO EXORCISE THAT BASARA.
FRZZZ
YOU MUST HAVE WASTED 20... NO, 30 PERCENT OF YOUR SPIRITUAL POWER ALREADY.
AND THAT'S WHY TODAY...
...IS THE END FOR TSUCHI-MIKADO ISLAND!

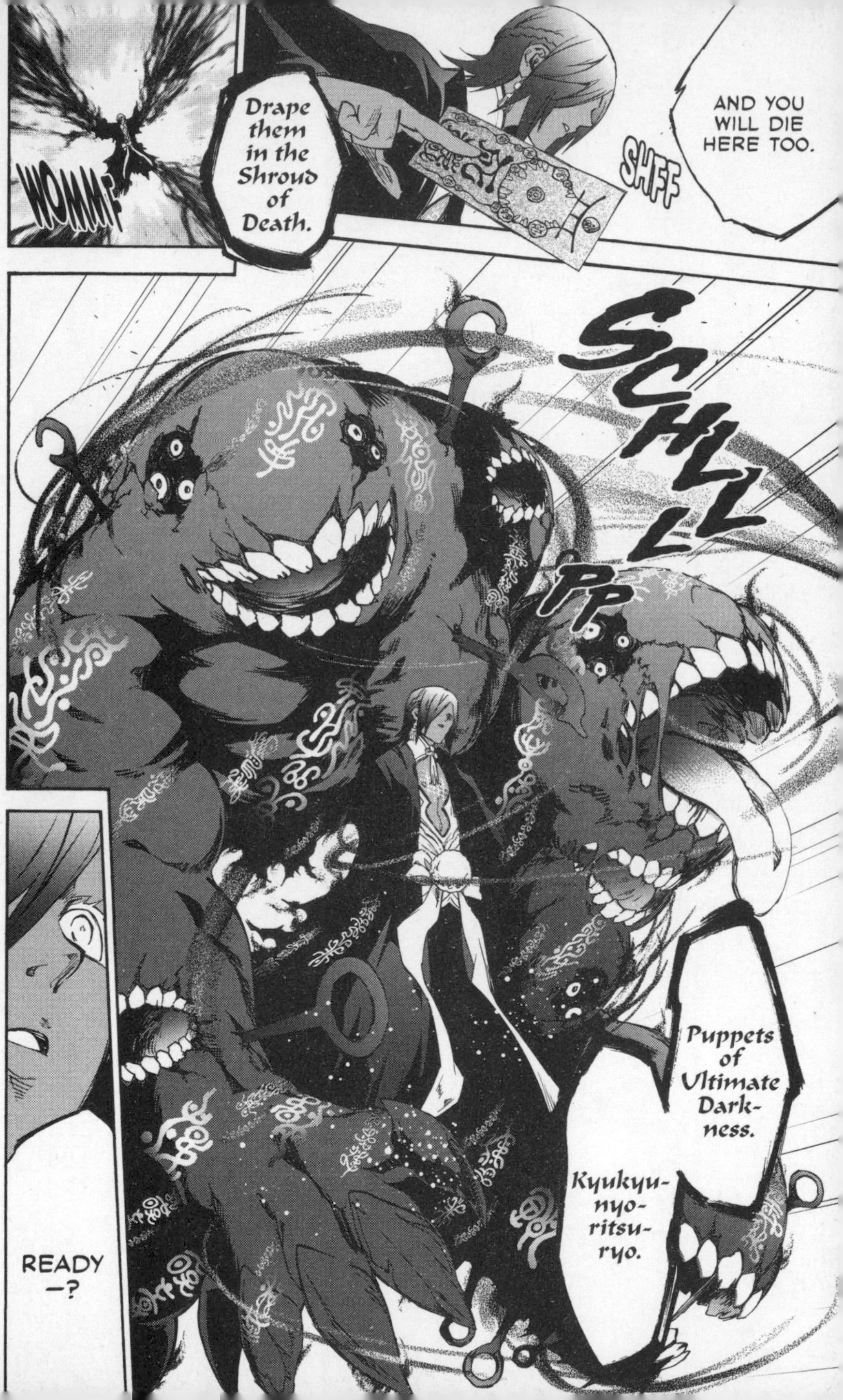
AND YOU WILL DIE HERE TOO.
SHFF
Drape them in the Shroud of Death.
WOMMF
SCHLLLPP
Puppets of Ultimate Dark-ness.
Kyukyu-nyo-ritsu-ryo.
READY —?

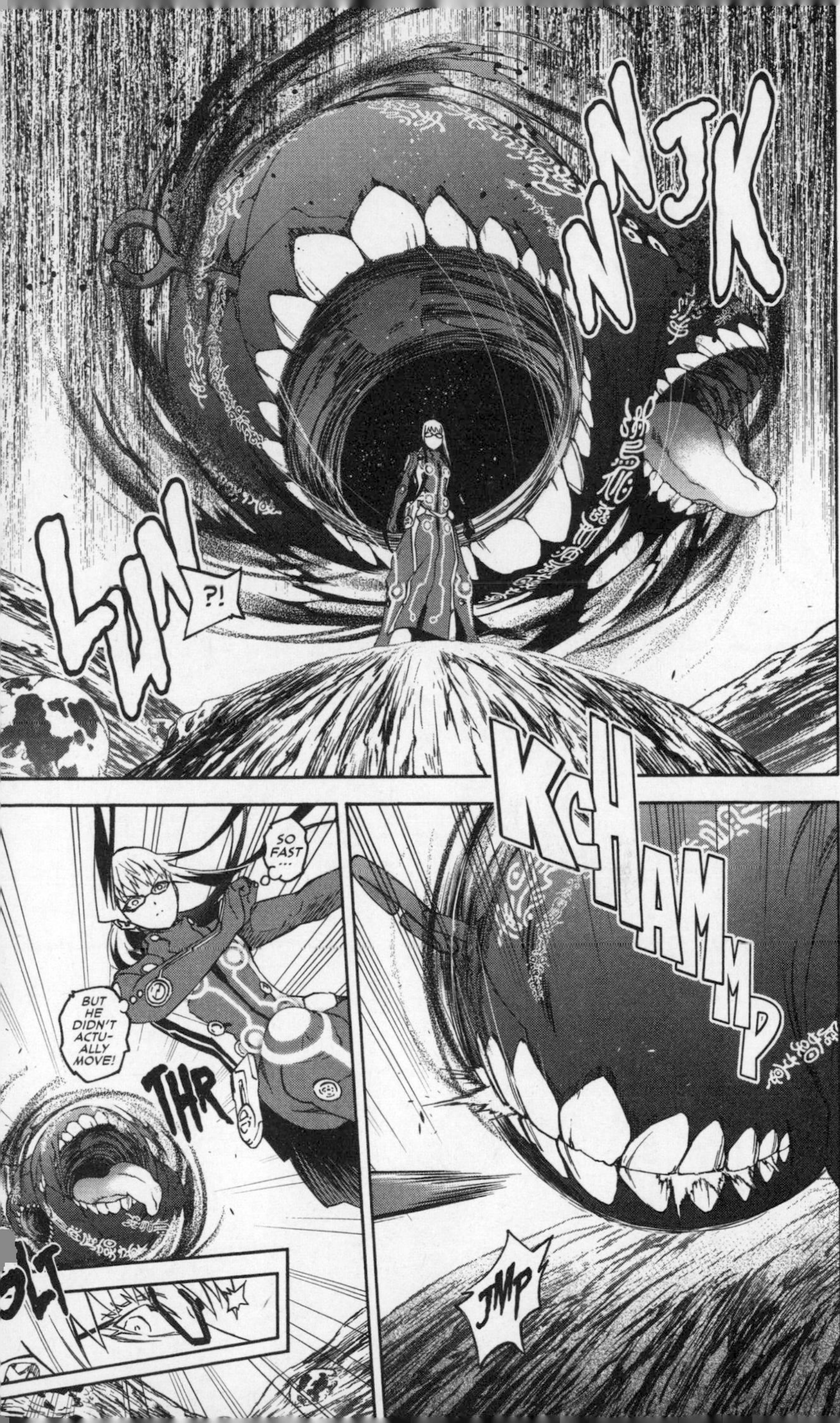
NNJK
?!
KCHAMMP
JMP
SO FAST...
BUT HE DIDN'T ACTU-ALLY MOVE!
THR

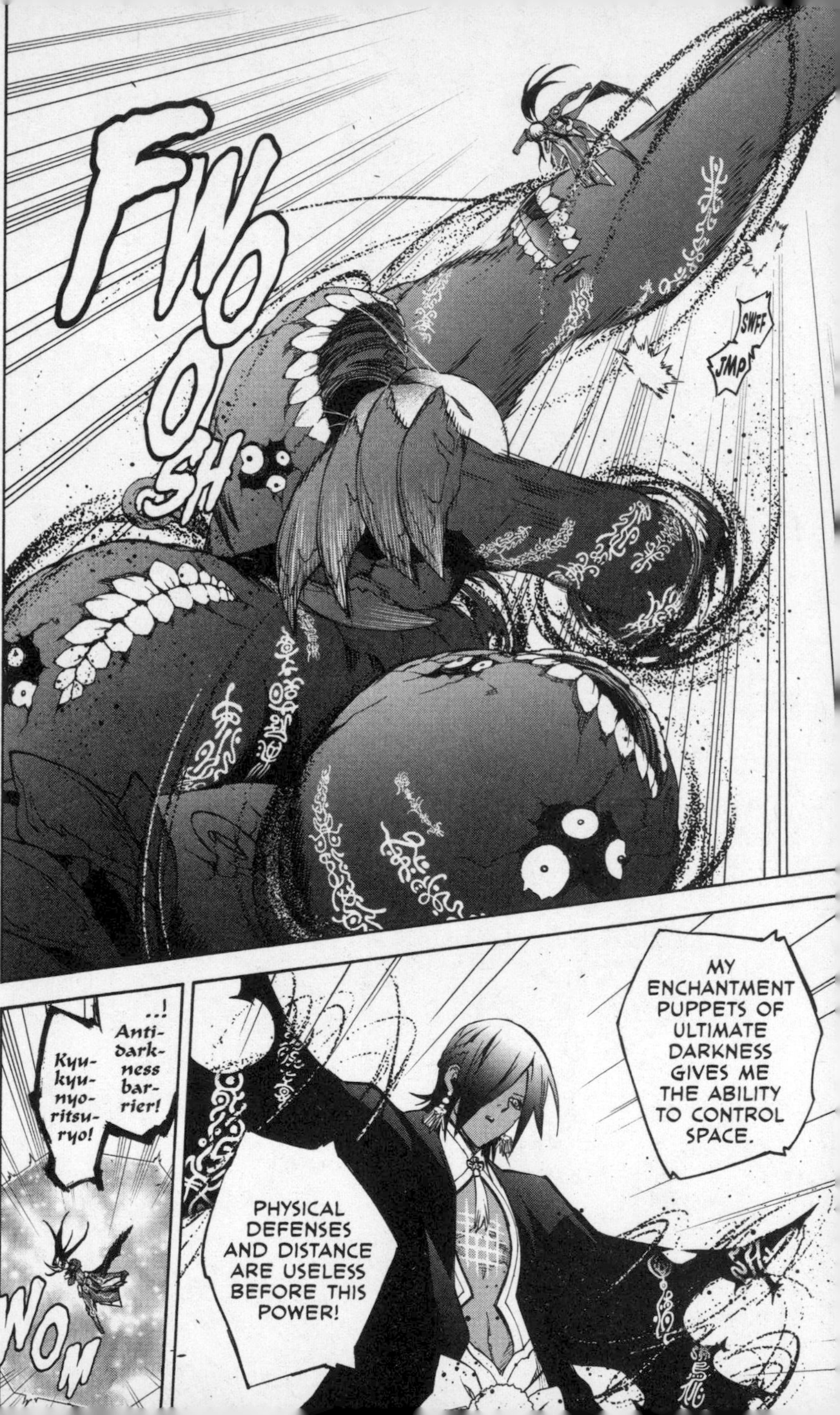
FWOOOSH
SWFF
JMP
MY ENCHANTMENT PUPPETS OF ULTIMATE DARKNESS GIVES ME THE ABILITY TO CONTROL SPACE.
PHYSICAL DEFENSES AND DISTANCE ARE USELESS BEFORE THIS POWER!
...! Anti-darkness barrier!
Kyukyunyoritsuryo!
WOM

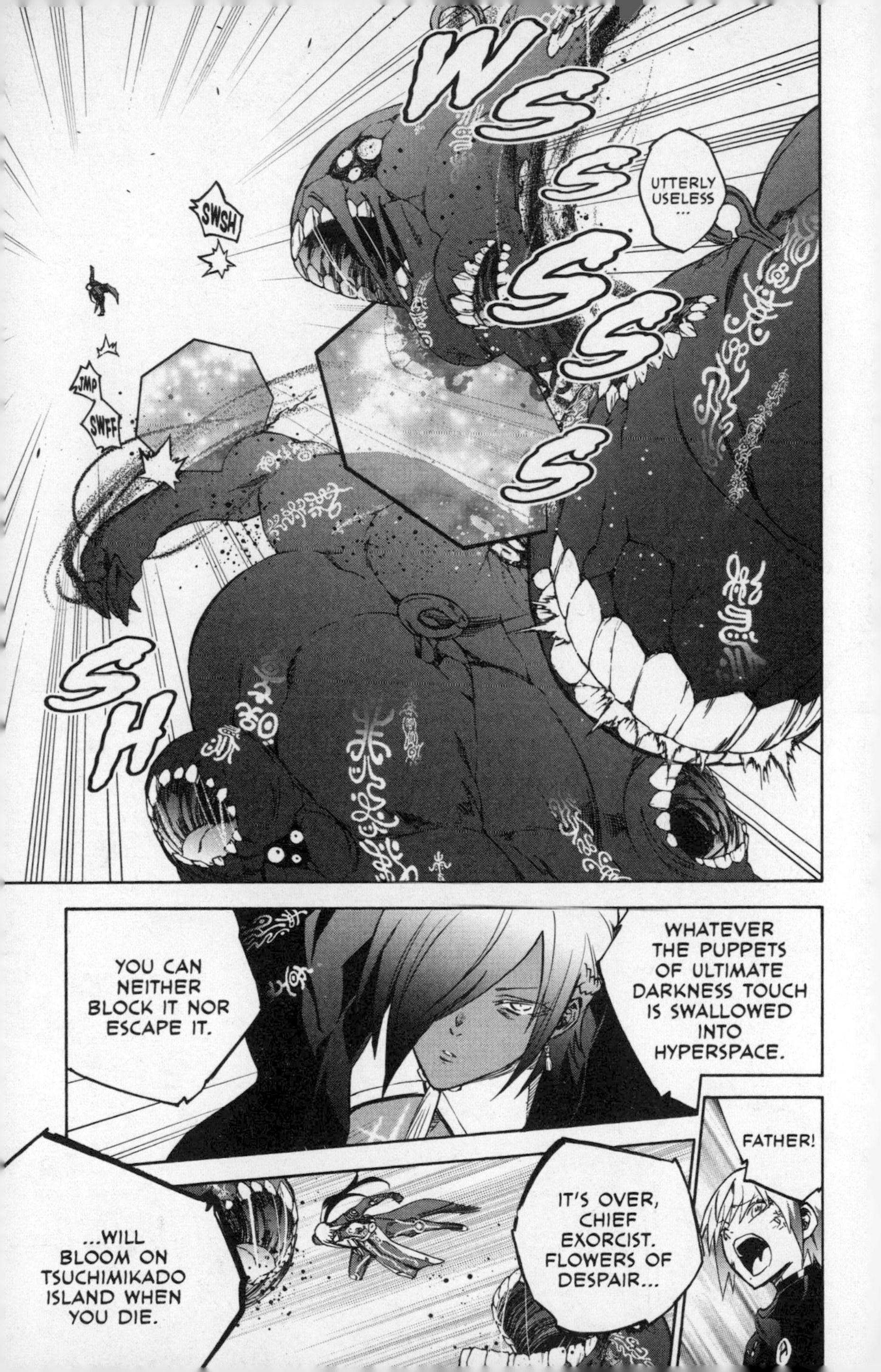
WSSSSSS
UTTERLY USELESS...
SWSH
JMP
SWFF
SH
WHATEVER THE PUPPETS OF ULTIMATE DARKNESS TOUCH IS SWALLOWED INTO HYPERSPACE.
YOU CAN NEITHER BLOCK IT NOR ESCAPE IT.
FATHER!
IT'S OVER, CHIEF EXORCIST. FLOWERS OF DESPAIR...
...WILL BLOOM ON TSUCHIMIKADO ISLAND WHEN YOU DIE.

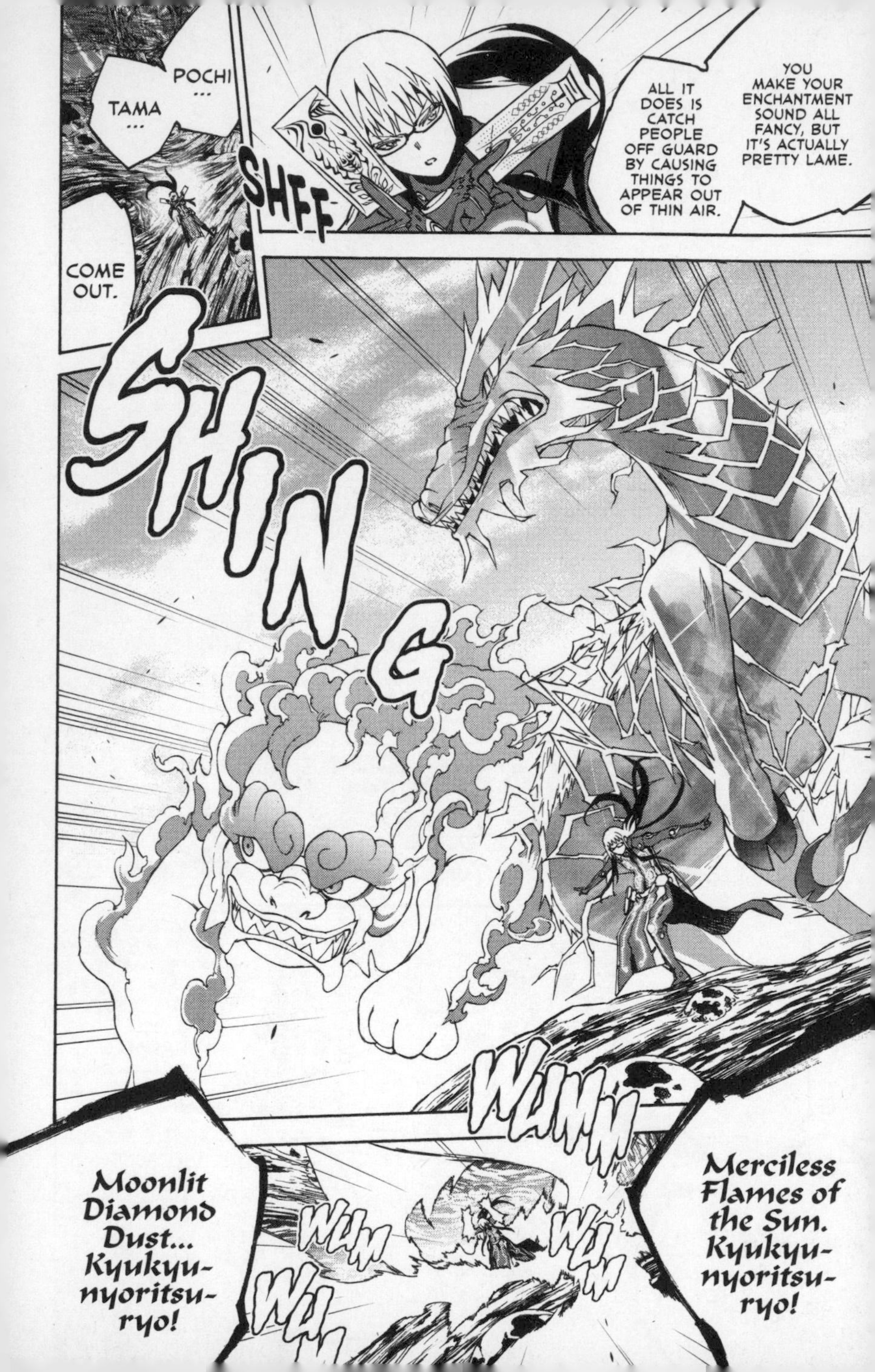
YOU MAKE YOUR ENCHANTMENT SOUND ALL FANCY, BUT IT'S ACTUALLY PRETTY LAME.
ALL IT DOES IS CATCH PEOPLE OFF GUARD BY CAUSING THINGS TO APPEAR OUT OF THIN AIR.
SHFF
POCHI ...
TAMA ...
COME OUT.
SHING
WUMM
Merciless Flames of the Sun. Kyukyu-nyoritsu-ryo!
Moonlit Diamond Dust... Kyukyu-nyoritsu-ryo!

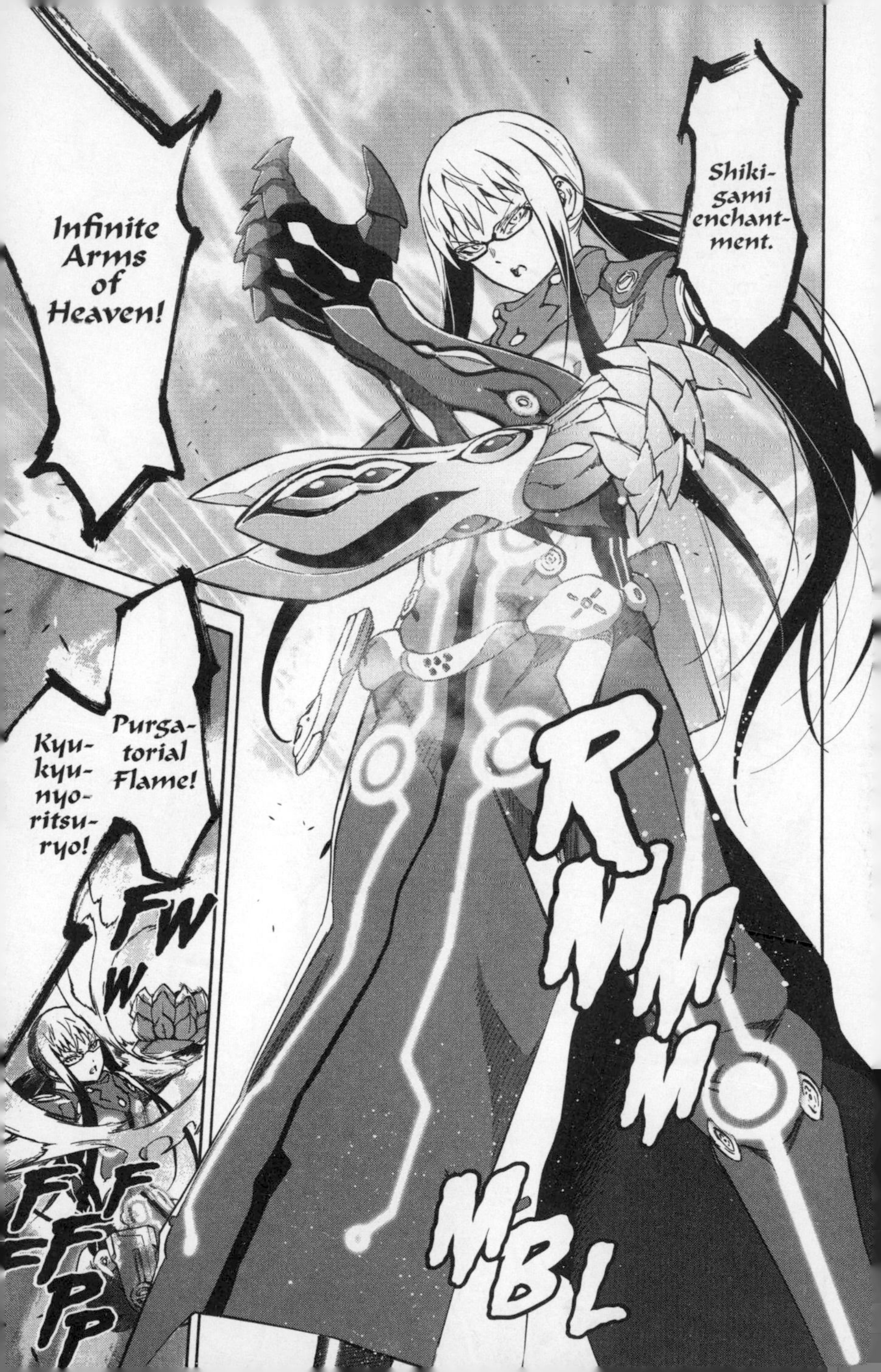
Shiki-gami enchant-ment.
Infinite Arms of Heaven!
RMMMMBL
Purga-torial Flame!
Kyu-kyu-nyo-ritsu-ryo!
FWW
FFFPP

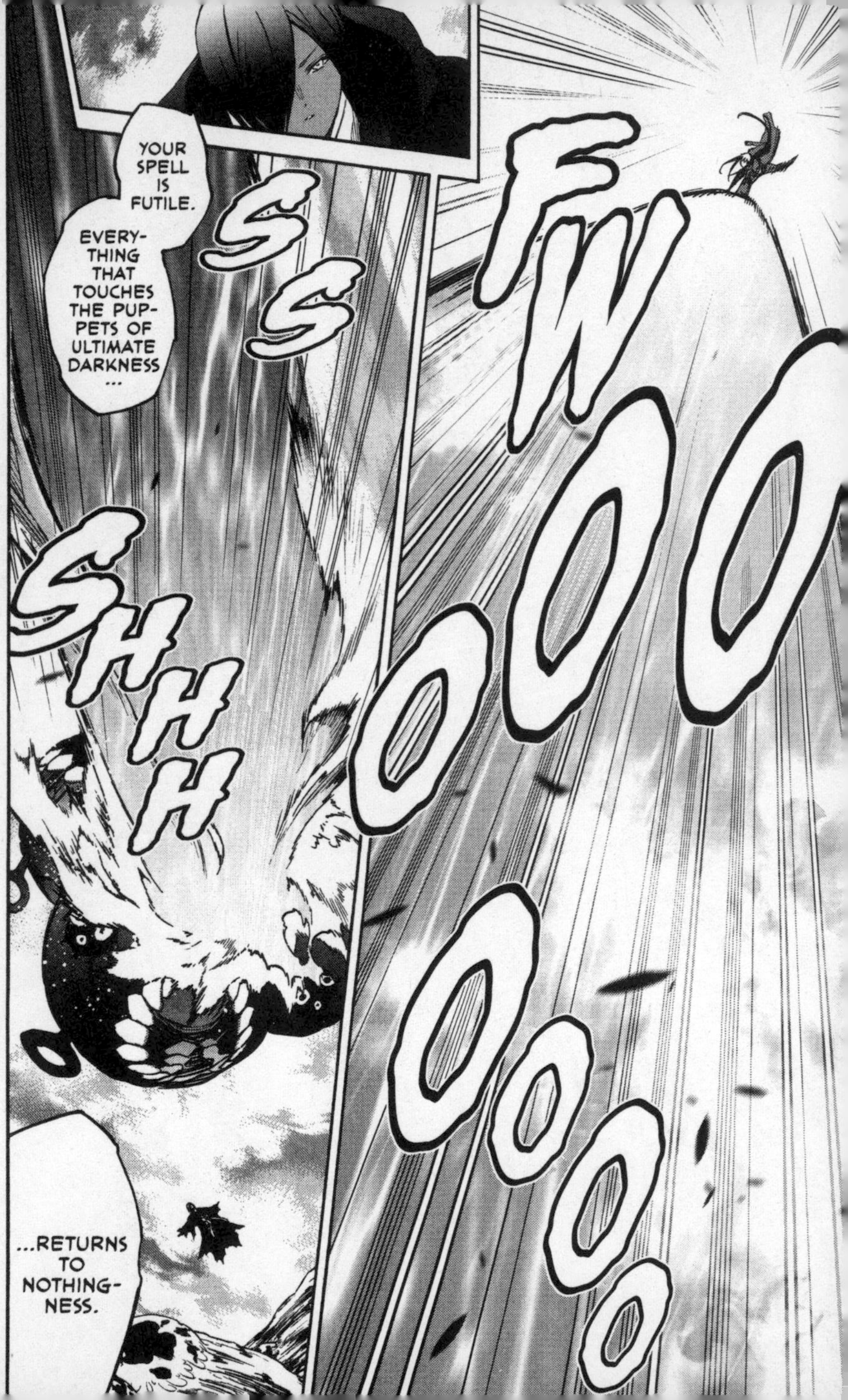
FWOOOOOOOOO
YOUR SPELL IS FUTILE.
EVERY-THING THAT TOUCHES THE PUP-PETS OF ULTIMATE DARKNESS...
SSS
SHHH
...RETURNS TO NOTHING-NESS.

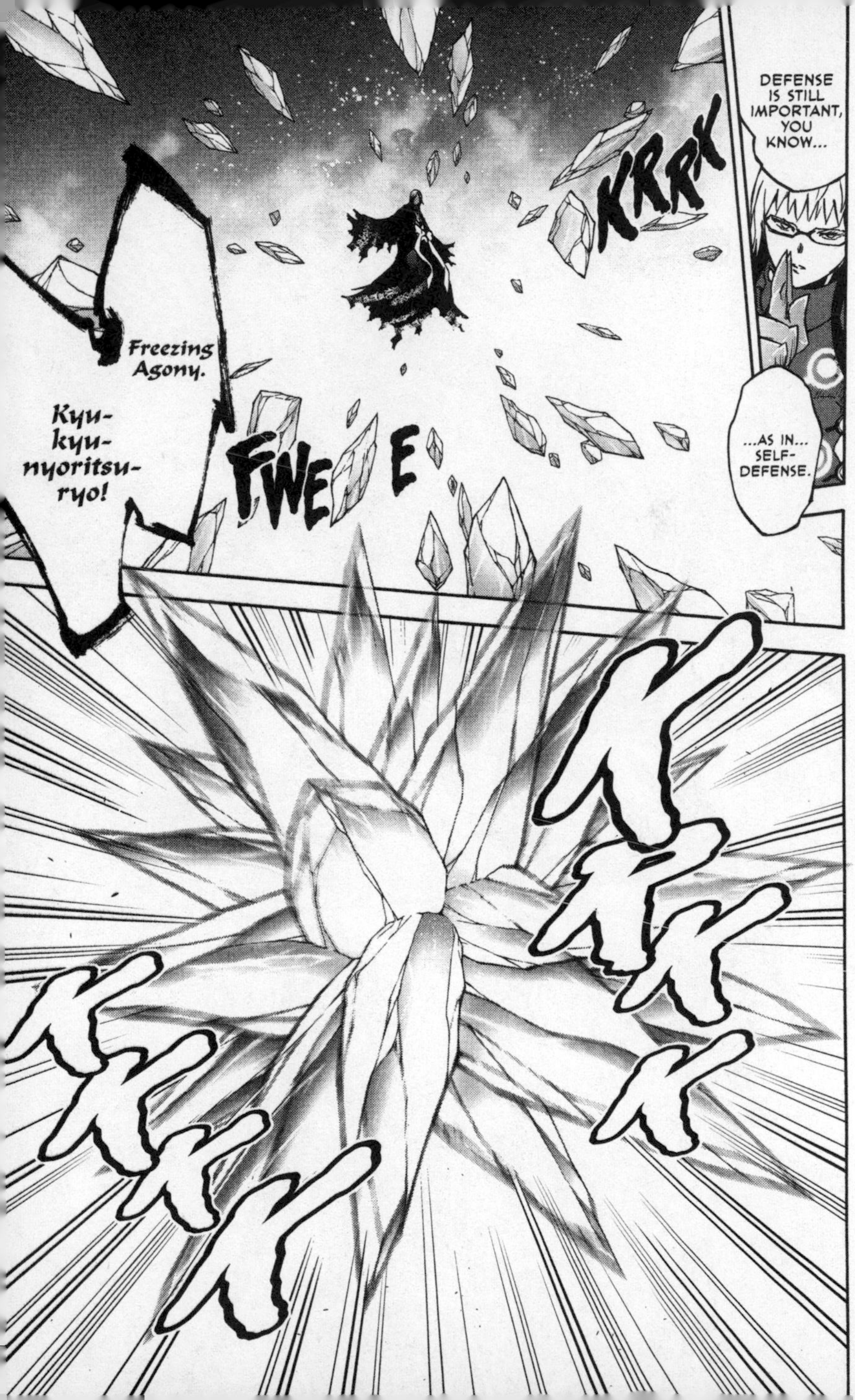
DEFENSE IS STILL IMPORTANT, YOU KNOW...
...AS IN... SELF-DEFENSE.
KRRK
Freezing Agony.
Kyu-kyu-nyoritsu-ryo!
FWE E

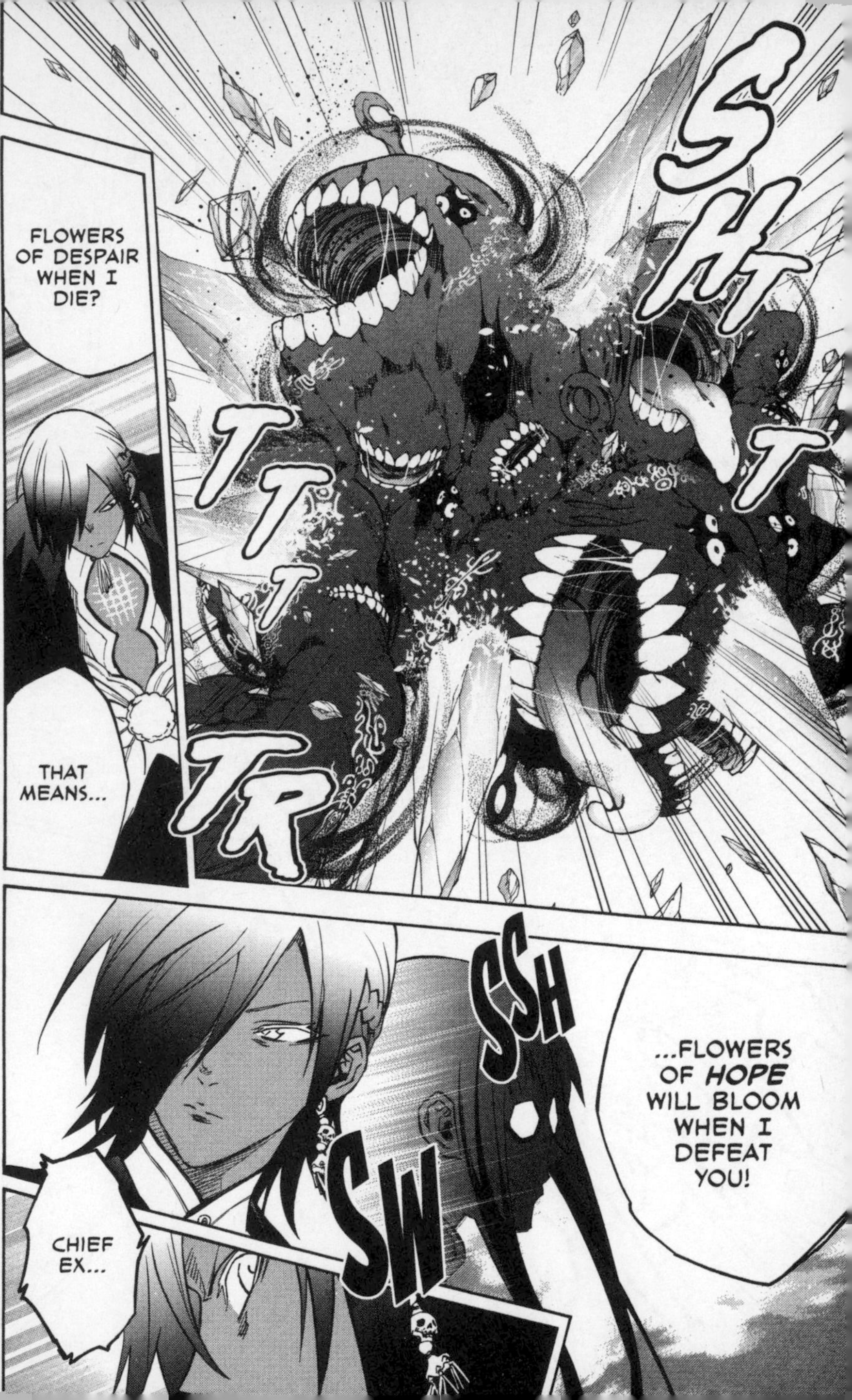
SHT
T
FLOWERS OF DESPAIR WHEN I DIE?
T
T
T
TR
THAT MEANS...
SSH
...FLOWERS OF *HOPE* WILL BLOOM WHEN I DEFEAT YOU!
SW
CHIEF EX...

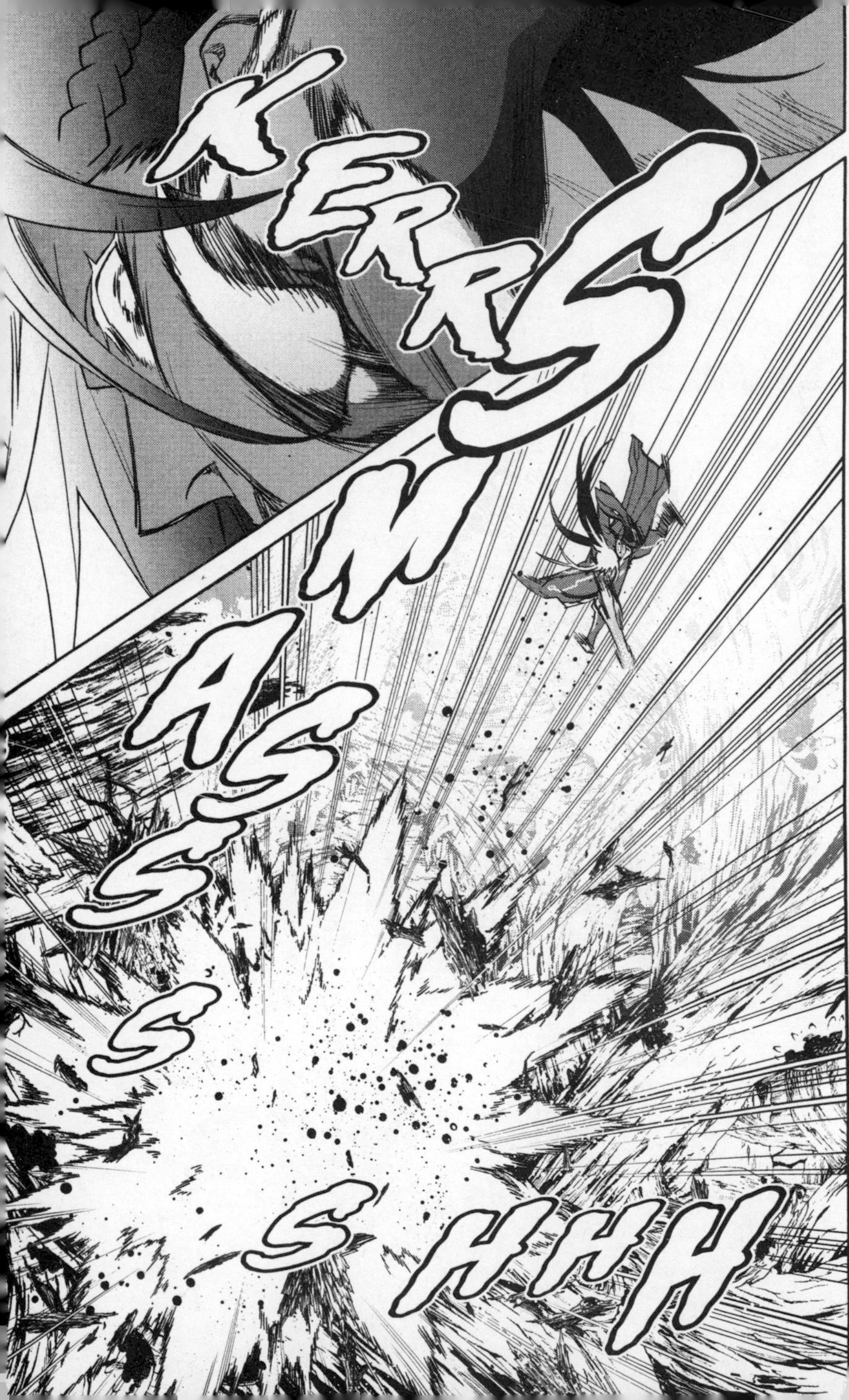
KERRSMASSSSHHH

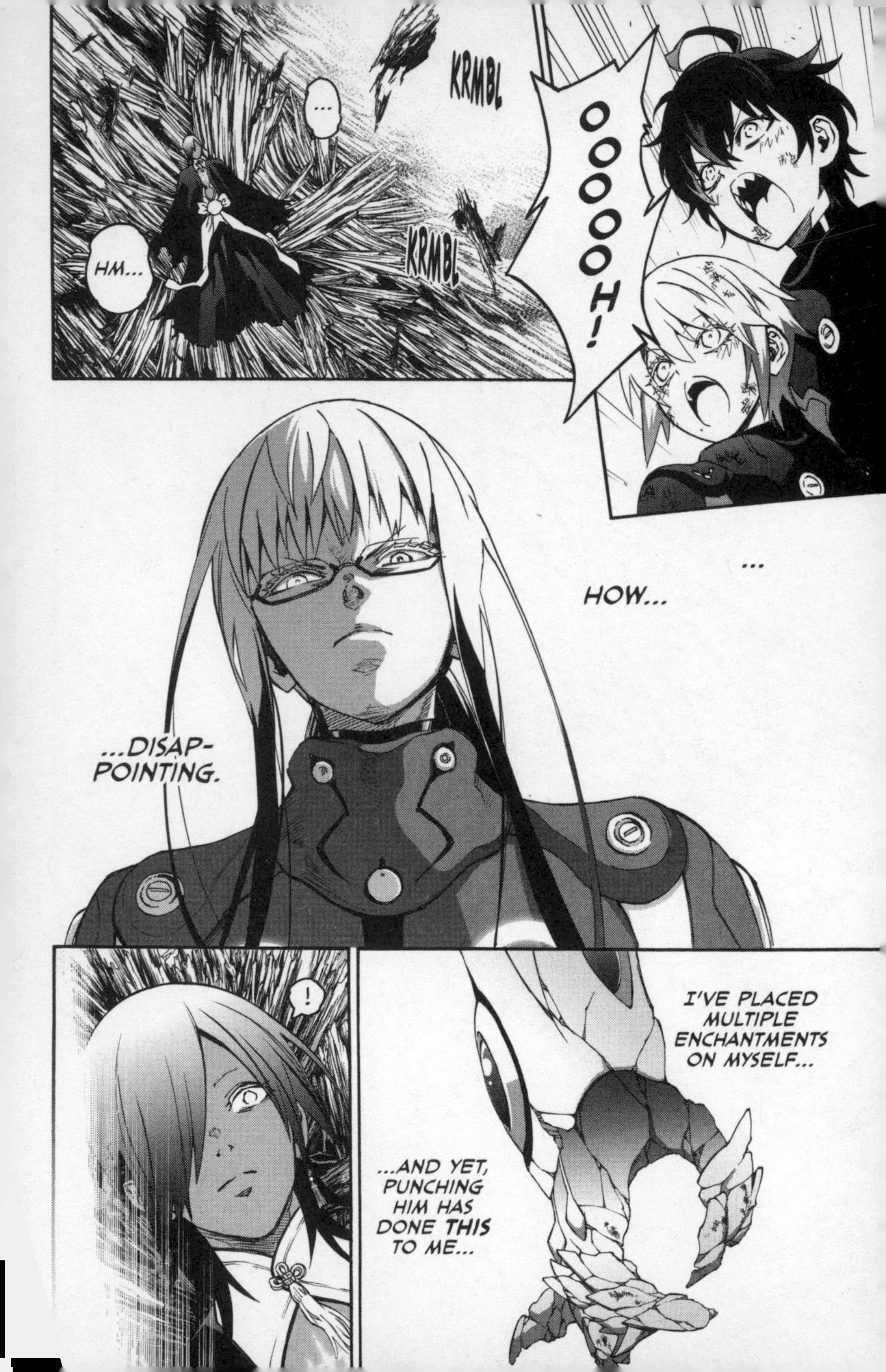
OOOOOOH!
...
KRMBL
KRMBL
HM...
...
HOW...
...DISAP-POINTING.
I'VE PLACED MULTIPLE ENCHANTMENTS ON MYSELF...
...AND YET, PUNCHING HIM HAS DONE THIS TO ME...
!

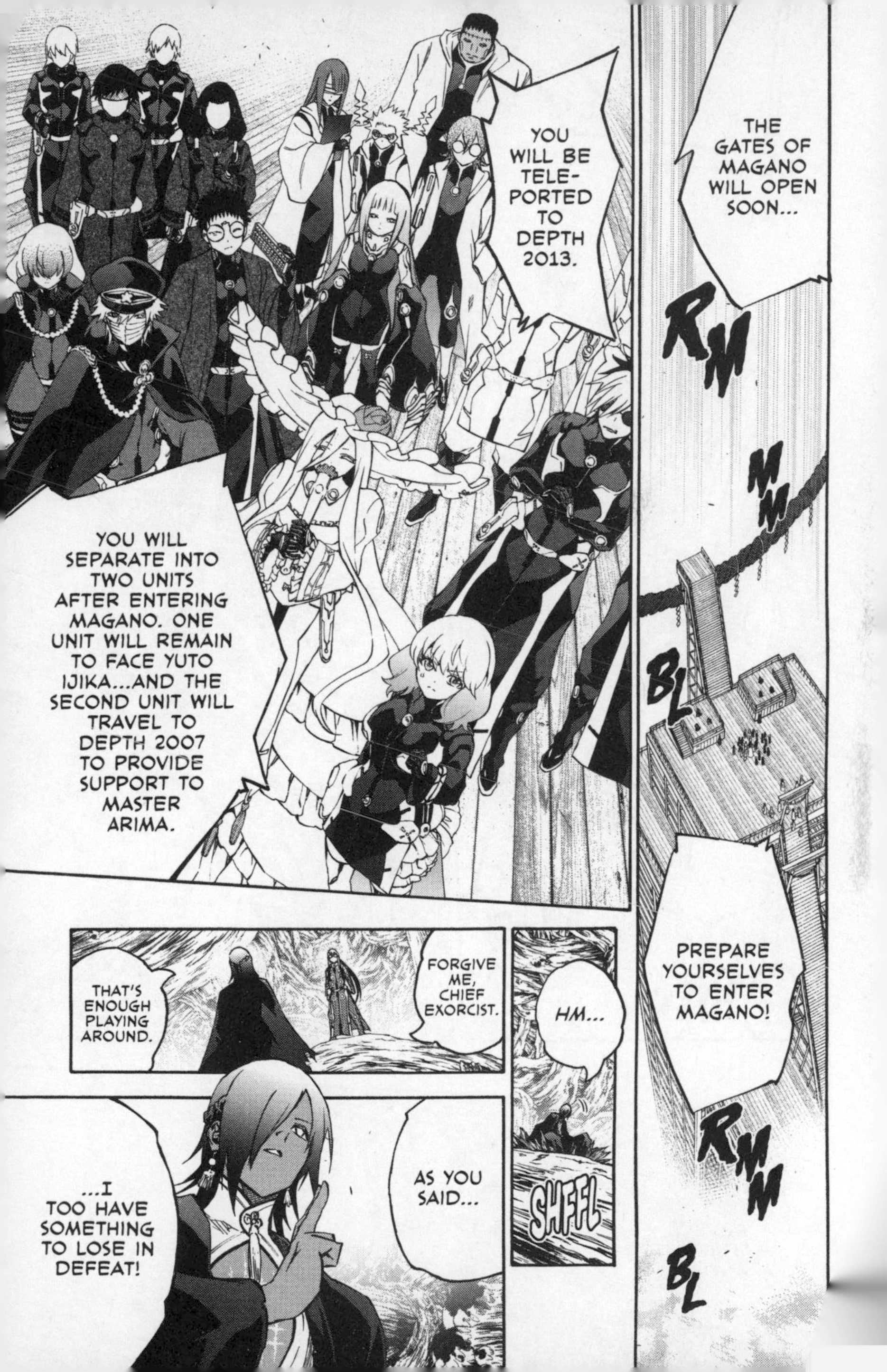
THE GATES OF MAGANO WILL OPEN SOON...
RMMMM
BL
PREPARE YOURSELVES TO ENTER MAGANO!
RMMM
BL
YOU WILL BE TELE-PORTED TO DEPTH 2013.
YOU WILL SEPARATE INTO TWO UNITS AFTER ENTERING MAGANO. ONE UNIT WILL REMAIN TO FACE YUTO IJIKA...AND THE SECOND UNIT WILL TRAVEL TO DEPTH 2007 TO PROVIDE SUPPORT TO MASTER ARIMA.
HM...
SHFFL
FORGIVE ME, CHIEF EXORCIST.
THAT'S ENOUGH PLAYING AROUND.
AS YOU SAID...
...I TOO HAVE SOMETHING TO LOSE IN DEFEAT!

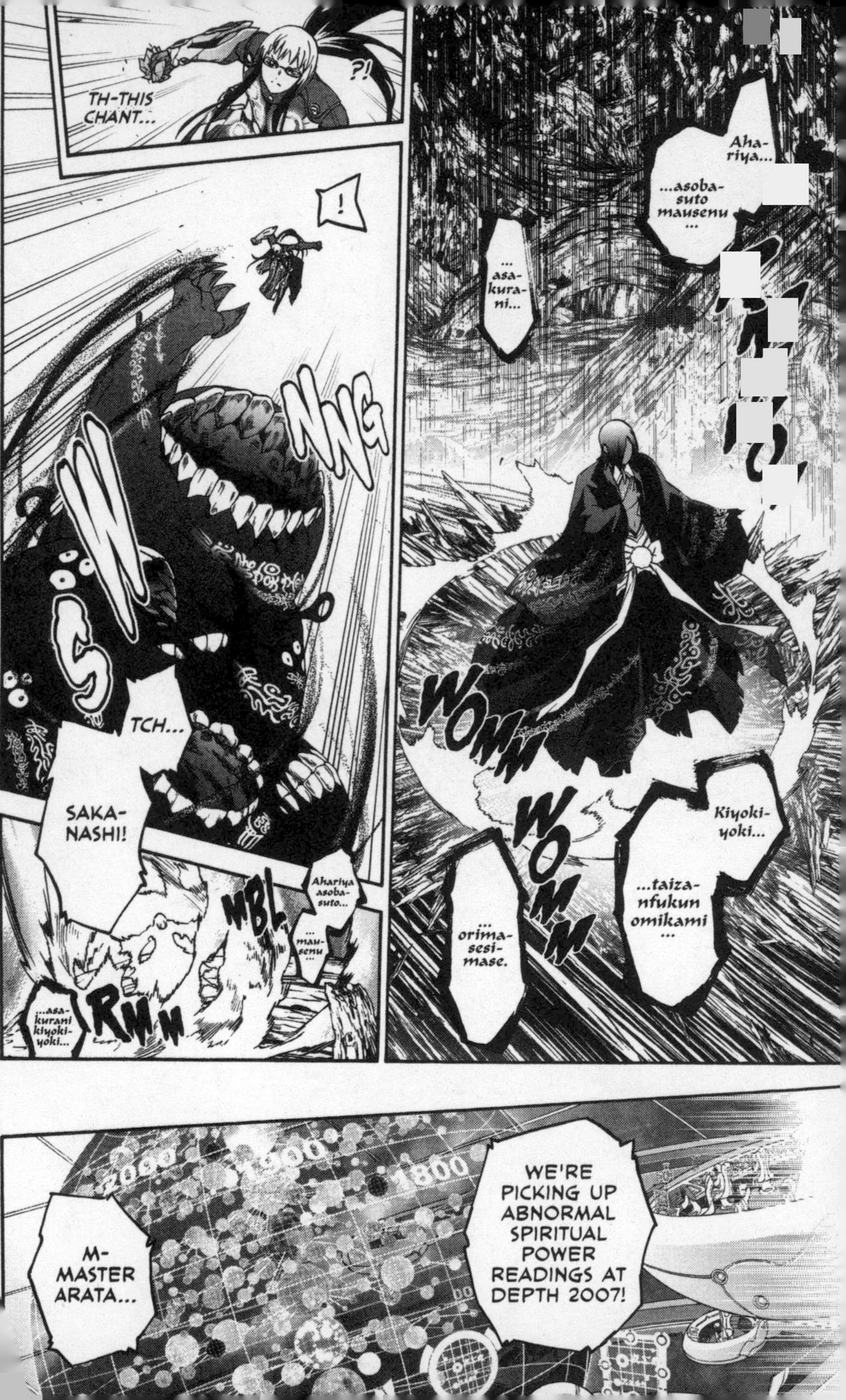

Ahariya...
...asobasuto mausenu...
...asakurani...
WOMM
Kiyokiyoki...
...taizanfukun omikami...
WOMM
...orimasesimase.
?!
TH-THIS CHANT...
!
SWNNG
TCH...
SAKANASHI!
Ahariya asobasuto...
...mausenu...
MBL
RMM
...asakurani kiyokiyoki...
2000
1900
1800
WE'RE PICKING UP ABNORMAL SPIRITUAL POWER READINGS AT DEPTH 2007!
M-MASTER ARATA...

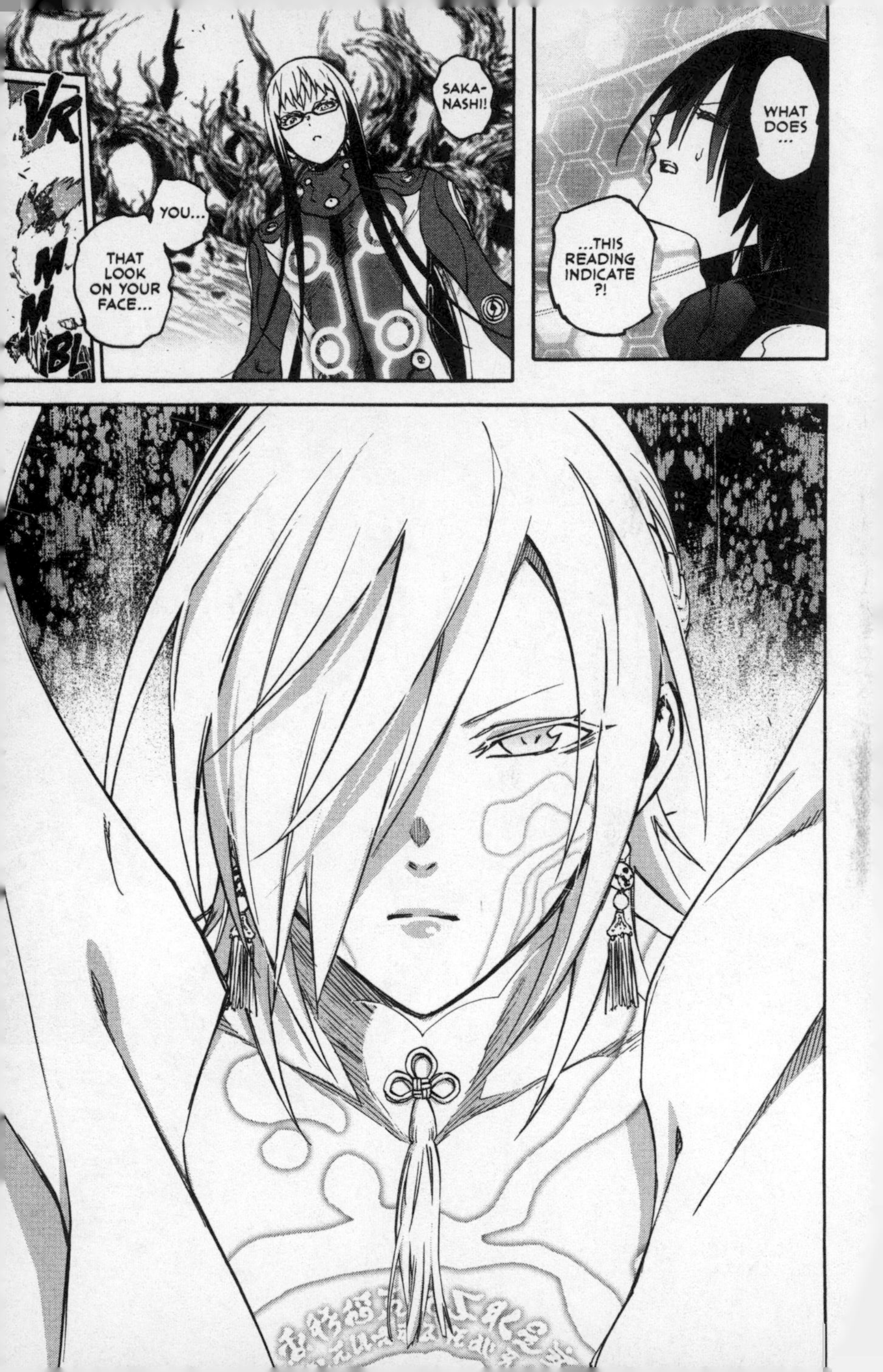
WHAT DOES...
...THIS READING INDICATE?!
SAKA-NASHI!
YOU...
THAT LOOK ON YOUR FACE...
VRMMBL

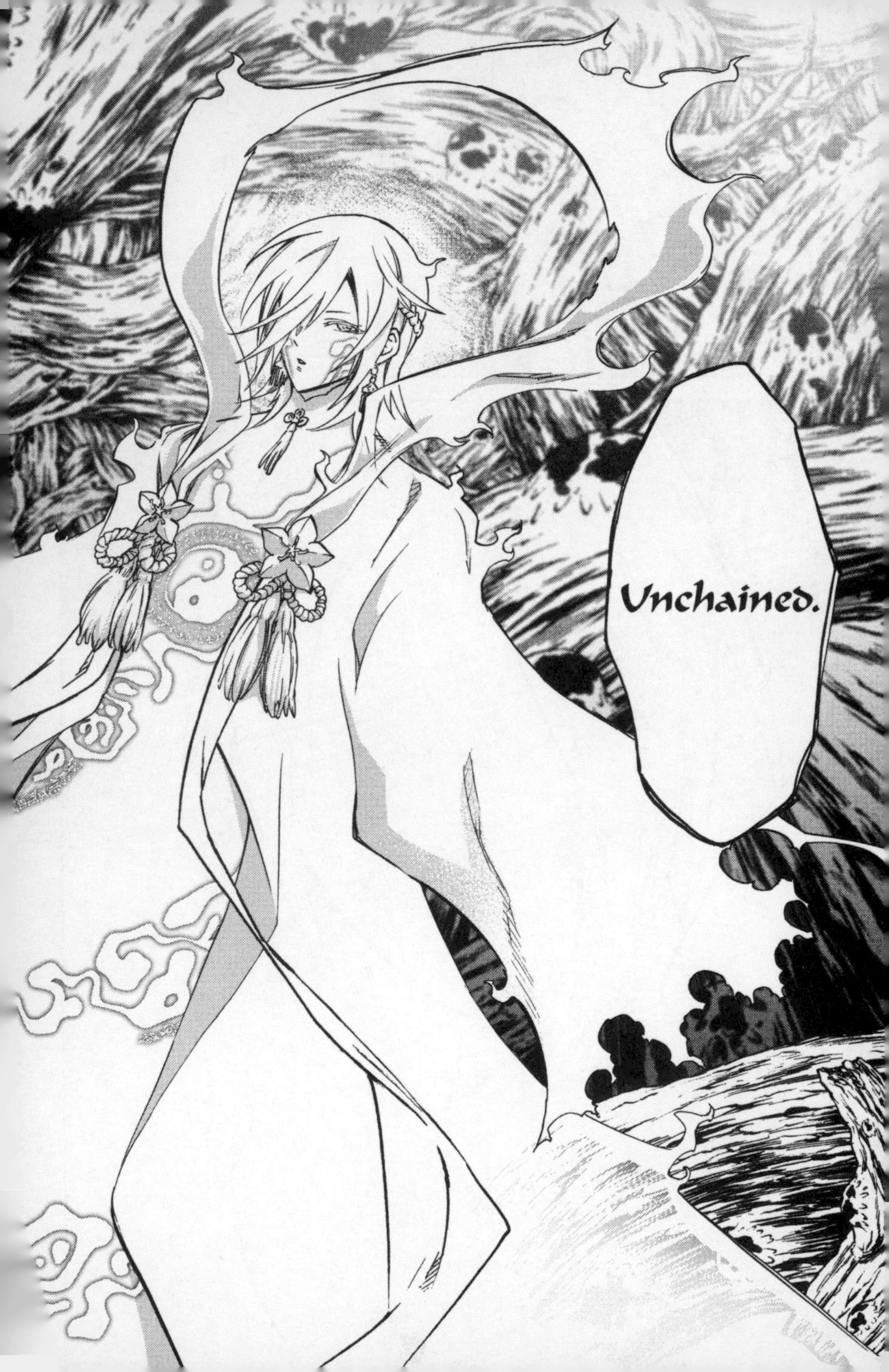
Unchained.

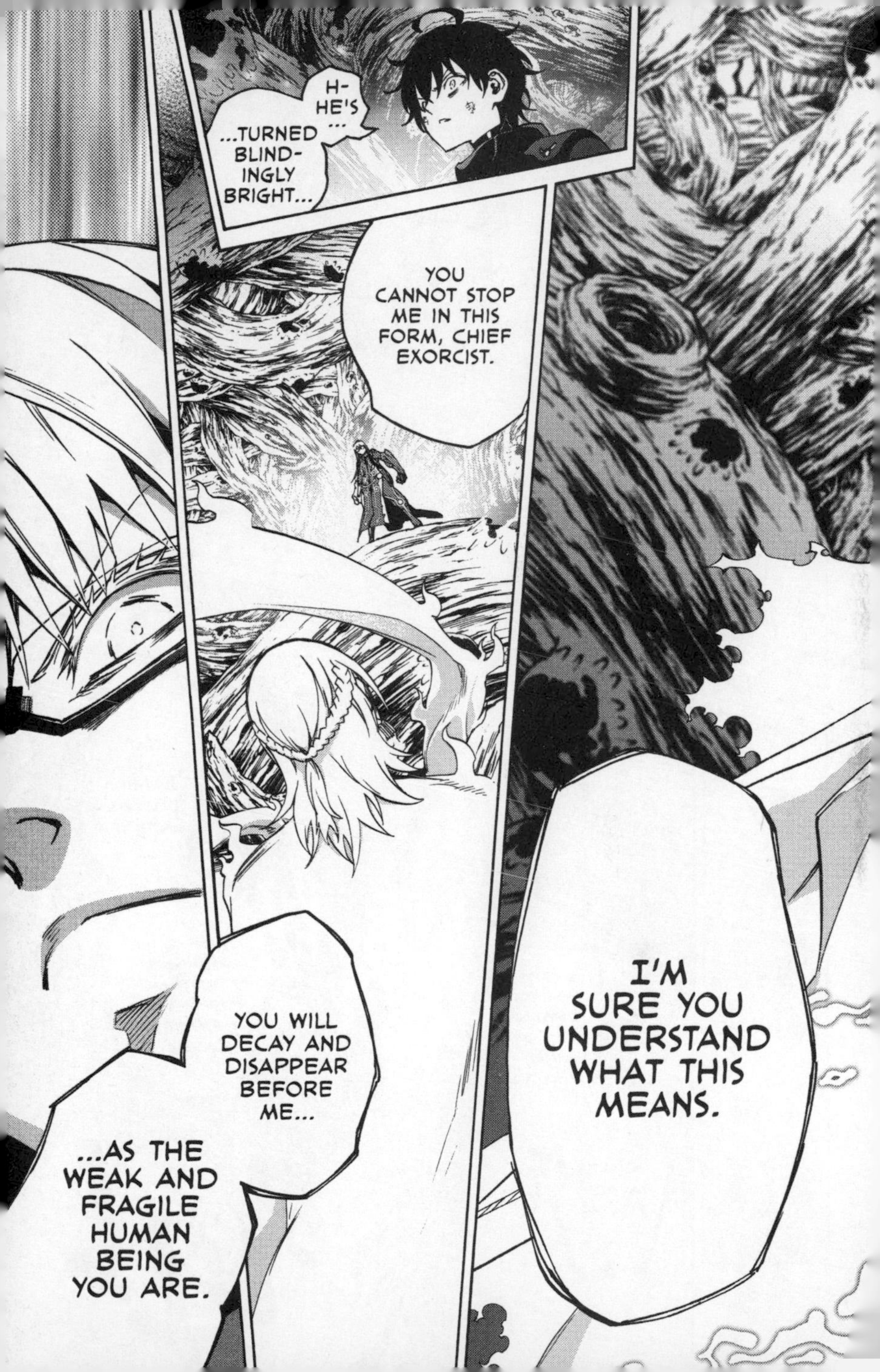
H-HE'S...
...TURNED BLINDINGLY BRIGHT...
YOU CANNOT STOP ME IN THIS FORM, CHIEF EXORCIST.
I'M SURE YOU UNDERSTAND WHAT THIS MEANS.
YOU WILL DECAY AND DISAPPEAR BEFORE ME...
...AS THE WEAK AND FRAGILE HUMAN BEING YOU ARE.

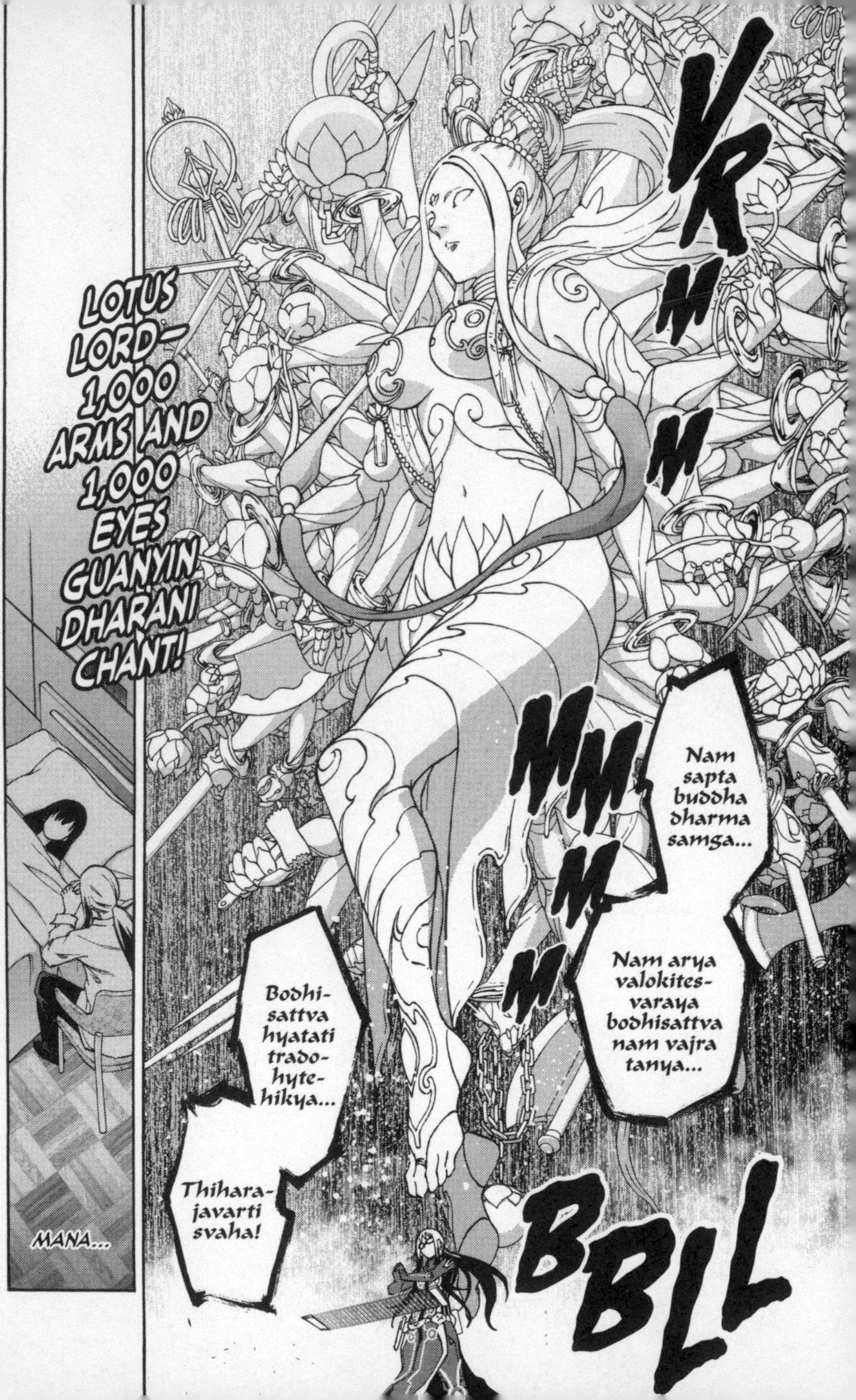
VRMMM
LOTUS LORD—1,000 ARMS AND 1,000 EYES GUANYIN DHARANI CHANT!
MMMM
Nam sapta buddha dharma samga...
Nam arya valokites-varaya bodhisattva nam vajra tanya...
Bodhi-sattva hyatati trado-hyte-hikya...
Thihara-javarti svaha!
BBLL
MANA...

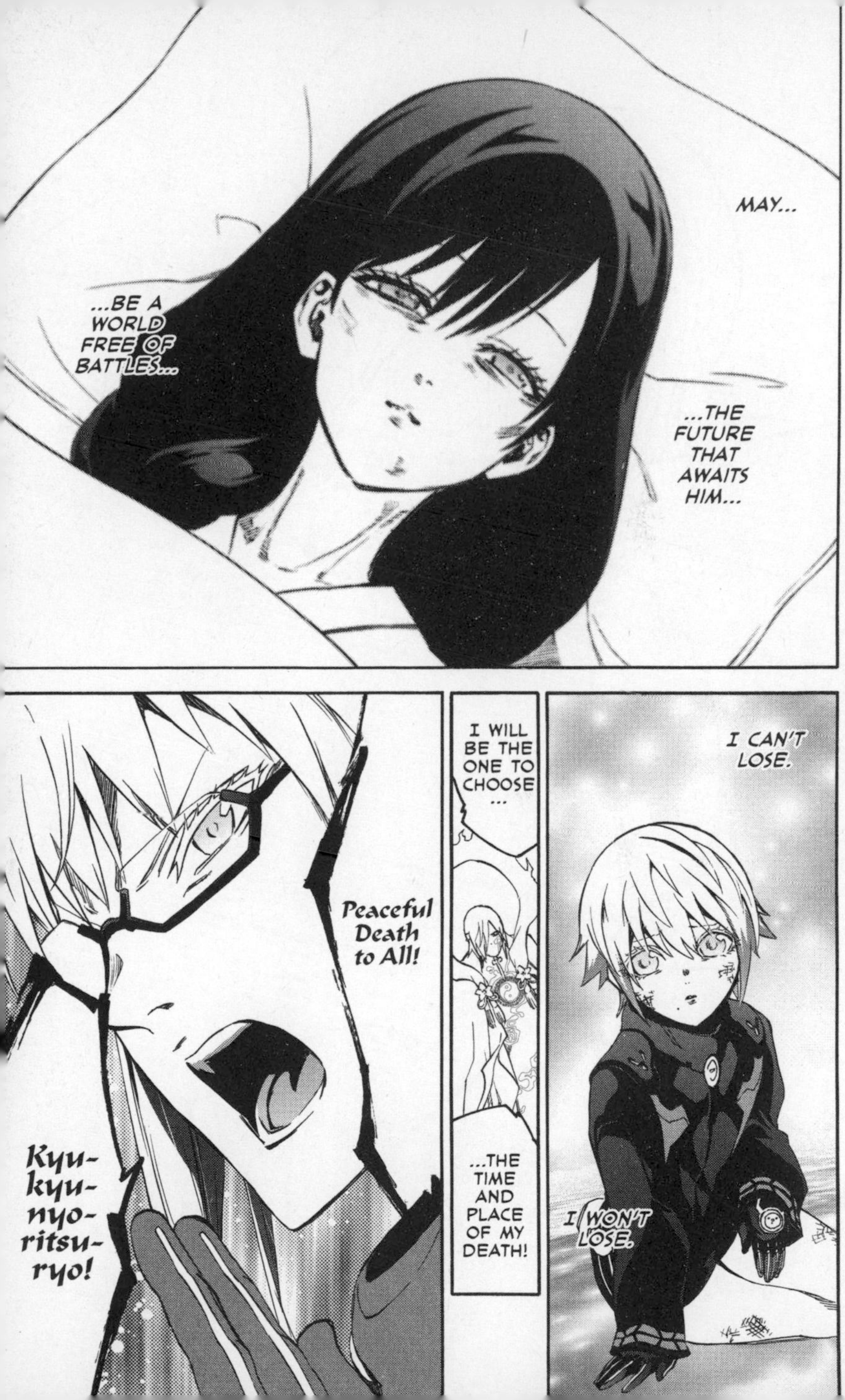
MAY...
...THE FUTURE THAT AWAITS HIM...
...BE A WORLD FREE OF BATTLES...
I CAN'T LOSE.
I WON'T LOSE.
I WILL BE THE ONE TO CHOOSE ...
...THE TIME AND PLACE OF MY DEATH!
Peaceful Death to All!
Kyu-kyu-nyo-ritsu-ryo!

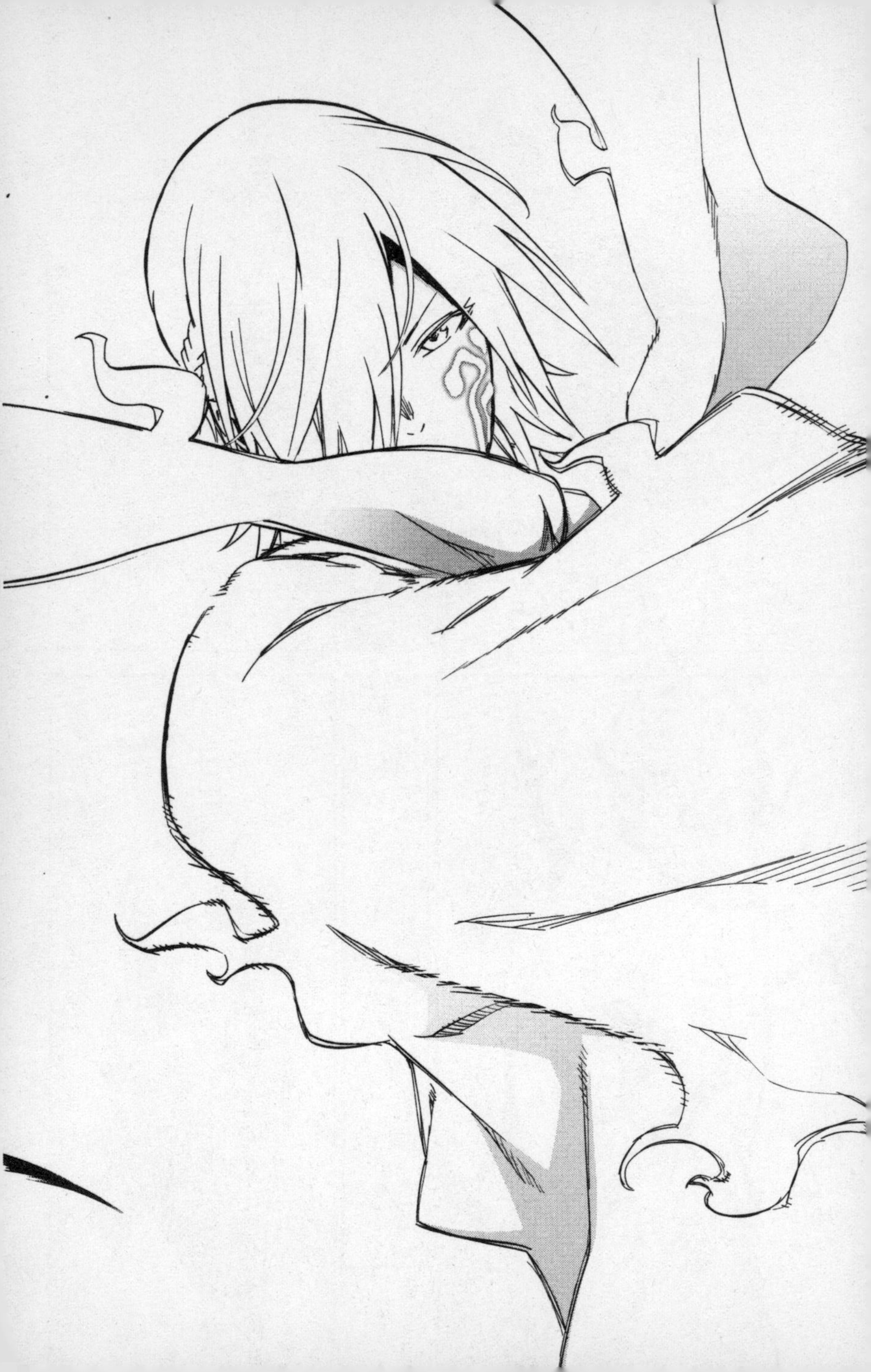

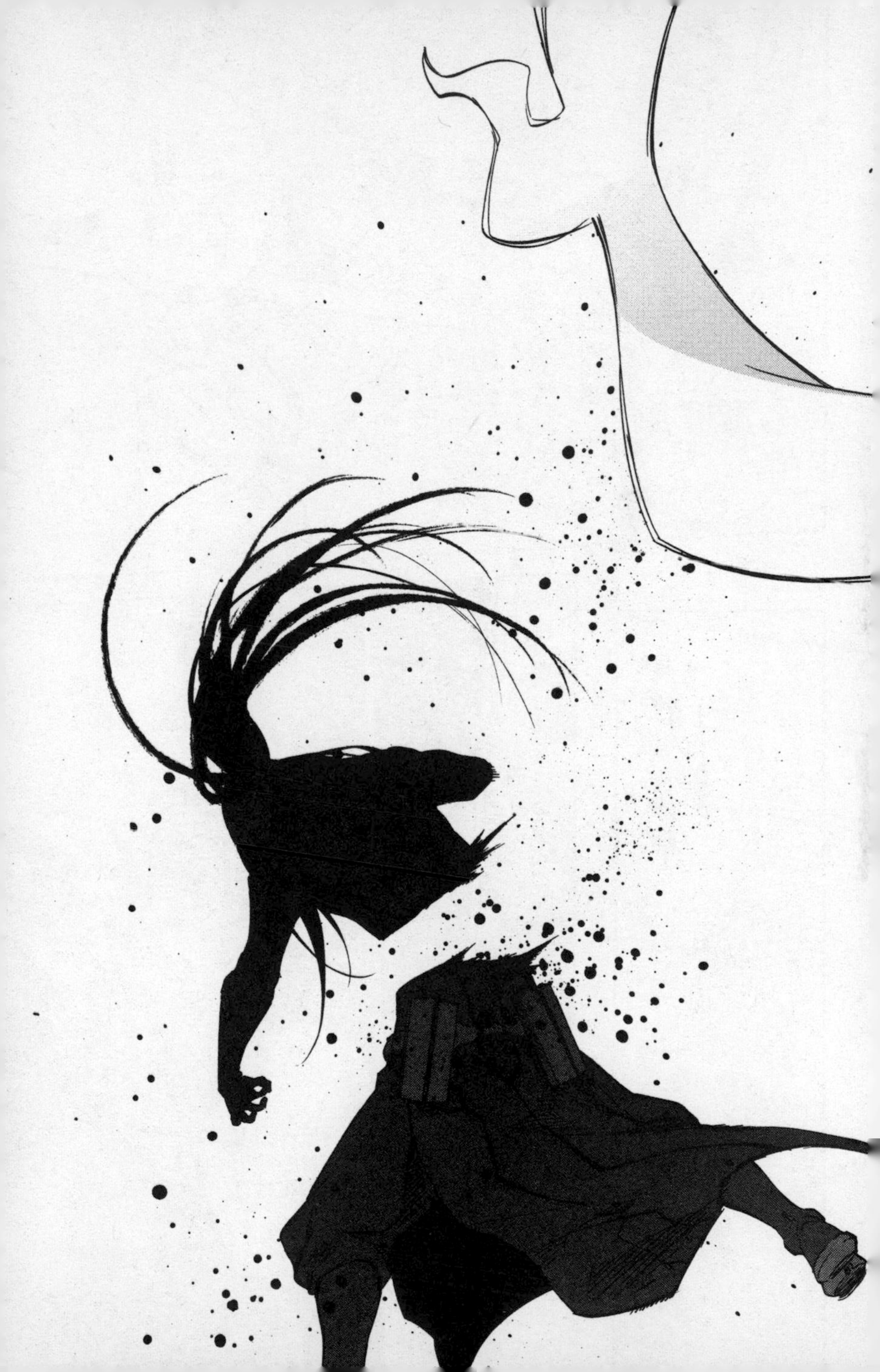

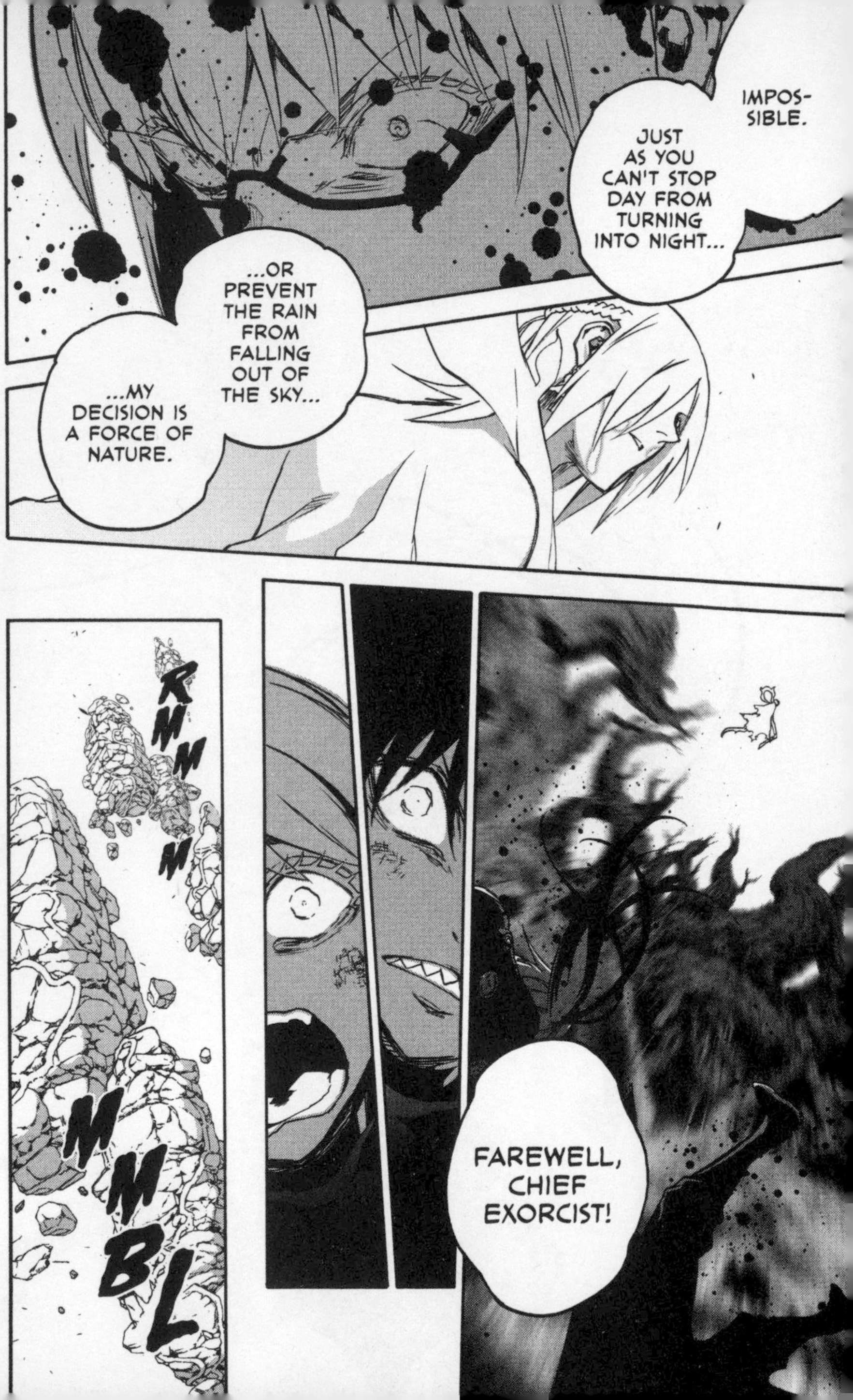
IMPOSSIBLE.
JUST AS YOU CAN'T STOP DAY FROM TURNING INTO NIGHT...
...OR PREVENT THE RAIN FROM FALLING OUT OF THE SKY...
...MY DECISION IS A FORCE OF NATURE.
FAREWELL, CHIEF EXORCIST!
RMMM
MMBL

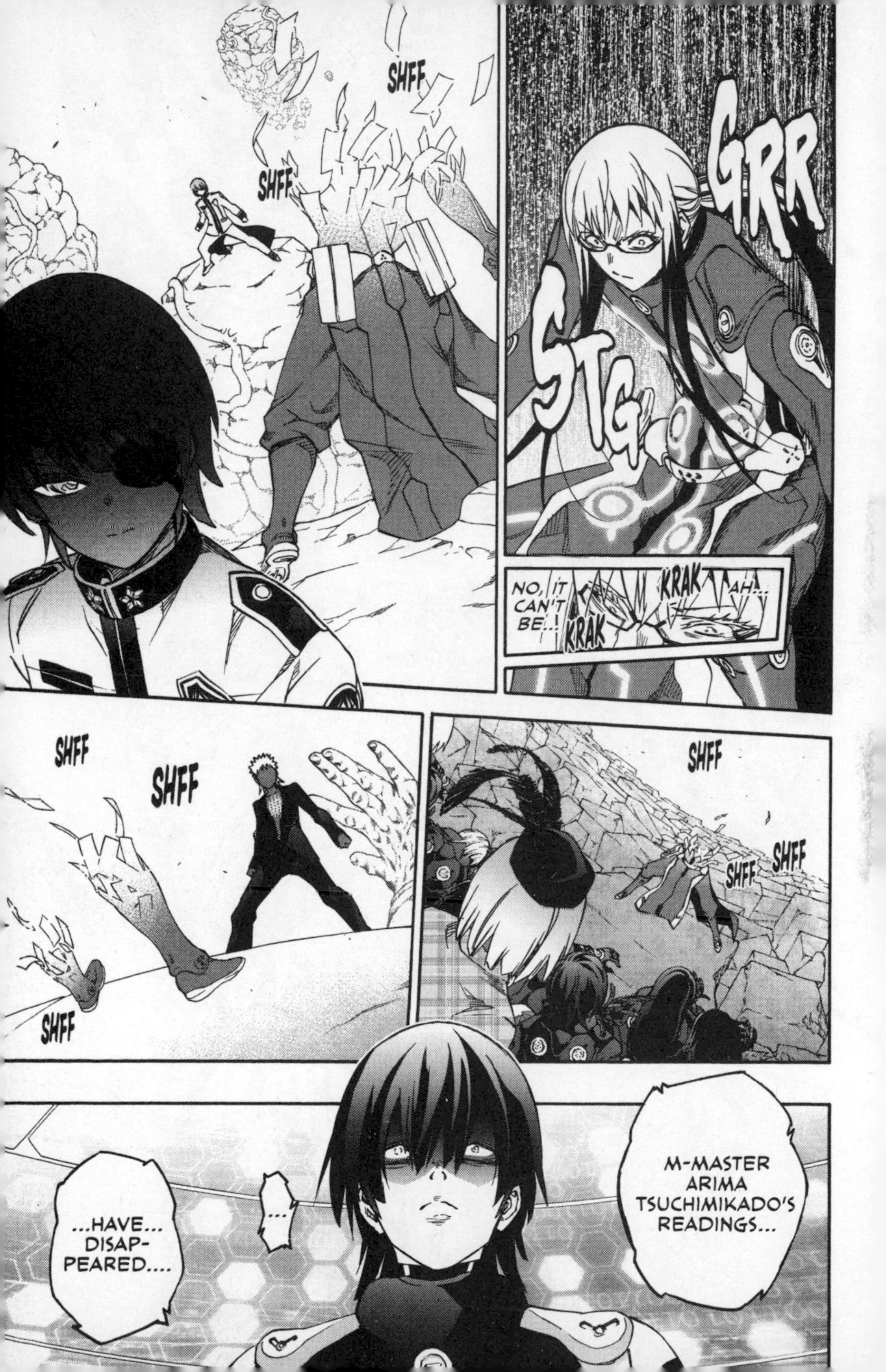
GRR
STG
AH...
KRAK
NO, IT CAN'T BE..!
KRAK
SHFF
SHFF
SHFF
SHFF
SHFF
SHFF
SHFF
SHFF
M-MASTER ARIMA TSUCHIMIKADO'S READINGS...
...
...HAVE... DISAP-PEARED....

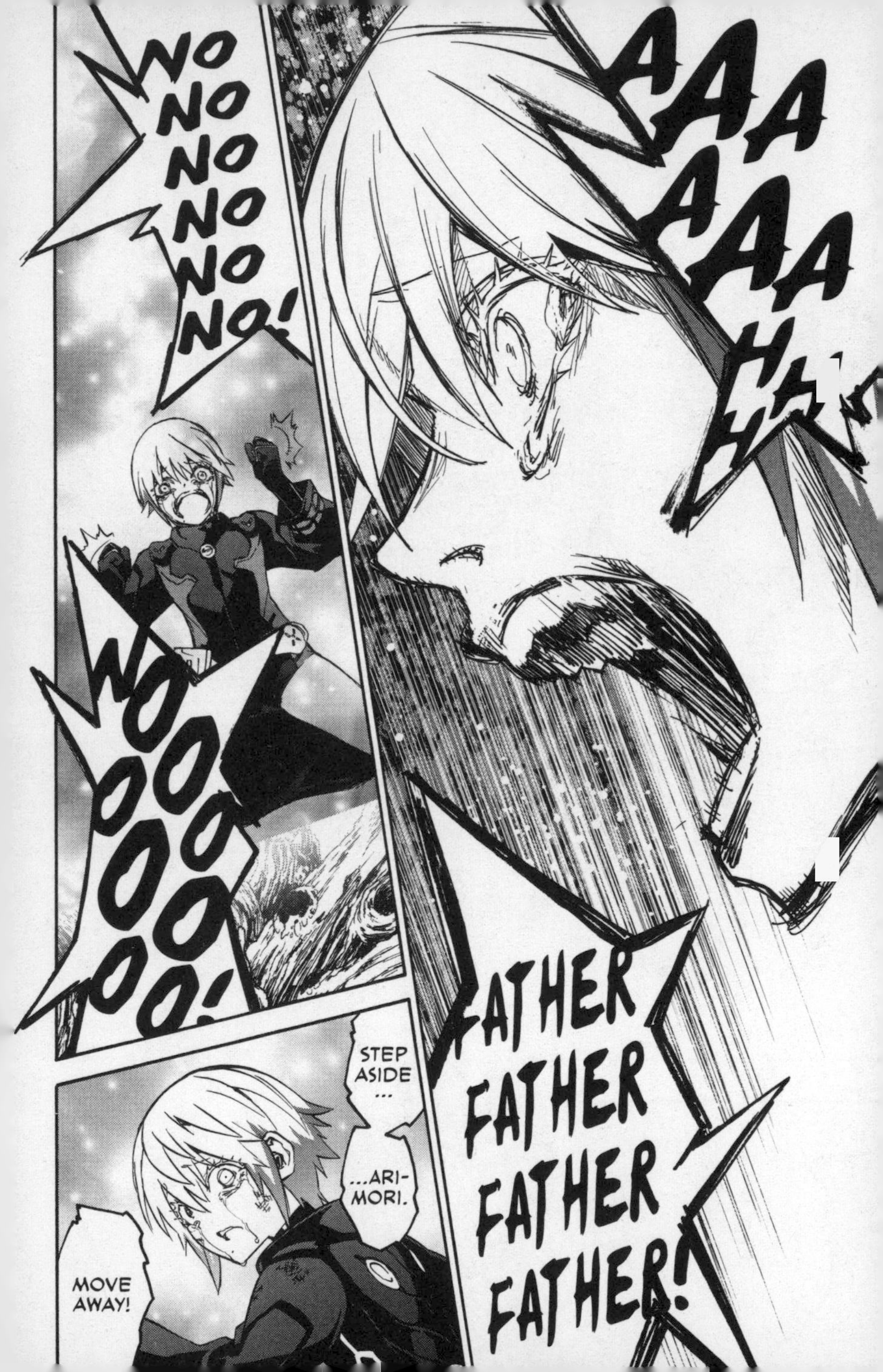
AAAAAAHHH
FATHER FATHER FATHER FATHER FATHER!
NO NO NO NO NO NO NO!
NOOOOOOOOOOO!
STEP ASIDE...
...ARI-MORI.
MOVE AWAY!

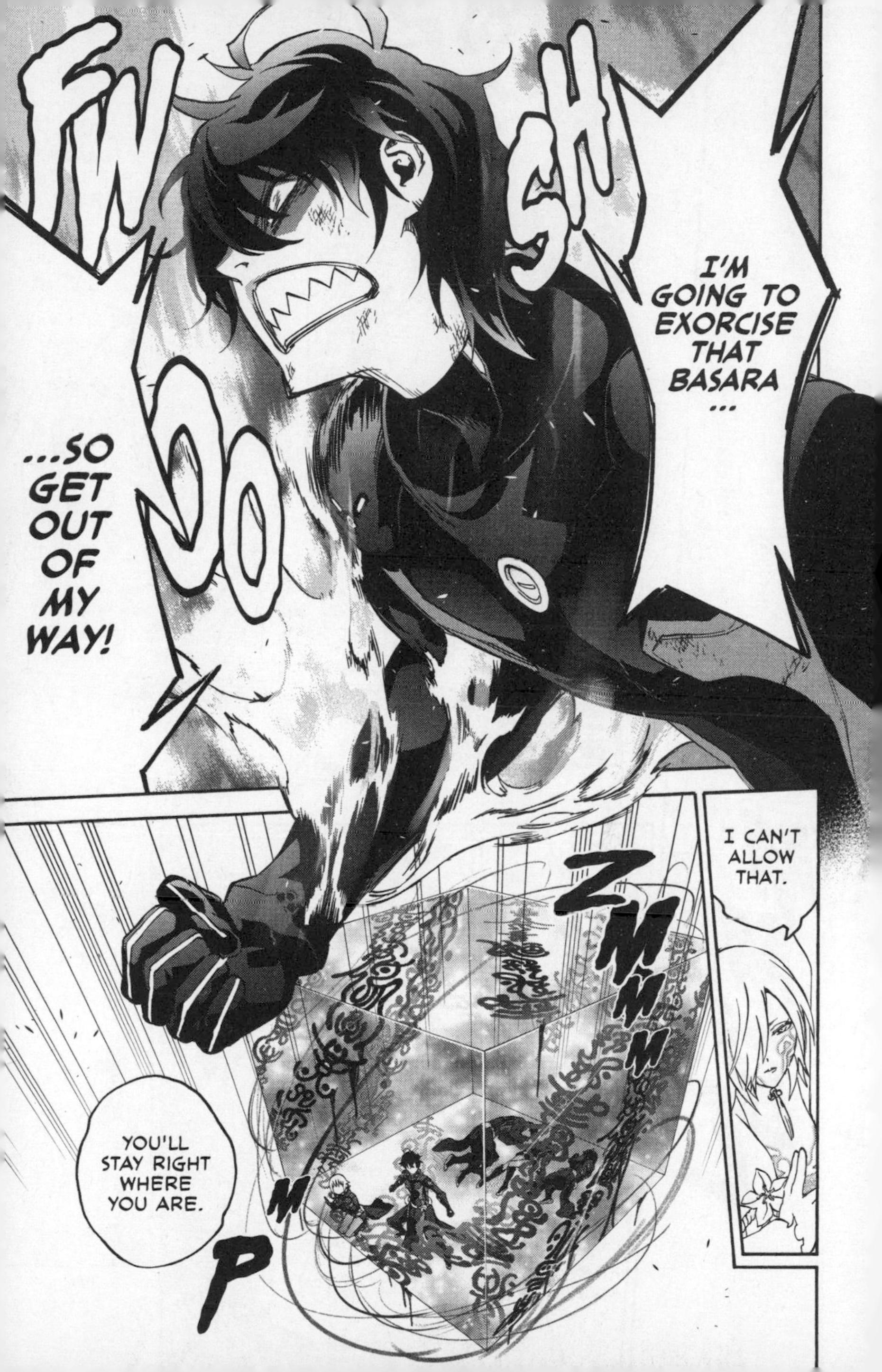
FWOOSH
I'M GOING TO EXORCISE THAT BASARA...
...SO GET OUT OF MY WAY!
I CAN'T ALLOW THAT.
ZMMMM
YOU'LL STAY RIGHT WHERE YOU ARE.
MP

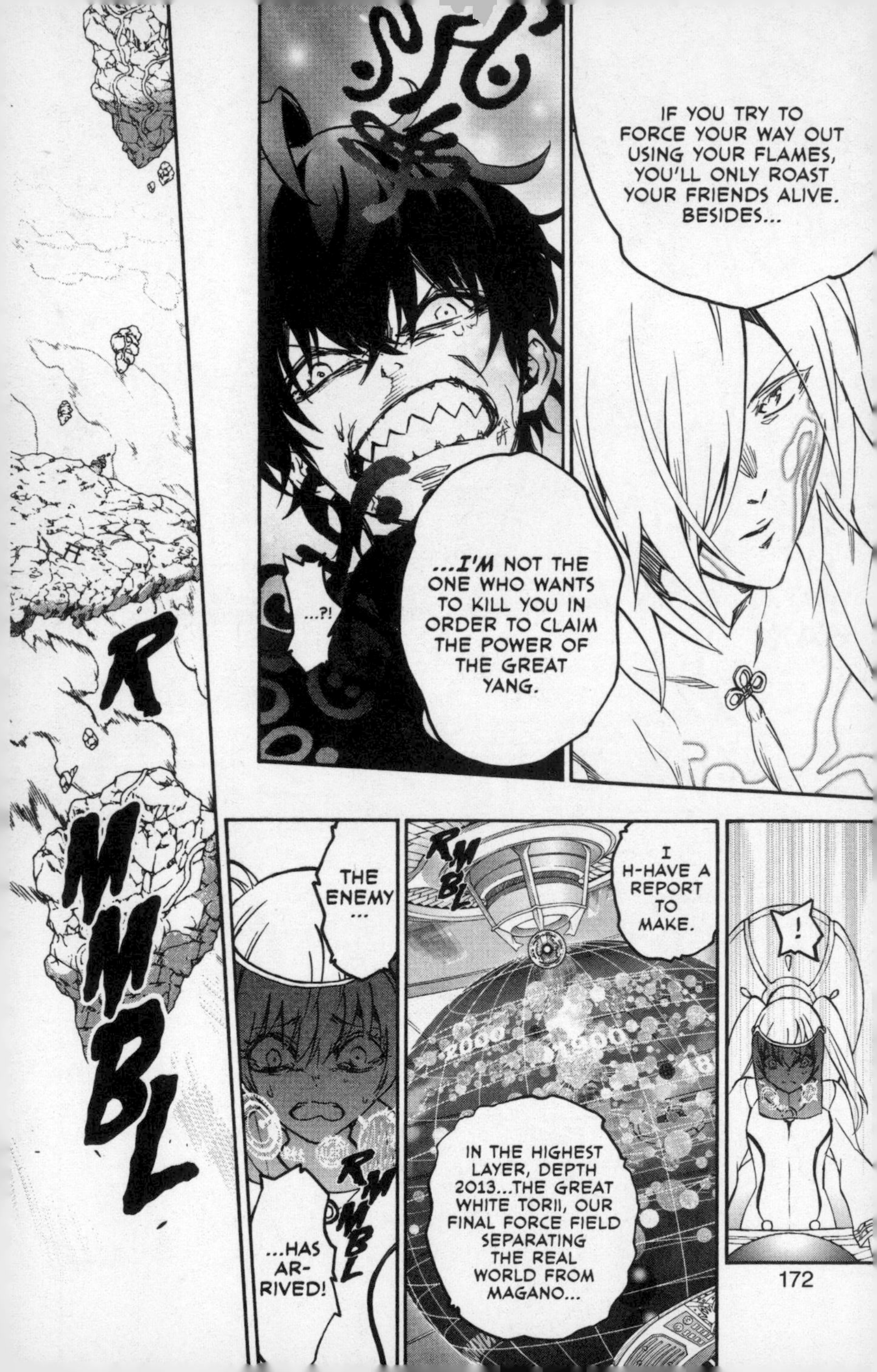

IF YOU TRY TO FORCE YOUR WAY OUT USING YOUR FLAMES, YOU'LL ONLY ROAST YOUR FRIENDS ALIVE. BESIDES...
...I'M NOT THE ONE WHO WANTS TO KILL YOU IN ORDER TO CLAIM THE POWER OF THE GREAT YANG.
...?!
!
I H-HAVE A REPORT TO MAKE.
RMBL
IN THE HIGHEST LAYER, DEPTH 2013...THE GREAT WHITE TORII, OUR FINAL FORCE FIELD SEPARATING THE REAL WORLD FROM MAGANO...
2000
1900
THE ENEMY...
RMMBL
...HAS ARRIVED!
RMMBL

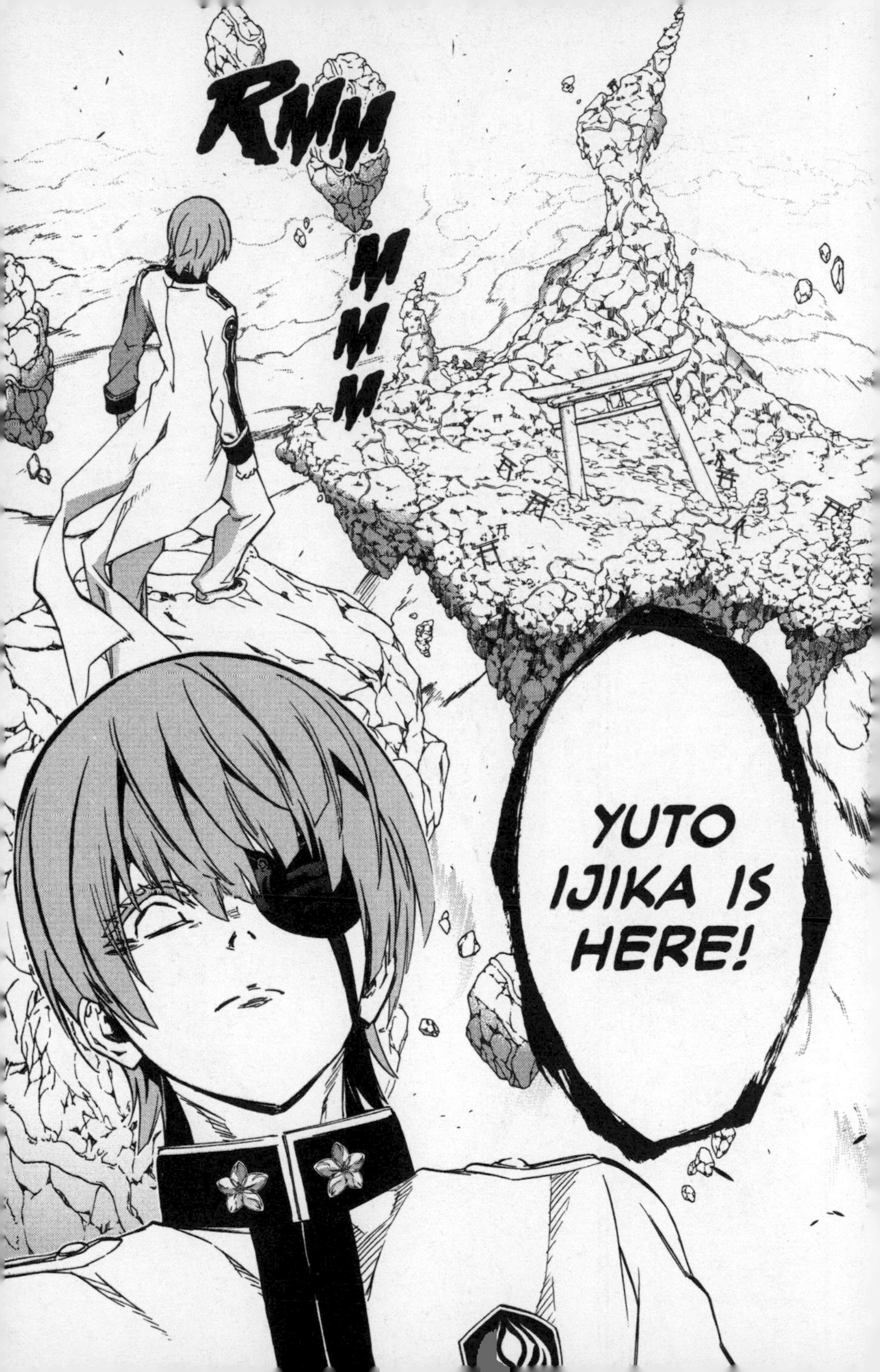
RMM
MMMM
YUTO IJIKA IS HERE!

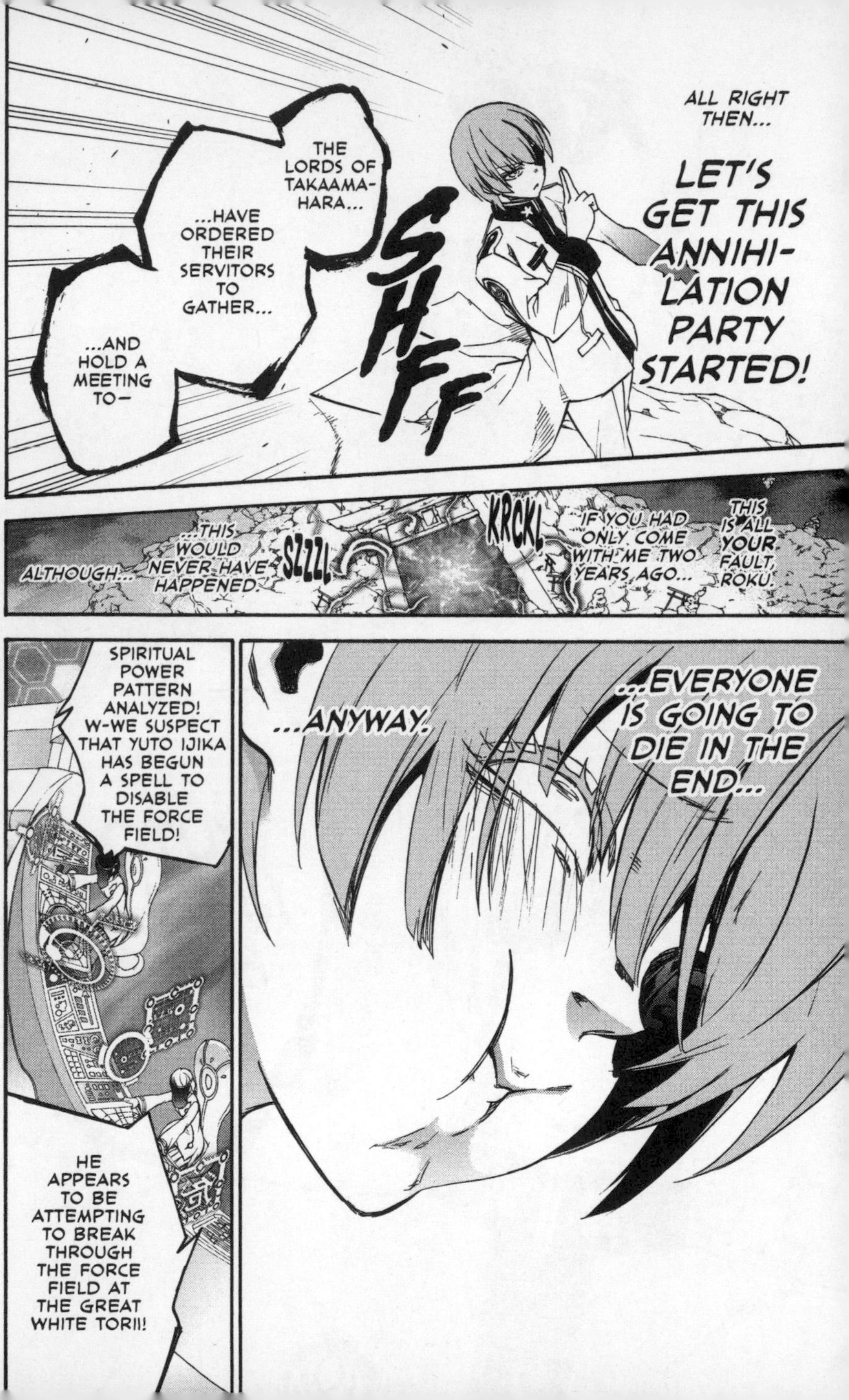
ALL RIGHT THEN...
LET'S GET THIS ANNIHI-LATION PARTY STARTED!
SHFF
THE LORDS OF TAKAAMA-HARA...
...HAVE ORDERED THEIR SERVITORS TO GATHER...
...AND HOLD A MEETING TO—
THIS IS ALL YOUR FAULT, ROKU.
IF YOU HAD ONLY COME WITH ME TWO YEARS AGO...
KRCKL
...THIS WOULD NEVER HAVE HAPPENED.
SZZZL
ALTHOUGH...
...EVERYONE IS GOING TO DIE IN THE END...
...ANYWAY.
SPIRITUAL POWER PATTERN ANALYZED! W-WE SUSPECT THAT YUTO IJIKA HAS BEGUN A SPELL TO DISABLE THE FORCE FIELD!
HE APPEARS TO BE ATTEMPTING TO BREAK THROUGH THE FORCE FIELD AT THE GREAT WHITE TORII!

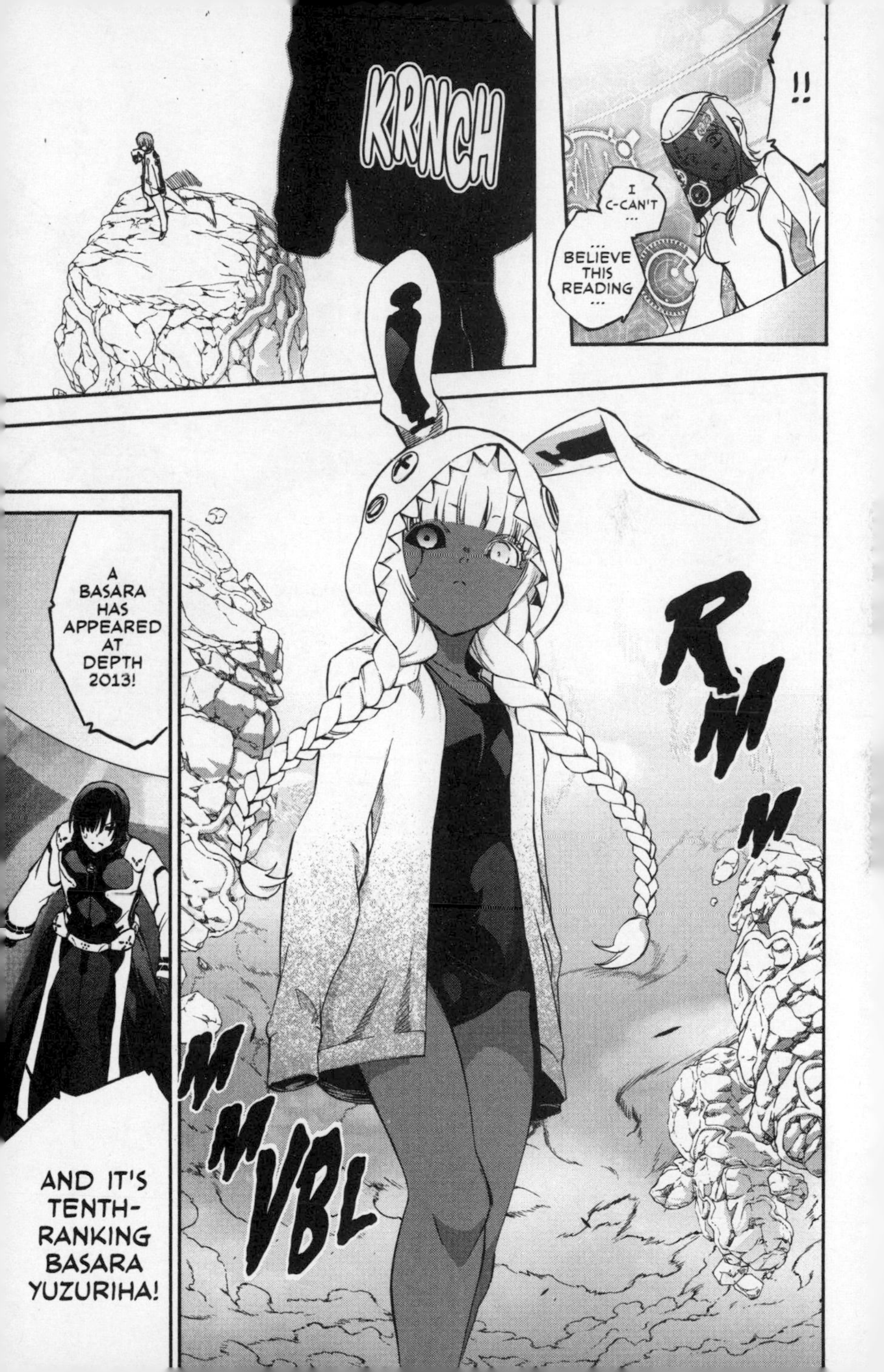
!!
I C-CAN'T... ...BELIEVE THIS READING...
KRNCH
RMM
A BASARA HAS APPEARED AT DEPTH 2013!
MMVBL
AND IT'S TENTH-RANKING BASARA YUZURIHA!

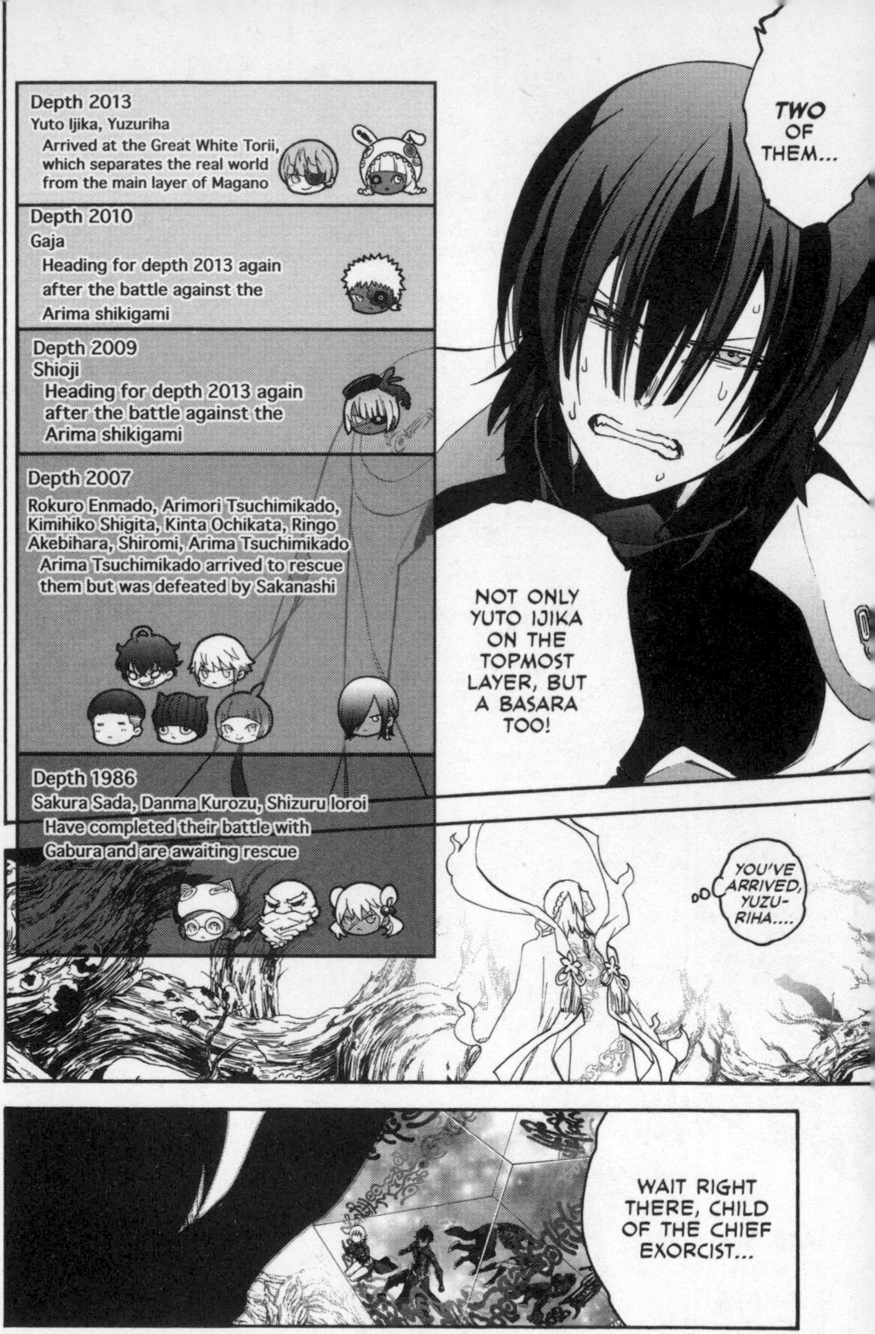
TWO OF THEM...
NOT ONLY YUTO IJIKA ON THE TOPMOST LAYER, BUT A BASARA TOO!
Depth 2013
Yuto Ijika, Yuzuriha
Arrived at the Great White Torii, which separates the real world from the main layer of Magano
Depth 2010
Gaja
Heading for depth 2013 again after the battle against the Arima shikigami
Depth 2009
Shioji
Heading for depth 2013 again after the battle against the Arima shikigami
Depth 2007
Rokuro Enmado, Arimori Tsuchimikado, Kimihiko Shigita, Kinta Ochikata, Ringo Akebihara, Shiromi, Arima Tsuchimikado
Arima Tsuchimikado arrived to rescue them but was defeated by Sakanashi
Depth 1986
Sakura Sada, Danma Kurozu, Shizuru Ioroi
Have completed their battle with Gabura and are awaiting rescue
YOU'VE ARRIVED, YUZURIHA....
WAIT RIGHT THERE, CHILD OF THE CHIEF EXORCIST...

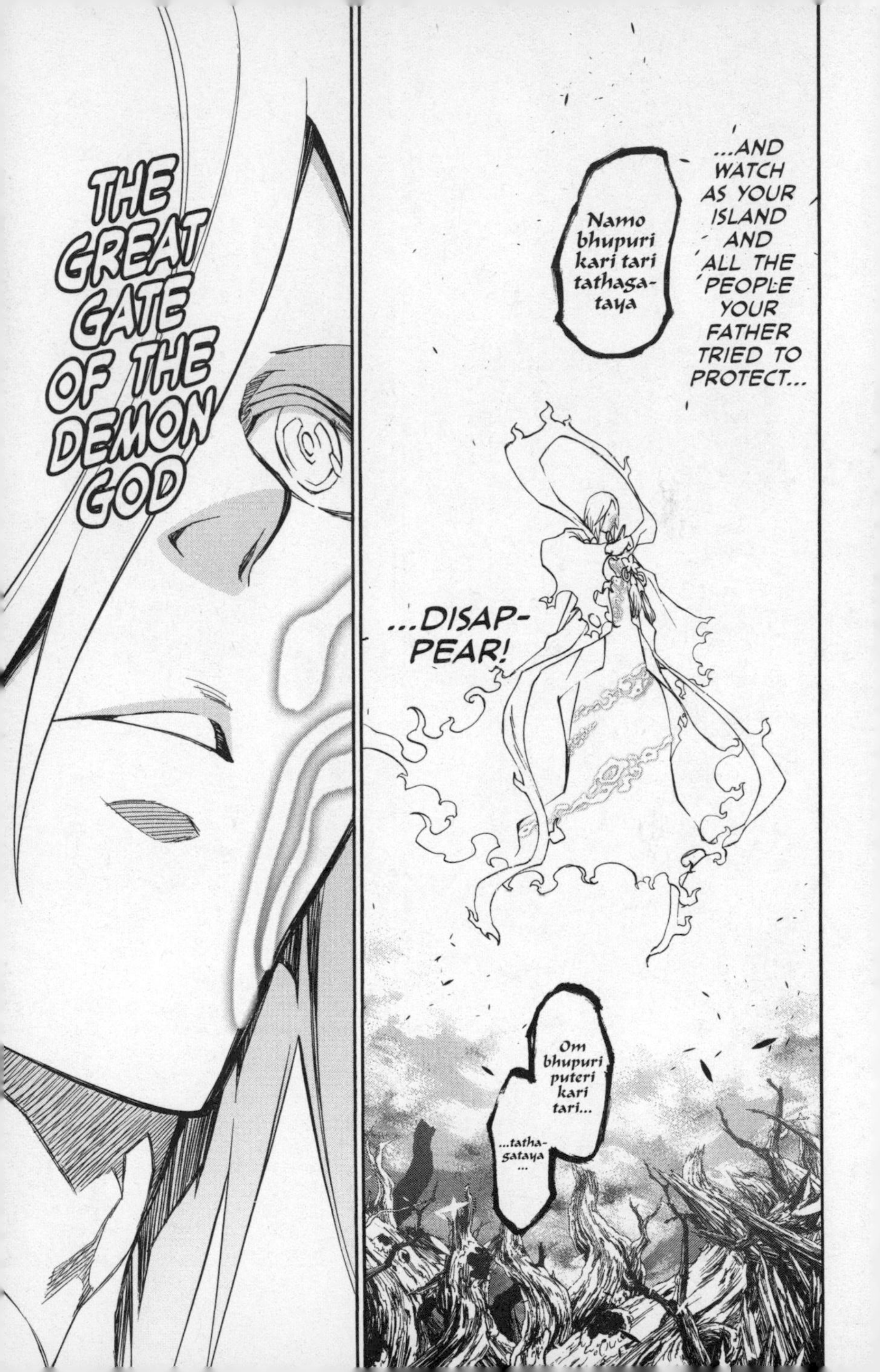
...AND WATCH AS YOUR ISLAND AND ALL THE PEOPLE YOUR FATHER TRIED TO PROTECT...
Namo bhupuri kari tari tathaga-taya
...DISAP-PEAR!
Om bhupuri puteri kari tari...
...tatha-gataya ...
THE GREAT GATE OF THE DEMON GOD

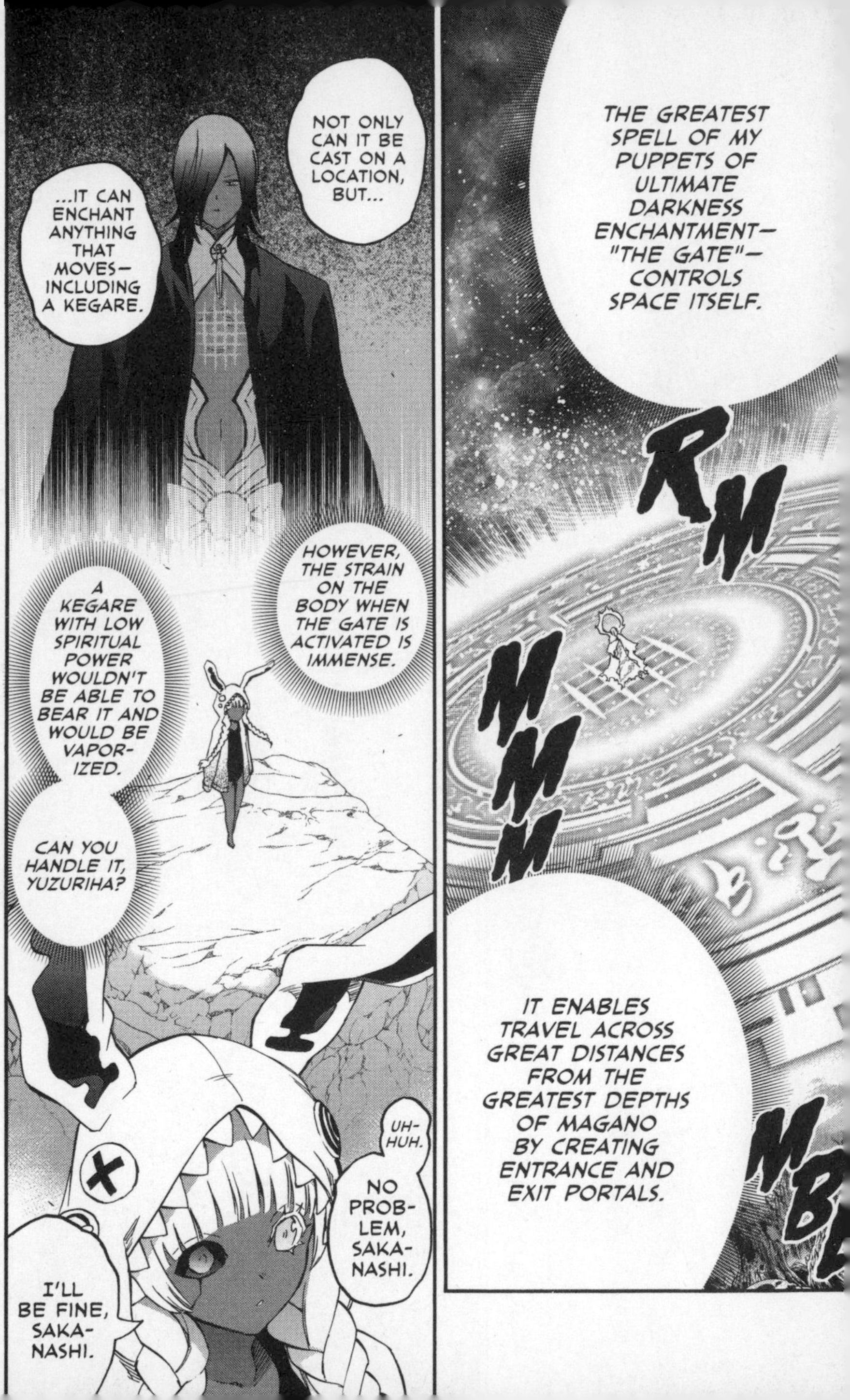
THE GREATEST SPELL OF MY PUPPETS OF ULTIMATE DARKNESS ENCHANTMENT—"THE GATE"—CONTROLS SPACE ITSELF.
RMMMMM
IT ENABLES TRAVEL ACROSS GREAT DISTANCES FROM THE GREATEST DEPTHS OF MAGANO BY CREATING ENTRANCE AND EXIT PORTALS.
MBL
NOT ONLY CAN IT BE CAST ON A LOCATION, BUT...
...IT CAN ENCHANT ANYTHING THAT MOVES—INCLUDING A KEGARE.
HOWEVER, THE STRAIN ON THE BODY WHEN THE GATE IS ACTIVATED IS IMMENSE.
A KEGARE WITH LOW SPIRITUAL POWER WOULDN'T BE ABLE TO BEAR IT AND WOULD BE VAPORIZED.
CAN YOU HANDLE IT, YUZURIHA?
UH-HUH.
NO PROBLEM, SAKANASHI.
I'LL BE FINE, SAKANASHI.

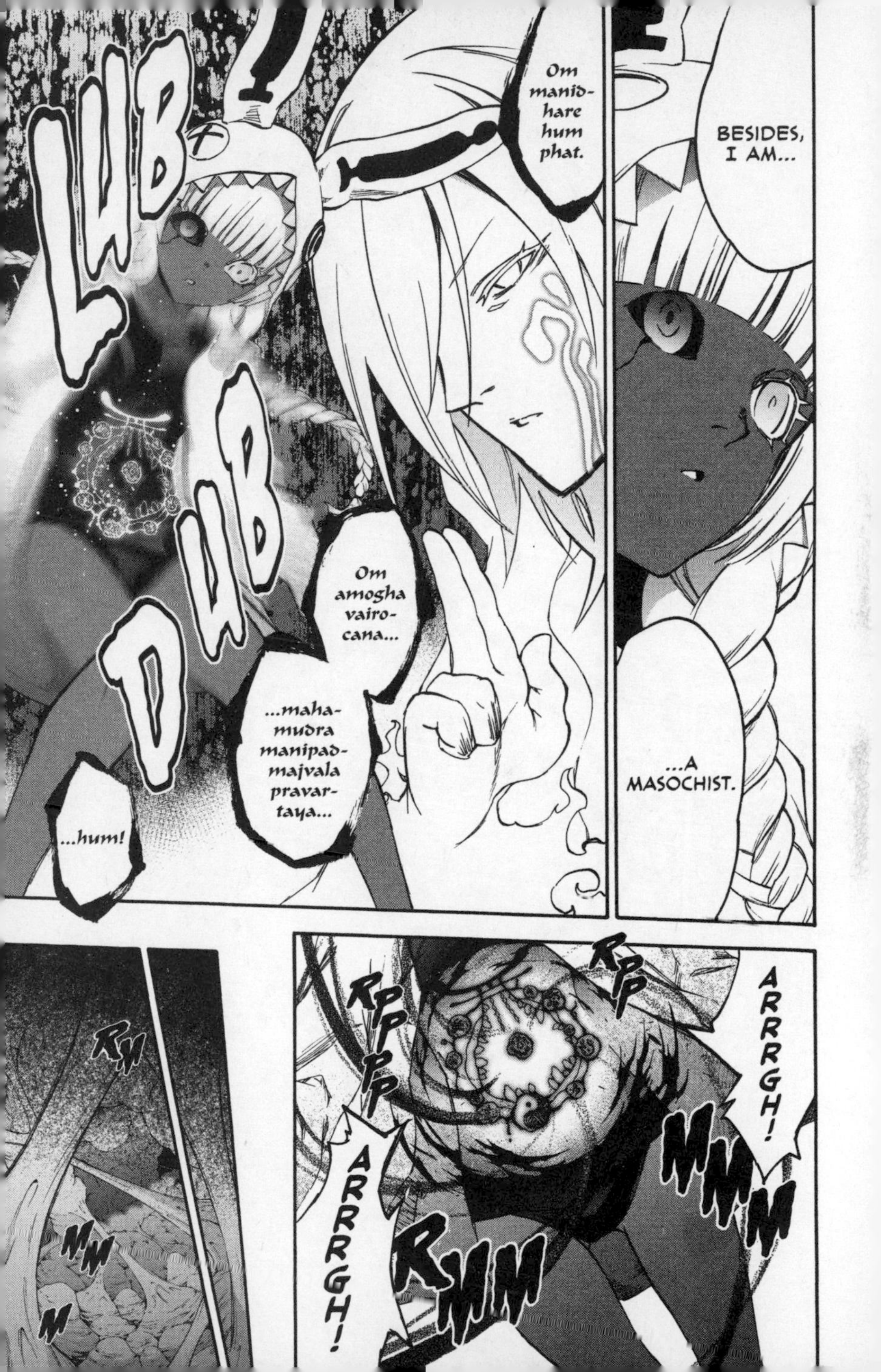
BESIDES, I AM...
...A MASOCHIST.
Om manid-hare hum phat.
LUB DUB
Om amogha vairo-cana...
...maha-mudra manipad-majvala pravar-taya...
...hum!
RPP
RPPPP
ARRRGH!
MMMM
ARRRGH!
RMM
RM
MMMM

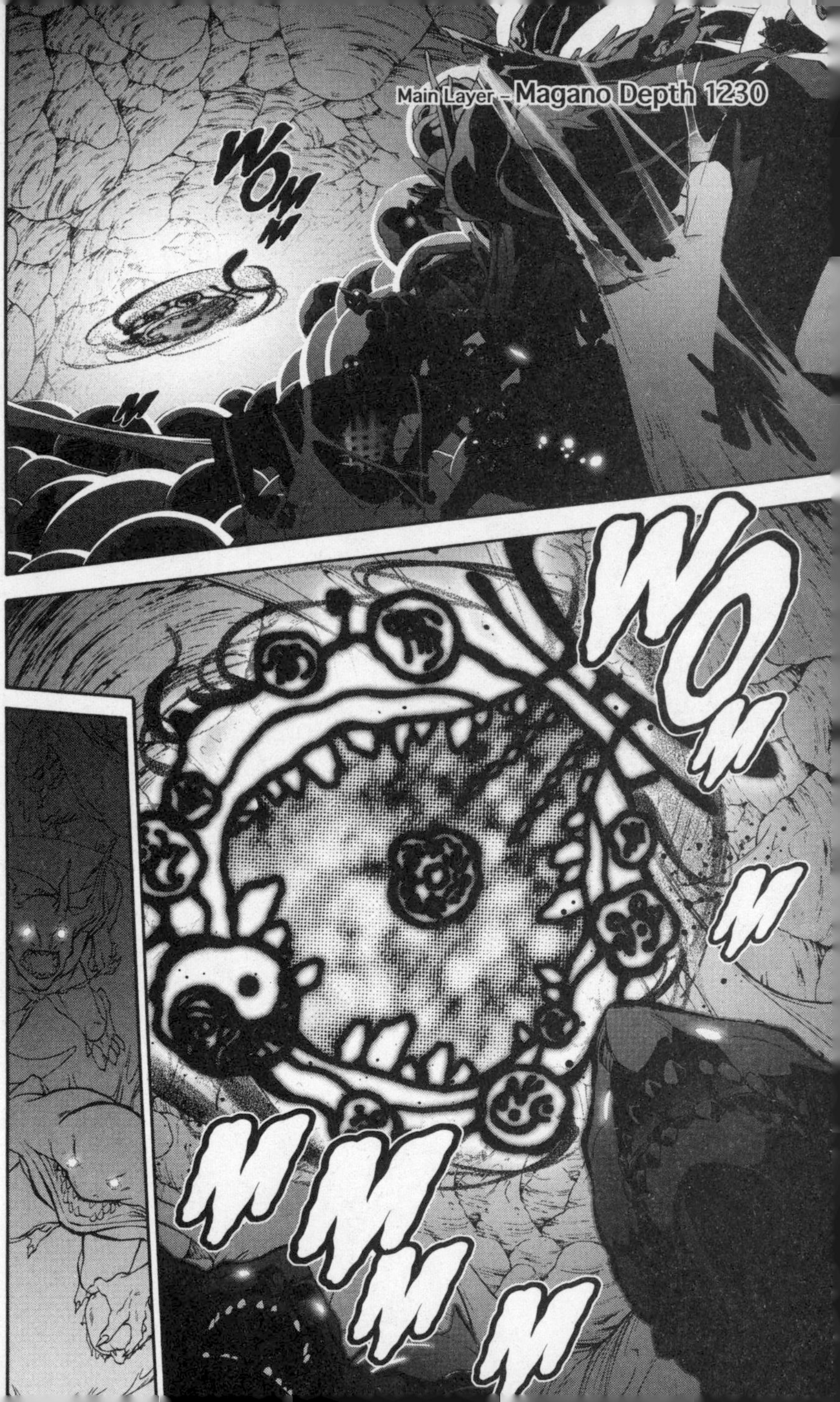
Main Layer – Magano Depth 1230
WOMMM
WOMMM
MMMM

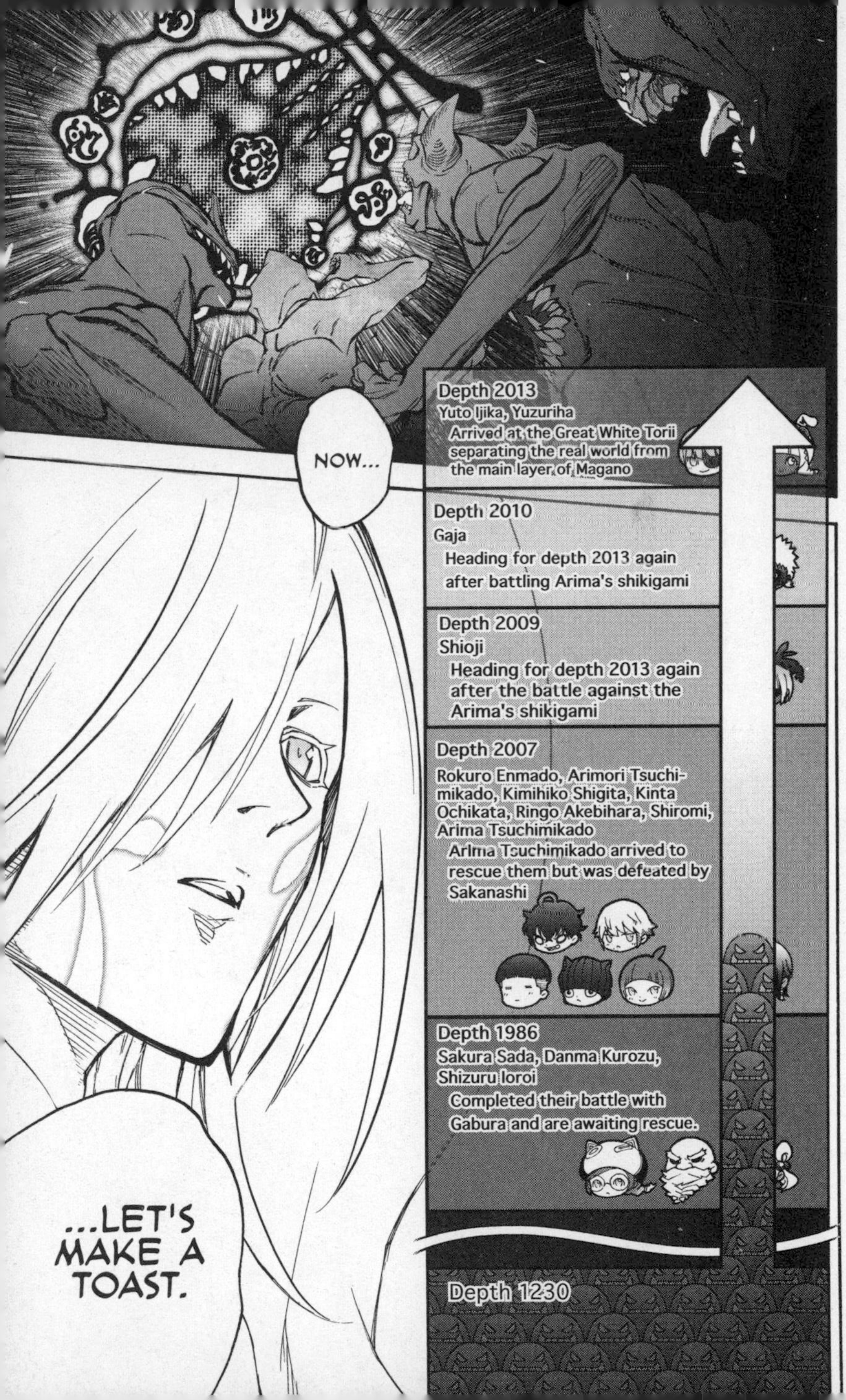
Depth 2013
Yuto Ijika, Yuzuriha
Arrived at the Great White Torii separating the real world from the main layer of Magano
Depth 2010
Gaja
Heading for depth 2013 again after battling Arima's shikigami
Depth 2009
Shioji
Heading for depth 2013 again after the battle against the Arima's shikigami
Depth 2007
Rokuro Enmado, Arimori Tsuchimikado, Kimihiko Shigita, Kinta Ochikata, Ringo Akebihara, Shiromi, Arima Tsuchimikado
Arima Tsuchimikado arrived to rescue them but was defeated by Sakanashi
Depth 1986
Sakura Sada, Danma Kurozu, Shizuru Ioroi
Completed their battle with Gabura and are awaiting rescue.
Depth 1230
NOW...
...LET'S MAKE A TOAST.

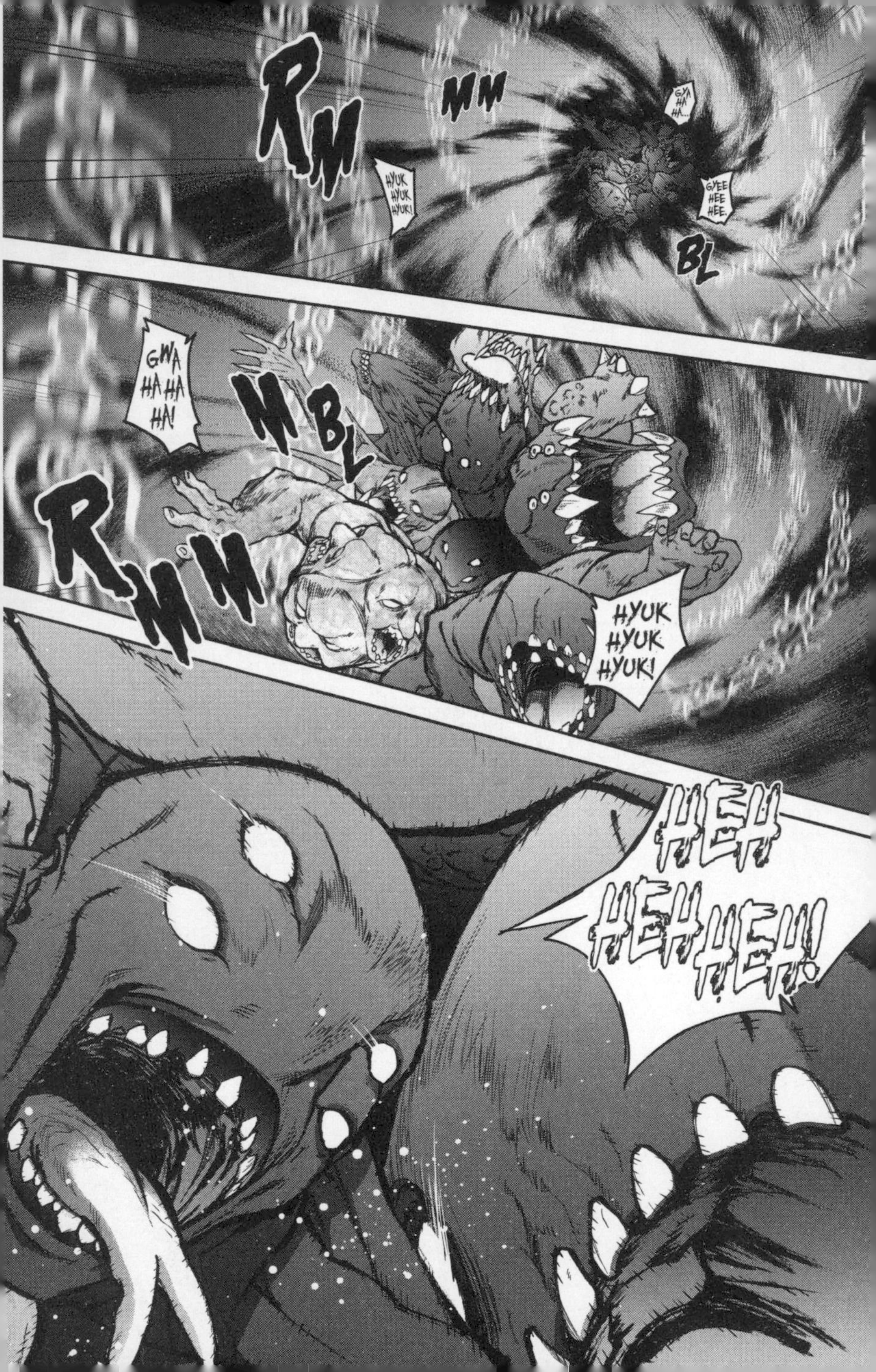
GYA HA HA...
GYEE HEE HEE.
BL
MM
HYUK HYUK HYUK!
RM
HYUK HYUK HYUK!
MBL
GWA HA HA HA!
RMMM
HEH HEH HEH HEH!

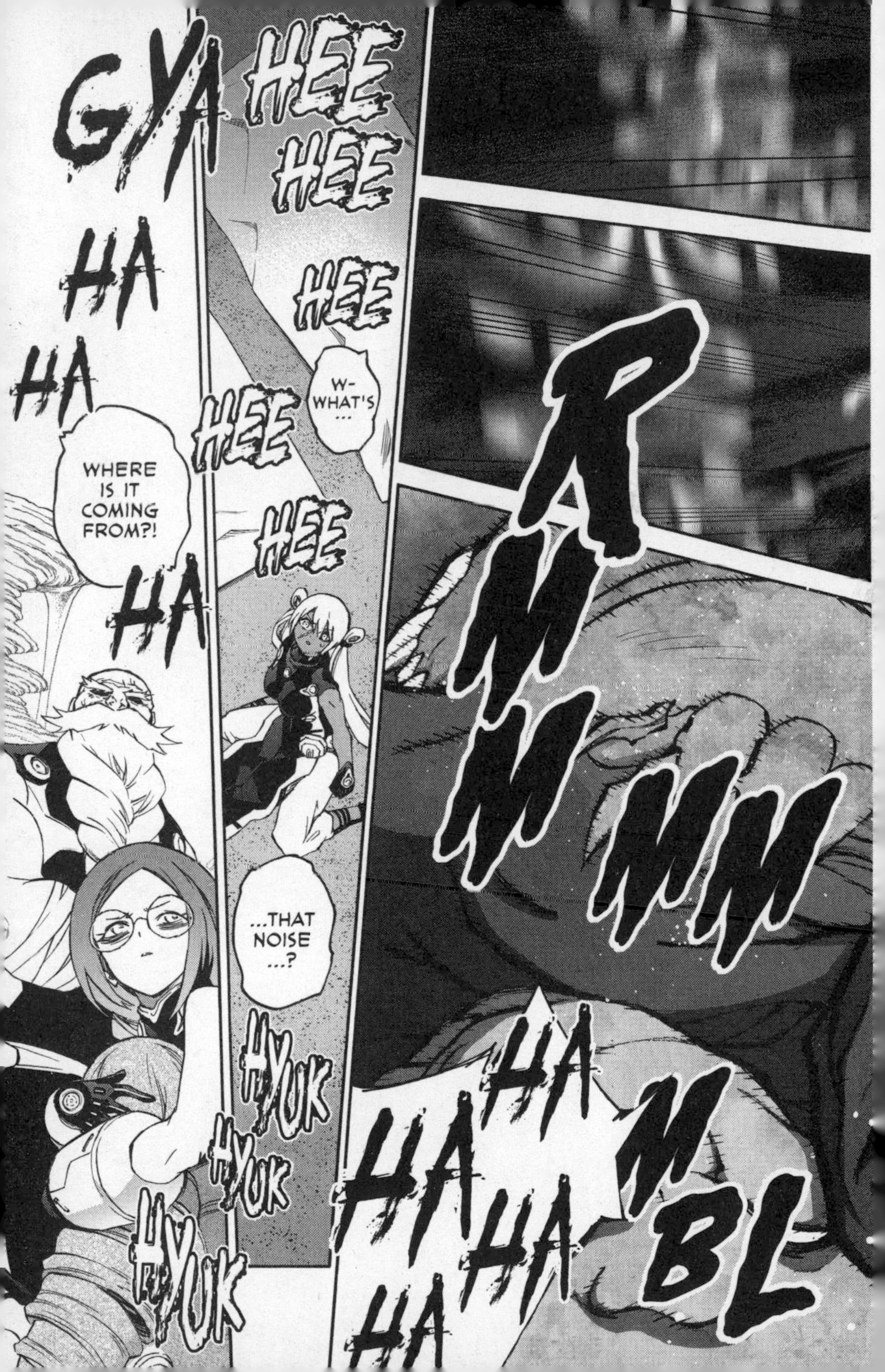
RMMMMM
HAHAHAHA
MBL
HEE HEE HEE
HEE
W-WHAT'S...
HEE
HEE
...THAT NOISE...?
HYUK HYUK HYUK
GYA HA HA
WHERE IS IT COMING FROM?!
HA

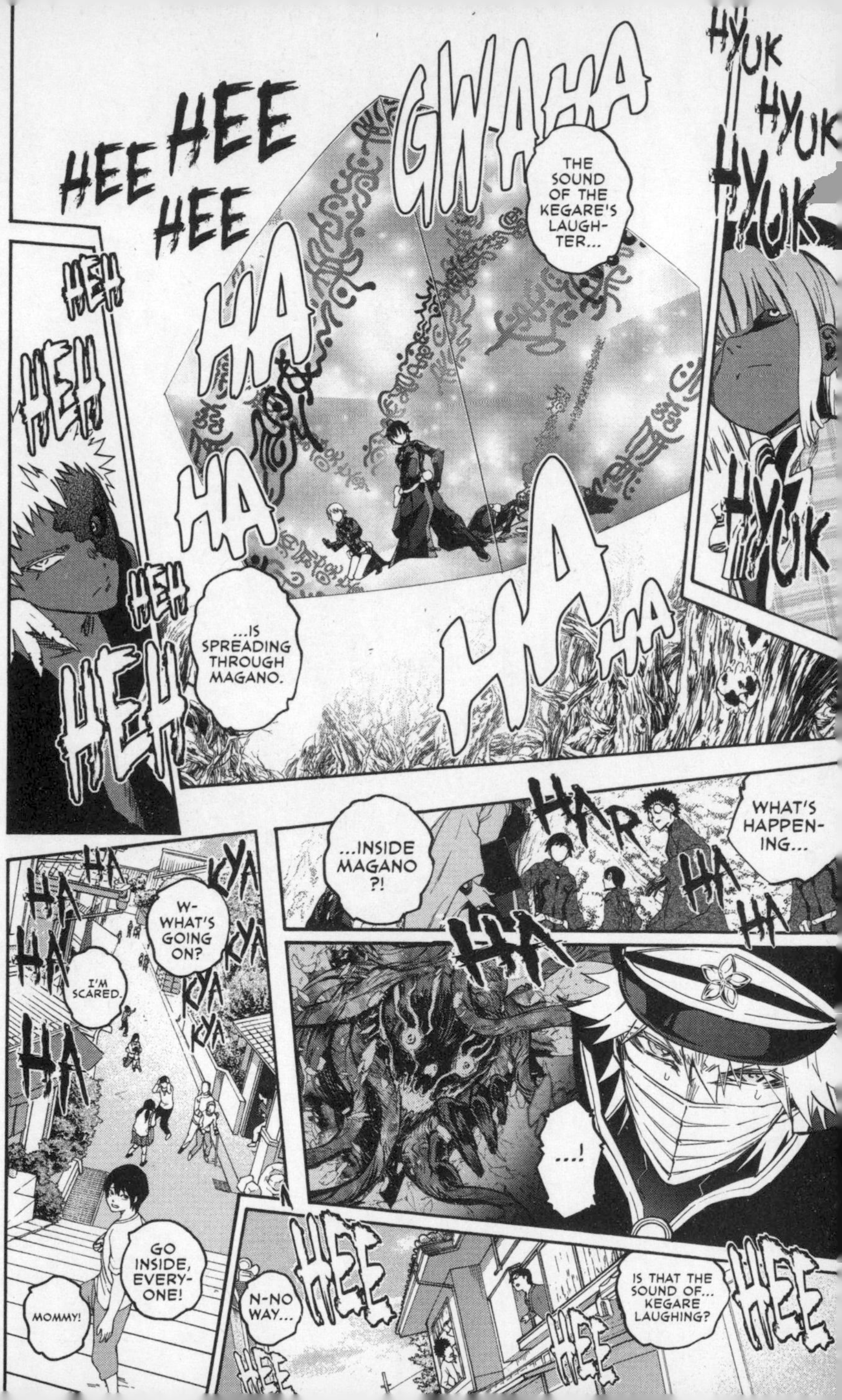
HYUK HYUK HYUK HYUK HYUK HYUK
GWAHA
HEE HEE HEE
THE SOUND OF THE KEGARE'S LAUGH-TER...
HA HA
HEH HEH
HEH HEH
HA HA HA
...IS SPREADING THROUGH MAGANO.
WHAT'S HAPPEN-ING...
HAR HA HA
...INSIDE MAGANO?!
HA
...!
HEE HEE
IS THAT THE SOUND OF... KEGARE LAUGHING?
HEE HEE
N-NO WAY...
KYA KYA KYA KYA
W-WHAT'S GOING ON?
HA HA HA HA
I'M SCARED.
HA
GO INSIDE, EVERY-ONE!
MOMMY!

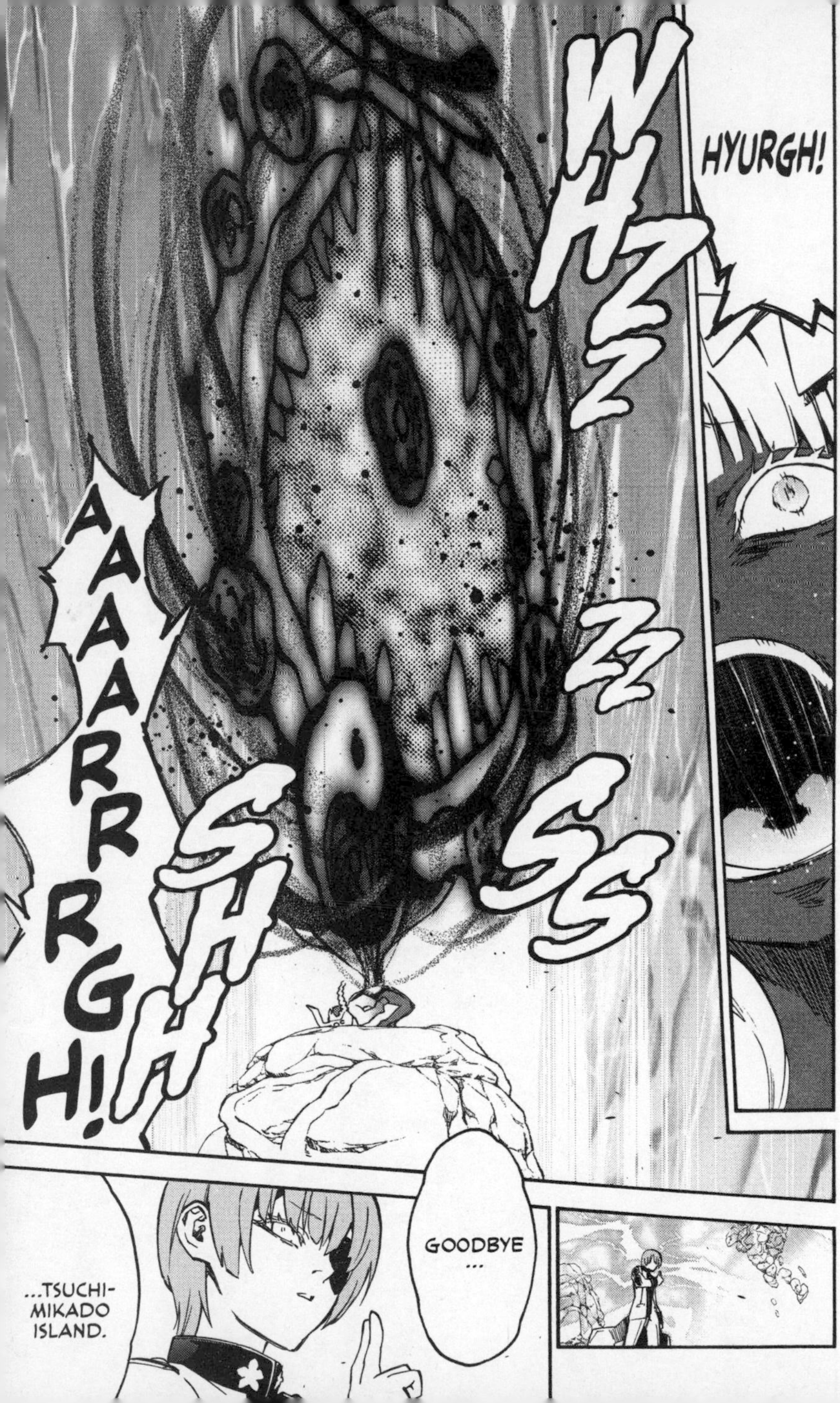
HYURGH!
WHZZZZSS
SHHH
AAAARRRGH!
GOODBYE ...
...TSUCHIMIKADO ISLAND.

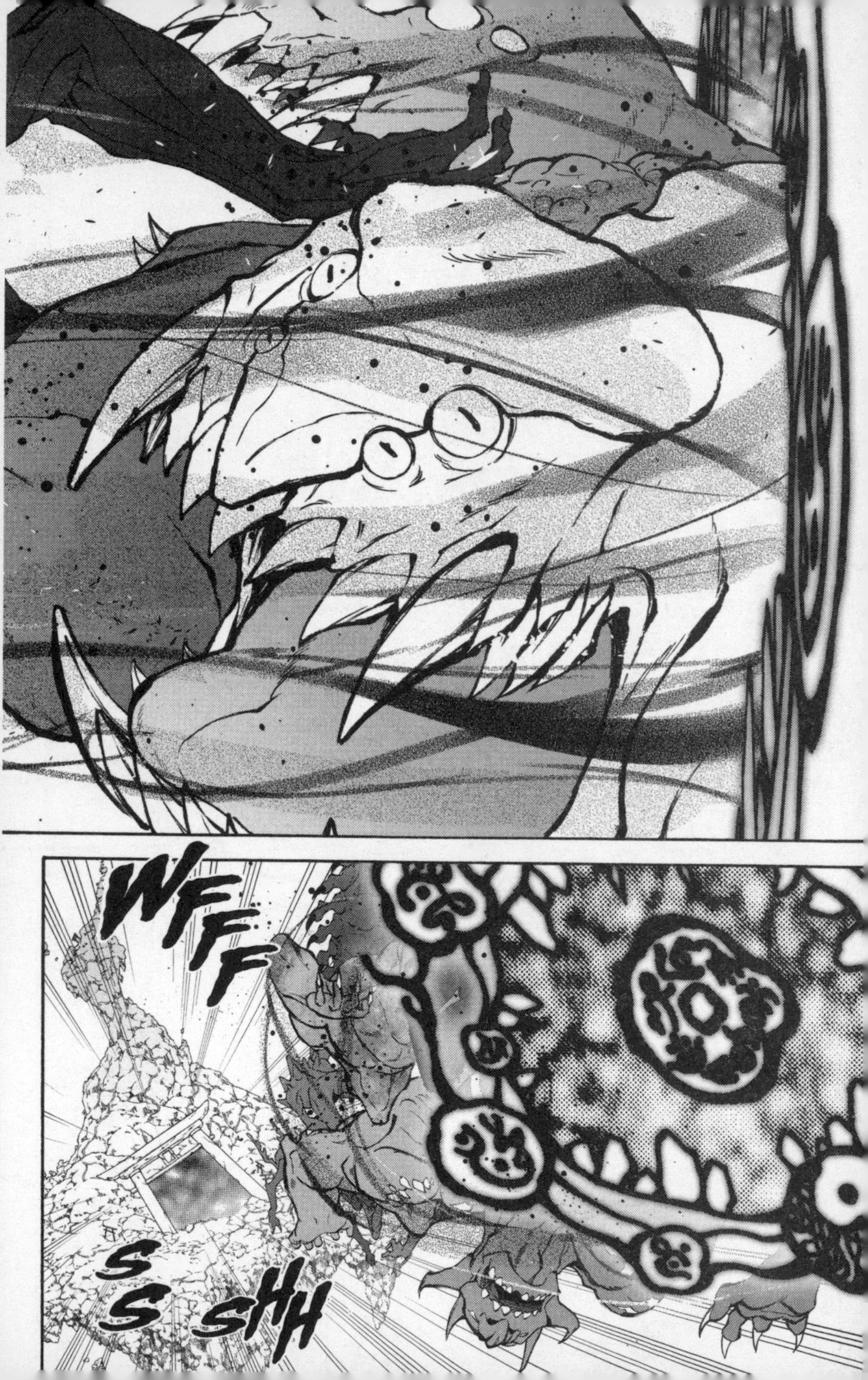
WFFF
SSSHH

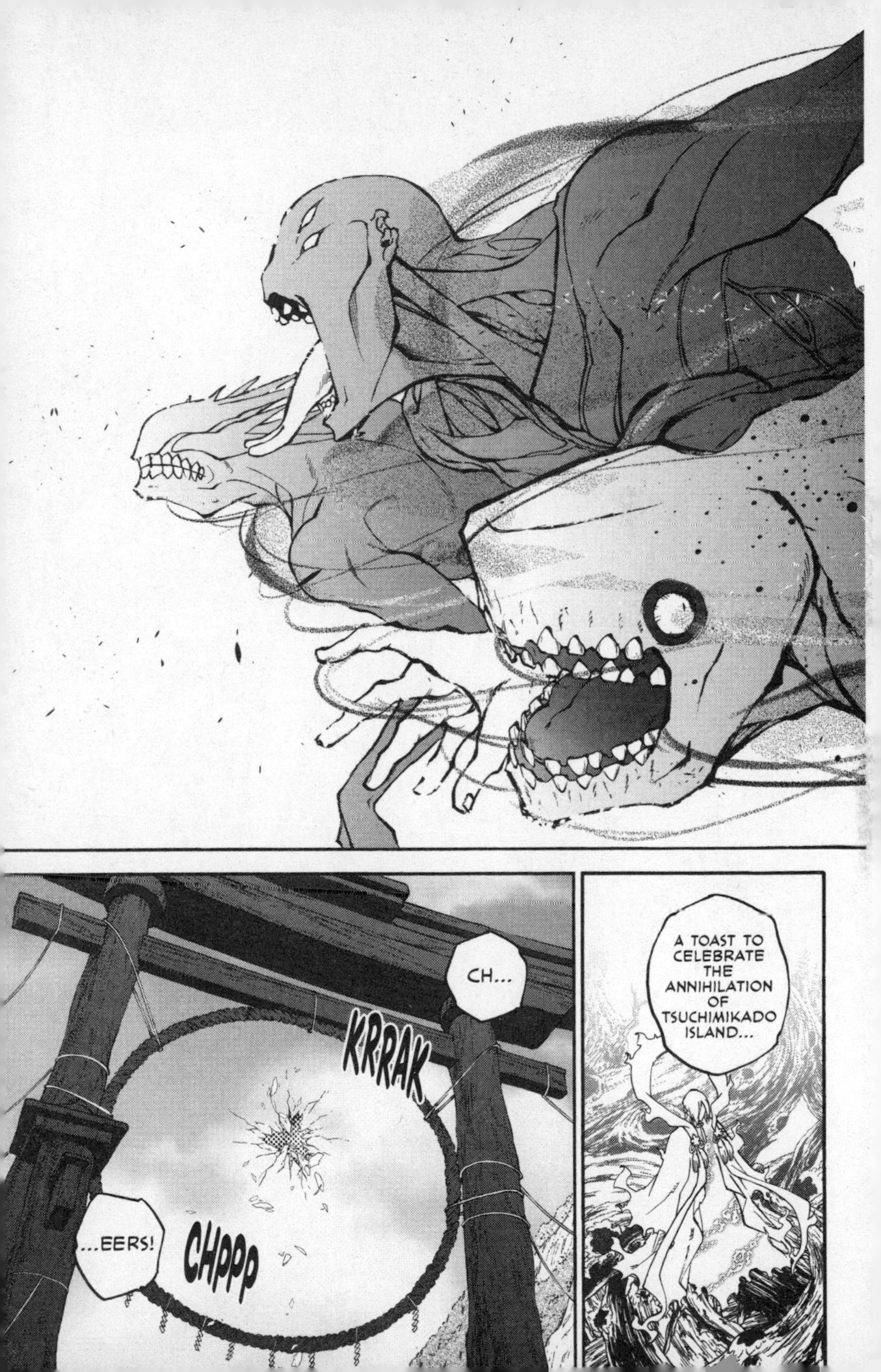
A TOAST TO CELEBRATE THE ANNIHILATION OF TSUCHIMIKADO ISLAND...
CH...
KRRAK
...EERS!
CHPPP

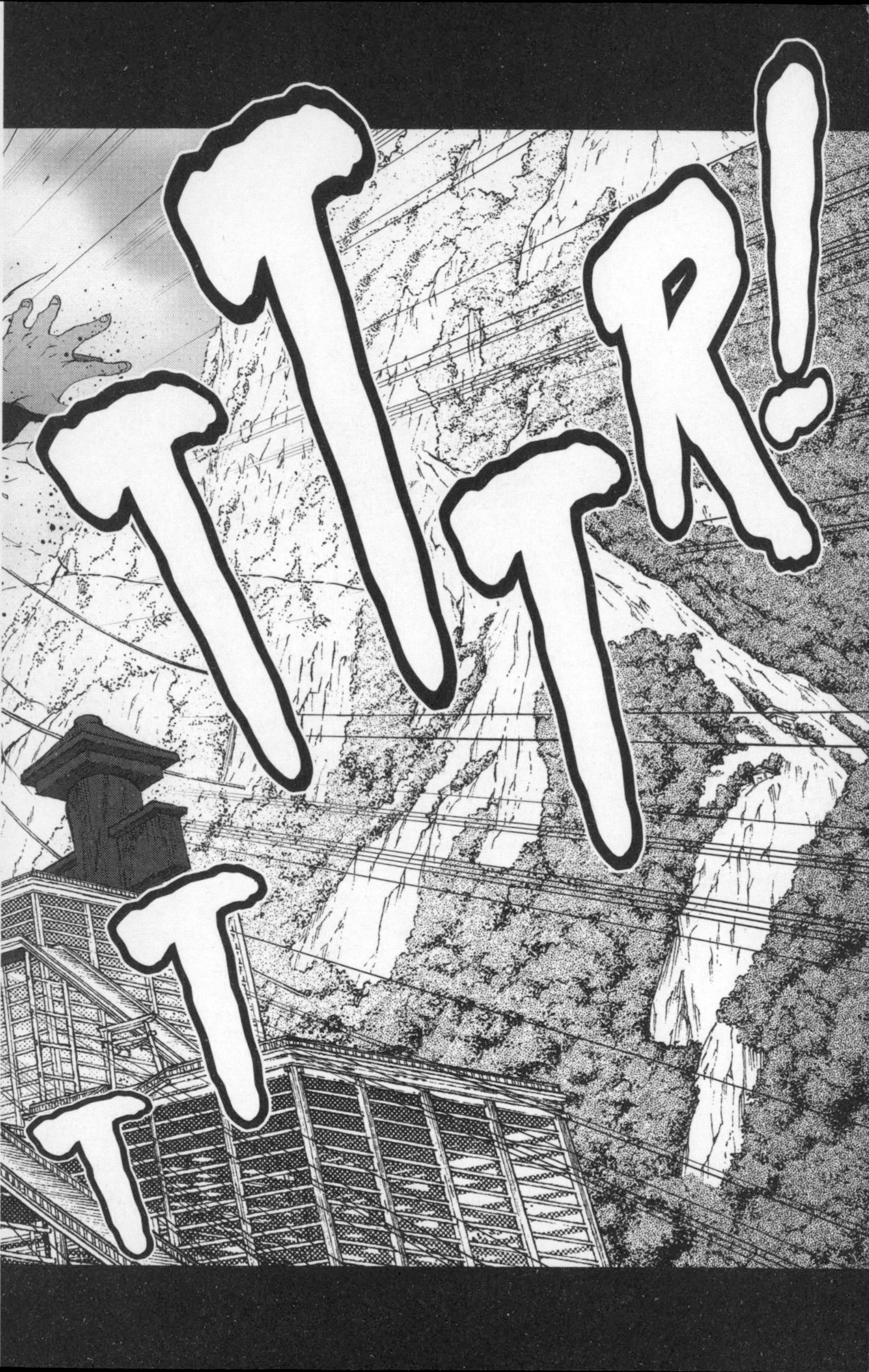
TTTTTR!

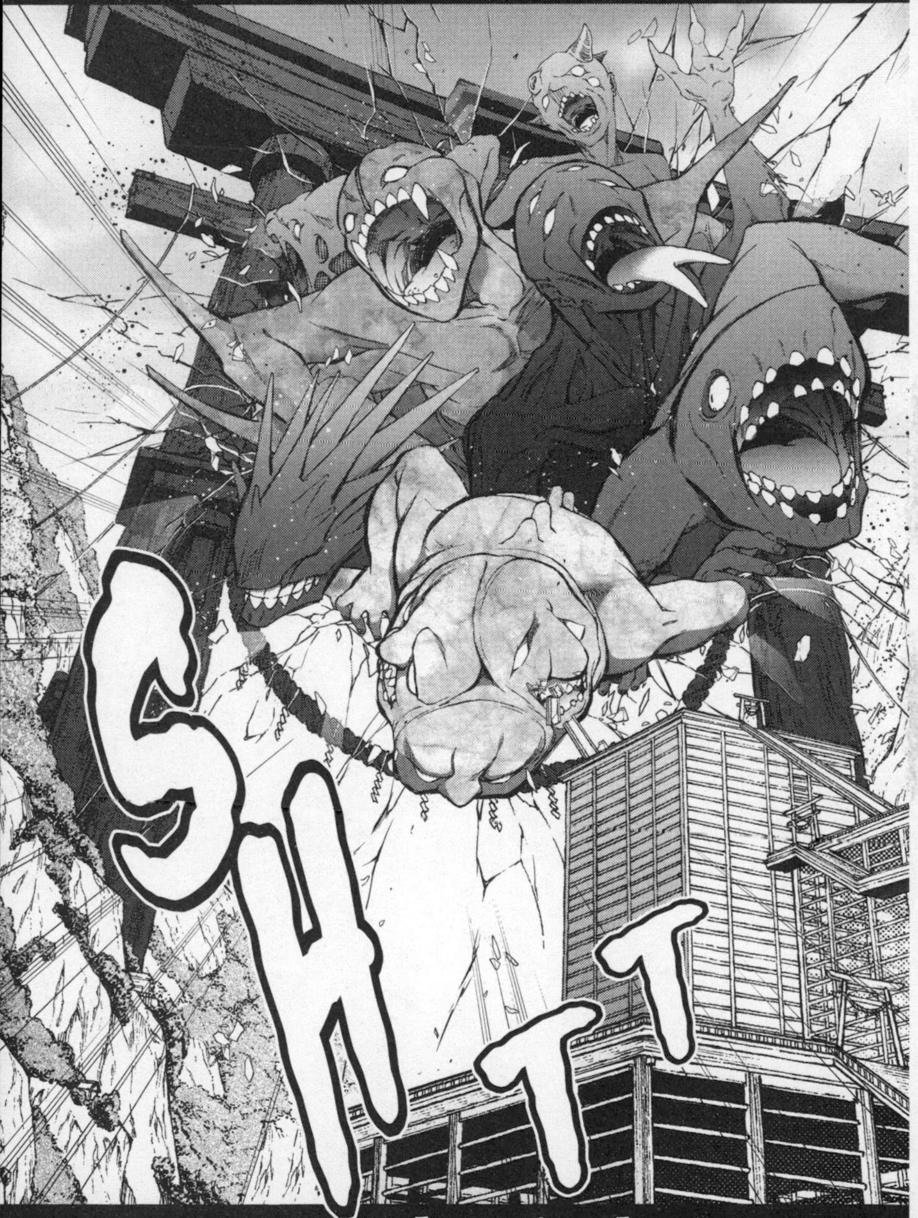
SHTT

To be continued...

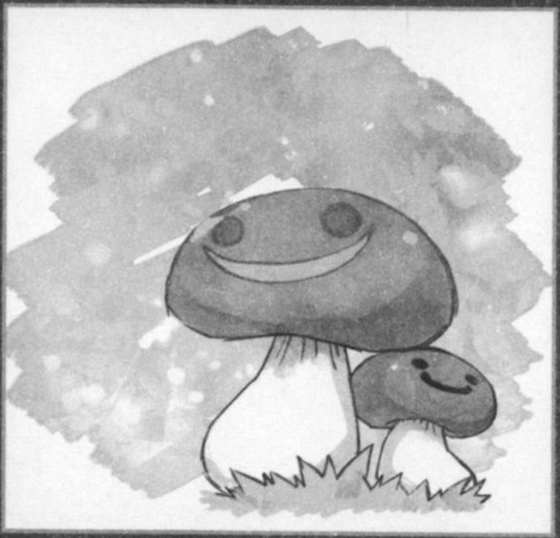

Twin Star Exorcists has been running for over five years already. *Binbougami ga!* lasted five years and two months, so my current series is going to surpass my previous one. There are still a lot of images I'm looking forward to drawing. I know this is a stereotypical thing to say, but I promise to give this my all, so please continue to support me.

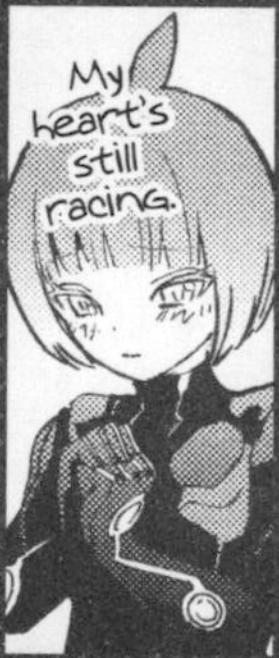
My heart's still racing.

YOSHIAKI SUKENO was born July 23, 1981, in Wakayama, Japan. He graduated from Kyoto Seika University, where he studied manga. In 2006, he won the Tezuka Award for Best Newcomer Shonen Manga Artist. In 2008, he began his previous work, the supernatural comedy *Binbougami ga!*, which was adapted into the anime *Good Luck Girl!* in 2012.

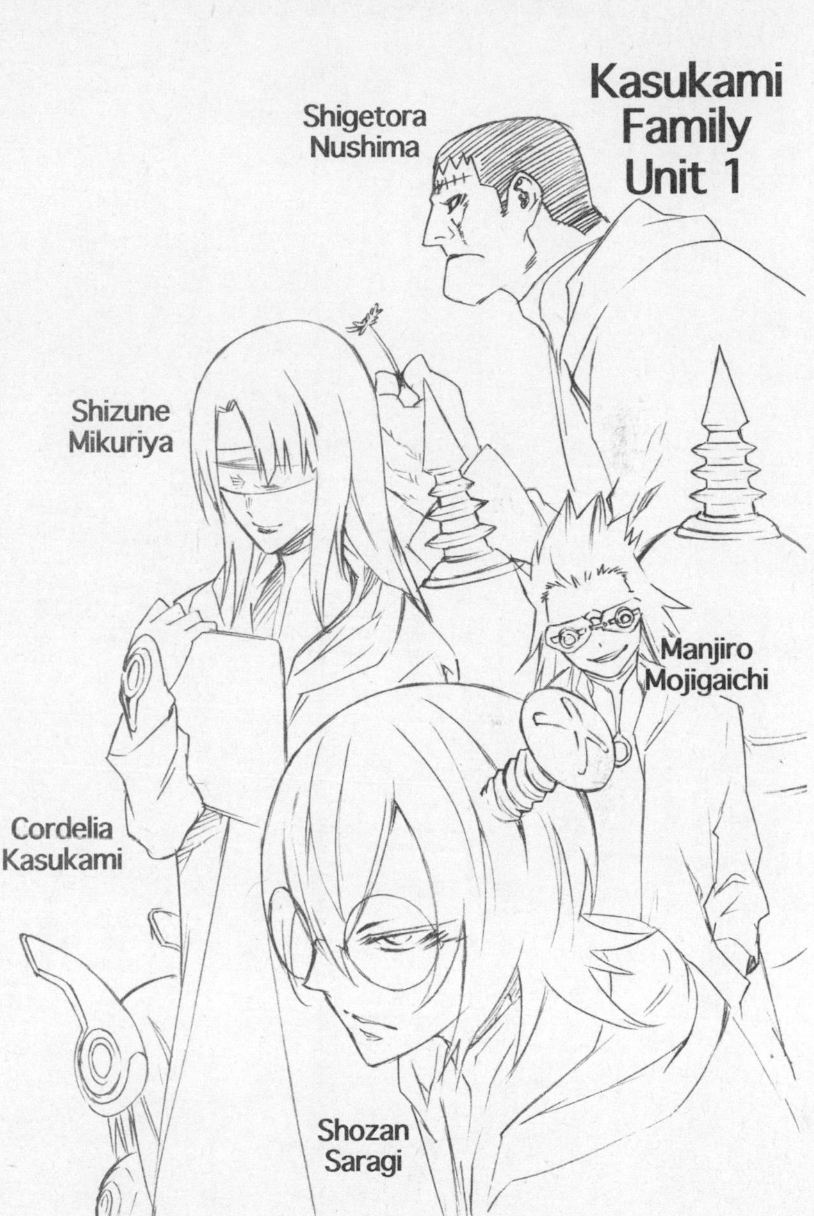
Kasukami Family Unit 1
Shigetora Nushima
Shizune Mikuriya
Manjiro Mojigaichi
Cordelia Kasukami
Shozan Saragi

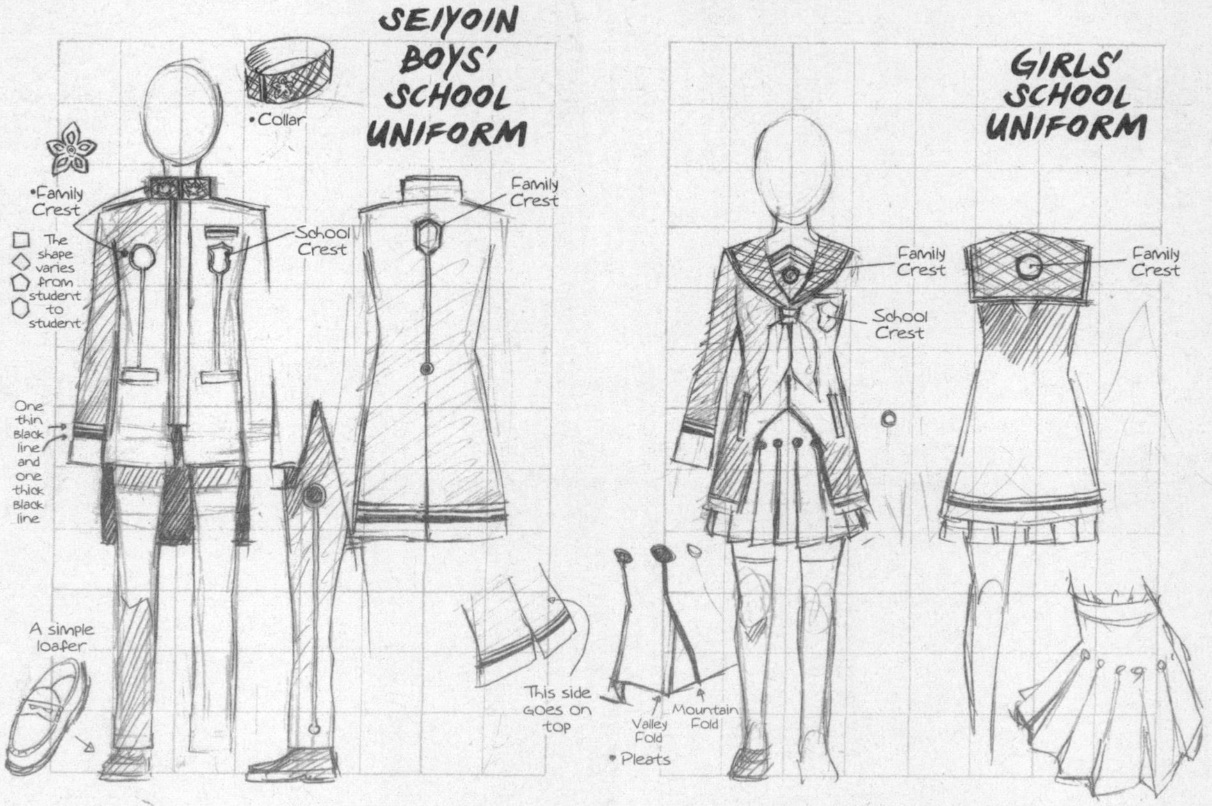
SEIYOIN BOYS' SCHOOL UNIFORM
•Collar
•Family Crest
The shape varies from student to student
School Crest
Family Crest
One thin Black line and one thick Black line
A simple loafer
This side goes on top
Valley Fold
Mountain Fold
• Pleats
GIRLS' SCHOOL UNIFORM
Family Crest
School Crest
Family Crest

17

—SHONEN JUMP Manga Edition—

STORY & ART **Yoshiaki Sukeno**

TRANSLATION **Tetsuichiro Miyaki**
ENGLISH ADAPTATION **Bryant Turnage**
TOUCH-UP ART & LETTERING **Stephen Dutro**
DESIGN **Shawn Carrico**
EDITOR **Annette Roman**

SOUSEI NO ONMYOJI © 2013 by Yoshiaki Sukeno
All rights reserved.
First published in Japan in 2013 by SHUEISHA Inc., Tokyo.
English translation rights arranged by SHUEISHA Inc.

Printed in the U.S.A.

Published by VIZ Media, LLC
P.O. Box 77010
San Francisco, CA 94107

10 9 8 7 6 5 4 3 2 1
First printing, February 2020

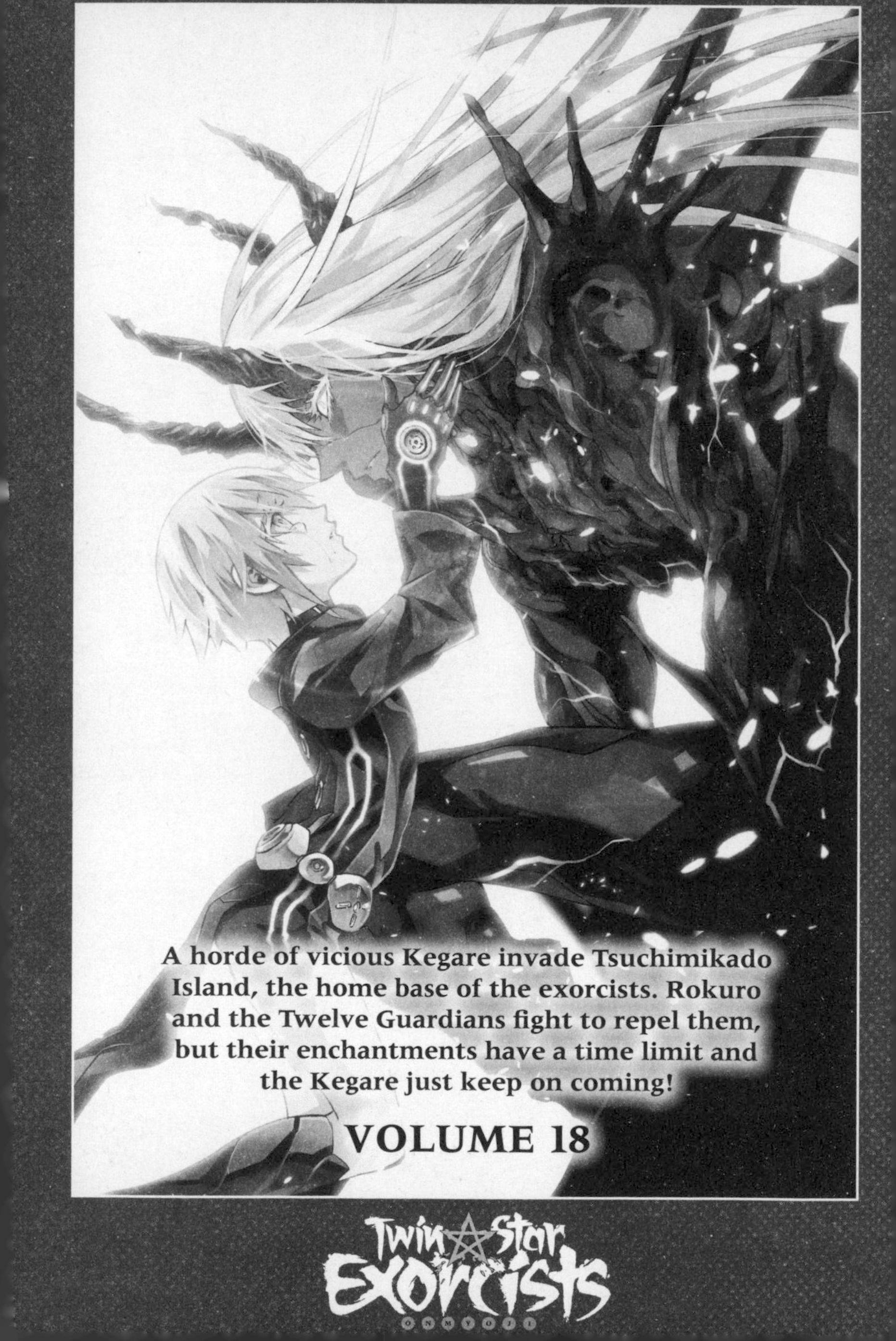

A horde of vicious Kegare invade Tsuchimikado Island, the home base of the exorcists. Rokuro and the Twelve Guardians fight to repel them, but their enchantments have a time limit and the Kegare just keep on coming!

VOLUME 18

Twin Star Exorcists

ONMYOJI

THE PROMISED NEVERLAND

STORY BY **KAIU SHIRAI**
ART BY **POSUKA DEMIZU**

Emma, Norman and Ray are the brightest kids at the Grace Field House orphanage. And under the care of the woman they refer to as "Mom," all the kids have enjoyed a comfortable life. Good food, clean clothes and the perfect environment to learn—what more could an orphan ask for? One day, though, Emma and Norman uncover the dark truth of the outside world they are forbidden from seeing.

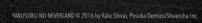

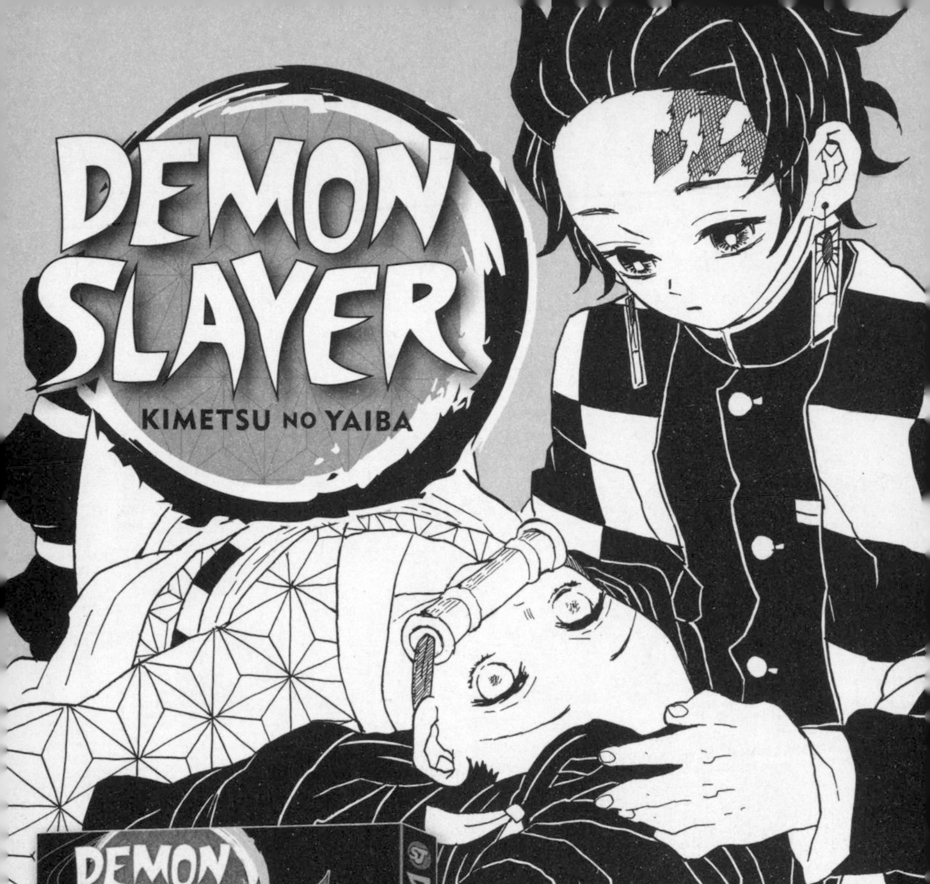
DEMON SLAYER
KIMETSU NO YAIBA

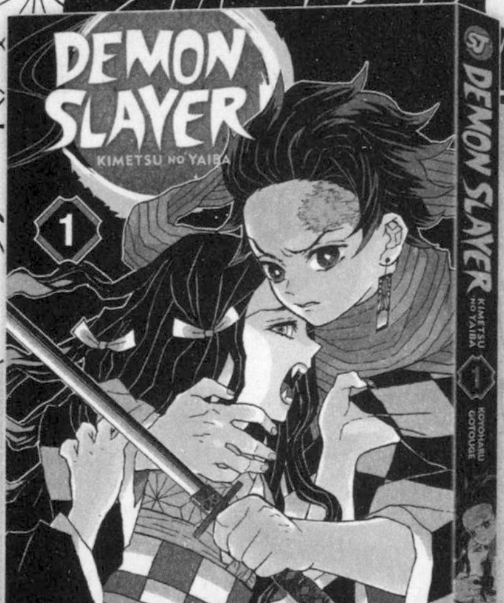
DEMON SLAYER
KIMETSU NO YAIBA
1
Story and Art by
KOYOHARU GOTOUGE
DEMON SLAYER
KIMETSU NO YAIBA
KOYOHARU GOTOUGE
VIZ

Story and Art by

KOYOHARU GOTOUGE

In Taisho-era Japan, kindhearted Tanjiro Kamado makes a living selling charcoal. But his peaceful life is shattered when a demon slaughters his entire family. His little sister Nezuko is the only survivor, but she has been transformed into a demon herself! Tanjiro sets out on a dangerous journey to find a way to return his sister to normal and destroy the demon who ruined his life.

RATED T TEEN

VIZ